5⁰⁰

ABC

THE HOOVER COMMISSION REPORT

THE COMMISSION

HERBERT HOOVER, *Chairman*
DEAN ACHESON, *Vice Chairman*

ARTHUR S. FLEMMING
JAMES FORRESTAL
GEORGE H. MEAD
GEORGE D. AIKEN
JOSEPH P. KENNEDY

JOHN L. McCLELLAN
JAMES K. POLLOCK
CLARENCE J. BROWN
CARTER MANASCO
JAMES H. ROWE, JR.

The Hoover Commission Report

ON ORGANIZATION

OF THE EXECUTIVE BRANCH OF

THE GOVERNMENT

081224

McGRAW-HILL BOOK COMPANY, INC.

New York, Toronto, and London

Second Printing
Printed in the United States of America

PREFACE

The reader may wisely bear in mind two factors which distinguish this book. First, few Government reports are "best sellers." Second, few attempts to reorganize the Federal Government have greatly excited public interest. Yet this report, in a far less manageable form, has already had wide circulation. It is believed that this is due to a public demand for information about Government reorganization that is without precedent.

Now for a guess at the reasons. It is worth noting that the unofficially famous "Hoover Commission" was officially christened, by the Congress which created it, "The Commission on Organization of the Executive Branch of the Government." Observe that this avoids the commonly used term, "reorganization," and hews to the real point which seems to be this: The Executive Branch has *never* been organized.

Here we speak of "organization" in common-sense business terms. The Government was not organized in George Washington's day nor was it in the time of Andrew Jackson. This worried Jackson and he tried to do something about it. Most Presidents have worried and tried since then. Among them were Presidents Taft, Wilson, Hoover, Roosevelt, and Truman. In turn they attempted to solve the problem by means of commissions, executive orders, and legislation. All met with scant success.

The Executive Branch under Mr. Hoover cost $4 billion a year to operate, and employed 600,000 persons. Lacking proper organization, it laid, even then, a great burden upon the Executive. Today, it requires an annual budget of $42 billion and employs 2,100,000 persons in an intricate structure of 1,816 assorted departments, bureaus, sections, divisions, administrations, etc. Manifestly no mere mortal President can carry the responsibility for personal direction of this establishment and have any time left for the broader duties of his office. What he cannot delegate officially he is forced either to delegate unofficially or neglect completely. The result, in either instance, is bound to be just what we have—duplication, overlapping, and administrative turmoil. We may have come at last to the point where officials and legislators will agree that "something must be done."

More importantly, the average citizen has become uncomfortably conscious of the vast size of our Government. We all want and expect many services from the Government, to be sure; but we are baffled by its magnitude, puzzled by its complexities, and frightened by its cost. Instinctively we see a possible danger to democracy itself.

Probably we, as citizens, have been looking unconsciously for something like the Hoover Commission Report, something that promises us a chance to see and understand the Government in Town Hall terms. If that is the case, it was no accident that the creation of the Commission and the publication of its report made national news from the start.

Most readers know the history of the Commission. It was created by unanimous vote of the Congress in July, 1947. The Lodge-Brown Act, which brought it into being, conceived of its mission on the highest possible plane. The Commission was bipartisan, with six members from each party. Four Commissioners each were chosen by the President of the Senate, the Speaker of the House of Representatives, and President Truman.

The choice of Mr. Hoover as Chairman was of course inspired. Always rated among the ablest administrators of all times, he alone, among living Americans, knows intimately the real problems which confront President Truman. Moreover, few men in our or any other day are so well qualified to execute a massive assignment in research. Many scholars still treasure his monumental reports on "Recent Economic Changes" and "Recent Social Trends," which this company had the privilege of publishing some years ago.

The Hoover Commission made a characteristically thorough and thoughtful approach to its mighty task. It began by defining some 24 of the principal problems of government and management. These included such things as personnel, budgeting and accounting, the Post Office, the National Security Organization, the State Department, and many other matters bearing on the assignment.

Having thus cut its cloth, the Commission created special research committees, called "task forces." These comprised some of the most eminent specialists available in each field. The task forces were given time, opportunity, and staffs with which to pursue their inquiries until they got to the general heart of each problem. Then, after periods of 10 to 14 months, they returned to the Commission with their findings in each field.

The result was the most imposing collection of facts, figures, and opinions on Government that has ever been assembled. It amounted, in fact, to some 2,500,000 words of basic data of the most valuable sort.

From this massive bulk the Commission then prepared to carve out the model of a streamlined, modern Government. For several months the Commissioners met at least three days each week. Taking each of the task force reports in turn, they selected the material of greatest value, considered all component parts with care, and brought them into an integrated whole.

To put it another way, Herbert Hoover and associates, as consulting engineers, have presented the American people with a blueprint for good government. In one sense it is the sort of report that an alarmed board of directors would hasten to obtain for the salvation of a rickety business. On a business basis alone, the Hoover Commission Report promises cash savings which have been estimated at more than $3 billion a year.

In human terms, the report has greater significance than any price tag can impart. As a people, we have reached the point at which the size and cost of government can easily impair the effectiveness of our economy, lower our standards of living, and weaken our effort to lead the free peoples of the world to safety from the encroachment of totalitarianism.

Mr. Hoover himself has put it this way: "Our field of inquiry not only concerns every citizen, it concerns the very strength and vitality of democracy itself. The success of this mission may well set the pattern for future joint participation by private citizens and Government representatives on matters affecting national welfare."

This volume is printed as a tool for the use of citizens, legislators, and Government officials in what may well prove to be—the times and the new attitude of the public considered—a genuine forward move in the direction of lasting good government. Certainly it is generally realized that fundamental reform of the Executive Branch is not the work of a moment. Suppose citizens and officials were to determine unanimously to put the Hoover report into effect at the earliest possible date. Even then the sheer mechanics of readjusting the huge and cumbersome governmental machine would take years to evolve. Meanwhile, a convenient reference work will be needed by all those who participate in the task.

We hope this book will help in that task. It presents the essence of the Commission's findings. Plucked from the heart of a vast body of task force research, it has also been stripped of the dissents, additional comments, and minority views of the various Commissioners. Note well that some of these reports were unanimously arrived at, while others were not. It would be strange, indeed, if 12 able men of diverse background and experience were to agree unanimously on all points of a program so vast and so varied. The Commissioners disagreed quite frequently. The dissents were fairly numerous and they had, like Supreme Court dissents, real value as commentaries on the problem.

There is a necessity, however, for a single volume which quickly answers the question: "What did the majority of the Commission determine?" It is to meet this need that we present this volume. We hope it may prove useful to those who work to make a lasting reality of this design for a Government which will forever be the servant, not the master, of our people.

THE PUBLISHERS

CONTENTS

FIRST LETTER OF TRANSMITTAL

WASHINGTON, D. C.,
5 February, 1949.

DEAR SIRS: In accordance with Public Law 162, Eightieth Congress, approved July 7, 1947, the Commission on Organization of the Executive Branch of the Government submits herewith its first report.

This report relates to the General Management of the Executive Branch.

We shall, as rapidly as possible, send to the Congress our reports and recommendations upon the various functions and departments with some annexes and the related task force reports.

The Commission wishes to express its appreciation for the work of its task forces in the area of general management of the executive branch and for the cooperation of the officials of departments and agencies included in this report.

Respectfully,

HERBERT HOOVER
Chairman.

The Honorable
The President of the Senate
The Honorable
The Speaker of the House of Representatives

REORGANIZATION POWERS

In our letter of January 13, 1949, addressed to the President Pro Tempore of the Senate and to the Speaker of the House of Representatives, the Commission on Organization of the Executive Branch of the Government recommended that the President be granted reorganization powers. To complete the record, we repeat this letter here.

Recommendation to the Congress

The necessity for reorganization of the executive branch of the Government was clearly recognized by the Congress when it created this Commission in July, 1947, with the full approval of the President. Congress assigned the Commission the duty of examination and recommendation under the following statement from the act creating the Commission:

> It is hereby declared to be the policy of Congress to promote economy, efficiency, and improved service in the transaction of the public business in the departments, bureaus, agencies, boards, commissions, offices, independent establishments, and instrumentalities of the executive branch of the Government by—
>
> 1. Limiting expenditures to the lowest amount consistent with the efficient performance of essential services, activities, and functions;
>
> 2. Eliminating duplication and overlapping of services, activities, and functions;
>
> 3. Consolidating services, activities, and functions of a similar nature;
>
> 4. Abolishing services, activities, and functions not necessary to the efficient conduct of Government.
>
> 5. Defining and limiting executive functions, services, and activities.

This concern of Congress for economy and efficiency reflects the overwhelming interest of every thoughtful citizen and taxpayer in the land.

The writing and adoption of the Federal Constitution proved that a republic could deliberately analyze its political institutions and redesign its Government to meet the demands of the future. The broad pattern that America then selected is sound. Today we must deal with the infinitely more complicated Government of the twentieth century. In doing so, we must reorganize the executive branch to give it the simplicity of structure, the unity of purpose, and the clear line of executive authority that was originally intended under the Constitution.

As a result of depression, war, new needs for defense, and our greater responsibilities in the foreign field, the Federal Government has become the most gigantic business on earth. In less than 20 years the number of its civil employees has risen from 570,000 to over 2,100,000. The number of bureaus, sections, services, and units has increased fourfold to over 1,800. Annual expenditures have increased from about $3,600,-000,000 to over $42,000,000,000. The national debt per average family has increased from about $500 to about $7,500. Such rapid growth could not take place without causing serious problems. Organizational methods, effective 20 years ago, are no longer applicable. The growth of skills and methods in private organization has long since outmoded many of the methods of the Government.

This Commission has found that the United States is paying heavily for a lack of order, a lack of clear lines of authority and responsibility, and a lack of effective organization in the executive branch. It has found that great improvements can be made in the effectiveness with which the Government can serve the people if its organization and administration are overhauled.

This Commission has been engaged in its task for the last 16 months and is reaching its conclusions only after the most painstaking research. We decided at an early date that we must have the aid of leading and experienced citizens to assist us in making findings of fact and recommendation of remedies. The Commission, therefore, divided its work into functional and departmental segments; it created 24 "task forces" with authority to engage such research aid as they might require. About 300 outstanding men and women, expert and experienced in the fields to which they were assigned, have now submitted to us their findings and recommendations. Thanks are due them. They brought great talent and diligence to their work. Their findings will be found useful by the Congress and the executive branch in solution of the problems considered.

Some of the recommendations contained in the volumes of our report, which we plan to file from time to time between now and the expiration of the life of the Commission, can be put into effect only by legislation. Others can be accomplished by executive action. But many of the most important can probably be accomplished only if the Congress reenacts and broadens the power to initiate reorganization plans which it had previously granted to the President under an act which expired on March 31, 1948.

The Commission recommends that such authority should be given to the President and that the power of the President to prepare and transmit plans of reorganization to the Congress should not be restricted by limitations or exemptions. Once the limiting and exempting process is begun it will end the possibility of achieving really substantial results.

But, in saying this, the Commission should not be understood as giving sweeping endorsement to any and all reorganization plans. It does believe that the safeguard against unwise reorganization plans lies both in a sound exercise of the President's discretion and in the reserved power in the Congress by concurrent resolution to disapprove any proposed plan.

Limitations or exemptions upon this power to reorganize should not be imposed other than that of Congressional disapproval. They have arisen in the past chiefly in connection with the regulatory commissions. In one of its reports the Commission will discuss these regulatory commissions in detail. It will point out in each case those regulatory functions which it is believed should continue to be performed independently. The Commission will also point out certain other functions which are of a different nature and which can be more efficiently and economically performed by purely executive officials. The inclusion in a reorganization act of provisions exempting certain agencies from its terms would prevent changes which are in accord with established principles in this field and which in no way impair the maintenance of independence and impartiality in the exercise of the great regulatory functions.

Similarly, the inclusion of general language, like that contained in section 5 (a) (6) of the Reorganization Act of 1945,[1] intended to prevent

---

[1] "Sec. 5. (a) No reorganization plan shall provide for, and no reorganization under this Act shall have the effect of— . . .(6) imposing, in connection with the exercise of any quasi-judicial or quasi-legislative function possessed by an independent agency, any greater limitation upon the exercise of independent judgment and discrtion, to the full extent authorized by law, in the carrying out of such function, than existed with respect to the exercise of such function by the agency in which it was vested prior to the taking effect of such reorganization; except that this prohibition shall not prevent the abolition of any such function; . . ."

the submission of any plan which imposes limitations upon the independent exercise of quasi-legislative or quasi-judicial functions, would, in the Commission's judgment, be unwise. The phrases are extremely vague and of uncertain meaning. Ingenious and plausible arguments can be made to apply them to a wide range of functions which should clearly be subject to reorganization procedure. Such arguments would not be matters of purely theoretical concern or legislative debates, for the validity of reorganization could be made the subject of protracted litigation by private interests resisting the acts of a reorganized agency on the ground that it was illegally constituted. It might take several years of litigation to lay down interpretations of these general phrases and even then, uncertainty would remain.

The Commission, in accordance with the act of Congress creating it (P. L. 162, as amended), will file a series of reports, the last of which will be delivered within 70 days of the organization of the Eighty-first Congress. These reports will contain its findings and recommendations. They will begin with the top organization and structure of the executive branch and proceed through the services which are common to the whole executive branch to the reorganizations recommended for particular agencies and groups of agencies.

I

General Management of the Executive Branch

Chapter One

INTRODUCTION

In this part of its report, the Commission on Organization of the Executive Branch of the Government deals with the essentials of effective organization of the executive branch. Without these essentials, all other steps to improve organization and management are doomed to failure.

The President, and under him his chief lieutenants, the department heads, must be held responsible and accountable to the people and the Congress for the conduct of the executive branch.

Responsibility and accountability are impossible without authority—the power to direct. The exercise of authority is impossible without a clear line of command from the top to the bottom, and a return line of responsibility and accountability from the bottom to the top.

The wise exercise of authority is impossible without the aids which staff institutions can provide to assemble facts and recommendations upon which judgment may be made and to supervise and report upon the execution of decisions.

Definite authority at the top, a clear line of authority from top to bottom, and adequate staff aids to the exercise of authority do not exist. Authority is diffused, lines of authority are confused, staff services are insufficient. Consequently, responsibility and accountability are impaired.

To remedy this situation is the first and essential step in the search for efficiency and economy in the executive branch of the Federal Government.

The critical state of world affairs requires the Government of the United States to speak and act with unity of purpose, firmness, and restraint in dealing with other nations. It must act decisively to preserve its human and material resources. It must develop strong machinery for the national defense, while seeking to construct an enduring world peace. It cannot perform these tasks if its organization for development and execution of policy is confused and disorderly, or if the Chief Executive is handicapped in providing firm direction to the departments and agencies.

If disorder in the administrative machinery makes the executive branch of the Government work at cross purposes within itself, the Nation as a whole must suffer. It must suffer—if its several programs conflict with each other and executive authority becomes confused— from waste in the expenditure of public funds, and from the lack of national unity that results from useless friction.

An energetic and unified executive is not a threat to free and responsible government, as Alexander Hamilton pointed out in "The Federalist" (No. 70). He declared that the ingredients of "safety in the republican sense" are "first, a due dependence on the people; secondly, a due responsibility." Strength and unity in an executive make clear who is responsible for faults in administration and thus enable the legislature better to enforce accountability to the people.

Findings

The Commission has found that violation of these principles results from the conditions stated in the following findings.

First Finding. **The executive branch is not organized into a workable number of major departments and agencies which the President can effectively direct, but is cut up into a large number of agencies, which divide responsibility and which are too great in number for effective direction from the top.**

Thousands of Federal programs cannot be directed personally by the President. They must be grouped by related function and divided among a small number of principal assistants who are the heads of departments.

If the number gets too large, the President cannot control or supervise them. Yet, at the present time, we have a large number of agencies subject to no direction except that of the President. In many cases several agencies each have a small share in carrying out a single major policy which ought to be the responsibility of one department. Until these dispersed units are pulled together, and authority is placed in

4

department heads as chief assistants to the President, there will be conflict, waste, and indecisiveness in administration.

Second Finding. **The line of command and supervision from the President down through his department heads to every employee, and the line of responsibility from each employee of the executive branch up to the President, has been weakened, or actually broken, in many places and in many ways.**

That line of responsibility still exists in constitutional theory, but it has been worn away by administrative practices, by political pressures, and by detailed statutory provisions. Statutory powers often have been vested in subordinate officers in such a way as to deny authority to the President or a department head. For example, the statute governing the sale of helium to a foreign nation gave the Secretary of the Interior the authority to control such sales regardless of the opinion of the President. The Corps of Engineers of the United States Army, in another case, has the statutory duty of preparing river development plans, and the Secretary of the Army is not responsible for its selection of projects.

Some administrative or operating tasks are given to boards instead of to single executives, and the President's authority to appoint and remove the members of those boards is restricted. The United States Maritime Commission, which has a high degree of independence as a Commission because of its regulatory functions, also has statutory authority to conduct a great business enterprise and to make executive decisions affecting our foreign policy.

On some occasions the responsibility of an official to his superior is obscured by laws which require him, before acting, to clear his proposals with others. This breaks the line of responsibility, and encourages indecision, lack of initiative, and irresponsibility.

Third Finding. **The President and the heads of departments lack the tools to frame programs and policies and to supervise their execution.**

No executive, public or private, can manage a large and complex establishment without staff assistance. Staff agencies must keep the President informed on the way in which the various departmental programs are related to each other, assist in defining specific programs pursuant to the instructions of the Congress, and help him supervise the execution of these programs.

Staff agencies do this by helping the President control the common requirements of all Government programs—funds spent, legislation requested, personnel required, the relation of each program to others and to the national interest. The President's staff agencies can best help him by keeping in close touch with their counterparts in the departments.

Despite improvements during the past decade, these staff agencies are still less effective than they should be. Detailed recommendations on this subject appear in our report on The Executive Office of the President.

Fourth Finding. **The Federal Government has not taken aggressive steps to build a corps of administrators of the highest level of ability with an interest in the program of the Government as a whole.**

Recommendations on this subject appear in our report on Personnel Management.

Fifth Finding. **Many of the statutes and regulations that control the administrative practices and procedures of the Government are unduly detailed and rigid.**

It is impossible to secure efficiency of administration unless administrators have enough authority and discretion to seize opportunities for economical and effective operation. Present laws and regulations establish patterns so detailed and rigid that department heads are granted almost no operational discretion or flexibility necessary to give real effect to the purpose of the Congress.

Instead of being unified organizations, many departments and agencies are but loose federations of bureaus and subdivisions, each jealously defending its own jurisdiction. Department heads will not be able effectively to aid the President in the coordination of administration unless reorganizations produce unity and integration in fact as well as in appearance.

Recommendations on this problem appear in our report on Departmental Management.

Sixth Finding. **Likewise, the budgetary processes of the Government need improvement, in order to express the objectives of the Government in terms of the work to be done rather than in mere classifications of expenditures.**

Recommendations on budgeting are presented in our report on Budgeting and Accounting.

6

Seventh Finding. The accounting methods in the executive branch require standardization and simplification and accounting activities require decentralization if they are to become effective tools of management and if great expense and waste are to be eliminated.

Accounting recommendations also are presented in our report on that subject.

Eighth Finding. General administrative services for various operating agencies—such as purchasing of supplies, maintenance of records, and the operation of public buildings—are poorly organized or coordinated.

At present some of these services are unduly centralized. Decentralization to operating departments, under proper performance standards, would achieve improvements. Moreover, some of these services are illogically scattered among independent agencies, or located in subdivisions of executive departments.

Recommendations appear in our report on The Office of General Services.

Summary

Any systematic effort to improve the organization and administration of the Government, therefore, must:

1. Create a more orderly grouping of the functions of Government into major departments and agencies under the President.

2. Establish a clear line of control from the President to these department and agency heads and from them to their subordinates with correlative responsibility from these officials to the President, cutting through the barriers which have in many cases made bureaus and agencies partially independent of the Chief Executive.

3. Give the President and each department head strong staff services which should exist only to make executive work more effective, and which the President or department head should be free to organize at his discretion.

4. Develop a much greater number of capable administrators in the public service, and prepare them for promotion to any bureau or department in the Government where their services may be most effectively used.

5. Enforce the accountability of administrators by a much broader pattern of controls, so that the statutes and regulations which govern

7

administrative practices will encourage, rather than destroy, initiative and enterprise.

6. Permit the operating departments and agencies to administer for themselves a larger share of the routine administrative services, under strict supervision and in conformity with high standards.

Only by taking these steps can the operations of the executive branch be managed effectively, responsibly, and economically.

Chapter Two

THE EXECUTIVE OFFICE OF THE PRESIDENT

The wise division of powers in the Constitution assigns the executive power to the President in unequivocal language: "The executive Power shall be vested in a President of the United States of America."

But the President has many other Constitutional responsibilities: "He shall take Care that the Laws be faithfully executed." He is Commander-in-Chief of the armed forces; he must conduct foreign relations; he must make legislative recommendations and approve or disapprove of legislative enactments. He is Chief of State, and he is the political symbol of the American people.

Beyond this is a function not foreseen by the Constitution: that of leadership of a political party—a function inseparable from the President's dealings with the Congress and his accountability to the people. All of these functions involve important decisions of policy.

On the President, along with whatever advisory and administrative staff is provided for him, falls the crushing burden of bringing all the units of the executive branch into harmony, and of fitting them together so that a unified program may be carried out.

The Presidential Staff

The historical development of aid to the President has not been exclusively through the expansion of departmental and agency assistance, but also through increases in his personal staff. However, until well into this century, the President's personal staff consisted of his secretary and an executive clerk, with assistants to take care of visitors

9

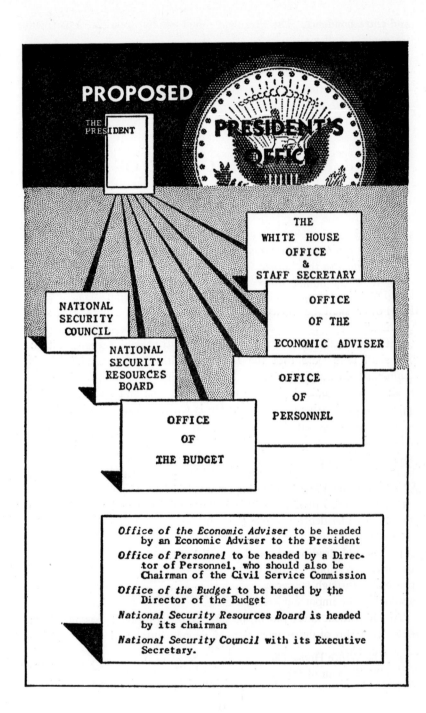

PROPOSED

THE PRESIDENT

PRESIDENT'S OFFICE

THE WHITE HOUSE OFFICE & STAFF SECRETARY

NATIONAL SECURITY COUNCIL

OFFICE OF THE ECONOMIC ADVISER

NATIONAL SECURITY RESOURCES BOARD

OFFICE OF PERSONNEL

OFFICE OF THE BUDGET

Office of the Economic Adviser to be headed by an Economic Adviser to the President

Office of Personnel to be headed by a Director of Personnel, who should also be Chairman of the Civil Service Commission

Office of the Budget to be headed by the Director of the Budget

National Security Resources Board is headed by its chairman

National Security Council with its Executive Secretary.

and correspondence. The President relied wholly upon the departments for general staff assistance.

The need of information for the solution of broad problems and the determination of Government-wide policies has gradually forced the development of better staff services for the President. The acute need for more adequate staff assistance during the Twenties was evidenced by the constant assignment of staff personnel from the departments to the White House and an increase in the use of committees, commissions, and conferences to develop facts and policies for the President.

The first real step in systematic aid to the President resulted from the enactment of the Budget and Accounting Act of 1921. Although the Bureau of the Budget was placed in the Treasury Department, the Director of the Budget became at once the President's immediate advisor in dealing with Government expenditures as a whole. Soon legislative reference work was undertaken, and some years later duties were assigned to this bureau for the study of management problems.

In 1928, the number of secretaries to the President was increased to three, and the White House work was departmentalized into correspondence, reception of visitors, economic research, legislative matters, and press relations. At this time, the purely social duties of the President's chief military and naval aides were changed by the Secretaries of War and the Navy through appointment of distinguished officers to the White House to aid the President on defense questions.

In 1939, the Bureau of the Budget was transferred from the Treasury Department to the Executive Office of the President, and its services were expanded to relieve the President further.

THE PRESENT STAFF

The President's personal staff now comprises three secretaries; an assistant to the President; six administrative assistants; a special counsel to the President; the executive clerk; and Army, Navy, and Air Force aides.

It has been traditional that the executive clerk and his aides should be career positions so that there might be continuity of White House procedure through successive administrations. The same has generally applied to the important employees in the White House residence.

At the present time, the President's immediate executive staff (aside from the heads of departments and agencies) consists of:

a. The White House Office
b. The Bureau of the Budget

c. The Council of Economic Advisers
d. The National Security Council
e. The National Security Resources Board

Recommendation No. 1

The Commission recommends the following additions to the Executive Office:

An Office of Personnel, headed by a director who should also be chairman of the Civil Service Commission.
A staff secretary in the White House Office, as described later.
The Commission also recommends certain further expansion in the work of the Bureau of the Budget.

Reasons for these proposals and further recommendations will be given in due course.

TERMS USED

At the outset it is desirable to clarify some problems of nomenclature as used in these reports. We will refer to the agencies above as the "President's Office" to avoid the confusion of the present official name, "The Executive Office of the President," with such expressions as "Executive Services," "Executive Office," "Executive Branch." The original name, Bureau of the Budget, should be changed to "Office of the Budget," which we shall use hereafter. To avoid the confusion in use of the terms "Executive Agencies," "Departments," "Administrations," we refer to the major agencies of the Government as "Departments and Agencies."

The Role of Staff Services in the President's Office

The purpose of the staff services in the President's Office is not to assume operating functions or to duplicate responsibilities of the operating departments. These services should exist only to give the President the greatest possible information on the activities of the Government as a whole, and to enable him to direct the policies of the departments and agencies.

Recommendation No. 2

Statutory authority over the operating departments should not be vested in any staff members or staff agency of the President's Office.

The Congressional requirement that personnel ceilings be fixed by the Office of the Budget is a case in point. This type of authority should be vested in the President.

Authority of the President to Organize His Staff

In the President's Office, the precise boundaries between one staff or advisory function and another cannot readily be fixed.

To enable the President to make use of the total staff resources in a flexible manner, he should be given complete freedom to adjust the internal relationships of the President's Office.

Recommendation No. 3

The President should not be prevented by statute from reorganizing the President's Office and from transferring functions and personnel from one part of it to another.

Appointments in the President's Office

The Congress, when it enacted the Budget and Accounting Act in 1921, wisely made the Director of the Bureau of the Budget a staff agent to the President, to be appointed by him without the Senate confirmation that properly goes with appointment of heads of the operating agencies. Similarly, it recently authorized the President to appoint the executive secretary of the National Security Council without Senate confirmation.

Recommendation No. 4

The head of each staff agency in the President's Office should be appointed by the President without confirmation by the Senate except the Civil Service Commission.

The Office of the Economic Adviser to the President

The Council of Economic Advisers was established as a part of the President's Office by the Employment Act of 1946. It is a council of three members appointed by the President subject to the advice and consent of the Senate.

The Council, with the aid of a small staff, supplies the President with economic information and advice.

Just as the budget is the responsibility of the President and not of the Office of the Budget, the annual economic report is the report of the President, not of the Council. Like the Office of the Budget, the Council should advise the President as a professional staff agency and should not take public leadership on issues of policy in its own right.

The Council is a relatively new agency. It has properly proceeded with considerable caution in developing its role. No one can judge its strength or weakness with confidence at this early stage of its existence. But it seems clear that, at least potentially, it is handicapped by being a multiheaded body, with the requirement that its members be confirmed by the Senate.

To put a full-time board at the head of a staff agency is to run the risk of inviting public disagreement among its members and of transplanting within the President's Office the disagreements on policy issues that grow up in the executive departments or in the Congress. It also makes cooperation with related staff agencies more difficult.

Recommendation No. 5

The Commission recommends that the Council of Economic Advisers be replaced by an Office of the Economic Adviser and that it have a single head.

Cabinet Committees

The members of the Cabinet are the primary advisers to the President. He is free to select them, to decide the subjects on which he wishes advice, and to follow their advice or not as he sees fit.

The Cabinet as a body, however, is not an effective council of advisers to the President and it does not have a collective responsibility for Administration policies. That responsibility rests upon the President. The Cabinet members, being chosen to direct great specialized operating departments, are not all fitted to advise him on every subject.

For many years, Presidents have assigned problems involving more than one department to committees of the Cabinet whose experience bears on particular problems. In crucial areas in the conduct of national affairs, where Presidential consideration or decision is required, the creation of Cabinet committees is desirable to advise the President on both the foreign and domestic aspects of the important problems. Sound high-level foreign policies, for instance, can only be formed by placing side by side for comparison a financial outlook, a natural resources outlook, a transportation outlook, a manpower outlook, and a security outlook.

These Cabinet committees should be established by, and function directly under, the President. They should not be part of the Cabinet. Creation of specific committees by statute should be avoided because the resulting framework is too rigid and, in any event, the President should not be directed to receive advice from designated sources.

Recommendation No. 6

The membership and assignment of any Cabinet committee set up to advise the President on important policy issues should be determined by the President.

The National Security Council
The National Security Resources Board
The National Advisory Council

The two most conspicuous Cabinet-level committees are the National Security Council and the National Security Resources Board, which were made advisory agencies to the President by the National Security Act of 1947. They are located in the same building with the agencies of the President's Office, and to all intents and purposes are part of that Office. A third statutory committee, the National Advisory Council on International Monetary and Financial Problems, in practice, has been under the aegis of the Treasury Department, but it also gives advice to the President as part of its duties.

Each of these agencies consists of an interdepartmental committee (composed primarily of the heads of departments), and a small planning staff and secretariat. The memberships of the National Security Resources Board and the National Security Council are largely fixed and flexible only to the extent that the President can add to the statutory members of the Council and designate the department heads to serve on the Board.

The National Security Council deals with national security matters with strong foreign policy overtones, but its emphasis on security considerations may result in insufficient attention to other considerations, such as natural resources or manpower.

The National Advisory Council views foreign affairs largely through the instrument of financial assistance and so tends to ignore the agricultural or mineral aspects of the Nation's economy.

The National Security Council is unduly weighted in its statutory membership on the side of the military departments. The executive secretary of the National Security Council is appointed by the President. So is the chairman of the National Security Resources Board, but with the added requirement of Senate confirmation.

The chairman of the National Advisory Council is, by statute, the Secretary of the Treasury. The work of this committee in connection with the International Monetary Fund and the International Bank for Reconstruction and Development requires such a close relationship with the Secretary of the Treasury that the present arrangements under which this committee operates may be left unchanged.

Recommendation No. 7

The inflexible composition of these Cabinet-level committees set up by statute should be revised so as to afford a flexible framework within which the President can determine their membership and assignments.

The National Security Council and the National Security Resources Board, in supervising their respective staffs and in dealing with the department heads who are members of their committees, are similar to the other assistants in the President's office and to the heads of his other staff agencies.

The National Security Council and the National Security Resources Board, with their respective staffs, should be made, formally as well as in practice, a part of the President's office.

Interdepartmental Committees below Cabinet Level

Interdepartmental committees are helpful in coordinating the programs of departments and agencies.

The report of our Foreign Affairs task force indicates the existence of some 30 interdepartmental committees in the foreign affairs area alone. There are many more such committees in the domestic area. As a result of their multiplication, there is a need for coordination to prevent both confusion and waste.

The work of these committees should be integrated. While they were initially created for some specific purpose, they tend to become permanent and to waste time and personnel.

Recommendation No. 8

There should be an inventory of interdepartmental committees by the President's office at least once a year and those whose work is complete should be terminated.

Special Advisers to the President

The President has often made good use of special citizen advisory commissions or has called on private citizens of eminence and prestige for advice.

Recommendation No. 9

The President should be given adequate funds to make it possible for him to use advisory commissions and to employ consultants or personal advisers from time to time.

A New Staff Secretary

At present there is no one place in the President's Office to which the President can look for a current summary of the principal issues with which he may have to deal in the near future; nor is a current summary of the staff work available on problems that have been assigned to his advisers, his staff agencies, or the heads of departments and agencies.

To meet this deficiency, the Commission proposes the addition of a staff secretary. He would not himself be an adviser to the President on any issue of policy, nor would he review (in a supervisory capacity) the substance of any recommendation made to the President by any part of his staff.

The Commission believes that this recommendation will facilitate teamwork among the President's staff, the agencies of the President's Office, and any Cabinet or interdepartmental committees which are studying problems for the President.

If possible the staff secretary, like the executive clerk, should be a career public servant.

The staff secretary should keep the President currently informed of work which has been undertaken by various parts of the President's Office, by the Cabinet committees, or by interdepartmental committees or special advisory committees. He should inform the President of any difficulties which have arisen because of the overlapping of assignments or conflicts of policy. He should make the inventory of interdepartmental committees referred to in Recommendation No. 8 above.

Recommendation No. 10

The President should be given funds to provide a staff secretary, in addition to his present principal Secretaries, to assist him by

clearing information on the major problems on which staff work is being done within the President's Office, or by Cabinet or interdepartmental committees.

The Office of Personnel

The Federal Government, functioning in its capacity as an employer, finds itself faced with more complex and difficult problems in the personnel field than any other employer in the Nation today.

Unless these problems are solved effectively, programs for strengthening the management side of Government will be worthless.

The President of the United States, under the law and in accordance with sound principles of management, is in the final analysis, responsible for seeing to it that these problems are solved.

If the President is to discharge this responsibility in an effective manner, he should receive continuous staff advice and assistance from someone who is in close touch with the civilian career service of the Government.

The Commission has concluded, therefore, that an Office of Personnel should be established within the President's Office. We have also concluded that the director of this office should be the Chairman of the Civil Service Commission.

The director of the Office of Personnel, within the President's Office should function as the principal staff adviser to the President in connection with problems related to the career civilian service of the Federal Government. He should, for example, be responsible for keeping in close touch with the work of the various offices of personnel within the departments and agencies.

Also, the director should advise the President on ways and means of identifying exceptional talent within the Federal Civil Service in professional, scientific, and executive posts, and of making sure that this talent is being utilized in the most effective possible manner.

Furthermore, the director of personnel should be in such close touch with the conditions surrounding employment in the Federal service that he will always be in a position to advise the President as to the steps which need to be taken to put the Government in a position where it will be looked upon as one of the most progressive employers in the Nation.

Our later report on personnel recommends, in addition to the specific recommendation we are including in this report, a series of basic changes in the field of personnel administration.

Recommendation No. 11

An Office of Personnel should be established in the President's Office under the direction of the Chairman of the Civil Service Commission in order to provide the President with continuous staff advice and assistance relative to matters affecting the career civilian service of the Federal Government.

The Office of the Budget

Since 1921 the Office of the Budget has developed into the President's largest and most important staff agency. We discuss in another report the internal organization of the Office of the Budget, the functions which it performs, the process of budgeting, and the form in which the budget should be presented to the Congress. Important recommendations for action appear in that report.

Here we wish to stress the vital role which the Office of the Budget now plays, and which it should be equipped to play even more effectively in the future. It is a misconception to think of this office merely as an agency for the collection and compilation of estimates in the annual preparation of the budget document. Its functions go far beyond strictly budgetary matters. It is the President's main reliance as an instrumentality for the improvement of management and the attainment of economy and efficiency throughout the executive branch. Our purpose is not only to perfect the work of the Office of the Budget in budgetary operations as such, but to strengthen it as the managerial arm of the President.

It is for this reason that we have not adopted the recommendation of our task force on fiscal, budgeting, and accounting activities that the Office of the Budget should be transferred back to the Treasury Department. When the budget agency was shifted in 1939 from that department to the Executive Office of the President, the transfer was based on a recognition of the close working relationship which had grown up between the President and the Office of the Budget, and of the desirability of making the resources of that agency directly available for the use of the President. We believe, in view of past developments, and in the light of our conception of the role of the Office of the Budget, that it would be a step backward to remove it from the President's Office.

The primary function of the Office of the Budget is, of course, the preparation of the budget for submission annually by the President to the Congress. The first step in the budgetary process is a preview of financial requirements for the Government and the determination of target figures for transmission to the departments. As a second step, the Office of the Budget must assemble and analyze the resulting departmental estimates containing the requests of the various executive agencies for appropriations. The third step is the formulation of an over-all program of fiscal needs for the entire executive branch which harmonizes the agency requests.

Beyond these primary budgetary duties, the Office of the Budget has additional vital responsibilities.

It furnishes advice to the President as to ways and means for the improvement of management in governmental operations, both in the central offices in Washington and in the field offices.

It develops plans for reorganization of executive agencies to keep the structure of the executive branch in line with changing programs of operation.

It serves as a clearing house for proposals for legislative enactment, in order to advise the departments and Congress as to what proposed legislation is in accord with the program of the President.

It provides a means for coordinating services which are common to many or all executive agencies, such as statistics and publications.

A revitalized Office of the Budget will show improved performance in all these aspects of its work. Our subsequent recommendations are intended to achieve such a well-rounded and balanced budget agency, with particular emphasis given to the development of a more comprehensive program for the improvement of administrative management in the executive branch under the auspices of the Office of the Budget.

Office of General Services

In the direction and supervision of the operations of the executive branch, the President needs an organization which will include some of the agencies that serve all the departments. This is discussed in a later report.

Chapter Three

DEPARTMENTAL MANAGEMENT

The great executive departments and agencies are the operating units of the executive branch. The effectiveness of Presidential direction and supervision and the efficiency of administrative operations depend primarily upon the satisfactory management of these operating units. The heads of these agencies have a dual role. They are the advisers of the President upon policies; they are also the administrators of great operating agencies.

The Congress, and sometimes the President, have set up a maze of independent agencies reporting directly to the President; and the Congress frequently has fixed by statute the internal organization of departments and agencies and has given authority directly to subordinate officers. As a result, instead of being a unified organization, responsible to the executive direction of the President and accountable to the Congress for the use of the powers and funds granted by law, the executive branch is a chaos of bureaus and subdivisions.

The responsibility, the vigor of executive leadership, and the unity of administration of the executive branch as planned by the Constitution must be restored.

What Is Wrong with the Executive Departments and Agencies

a. The gigantic and sudden growth of the executive branch has produced great confusion within the departments and agencies as well as in their relations to the President and to each other.

b. There are too many separate agencies, several of which are not combined in accordance with their major purposes. Consequently, there are overlaps, duplications, and inadequacies in determination of policies,

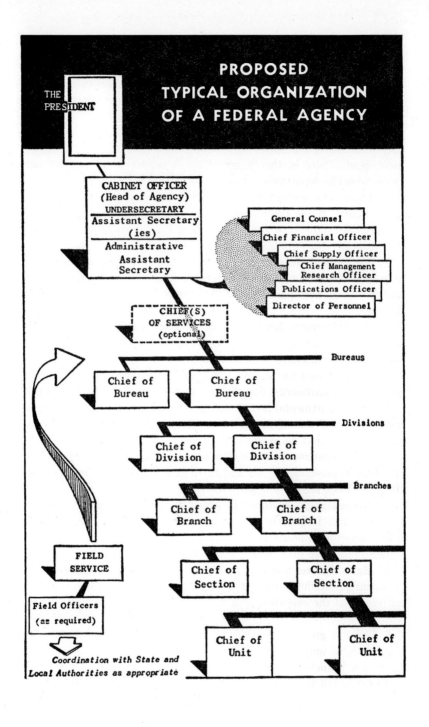

PROPOSED
TYPICAL ORGANIZATION
OF A FEDERAL AGENCY

THE
PRESIDENT

CABINET OFFICER
(Head of Agency)
UNDERSECRETARY
Assistant Secretary
(ies)
Administrative
Assistant
Secretary

General Counsel
Chief Financial Officer
Chief Supply Officer
Chief Management
Research Officer
Publications Officer
Director of Personnel

CHIEF(S)
OF SERVICES
(optional)

Bureaus

Chief of
Bureau

Chief of
Bureau

Divisions

Chief of
Division

Chief of
Division

Branches

Chief of
Branch

Chief of
Branch

FIELD
SERVICE

Chief of
Section

Chief of
Section

Field Officers
(as required)

Chief of
Unit

Chief of
Unit

Coordination with State and
Local Authorities as appropriate

and in the execution of programs with a resultant lack of a clear-cut mission for each department.

c. The line of authority from departmental heads through subordinates is often abridged by independent authorities granted to bureau or division heads, sometimes through congressional act or stipulations in appropriations. Department heads, in many instances, do not have authority commensurate with their responsibilities. Such bureau autonomy undermines the authority of both the President and the department head. There is, therefore, a lack of departmental integration in performing the department's major mission.

d. There is no uniformity in the method of appointing departmental subordinates. While Under Secretaries and Assistant Secretaries should properly be subject to Senate confirmation, about one-third of the bureau heads (or equivalent officials) must now also be so confirmed.

e. The Federal Government has failed to develop an aggressive program for building a corps of administrators of the highest level of ability. It is not quantity of administrators that is required, it is quality.

f. The department heads in most cases lack sufficient authority to assign within their departments such responsibility as would promote economy and efficiency.

g. While a common pattern of internal organization cannot be applied to all departments, there is less uniformity than there should be.

h. Such departmental housekeeping services as personnel, accounting, budgeting, and management research are overcentralized in outside agencies or subject to overly strict controls.

i. Some department heads lack adequate staffs to administer decentralized housekeeping services or to coordinate these functions with the President's staff.

j. Detailed appropriations assigned to individual agencies by the Congress lead frequently to increasing the number of employees because department heads lack authority to assign work directed by the Congress to those units where it can be performed most effectively.

k. Many statutes and departmental regulations that control the department's procedures are unduly complicated. They set up such rigid patterns that the execution of a congressional purpose is inefficient and wasteful.

l. There is great duplication in departmental field services. Many bureaus have unnecessary field services duplicating others, and many have more branches in the field than are at all necessary. Some department heads fail to delegate authority adequately to field officials.

23

m. Confusion in the Government agencies bewilders the citizen in his contacts with the Government.

The Reforms Recommended

The direction of necessary reforms is amply indicated by the above recitation of deficiencies. The Commission's recommendations follow:

Recommendation No. 12

The numerous agencies of the executive branch must be grouped into departments as nearly as possible by major purposes in order to give a coherent mission to each department.

By placing related functions cheek-by-jowl the overlaps can be eliminated, and, of even greater importance, coordinated policies can be developed.

Recommendation No. 13

Within each department, the subsidiary bureaus should also be grouped as nearly as possible according to major purposes.

Recommendation No. 14

Under the President, the heads of departments must hold full responsibility for the conduct of their departments. There must be a clear line of authority reaching down through every step of the organization and no subordinate should have authority independent from that of his superior.

Recommendation No. 15

There must be more decentralization into the operating agencies of such services as accounting, budgeting, recruiting and managing of personnel, under common standards and supervision established for the entire executive branch.

Recommendation No. 16

Department heads must have adequate staff assistance if they are to achieve efficiency and economy in departmental operations.

Reasons for Recommendations

GROUPING OF AGENCIES

A primary essential for the better organization of the whole executive branch is consolidation and unification into a more simple structure. This is the first necessity for the establishment of efficient and economical functioning of the Government. This step is also necessary in order to relieve the President of onerous administrative detail which arises from lack of unification.

At the present time there are 65 departments, administrations, agencies, boards, and commissions engaged in executive work, all of which report directly to the President—if they report to anyone. This number does not include the "independent" regulatory agencies in their quasi-judicial or quasi-legislative functions. It is manifestly impossible for the President to give adequate supervision to so many agencies. Even one hour a week devoted to each of them would require a 65-hour week for the President, to say nothing of the time he must devote to his great duties in developing and directing major policies as his constitutional obligations require.

Recommendation No. 17

Therefore, we recommend that these various agencies be consolidated into about one-third of the present number.

With the complicated activities of the Federal Government, it is not possible to arrive at perfection in carrying out these principles. An agency may of necessity have work related to that of any other agencies not in the same group. The determination of the major group in which such an agency shall be included becomes a matter of over-all judgment. Such instances, however, are exceptional.

DEPARTMENTAL STAFF

In order that the dual function of heads of departments as advisers to the President and administrators of the departments may be accomplished, they must have competent staff assistance.

Some of these departments are larger than the whole Government was 20 years ago. Some of them have far less management staff than industrial enterprises of half the size.

Recommendation No. 18

Each department head should receive from the Congress administrative authority to organize his department and to place him in control of its administration.

The following will indicate the opinions of the Commission as to the organization of the departments. Some of this set-up is already in effect. We are, however, setting no hard and fast rule. Each department head should determine the organization and be free to amend it.

In general, we recommend that the following top executive staff which now exists in many departments should be preserved and extended to all major agencies.

a. A cabinet officer or administrator as the head of the agency with his personal staff.

b. An under secretary (or equivalent official) who shall assume the duties of the departmental head in his absence and who can undertake general supervision of the department.

c. Such number of assistant secretaries (or equivalent officials) as may be necessary with functions assigned by the head of the department.

d. These officials, being of policy rank, should be appointed by the President and confirmed by the Senate.

In addition there should generally be an administrative assistant secretary who might be appointed solely for administrative duties of a housekeeping and management nature and who would give continuity in top management. They and certain other officials, as in the Treasury Department, where length of tenure makes appointment from the career service preferable, should be appointed from that service.

In addition to the under secretary and assistant secretaries referred to above, we recommend that the heads of all of the major executive agencies should be equipped, as some now are, with such staff assistants as:

a. GENERAL COUNSEL

b. FINANCIAL OFFICER (accounting, budgeting, and disbursements)

c. PERSONNEL OFFICER

d. SUPPLY OFFICER

e. MANAGEMENT RESEARCH OFFICER

f. INFORMATION AND PUBLICATIONS OFFICER

g. CONGRESSIONAL LIAISON OFFICER

We wish to emphasize especially the importance of staff members assigned to management research and review. The enormous operations of the executive agencies require constant reexamination.

These staff assistants, like those to the President, should not be assigned operating duties. Such duties must lie with the bureau or service directors.

The duties of these officers are indicated by their titles. It is necessary for department heads to make appropriate arrangements for constant review of department policies and programs. These responsibilities must be performed by senior departmental officials.

26

Recommendation No. 19

We recommend that, to lay the foundations of authority and discipline, the staff officials and, as a rule, bureau chiefs should be appointed by the department heads, and that proper consideration be given to the promotion of career employees.

Recommendations in Subsequent Reports Affecting Departmental Management

We present here, as an essential part of departmental management, recommendations which we make in our other reports on special subjects.

a. The Government must develop an aggressive program for building a corps of departmental administrators of the highest level of ability, and must develop a career service that will attract our best young men and women.

b. Exceptional administrative ability in employees should be recognized, and their transfer or promotion from one agency to another should be made possible in order to avoid blind alleys in promotion of talented public servants.

c. The recruitment and examination of civilian employees, except for positions in lower grades common to most departments, should be decentralized into the departments and the agencies. These selections should be based upon procedures and standards of merit proposed by the department, but approved and enforced by the Civil Service Commission.

d. The process of eliminating inefficient or incompatible employees should be greatly simplified, with adequate protection against injustice.

e. The whole budgeting function of the Government should be strengthened and simplified. A "performance budget" should be substituted for the present cumbersome procedure.

f. Federal accounting should be simplified and standardized. This function is a managerial necessity especially at the executive-agency level. It requires expedition, simplification, and the elimination of red tape.

g. The "management function" should be given more emphasis in the executive agencies and coordinated with that function in the Office of the Budget.

h. The procurement and handling of supplies (except for articles of common use) should be decentralized into the departments under standards and procedures to be established in the Office of General Services. That Office should also coordinate use of building space, management of records and other general services.

The application of the methods mentioned above requires important reorganization of the internal structure and methods in many of the executive agencies.

Authority

Recommendation No. 20

We recommend that the department head should be given authority to determine the organization within his department. He should be given authority to assign funds appropriated by the Congress for a given purpose to that agency in his department which he believes can best effect the will of Congress.

After all, it is he who must appear before Congress and account for his stewardship.

Standard Nomenclature

Recommendation No. 21

The Commission recommends that the internal operating organization of each department should follow a standard nomenclature as follows:

> **Service**
> **Bureau**
> **Division**
> **Branch**
> **Section**
> **Unit**

In general the principal operating unit of a department should be labeled a bureau. In those instances where a number of bureaus may be consolidated into one operating group, or where an individual bureau is particularly large, then the Commission believes that the designation "Service" should be injected into the operating structure.

The term "Office," as used in this report, refers to staff agencies, which serve the President or his department heads.

Federal Field Services

The business of the Federal Government is primarily transacted by field offices. Nearly 90 percent of all Federal employees work outside of Washington. There must be some official in the Government responsible for constant study and simplification and coordination of departmental work in the field.

The findings of our task forces indicate the direction for reorganization and improvement. Among these findings, there are listed the following deficiencies.

a. Too many separately organized, highly specialized field offices representing individual departments, their bureaus, and even different units of one bureau.

b. The ineffectiveness of field offices in dealing with operating problems because headquarters fail to delegate authority.

c. Confused lines of direction and supervision between specialized headquarters units and the field.

d. Inadequate systems of reporting and inspection which prevent administrative officials from knowing how effectively and efficiently their field organization is performing.

e. Lack of coordination of effort among the various Federal field offices, both within the same agency and between different agencies.

f. Failure to make the most of potential cooperation from State and local governments and private organizations.

This Commission is not in a position to make individual recommendations regarding the several hundred different field services of Federal departments and agencies. The proper distribution, supervision, and coordination of these field offices is essentially a problem for the President and the head of each department, with the cooperation of the Congress.

Recommendation No. 22

Administrative regions and regional headquarters should be more nearly comparable geographically.

The present regional districts of Federal bureaus and agencies, if superimposed, one on the other on a map, would show an unbelievable spider-web pattern of regional boundaries. If this situation were improved, service to the public would be far more satisfactory.

Recommendation No. 23

Greater utilization should be made of pooled centralized administrative services.

Now agencies separately provide their own supply, motor transport, space, and other services. Substantial savings in overhead cost are possible.

Recommendation No. 24

Reporting and inspection practices should be strengthened.

At present the relative effectiveness of field offices is most difficult to determine.

Recommendation No. 25

Field relationships with State and local officials should be standardized.

This problem is particularly serious where there are grant-in-aid programs, for frequently one program deals with numerous State and local agencies under one set of terms and conditions; whereas another agency may have quite different operating requirements.

Recommendation No. 26

The responsibility now vested in the Public Buildings Administration for providing certain types of space necessary to meet the field requirements of Federal agencies should be expanded.

Recommendation No. 27

Manuals of instructions now in use should be revised and simplified and their self-defeating degree of detail eliminated.

A major effort should be made to bring the Federal Government closer to the public served. Many department and agency heads have neglected this matter, and the result is that departmental people are isolated from field officials and from the public.

It should always be remembered that the purpose of any democratic government is to serve the people and that the personnel in Federal field offices are the Government's instrument in its dealings with the citizens.

Conclusions

The above is a general skeleton which we will fill out by supplemental reports on each of the major activities. These reports will contain detailed recommendations for assignments of functions and reduction of overlap and red tape so as to obtain an efficient over-all organization. Statements of savings to be achieved will be included.

The savings to the American taxpayer can amount to billions.

II
Budgeting and
Accounting

Introduction

There are serious weaknesses in the internal operations of the Federal Government in the fiscal field. These weaknesses penetrate into the heart of every governmental transaction. The President's budget, as submitted to the Congress annually, does not indicate accurately what the costs of each activity will be over the coming year; and the Government's accounting system, outmoded and cumbersome, does not indicate what was accomplished with the money spent in the year past.

Some of the fiscal concepts of the Federal Government come down from Alexander Hamilton. They were archaic when the total expenditures of the Government were $4,000,000,000 per annum. Now, with a Government which expends over $40,000,000,000 per annum, they are totally inadequate. They have been patched up over the years, but, even so, they contribute to wasted effort, and even defeat the capable management and initiative of the best of officials.

The time has come when the budgeting and accounting system of the Federal Government must be modernized. Unless this is done, the Congress, the executive branch, and the public will be unable intelligently to judge the wisdom of the proposed expenditures and the effectiveness of past expenditures.

Reorganization of Budgeting and Accounting

Present budgeting and accounting procedures confuse the Congress and the public and make effective administration almost impossible of attainment.

With this unfortunate situation in mind, this Commission proposes a radical revision in the Federal Government's budgetary presentation and in its methods of accounting for past expenditures. The new structure we propose is intended to tell the Congress and the public two things:

1. *On budgeting:* **What is the money wanted for?**

2. *On accounting:* **What do the taxpayers get for it?**

These two question lie at the root of any fiscal system. The present budgeting and accounting system of the Federal Government either does not supply answers to these questions, or supplies "half answers." A good system would supply the right answers.

Budgeting and accounting go hand in hand. Sums budgeted in advance are subsequently accounted for as obligated and spent. The activities are the same and the accounts themselves must be the same. Only by making comparisons between similar activities, and between the same activity in one year against another year, can efficiency be tested. Only by making the head of each activity financially responsible for all the costs of his program, can he be held to account. Only by modernizing the Federal system of budgeting and accounting will it be possible to tell exactly how much any single program or project is costing. The Federal Government must be able to assess results intelligently.

By following our recommendations, the Congress, the executive branch, and the people will have not only the same information they have now, but more information, presented in a more intelligible fashion.

Our recommendations on budgeting are presented in Chapter One of the report, and those on accounting in Chapter Three. In Chapter Two, we discuss the internal organization of the Office of the Budget.

Chapter One

THE BUDGET

Reform of the Budget

The budget and appropriation process is the heart of the management and control of the executive branch.

There is a great need for reform in the method of budgeting and in the appropriation structure.

The Federal budget is an inadequate document, poorly organized and improperly designed to serve its major purpose, which is to present an understandable and workable financial plan for the expenditures of the Government. The document has grown larger and larger each year as the Government's requirements have increased, but its general framework and method of presentation have not changed. The latest budget document, that for 1949–50, contains 1,625 closely printed pages, with about 1,500,000 words, and sums covering thousands of specific appropriations.

There is no uniformity in the schedules of appropriations. Some appropriations represent huge sums, others small amounts. Appropriations for the same service appear in many different places. Much of this results from historical accident.

The Bureau of Indian Affairs, for example, had approximately 100 appropriation titles and subtitles for the expenditure during the fiscal year 1947–48 of about $50,000,000. The largest appropriation item for this bureau amounted to more than $11,000,000, while the smallest item was $114.53.

At the other extreme, perhaps, is the Veterans Administration, which has an appropriation item of more than a billion dollars for "salaries and expenses," a title which indicates nothing whatever of the work program of that organization.

35

A Performance Budget

Recommendation No. 1

We recommend that the whole budgetary concept of the Federal Government should be refashioned by the adoption of a budget based upon functions, activities, and projects: this we designate as a "performance budget."

Such an approach would focus attention upon the general character and relative importance of the work to be done, or upon the service to be rendered, rather than upon the things to be acquired, such as personal services, supplies, equipment, and so on. These latter objects are, after all, only the means to an end. The all-important thing in budgeting is the work or the service to be accomplished, and what that work or service will cost.

Under performance budgeting, attention is centered on the function or activity—on the accomplishment of the purpose—instead of on lists of employees or authorizations of purchases. In reality, this method of budgeting concentrates Congressional action and executive direction on the scope and magnitude of the different Federal activities. It places both accomplishment and cost in a clear light before the Congress and the public.

We give two examples of the different methods of presenting the budget estimates in Annex I. (pp. 56–63.) To indicate the deficiencies of existing practices, we may cite here the National Naval Medical Center at Bethesda. This hospital now receives allotments from 12 different Navy appropriation titles such as:

SECRETARY'S OFFICE—Miscellaneous Expenses, Navy
BUREAU OF SHIPS—Maintenance
BUREAU OF ORDNANCE—Ordnance and Ordnance Stores
BUREAU OF SUPPLIES AND ACCOUNTS—Pay, Subsistence, and Transportation
BUREAU OF SUPPLIES AND ACCOUNTS—Maintenance
BUREAU OF SUPPLIES AND ACCOUNTS—Transportation of Things
BUREAU OF MEDICINE AND SURGERY—Medical Department, Navy
FIVE OTHER SIMILAR APPROPRIATION TITLES

There is no one title in the present Budget where the total cost of operating a Navy hospital is shown.

We propose, for instance, that by using performance budgeting, the costs of operating the Bethesda Center, along with those of

other comparable Naval hospitals, would be shown as an identifiable program under one appropriation title for "Medical Care."

This is illustrated in the first example in Annex I. (p. 56.)

The idea of a performance budget is not new. It has been adopted in the modernization of budgets by some States and several municipalities.

The performance budget does not change or shift legislative responsibility; control by the Congress still lies in the power to limit expenditures by appropriations. Performance budgeting gives more comprehensive and reliable information to the President, the Congress, and the general public, and helps the individual congressman to understand what the Government is doing, how much it is doing, and what the costs are. Supporting schedules can be fully provided, and in more understandable and effective form.

One of the primary purposes of the performance budget would be to improve Congressional examination of budgetary requirements. Such examination should be largely on the level of accomplishment, and for this reason the Congress needs to know clearly just what the whole of the expenditures is and what the executive and administrative agencies propose to do with the money they request. In the Bethesda case mentioned above, the Congress under the new system would have presented the cost of operating the hospital in detail, so that the Congress might readily compare such cost with that of the preceding year or with the costs of other comparable hospitals.

The Bureau of Ships in the Navy Department, for example, is financed by 27 appropriations, many of which, as shown in the budget, have no apparent connection with the Bureau. Efforts have been made to resolve this confusion through the working out of an adequate budget structure. The ideas thus developed have been applied in part to the new Air Force estimates as set forth in the budget in 1949–50.

In a detailed example, given at the end of this part of the report, of the effect of performance budgeting on the Forest Service, our task force points out that the real operating cost of the Forest Service for the management and protection of the national forests does not appear in full under that heading in the budget, but actually is included in several other places. The total operating cost for the national forests, as displayed by the performance budget, would be shown as about $43,000,000 instead of only $26,000,000 as indicated under the present appropriation headings in the budget.

The New Approach

Indeed, the first task of the Appropriations Committees is to review what has been accomplished and what is proposed for the future period, the latter always being examined in the light of the past experience. The approach which we propose should enable these committees more easily to decide the basic expenditure issue each year; namely, just what should be the magnitude of the many Federal programs.

The performance budget would make it possible for the budget document to be submitted and acted upon in a shorter length of time. It would not delay or hamper the action of the Congress on the budget. It would assure more complete expenditure estimates and more accurate revenue figures for the next budget period.

Executive and legislative review of functional estimates and program justifications under the performance budget should center around two basic questions:

First: What is the desirable magnitude of any major Government program or function in terms of need, relation to other programs, and proportion of total governmental expenditures? This is essentially a question of public policy, and must be answered by the responsible officials of the executive branch and eventually by the Congress.

Second: How efficiently and economically can an approved Government program be executed? In other words, can the same amount of work be performed satisfactorily under different arrangements or through improved procedures at less cost?

The performance budget would enable administrators to place responsibility upon subordinate officials for the clear execution of the provisions made by the Congress. It would also simplify the reporting and accounting system.

Appropriation Structure and Performance Budgeting

The present appropriation structure underlying the budget is a patchwork affair evolved over a great many years and following no rational pattern. In some areas of the budget, there are entirely too many appropriation items; in others perhaps too few. Some appropriation items are exceedingly broad in scope; others are narrow on account of excessive itemization. Appropriations for a particular function appear in different places. In spite of recent simplifications, the language of some appropriation items remains a jungle of detailed provisions. Many of these

38

detailed prescriptions would seem to be susceptible of more or less uniform treatment in codified form.

The appropriation structure not only affects the presentation of the budget estimates, but runs to the root of management and fiscal responsibility. Departmental management is complicated and fiscal responsibility is diffused when single bureaus or functions are financed from diverse appropriations.

The appropriation structure is further complicated by several different kinds of authorizations such as annual, no-year, and permanent appropriations, reappropriations, contract authorizations, and appropriations to liquidate contract authorizations. Congress, the press, and the public are therefore often confused about the total amount of appropriations in any major appropriation bill. Certainly a comprehensive survey of existing appropriation practices looking towards simplification of appropriation structure, language, and procedure is long overdue. The revision of these practices should be made along the general lines and in accordance with the underlying purpose of the performance budget.

Recommendation No. 2

We recommend to the Congress that a complete survey of the appropriation structure should be undertaken without delay.

Checks against Deficits

The Congress has long been interested in seeing that agencies so spend their appropriations as not to incur deficits. Various actions have been taken both by the Congress and Presidents to achieve this end. These have finally resulted in a system of apportioning appropriations.

This system requires the spending agencies to submit to the Budget Bureau for its approval their requests for quarterly apportionments of their appropriations. Any revisions in the original apportionments require supplementary forms to be submitted to the Bureau for approval. A copy of the apportionments and any revisions goes to the Treasury for its information.

Each month the spending agencies are required to report on the status of their appropriations, including obligations and balances. But these reports on the status of appropriations are often misleading, since the spending agencies may report their obligations as they see fit. Neither the Budget Bureau nor the Treasury seems to have any direct check or control over what these agencies report. Furthermore, the administrative accounts, as prescribed by the Comptroller General, do not provide properly for the keeping of obligations under apportionments. Under these circumstances, the authority of the Budget Bureau to approve all apportionments on behalf of the President means very little in actually preventing current deficits.

This is the most glaring weakness of the present system of apportionments.

Much needed control cannot be effectively applied under the system of accounting presently employed by the operating departments and agencies. This is an important reason for our subsequent accounting recommendations.

Separation of Capital Outlays

There is, at present, constant confusion in Federal budgeting and accounting because current expenditures and capital outlays are intermingled. These two types of expenditures are essentially different in character, and should, therefore, be shown separately under each major function or activity in the budget. This is an important feature of performance budgeting.

The appropriations for capital purposes, provided each year, are usually only a part of the total cost of the numerous projects which the Federal Government is initiating or has under way. Many of these appropriations are made for a year's work on a given project without an adequate understanding of the total previous expenditure and the cost commitment which has been authorized in order to have a completed structure or improvement. This is not good business on the part of the Federal Government.

While capital projects may be carefully analyzed for usefulness, timeliness, and total probable costs at the time of original authorization, the total remaining costs of all capital projects should be set forth in the budget each year, together with costs incurred to date. These costs should be revised in succeeding years to keep them current with later developments.

Recommendation No. 3

We recommend that the budget estimates of all operating departments and agencies of the Government should be divided into two primary categories—current operating expenditures and capital outlays.

This Type of Budget Already in Use

The use of this type budgeting has been demonstrated by the budgeting of Government corporations under the Government Corporation Control Act of 1945. Government corporation budgeting practice at the present time amounts to a partial adoption of many of these simplifications based upon functional budgeting, accrual accounting and separation of capital outlays from current expenditures. It has greatly added to flexibility of management and to simplification of budgeting, accounting and audit.

Reductions in Appropriated Expenditures

Present law and practice are not clear on whether or not the Budget Bureau and the President have the right to reduce appropriated amounts during the year for which they were provided.

Recommendation No. 4

We recommend that it is in the public interest that this question be clarified and, in any event, that the President should have authority to reduce expenditures under appropriations, if the purposes intended by the Congress are still carried out.

Chapter Two

OFFICE OF THE BUDGET

In its first report the Commission on Organization of the Executive Branch of the Government spoke of the essential role of the Office of the Budget as a staff agency to the President. Through this office the President exercises his authority over the preparation of appropriation requests and over the execution of expenditure programs. Through this office, also, he develops improvements in the management of the executive branch as a whole, receives advice upon reorganization of administrative practices, analyzes the legislative requests of departments, and obtains coordination of certain activities such as statistics.

The Office of the Budget can be the greatest instrumentality of the President for achieving continuous results in improved administrative efficiency.

The executive branch has grown so tremendously in size and complexity that efficiency and economy cannot be attained merely by an annual review of the departmental requests for funds. The review of these estimates is only the last in a series of steps, all of which are essential to the President's management of the executive branch. The President's staff must see that each department prepares its basic program in harmony with the general program of the administration; that it prepares a budget which would put that program into effect in the most economical manner possible; and that it continuously reviews its own organization and its management practices in order to make sure that its program is responsibly and effectively administered.

The Office of the Budget and the executive branch generally have been caught in a vicious circle. The weakness of management in the several departments and agencies, particularly the weakness of some budget offices, often throws too great a burden of review of the details of estimates on the Office of the Budget. As a result, the Office must devote too large a share of its energies and personnel to work on departmental estimates that should have been prepared properly in the first place by the departments and agencies themselves.

Moreover, the lack of a closely knit system of cooperation in developing a program for the executive branch as a whole has produced for many years a series of departmental budgets that it is difficult, if not impossible, to coordinate satisfactorily by a review and revision of the estimates.

All these difficulties are partly the cause, and partly the effect, of the way in which the estimates are presented to the Congress and the way in which funds are appropriated. Only the reform of the general budgetary system and the establishment of a program or performance budget will make it possible for the Office of the Budget to develop the kind of teamwork as a part of the President's Office that will let it serve the President most effectively.

The Estimates Division

The Budget Office's main job—the nucleus of all its work—is to review and revise the departmental estimates. This is primarily the work of the Estimates Division of the Office. It gives the Office the opportunity to examine every program of the executive branch.

This work gives it the information and the influence with which to help the President develop his program for the executive branch as a whole and to improve its organization and management.

Each of the other divisions deals with some aspect of Government-wide problems. The success of each of them depends to a great extent on close teamwork with the Estimates Division, since the budget examiners in the Estimates Division are most closely in touch with the several departments and their programs.

Recommendation No. 5

Therefore, the Commission recommends that the review and revision by the Estimates Division of the Office of the Budget be done from the first to the final stages in conjunction with representatives of the Administrative Management and Fiscal Divisions.

The review of the estimates must contribute to, and must in turn be supported by, three other principal types of staff work:

a. The development of a consistent policy and program for the executive branch as a whole.

43

b. The improvement of its organization and management.

c. The coordination of certain administrative activities which are common to various departments (such as statistics and reports).

The Legislative Reference Division

The first Director of the Budget and the Congressional committees with which he worked saw that the whole purpose of the budget system would fail if each department should independently recommend legislation which would later require appropriations and expenditures. They saw, moreover, that the work of the Congress and its committees would be infinitely more difficult if they had to consider great quantities of legislation, much of it on highly technical subjects, which had been prepared by a number of competing departments without any regard for the President's program.

The first Director of the Budget accordingly began the work which is now carried on in the Office of the Budget primarily by the Legislative Reference Division. This is the work of compiling information for the President on the departments' recommendations for legislation. This work is done partly to provide the President with full information on which he may decide whether to sign or veto an act, and partly so that the departments and agencies may be told how their legislative recommendations are related to the program of the President.

During the Eightieth Congress, the Bureau of the Budget had to advise the President or the executive departments on 5,992 bills, and had to give the President information on the 1,438 bills passed by the Congress.

The Fiscal Division

The clearance of legislative recommendations is one of the ways by which the Office of the Budget helps to develop a consistent program for the executive branch. A second way is to analyze the estimates of the several departments to see how their programs are related to each other, and how they may be shaped into a harmonious program and fiscal policy for the executive branch as a whole.

The difficulty here is twofold:

First, a fiscal policy for the executive branch depends less on how much money is appropriated than on how much money is spent in any one year. Appropriations and expenditures are not the same, and both must be analyzed to see the effect of Government expenditures on the economy of the Nation.

Second, both appropriations and expenditures are usually shown department by department, and bureau by bureau, whereas several bureaus in several different departments may all be engaged in different aspects of the same program (as several are, for example, in the development of natural resources). The adoption of our recommendations on the performance budget will call attention to this interrelation.

The Fiscal Division's most important accomplishment during the past few years has perhaps been the development of the Budget Preview, which sets forth in May the financial requirements of the Government for the Budget which is to be sent to the Congress the following January. This preview helps determine the President's policy on the next Budget, and helps set the "target figures" to govern the departments in the preparation of their estimates.

Recommendation No. 6

The Commission recommends the development of much closer relations between the constituent divisions of the Office of the Budget and with such agencies as the President's personal staff, the Treasury Department, the Economic Adviser, and the National Security Resources Board.

The Administrative Management Division

The Office of the Budget, primarily through its Administrative Management Division, advises the President on over-all organization and on management in the departments and agencies.

The Office of the Budget has appreciated the extent to which the Administrative Management Division must draw on the Estimates Division for information. It has not been able to take advantage to an equal extent of the contribution that administrative management work could make to the preparation of estimates and the attainment of economy in departmental expenditures.

The budget for the 1950 fiscal year is the first in which the Office of the Budget decided how much money each department needed partly on the basis of definite criteria that show how much personnel should be needed for a certain quantity of standard work. These criteria or "staffing guides" apply mainly to the common services such as personnel, accounting, and disbursing.

The only way by which the Office of the Budget can rescue itself from dealing with an unbearable quantity of budgetary detail is to put greater emphasis on the improvement of management in the departments—particularly the improvement of the departments' budget offices.

It is essential that each department and agency have a strong budget office and a strong program of management improvement. The Office of the Budget should be able to work with its counterpart in each department or agency so that the President may put into effect sound principles of organization and economical procedures of management throughout the executive branch. In our first report, the chapter dealing with Departmental Management describes in greater detail the reforms that are required.

The Government, by the common wish of the President and the Congress, is entering upon a period of vigorous reorganization. The President needs not only a grant of authority to carry out this reorganization, but competent staff work in his Office to put the necessary reforms into effect. The Administrative Management Division of the Office of the Budget, which supplied the technical assistance in preparing the reorganization plans under the Reorganization Acts of 1939 and 1945, must be the nucleus of such work.

This Division should be expanded and strengthened. But it must not be assumed that it can do the job by itself. The Administrative Management Division should be only the nucleus of the President's staff work for the improvement of organization and management.

A further problem in administrative management is that of the field services. Better provisions should be made for staff work on this problem in the Office of the Budget.

The business of the Federal Government is primarily transacted by Federal field services. Approximately 90 percent of all Federal employees are working outside of Washington. There must be some official in the Government responsible for constant study and simplification and coordination of field work.

The findings of our task force indicate that the field services sorely need attention. We dealt with this subject in our first report, in Chapter Three, "Departmental Management."

Recommendation No. 7

In dealing with the budgets of the executive departments and agencies, the Office of the Budget should place much greater emphasis on the developing of policies and standards to govern the preparation of estimates, and on the development of adequate budget work in the departments themselves, and comparatively

46

less on the review by its own staff of the details of departmental estimates. A program or performance budget should be the goal. Further emphasis should be placed on the management research function, particularly as it effects the field services.

Publications

There is need for stronger coordination of the publications of the executive branch. The total printing bill of the executive branch at the Government Printing Office in the 1947 fiscal year was about $47,500,000 for approximately 14 billion items. It represented an increase of $37,000,000 and 10.5 billion items in 20 years. In addition to the activities of the Public Printer, the separate executive agencies operate 133 printing plants and 256 duplicating plants at a cost of about $25,000,000 per annum.

The volume of document expansion is somewhat indicated by the increase in executive departmental free mail in recent years, for it rose from an estimated $9,347,505 in the fiscal year 1930 to approximately $76,608,338 in the fiscal year 1948.

There is need for review of these and other reports to eliminate duplication, to stop reports which are no longer necessary, and to coordinate the production of publications with the Public Printer. As most publications of the executive branch are of routine order, there would need to be only a small staff to effect great economies.

Recommendation No. 8

The commission recommends that the President be given the means and authority to supervise all publications of the executive branch and that he delegate this authority to a responsible official in the Office of the Budget.

Coordination of Statistical Services

Our task force on statistical agencies found that in the fiscal year 1947 about 10,500 employees in some 50 different civilian agencies of the Government were engaged in statistical work at a cost of about $43,000,000.

The statistical research and publications are the very basis of public administration and are essential to study and understanding of economic and social life. The services, however, have many defects. Deficiencies were found in the training of personnel. Other defects include

47

incomplete coordination, overlapping functions, jurisdictional conflicts, lack of comparability, lack of standard concepts, definitions, and classifications. There are conflicts between reports, faulty coverage in various areas and gaps in the statistics assembled. Other faults include excessive detail and delay in publication. Nine different congressional committees deal with these problems.

The Office of the Budget has a Division of Statistical Standards but the function requires more emphasis. Also, there is insufficient authority to compel reforms.

Recommendation No. 9

The Commission therefore recommends that authority be given to the President to effect improvements in statistical activities and that such authority be delegated to the Director of the Division of Statistical Services in the Office of the Budget. Thus responsibility for reforms would be definitely located.

The Commission's further recommendations are given in its report on Government Statistical Services which follows this report.

The Commission's investigation developed that by coordination and elimination of duplication and overlap through assignment of statistical functions, much might be saved annually and the statistical services would be made more efficient and more serviceable to the public.

Chapter Three

REORGANIZATION OF ACCOUNTING
IN THE GOVERNMENT

Accounting

The conduct of the accounting system of the Government affects all other administrative problems.

The financial operations of the Government must be controlled even more rigorously than those of private business. Maintenance of financial integrity affects the confidence of the Nation in itself and the moral standards of all the people. A failure of such integrity in private business affects the pocketbooks and slackens the morals of a few, but its failure in public business affects the morals of all.

Policies and methods in the handling of governmental funds must be clearly defined and responsibilities firmly fixed.

Nevertheless, the complicated checks and balances employed make for unnecessary inefficiency in every activity and one of the very first steps toward economy in governmental operations lies in improving the accounting system.

Over the past several years private business has developed a number of new accounting methods and devices, many of which should be adapted to governmental operations.

The situation has not gone unrecognized. Members of the Congress and the exectuive branch have repeatedly protested at many of the worst features of present budgeting and accounting practices.

Accounting Objectives

Governmental accounting must serve several purposes. It is an indispensable tool in the day-to-day management of the administrative affairs of the Government. It reveals the status of appropriations, the extent that revenue estimates are realized, the progress of actual expenditures and collections, and comparative operating and other costs. It provides the basis for the summary financial reports which the executive branch sends to the Congress and which are printed for public information. Last but not least, accounting provides for the fixing of responsibility in the handling and use of Government funds, thus enabling a check of administrative competence and fidelity to be made by a representative of the legislative branch, the Comptroller General.

The Present Accounting System

The accounting system of the Government, as it now exists, consists of two general types of accounts—fiscal accounts and administrative accounts.

The fiscal accounts are the over-all or general accounts which are kept mainly in the Treasury Department. These accounts comprehend the fiscal operations relating to revenues, custody of funds, disbursements, public debt, and currency. The Comptroller General does not ordinarily concern himself with the form of these accounts or the contents of the reports which are made from them. Nor is he concerned with property or cost accounts.

Section 309 of the Budget and Accounting Act of June 10, 1921, provides . . .

. . . The Comptroller General shall prescribe the forms, systems, and procedure for administrative appropriation and fund accounting in the several departments and establishments, and for the administrative examination of fiscal officers' accounts and claims against the United States. (31 U. S. C. sec. 49.)

The authority of the Comptroller General is thus, by law, limited to prescribing administrative accounts. He does not now have any authority over fiscal or other accounts.

He has from time to time issued regulations prescribing in detail the form of these accounts—the latest issue being "Regulation 100" of a few years ago. But the Comptroller General has not been particularly concerned with property accounts or with cost accounts. They have been developed chiefly by the departments with the assistance of the Treasury.

The development of a complete and up-to-date system of accounting for the Government comprehends both the fiscal or general accounts and the administrative or departmental accounts. All these systems of accounts should be prescribed by the same authority in order to have an integrated system. With some prescribed by the Treasury, some by the departments, and others by the Comptroller General, it has not been possible during the last 27 years, since the Budget and Accounting Act was passed, to work out a satisfactory system.

The present unsatisfactory situation has been recognized by the organization of a voluntary committee, comprising the Secretary of the Treasury, the Comptroller General, and the Director of the Bureau of the Budget, to arrive at mutually agreeable reforms in the accounting system.

The Comptroller General emphasized this situation in a letter of October 20, 1948, to the Government departments and agencies. In this letter he announced a broad program which . . .

. . . contemplates the full development of sound accounting within each agency, as a working arm of management, in terms of financial information and control. At the same time it envisions an integrated pattern of accounting and financial reporting for the Government as a whole responsive to executive and legislative needs. Balanced recognition will be given to the need for a flexible basis for accounting development within agencies in the light of varying types of operations and management problems and to over-all fiscal reporting, and audit responsibilities.

The Comptroller General further states:

I wish to deal with the concept of my responsibility in the prescribing of accounting systems. I believe this function should be exercised so as to provide all possible encouragement to the agencies to exercise their own initiative and responsibility in the solution of their accounting function. In line with this, it will be my objective as the program progresses to prescribe requirements largely in terms of standards, principles, and basic forms, procedures, and terminology.

These efforts are in the right direction. But this Commission feels that more than voluntary correctives are needed. A definite system should be established and given more permanence through legislation and organization. Indeed, the admirable work of the Secretary of the Treasury, the Comptroller General, and the Director of the Bureau of the Budget will be greatly aided if positive action be taken to establish a responsible official with authority to give continuous motive force to reform in accounting. Since accounting is primarily the responsibility of the executive branch, it is proposed that this official should be an Accountant General in charge of a new Accounting Service in the Treasury Department.

Recommendation No. 10

Therefore, the Commission recommends that:

a. **An Accountant General be established under the Secretary of the Treasury with authority to prescribe general accounting methods and enforce accounting procedures. These methods and procedures should be subject to the approval of the Comptroller General within the powers now conferred upon him by the Congress.**

b. **The Accountant General should, on a report basis, combine agency accounts into the summary accounts of the Government and produce financial reports for the information of the Chief Executive, the Congress, and the public. (See chart.)**

Our recommendation would create a single officer in the Treasury Department with authority to prescribe a single system of fiscal accounts and to represent the executive branch in working out an administrative accounting system with the Comptroller General. The Accountant General would further supervise all departmental accounting activities throughout the executive branch and assist departments in performing their accounting duties.

We believe there is no inherent conflict between the present position of the Comptroller General and our recommendation to create the position of Accountant General.

Settlement of Accounts and Claims

Section 305 of the Budget and Accounting Act of 1921 provides that:

. . . All claims and demands whatever by the Government of the United States or against it, and all accounts whatever in which the Government of the United States is concerned, either as debtor or creditor, shall be settled and adjusted in the General Accounting Office. (31 U. S. C. sec. 71.)

The meaning of this language has been determined over a period of years by various opinions and decisions of the Comptroller General. In

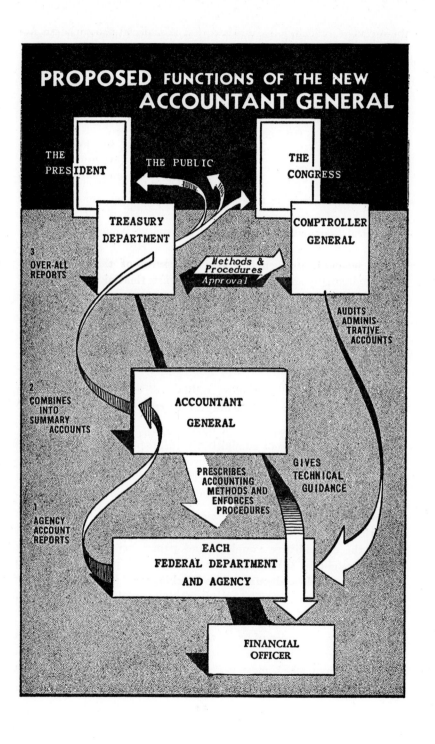

fulfilling his responsibilities under this section the Comptroller General now requires administrative agencies of the executive branch to submit all expenditure vouchers and supporting documents for every individual transaction to the General Accounting Office for examination and "settlement." This is a costly system. It means freight carloads of vouchers from all over the United States hauled to Washington for individual examination in the General Accounting Office.

The office now labors under a deluge of paper work of all kinds which requires about 10,000 people to examine. Over $30,000,000 is needed a year to operate the General Accounting Office on its present scale, and a whole new building is required to house personnel and papers. Of this number of persons and of these total costs, about half result from the central examination of individual expenditure vouchers and documents.

New arrangements should be made for the examination of vouchers at points mutually agreeable to the Comptroller General and the department heads concerned. This was done during the war in the case of the War Department.

Recommendation No. 11

Therefore, the Commission recommends:

a. **That the practice of sending millions of expenditure vouchers and supporting papers to Washington be stopped as far as possible.**

The Comptroller General must obviously continue to determine the adequacy and integrity of administrative fiscal practices; to check and make certain that laws governing appropriations are being properly interpreted; to check the efficiency of accounting and other administrative arrangements; and to report on these matters to the Congress.

b. **But this Commission recommends, in view of the fantastic growth of detail, that a spot sampling process at various places where the expenditure vouchers and papers are administratively checked might be substituted for much of the present procedure of bringing all these documents to Washington.**

This recommendation is not intended to weaken legislative control over expenditures, but (1) to free the General Accounting Office from the overwhelming burden of paper work required of the executive branch and (2) to simplify the work of executive agencies in handling expenditure transactions which must be "settled" by the General Accounting Office.

54

Other Recommendations

Our task force on accounting recommends that the accrual basis of accounting should be applied to both revenues and expenditures. It recommends simplification or elimination of the present warrant system. It proposes uniform departmental practices, procedures, nomenclature, better inventory and public debt accounting, which would greatly reduce staff and red tape.

Recommendation No. 12

The Commission endorses these recommendations.

Surety bonding, as at present practiced, adds greatly to departmental red tape and cost, especially in the Treasury Department where lists of bonding companies and surety bonds in force are maintained.

Under the present procedure about 558,000 accountable officers are required to pay for their own surety bonds provided by private companies at an aggregate annual premium cost of about $2,000,000, while recoveries average only about $230,000 annually.

The problem, it seems, could be better solved by establishing a fidelity insurance fund in the Treasury to which accountable officers would be required to contribute.

Recommendation No. 13

We further recommend that the Congress continue its study of the whole question of fidelity insurance for the accountable officers of the Government in order to arrive at a simpler and less expensive procedure.

Annex I

EXAMPLES OF PERFORMANCE BUDGET

Example 1.—Navy Medical Service

Our first example of the application of performance budgeting is presented on the accompanying chart, which shows the Medical Service of the Navy Department as it appears in the budget for 1947–48 (pp. 661–662) and as it would appear in a performance budget.

THE PRESENT METHOD OF BUDGETING THE MEDICAL SERVICE

Column one reproduces that part of the Federal Budget document which covers the major requirements of the Navy Medical Service. It will be observed that other requirements of the Medical Service were provided for elsewhere in the Navy budget, although such requirements are not directly indentifiable. An examination of this column will reveal that little or no information appears in the present budget presentation to afford an understanding of the various programs of Navy Medical Service, or what that service is accomplishing.

SUGGESTED PERFORMANCE BUDGET FOR THE MEDICAL SERVICE

Column two of the chart shows the over-all operating program of the Navy Medical Service divided into its principal subprograms. The established subprograms are based upon the requirements of management for effective operating purposes. In the narrative description an outline is given of the nature of the work to be performed, the principal elements of cost involved, as well as the total dollar requirements for each of the major elements.

This form of budget presentation would greatly facilitate subsequent accounting and reporting, enabling actual progress and accomplishments to be shown. It would also assist in fixing administrative responsibility for the work to be done, which is of prime importance.

Such capital items as may be required for the Medical Service would appear separately under the capital outlay sections of the Navy budget, designated as "Facilities for the Medical Service."

SUPPORTING SCHEDULES AND INFORMATION FOR PERFORMANCE BUDGET

Column three of the chart shows the type of supporting information which would be submitted to the Appropriations Committees of the House and the Senate for inclusion in their published hearings. Additional data as desired by these Committees or as brought out at Committee hearings would also be included.

Supporting detail submitted initially would include a narrative explanation of the significance and scope of each subprogram—by activity or subunit when appropriate—changes in emphasis over previous years, together with a progress report of work accomplished or under way. Additional data would be set forth in tabular form showing comparative work load, unit costs, and such other yardsticks as might be necessary to evaluate any elements of the appropriation request. We have shown on the chart how these data may be developed for a Naval hospital.

Example 2.—The Forest Service

To illustrate further the application of the performance budget, we take the Forest Service in the Department of Agriculture and show (1) how it is budgeted at present in the 1949–50 budget document and (2) how it can be budgeted on a performance basis.

THE PRESENT METHOD OF BUDGETING THE FOREST SERVICE

As budgeted at the present time, the estimates of the Forest Service cover 18½ closely printed quarto pages of the budget document. The estimates are built around 16 separate items, each of which constitutes an appropriation. Each item has an average of about a page of supporting schedules, setting forth detailed information, principally according to an object classification.

These 16 items or groups now making up the estimates are more or less chance creations; they do not follow either organizational or functional lines. They do not specify accomplishments or indicate performances. Only as one can read meaning into three vertical columns of figures set up on the objective basis can one have any idea of the essential programs, the extent to which these programs succeed or fail, and the effect of changing conditions upon the future character of the programs.

The 16 groups do not make any distinction between current operating costs and capital outlays. Some headings indicate that the amounts requested are to be spent mainly for capital acquisitions; others clearly signify operating costs but, when analyzed, show capital outlays to be included.

The Forest Service has about $24,000,000 of receipts annually which should be indicated in connection with its budget, since percentages of these receipts enter into certain appropriation items, as noted below.

Finally, the 16 items of appropriations made to the Forest Service do not carry all the funds which are required for its operation. Several other appropriations, some of them made directly to the Secretary of Agriculture, contribute to the funds of the Forest Service. By reason of these additional funds the operating requirements of the Service are much larger than actually indicated in the budget. This administrative transfer of funds which takes place on a wide scale within all large governmental departments and agencies makes the present method of budgeting more or less meaningless and defeats the present scheme of appropriations which Congress follows. Only functional budgeting will expose this situation, and allow it to be corrected.

FOREST SERVICE

As Set Up in the Present 1949–50 Budget

(Material in italics below is the Commission's comment and does not appear in the budget quoted.)

1949–50 Requests

1. General administrative expenses .... $ 655,000
   (This item does not by any means include all administrative expenses of the Service. It has not increased appreciably for several years.)

2. National forests protection and management 26,489,500
   (This item contains the bulk of the Service's operating expenses, and it includes considerable capital outlays.)

58

3. Fighting forest fires 100,000
   (*This is a nominal figure. Receipts from payments
   for the suppression of forest fires on State and private lands are also made available.*)

4. Forest research into forest and range management 2,812,500
   (*This item covers research into fire control, silvi-
   culture, watershed control, and forest and range
   management. Receipts from the rental and sale of
   equipment and supplies to non-Federal agencies
   which cooperate with the Forest Service in fire control are included.*)

5. Forest products 1,172,000
   (*This item includes the operation of the great
   Forest Products Laboratory located in Wisconsin,
   but there are no indications as to the volume and
   general character of its work, the nature of the ex-
   periments and tests being conducted, or the discov-
   eries which have resulted.*)

6. Forest resources investigations 866,000
   (*This item provides for a comprehensive forest survey and investigation of forest economics. Receipts
   are also available, as under Item 4 above.*)

   SUBTOTAL annual specific appropriations $32,095,000

7. Forest development roads and trails 9,752,000
   (*This item is for the construction, reconstruction,
   and maintenance of roads and trails (not main thor-
   oughfares) in national forests. Receipts are also
   available, as under Item 4 above.*)

8. Forest fire cooperation 9,000,000
   (*This item is the contribution of the Federal Government to the States for fire control in timbered
   and cut-over lands.*)

9. Farm and other private forestry cooperation 814,500
   (*This item is for advice to farmers and other private
   forest owners on sustained-yield management and
   proper utilization of timber resources.*)

10. Acquisition of lands for national forests 401,000
    (*This item is for the acquisition of forest lands
    under the Weeks Act (1911). It includes the costs
    of surveys.*)

11. Acquisition of forest land, Superior National Forest, Minnesota 100,000
  (*This item is for the acquisition of forest lands, including surveys, under an Act of 1948.*)

12. Acquisition of lands (in connection with seven National forests in three western states, Utah, Nevada, and California) 142,000
  (*This item includes land appraisal and other work in acquiring lands.*)
      (*Transfers of funds to and from the Forest Service require four pages of schedules at this point.*)

TOTAL annual specific appropriations $52,304,500

13. Payment to school funds of Arizona and New Mexico. 55,000
  (*This is a permanent appropriation from the general fund.*)

14. Payment to States and Territories 5,995,000
  (*This is a permanent appropriation, consisting of 25% of the net revenue from National forests, paid to states in which the forests are located.*)

15. Roads and trails for States 2,398,000
  (*This is a permanent appropriation, consisting of 10% of the net revenue from National forests, paid to states in which the forests are located.*)

TOTAL permanent appropriations .... $ 8,448,000

TOTAL Forest Service, general and specific accounts $60,752,500

16. Cooperative work 5,300,000
  (*This item is from privately contributed (trust) funds by users of the forests. It is used for various purposes that benefit both the National and privately owned forests.*)

GRAND TOTAL, Forest Service $66,052,500

The above numbered headings are supported by schedules, mostly on an object basis, amounting to about 18½ closely printed quarto pages of text.

SUGGESTED PERFORMANCE BUDGET FOR THE
FOREST SERVICE

It is proposed in the outline below that the two major functions of the Forest Service should be (1) the protection and management of the National forests and (2) forest research.

As far as possible from the facts and figures in hand, all expenditure estimates for each of these functions have been assembled. The first major function has been roughly divided between current operating costs and capital outlays, to illustrate how such a division may be made. The current operating costs, under "protection and management," have then been divided into 10 operating functions or programs. Many of these may be subdivided for purposes of showing important subprograms. In each case, the nature of the work should be explained briefly, the elements involved in carrying it on, some appraisal of results, and the scope or trend of future work. This explanation or justification of the operating programs should be satisfactorily set forth on 4 or 5 pages of the budget document.

The headings under capital investments and improvements indicate the general classes of outlays for which the Forest Service spends funds. It has not been possible to segregate maintenance and other expenses which are frequently included in the capital items; hence the figures are only approximate.

In the total for the national forests, we do, however, show a figure that includes approximately all of the operating costs and outlays in connection with these forests. Some of the programs, like white pine blister rust, pest control, and flood control, are now financed from appropriations made elsewhere in the Department of Agriculture.

Under the second major function of the Forest Service, that of forest research, we show the major subfunctions or subprograms. These are to be treated in the same way as the operating programs under National forests.

Two other major items make up the grand total under the Forest Service. These are (1) cooperative work with the private users of the national forests, and (2) payments under acts relating to State and private cooperation in the forestry field. These items are set up separately because the first involves the use of private or trust funds, and the second is in the nature of a subsidy for promoting certain work with the States and private owners of forests.

FOREST SERVICE

Suggested Set-up under a Performance Budget
(Figures used are approximate)

I. *The national forests*

*1949–50 Figures
Redistributed*

A. Protection and management

1. Over-all managerial and custodial activities.. $ 7,300,000
2. Forest fire control *7,400,000
3. Insect pest and disease control 2,276,650
4. Timber management (growing and cutting) .. 4,300,000
5. Range management (grazing) 1,097,000
6. Recreation use (health and safety measures). 599,000
7. Land-use management 620,000
8. Water resources management 44,000
9. Maintenance of improvements 13,297,000
10. Payments to states in lieu of taxes 6,050,000

TOTAL protection and management $42,983,650

B. Capital investments and improvements

1. Acquisition of lands for national forests $1,225,750
2. Flood control works 1,941,600
3. Construction of roads and trails 1,752,000
4. Construction of other improvements 213,000
5. Reforestation of forest lands 1,268,000
6. Revegetation of forest lands 758,000

TOTAL capital investments and improvements $ 7,158,350

GRAND TOTAL national forests...... $50,142,000

REVENUES, national forests, from use of
lands and sale of products $23,980,000

*Estimated supplement of $4,000,000 additional needed for fire control.

II. *Forest research*

A. Forest and range management research.......... $2,862,000
B. Forest products utilization 1,200,950
   1. Forest Products Laboratory ($858,000)
C. Forest resources surveys 885,300

TOTAL forest research $4,948,250

III. Cooperative work—Forest Service and private users of national forests

	1949–50 Figures Redistributed
A. Protection and management	
1. Forest and range management	$ 275,000
2. Custodial services	109,000
3. Forest fire control	985,000
4. Maintenance of improvements	550,000
5. Timber management	2,736,000
6. Refunds to cooperators	100,000
TOTAL protection and management	$4,755,000
B. Capital improvements	
1. Construction of improvements	$ 520,000
2. Reforestation	25,000
TOTAL capital improvements	$ 545,000
TOTAL cooperative work (trust account)..	$5,300,000

IV. State and private cooperation

A. Forest fire prevention and protection .... (Clarke-McNary Act)	$9,000,000
B. Farm and other private forestry .... (Clarke-McNary and Norris-Doxey Acts)	814,500
TOTAL State and private cooperation	$9,814,500

Each of these programs or projects is to be accompanied by appropriate explanatory text and supporting schedules.

III
Statistical Activities

Government Statistical Activities

Americans are a fact-minded people. They want to know the magnitude of every facet of national life. They want to measure everything in which they are interested.

Historically, statistical information was one of the first services the Federal Government was called upon to provide. The Constitution itself directed a census to be taken every 10 years. Various acts of Congress thereafter set up agencies to collect and disseminate statistics on agriculture, commerce, labor, and many other activities. There are about 10,500 full-time employees in the Federal Government engaged in statistical activities outside the National Military Establishment, and the estimated annual over-all cost of these statistical activities is about 43 million dollars.

A host of private and public decisions is being made every day based upon statistical data.

Government policy depends upon much detailed knowledge about the Nation's employment, production, and purchasing power. The formulation of legislation and administrative programs on conservation, crime suppression, public health, education, housing, industrial relations, and economic stabilization must stem from accurate up-to-date information. The supervision of various carriers of interstate commerce and of other public utilities, the regulation of banking and the issue of capital stock, and the control of unfair competition must be guided by knowledge of a wide range of relevant facts. Today as never before, statistical data play a major role in the supervision of Government activities. Administrators not only make plans in the light of known facts in their field of interest, but also they must have reports on the actual progress achieved in accomplishing their goals. The public likewise wants to know what its administrative officials accomplish with the funds they spend.

The statistical activities of the Federal Government are complex and far-flung. Statistical releases range from the comprehensive decennial census to monthly, weekly, and daily reports. They cover population and vital statistics, the weather, national income and its distribution, production and distribution of goods, imports and exports, employment, wages, money supply, immigration, Government finances, and a multitude of other subjects.

This work in statistical collection and publication is performed by many administrative agencies, which may be divided into four general types.

1. A number of agencies have a primary function of collecting statistics; such as the Bureau of the Census, the Bureau of Agricultural Economics, the Bureau of Labor Statistics, and the Office of Vital Statistics.

2. Many administrative and regulatory agencies provide important general statistical data as a "byproduct" of their work; agencies such as the Bureau of Internal Revenue, the Social Security Administration, the Interstate Commerce Commission, and the Securities and Exchange Commission.

3. A number of agencies analyze statistical data collected by other agencies; for example, the Division of Research and Statistics under the Board of Governors of the Federal Reserve System, and the Council of Economic Advisers.

4. Two agencies in the Government give particular attention to research on improving statistical techniques. These are the Statistical Engineering Laboratory of the National Bureau of Standards and the Census Bureau. The Statistical Engineering Laboratory in particular has pioneered in conducting statistical tests in engineering and the physical sciences, and in applying standard procedures to the control of quality in industrial production.

The Division of Statistical Standards in the Bureau of the Budget exercises some supervision over the types of activities described above.

What Is Wrong with the System

1. The wide number of different statistical agencies inevitably produces overlappings and uncertainties about the primary responsibility for collecting data.

As examples of overlapping areas of statistical activity, our task force report cites employment and pay-roll data, "prevailing wage" inquiries, income distribution, consumption data, and construction and housing data. Moreover, since statistical activities have grown up piecemeal, some areas receive greater attention than others. There is no general scheme of priorities in assembling or analyzing statistical data.

2. There is useless duplication of reports, many of which are also published in unnecessarily large quantities.

These faults result primarily from a lack of adequate centralized management of the highly decentralized system of statistical activities in the executive branch of the Federal Government.

3. Many of the statistics gathered by the Federal Government are of questionable value and are sent to people who have little interest in reading them.

There is no group in the Government which attempts to appraise the worth of the statistics which are being gathered and sent out to the public.

4. There are delays in publishing and in revising statistical data, failures to relate statistical collection to informational needs, faulty coverage of some subjects, gaps in coverage, uneven development and application of modern techniques for collecting data, and inadequate coordination of Federal-State statistical activities.

In addition, many statistical series are not comparable in the absence of standard concepts, definitions, and procedures.

5. The Federal Government requires large numbers of statistical figures from businesses and individuals, thus imposing a financial burden upon them.

This is particularly true in the case of small business. This burden might be further reduced.

6. Much information which is of great value to particular groups is given out by the Government without charge when the recipients should pay for it.

Our task force found it impossible to determine exactly how much the gathering, compiling, and publishing of statistics by the Federal Government cost the taxpayers.

Recommendations

The organizational difficulties of the statistical system might be met in one of two ways. The first possibility is to assign all statistical collection to a single agency. The other alternative is to introduce effective central management of statistical activities.

The first possibility is not feasible. Since so much of our statistical information is collected incidental to administering tax laws, social security laws, and other legislation, this work cannot be separated from the administrative processes of the various agencies involved. Moreover, since administrative agencies tend to develop their separate specialties they possess a unique knowledge of the statistical information they need for their operations. They also tend to know particular statistical needs of individual groups in the United States.

The only practical alternative, then, is effective central direction and supervision of statistical activities. But some official with authority must see that coordination is achieved.

Recommendation No. 1

The Commission recommends that the diverse system of collection and analyzing statistical data should be continued. It is suggested, however, that greater use should be made of the Census Bureau for the repetitive, large-scale tasks of primary collection and tabulation of statistical data.

Recommendation No. 2

Responsibility for the adequacy of the statistical system as a whole, for its economical operation, for coordinating the activities of statistical agencies, and for determining priorities among these activities should be fixed.

Recommendation No. 3

The costs of statistical services that are mainly of benefit to specific groups should, to the greatest extent possible, be shifted to the beneficiaries.

Recommendation No. 4

Forms and questionnaires sent to the public should be simplified and the Division of Statistical Standards should make a constant effort to relieve the burden of these reports on businesses and individuals.

Organizational Responsibility

Recommendation No. 5

Subject to the approval of the President, the Division of Statistical Standards of the Office of the Budget should be strengthened to perform this work.

The task force also makes a number of recommendations intended to improve the quality of statistical work in the Federal Government which the Commission believes to be desirable.

There is one objective mentioned by the task force to which the Commission wishes to call particular attention:

That, in view of the necessity for objectivity in the collection, organization, and presentation of the facts of national life, Federal statistical agencies should be clearly recognized as representatives of the public, and not regarded as agents of special groups nor as advocates of special interests.

Conclusion

Substantial savings, greater accuracy in statistics, greater speed in collection and analysis, and more proficient coverage—these are some of the benefits efficient centralized coordination could produce in filling the Nation's statistical requirements economically, efficiently, and adequately.

IV

Office of General Services

An Office of General Services

Three major internal activities of the Federal Government now suffer from a lack of central direction. These are Supply, Records Management, and the Operation and Maintenance of Public Buildings. These activities are carried on in several places within the executive branch with varying degrees of adequacy. While, as a general rule, centralized direction is lacking, there are some instances of the exact reverse of this situation in which operations are centrally controlled down to the smallest detail.

To the general public, the "housekeeping" activities listed above are little-known, but unless they are properly administered, the executive branch cannot be effectively managed. Moreover, huge sums are spent on these activities. Rents and utility services have cost in the neighborhood of $200,000,000 in each recent year. Civilian supply purchases alone total an estimated $900,000,000 per year, and this is exclusive of such large items as transportation of property and storage or handling costs.

Since these activities relate to all departments, there is only one place in the executive branch of the Government where authority should be vested. That is in the President, subject, of course, to appropriate legislative directions. Yet obviously the President personally cannot exercise this responsibility except in most unusual circumstances.

The principal issue affecting service activities is: How much of any such activity shall be centralized and how much shall be performed by the individual executive departments and agencies?

Undoubtedly, some housekeeping services must be performed centrally in order to avoid waste. On the other hand there is frequently too much centralization. In a large-scale effort like the Federal Government, too high a degree of centralization of services may result merely in congestion, red tape, and inefficiency. When highly specialized equipment must be purchased by a single agency only for its own use, for example, it is more reasonable and efficient for it to develop the specifications, negotiate the purchase contract, and inspect the delivered goods.

Two important questions about these housekeeping services must be determined.

First. Who shall decide what part of any service shall be centralized and what part shall be left to individual operating agencies?

Second. Who shall supervise the centralized services to make certain that they perform their work satisfactorily?

Recommendation No. 1

The Commission recommends that responsibility for these three internal service operations should be placed in an Office of General Services under a director appointed by the President.

The Office of General Services should be given authority, subject to the direction of the President, to prescribe regulations governing the conduct of these three activities by departments and agencies of the executive branch. However, the Office of General Services should, to the greatest extent possible, delegate responsibility for exercising these three functions to the departments and agencies.

In addition to these internal service operations, there are certain miscellaneous activities, primarily centered in and about the District of Columbia, which either report directly to the President or report to no one. These include the District of Columbia Government, the Smithsonian Institution, the National Capital Park and Planning Commission, the National Capital Housing Authority, and the Commission of Fine Arts. These activities have numerous relations with the executive branch; and there has never been anyone—other than the President—who has been responsible for handling their problems or for giving them such supervision as may be required under the law.

Recommendation No. 2

The Commission recommends that the relationship between these organizations and the executive branch be centered in the Office of General Services. All of the activities named above must be coordinated or directed from some central point with responsibility upon particular persons for their performance.

Recommendation No. 3

We recommend that the following functions, each under a director shall be placed in the Office of General Services.

    a. SUPPLY

    b. RECORDS MANAGEMENT

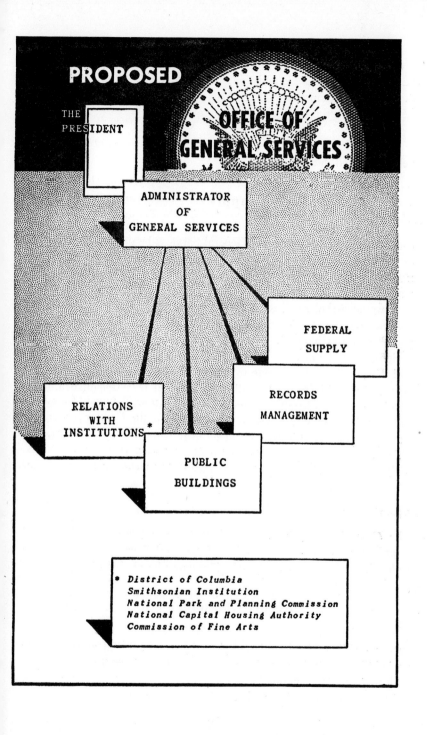

PROPOSED

OFFICE OF
GENERAL SERVICES

THE
PRESIDENT

ADMINISTRATOR
OF
GENERAL SERVICES

FEDERAL
SUPPLY

RECORDS
MANAGEMENT

RELATIONS
WITH
INSTITUTIONS *

PUBLIC
BUILDINGS

* District of Columbia
  Smithsonian Institution
  National Park and Planning Commission
  National Capital Housing Authority
  Commission of Fine Arts

c. OPERATION AND MAINTENANCE OF PUBLIC BUILDINGS

d. CERTAIN RELATIONS with the Smithsonian Institution, the National Parks and Planning Commission, the National Capital Housing Authority, the Commission of Fine Arts, and the District of Columbia (See chart, Proposed Office of General Services.)

The Commission's detailed recommendations on supply summarized below are filed in a separate report.

Supply

It is proposed, as discussed in our accompanying report, that the supply bureau in the Office of General Services be developed primarily, although not exclusively, for policy-making and coordination of the procurement of supplies and other supply functions for the executive departments.

It would assign responsibility for the purchase and storage of commodities peculiar to the use of an agency to the agency best suited to make such purchases or to store such commodities. It would also designate certain agencies to purchase specified supplies for all agencies and it would award contracts to vendors for common-use items. These contracts would be utilized by all agencies in the purchase of such items. The bureau would handle the purchase for small agencies when economical to do so. It would assure systematic handling and fundamental standards, and its objective would be to decentralize activities into the different departments, agencies and field office regions.

Civilian and military supply activities would be coordinated through a Supply Policy Committee.

Recommendation No. 4

The Commission recommends that a central Bureau of Federal Supply be created in the Office of General Services and that the Federal Bureau of Supply in the Treasury be abolished.

Records Management

The maintenance of records costs the Federal Government enormous sums annually. The records now in existence would fill approximately six buildings each the size of the Pentagon. (See chart, Two Decades of Federal Records Accumulation.)

In 1948, some 18 million square feet of space were filled with records.

78

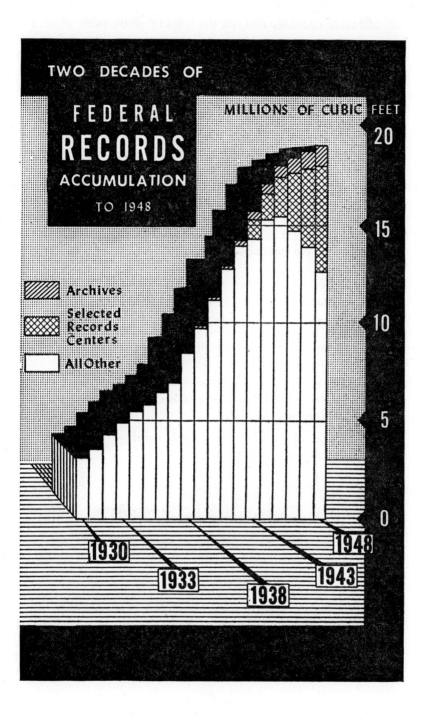

TWO DECADES OF

FEDERAL
RECORDS
ACCUMULATION
TO 1948

MILLIONS OF CUBIC FEET

20

15

10

5

0

Archives

Selected
Records
Centers

All Other

1930
1933
1938
1943
1948

Our task force estimates that, on the basis of rental value alone, the space costs for this volume of records is at least 20 million dollars annually. The filing equipment for handling these papers would be worth 154 million dollars at current prices.

A new central records service is needed to consolidate and reduce the records centers which various Government agencies now operate, and to direct the work of these regional records centers along with that of the National Archives in Washington.

More detailed recommendations to accomplish improved records management have been submitted by our task force. The task force report estimates that probably 50 percent of the total records of the average Government agency can be eliminated from the main office with a substantial savings of personnel, plant, equipment, and space. Every time the contents of one file cabinet are transferred to a records center, the Government can save approximately $27 a year in office cost. (See chart, How A Records Center Saves Money.)

Recommendation No. 5

We recommend:

a. **The creation of a Records Management Bureau in the Office of General Services, to include the National Archives.**

b. **Enactment of a new Federal Records Management Law to provide for the more effective preservation, management, and disposal of Government records.**

c. **Establishment of an adequate records management program in each department and agency.**

Operation and Maintenance of Public Buildings

Maintenance of buildings, allotment of space, and moving service in the District of Columbia and in some selected cities would be the responsibility of the third bureau in the Office of the General Services. Its work thus relates to all departments and agencies. It has the management of over 54 million gross square feet of Government-owned space and over 6 million gross square feet of leased space, of which 24 million square feet are outside the District of Columbia.

It is not proposed that space allotment in the Post Offices and the National Military Establishment should be made by this agency al-

HOW A RECORDS CENTER
SAVES MONEY

CONTENTS OF
FILE CABINET IN
OFFICE

TRANSFERRED TO
RECORDS CENTER

OCCUPIES ³⁄₁₀ AS
MUCH FLOOR SPACE

6 SQUARE FEET
OF SPACE

17½ SQUARE
FEET OF SPACE
HOLDS CONTENTS
OF 10 FILE
CABINETS

1 File Cabinet @ $50.00	
(Amortized 10 yrs) - - -	$5.00
6 sq. ft. of Space @ $2.50 per sq. ft.	$15.00
Overhead and Maintenance	
for 6 sq. ft. @ $1.50 per sq. ft.	$9.00

TOTAL COST
$29.00
IN OFFICE SPACE

SAVED $26.85 YEARLY

Every time the contents of a File
Cabinet are transferred to a
RECORDS CENTER

¹⁄₁₀ Steel Stack Section @ $32.00 = $3.20	
(Amortized 10 yrs) - - - - -	$0.32
6 Cardboard Cartons @ $0.15 = $0.90	
(Amortized 10 yrs) - - - - -	$0.09
¹⁄₁₀ of 17.5 sq. ft. of Space @ $0.50 per sq. ft.	$0.87
Overhead and Maintenance	
for ¹⁄₁₀ of 17.5 sq. ft. @ $0.50 per sq. ft. -	$0.87

TOTAL COST $2.15
IN RECORDS CENTER

though servicing by this agency of the buildings occupied by the Post Office and the Military Establishment is desirable. In any event, close cooperative arrangements should be established between this agency, the Post Office Department, and the National Military Establishment.

It is essential in these matters that authority be expanded and that there be a central agency (*a*) to prepare and issue standards of efficiency in the management of public buildings; (*b*) to supervise space allotments in Government buildings in towns where there are several large agencies (except in buildings of the National Military Establishment and the Post Office Department with which cooperative arrangements should be established); (*c*) to maintain and operate Government buildings; (*d*) to prepare standard forms of leases and deeds and maintain a record of leases and buildings owned by the Government.

Recommendation No. 6

The Commission recommends that the administration of the functions enumerated above be placed in the Office of General Services, but it expresses no opinion as to design and construction of buildings, and other functions of the Public Buildings Administration.

Relations with Certain Institutions

THE DISTRICT OF COLUMBIA

Under the Constitution the Congress has authority to "exercise exclusive legislation" over the District of Columbia. The District of Columbia Government is primarily supported by its own revenues, but the Federal Government makes annual contributions to it. The Federal contribution amounted to 12 million dollars in the fiscal year 1949. The budget of the District is transmitted with the President's budget message and appropriations for it are made by the Congress. Although the executive branch does not directly supervise the District of Columbia Government, departments and agencies and the District Government have many mutual contacts and problems for which there is no central clearing house other than the President himself.

Recommendation No. 7

The Commission recommends that matters involving Presidential action be referred by the District of Columbia officials to the Director of the Office of General Services.

THE SMITHSONIAN INSTITUTION

The Smithsonian Institution is one of the great scientific museums and research institutions of the country. It is partly endowed and partly supported by appropriations ($2,090,000 in 1949). The establishment has as its members the President of the United States, the Vice President, the Chief Justice, and the members of the President's Cabinet. The Institution is governed by a Board of Regents, comprised of the Vice President, the Chief Justice, three members each of the Senate and of the House of Representatives, and six citizens of the United States appointed by joint resolution of Congress. It cooperates with several Departments of the Government.

Recommendation No. 8

No change is proposed in the Institution, but when its officials need assistance from the Chief Executive or the departments, it is recommended that they consult with the Director of the Office of General Services.

OTHER NATIONAL CAPITAL ACTIVITIES

The following separate agencies perform activities in the District of Columbia:

THE NATIONAL PARK AND PLANNING COMMISSION
THE NATIONAL CAPITAL HOUSING AUTHORITY
THE COMMISSION OF FINE ARTS

Recommendation No. 9

These agencies should report to some responsible part of the executive branch. We recommend that they should report to the Director of the Office of General Services.

V
Federal Supply Activities

Chapter One

SCOPE OF SUPPLY ACTIVITIES

The Federal Government runs one of the greatest supply businesses in the world. It is spending more than 6 billion dollars a year for new material, supplies, and equipment for the regular activities of the civilian and military agencies. In addition, since 1941, the Federal Government has been engaged in enormous purchases for export in connection with lend-lease and foreign-aid programs. It makes huge purchases of strategic and critical materials from foreign sources, and imports them for the national stock pile.

The Federal Government also has in storage, in the continental United States, military and civilian inventories valued at 27 billion dollars. No one knows accurately the total worth of Government personal property currently being used, but its million or more motor vehicles, for example, have a value of at least 2 billion dollars. The Government also pays out more than 1 billion dollars yearly for transportation of property, and 440 million dollars in salaries of the nearly 150,000 employees working in supply operations.

While most of this supply activity is military, the Federal Government has important civilian supply functions in fields as diverse as the procurement of supplies used in building power dams, conducting research in atomic energy, and operating hospitals. It is the largest single user of office supplies. Total purchases by civilian agencies amount to about 900 million dollars a year.

As used in this report, the term "supply" refers to the task of providing personal property (supplies, materials, and equipment) required for the operation of the Federal Government. There are seven primary phases of the supply operation, which are as follows:

1. *Specification* or the task of establishing standards for property to be purchased.

2. *Purchasing* or the acquisition of property.

3. *Traffic management* or the transporting of property from the point of purchase or storage to the point of need.

4. *Inspection* or insuring adherence of property to purchase specifications.

5. *Property identification* or the task of cataloging property under a standard system so as to facilitate identification.

6. *Storage and issue* or the storing of necessary reserves of property and their distribution when needed.

7. *Property utilization* or the task of seeing that property is efficiently used and is suitably disposed of when no longer needed.

Chapter Two

WHAT IS WRONG WITH FEDERAL SUPPLY OPERATIONS

The numerous deficiencies in Federal supply operations are described in detail in the report of the Commission's Federal Supply Project which has been printed separately. It is sufficient to point out herein only a few of the major deficiencies:

1. Purchasing

One of the major weaknesses in Federal purchasing stems from the lack of any central body to coordinate Government purchasing activities. Small agencies buy for themselves, although the volume of their purchases does not permit the employment of a competent staff. In common-use items, consolidated orders for several agencies by a single purchasing office would achieve large savings. The Bureau of Federal Supply, which was established as the central supply organization, has insufficient funds to purchase on a centralized basis. A properly organized central supply service could almost completely eliminate purchasing offices in the smaller agencies.

a. Purchasing requires a high degree of professional competence, yet many purchasing offices are not manned with competent personnel.

b. Purchasing operations are unplanned.

As evidence of this it is estimated that approximately half of the several million purchase orders issued annually are for $10 or less. (See chart, When Federal Agencies Buy.)

Since the cost of processing a purchase transaction is greatly in excess of $10, the overhead cost is more than the cost of the goods.

WHEN FEDERAL AGENCIES BUY

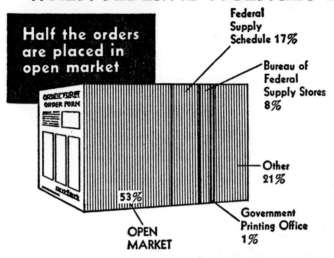

Half the orders are placed in open market

Federal Supply Schedule 17%

Bureau of Federal Supply Stores 8%

Other 21%

53%

OPEN MARKET

Government Printing Office 1%

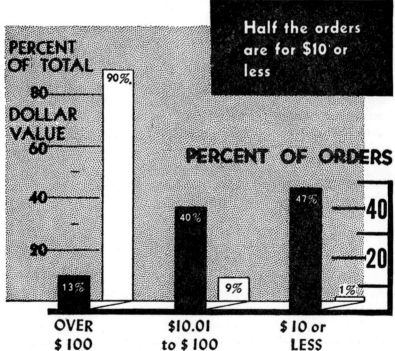

Half the orders are for $10 or less

PERCENT OF TOTAL
DOLLAR VALUE

80
60
40
20

90%
40%
13%

PERCENT OF ORDERS

40
20

47%
9%
1%

OVER $100 $10.01 to $100 $10 or LESS

SOURCE OF DATA: Bureau of Federal Supply, and the Bureau of Budget surveys of 19 agency supply facilities, February 1947 through June 1948.

c. Purchasing officers lack information and funds necessary to schedule purchases so as to take maximum advantage of favorable market conditions.

d. Purchasing officers have failed to develop cost records and other tools essential to an effective job of purchasing.

e. Purchasing operations have degenerated largely into the routine practice of soliciting bids and awarding contracts to the lowest bidder. An economical job cannot be expected unless purchasing officials are granted sufficient latitude to negotiate small purchases, to restrict competition to reliable vendors, and to give sufficient weight to quality of the product in awarding contracts.

2. Storage and Issue

It is estimated that over 100,000 employees whose total annual salary rate exceeds 270 million dollars are engaged in storage and issue activities in the military and civilian agencies.

a. There are too many storage warehouses. These warehouses maintain duplicating inventories.

For example, in the Washington metropolitan area alone there are 72 different activities of the Government which operate storage and issue facilities exclusive of the Bureau of Federal Supply and the Government Printing Office. In the field a similar situation exists. Six civilian agencies alone show a total of 748 stores facilities at field locations with inventories in excess of 180 million dollars.

b. A large part of the storage inventories are a long distance from the point of use so that issuance involves excessive transportation costs.

It has been estimated that 42 percent of the Washington stores inventories are for the benefit of field stations. Much of this stock could be delivered by vendors directly to field warehouses where they would be readily accessible to the establishments requiring them.

c. Practically every agency has excessive stocks of supplies.

These agencies are providing space and personnel to handle large quantities of supplies which, according to present rates of consumption, will be sufficient to meet their needs for periods of from 1 to 50 years. A study of the stock facilities of 10 civilian agencies by the Office of the Budget showed that excess stocks averaged 70 percent of the total stock inventories. (See chart, Excess Inventories in Civilian Agencies.)

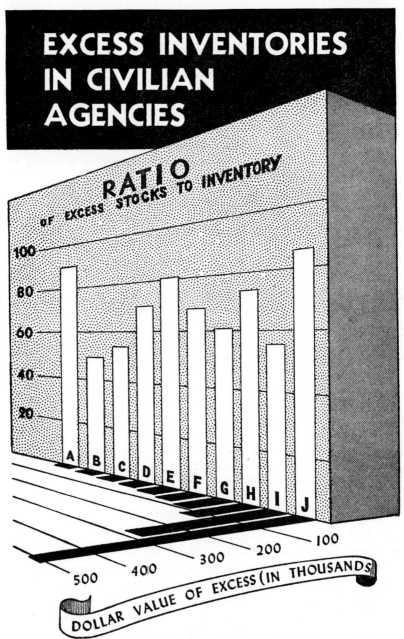

EXCESS INVENTORIES IN CIVILIAN AGENCIES

RATIO OF EXCESS STOCKS TO INVENTORY

100
80
60
40
20

A B C D E F G H I J

100
200
300
400
500

DOLLAR VALUE OF EXCESS (IN THOUSANDS)

SOURCE OF DATA: Bureau of Federal Supply, and the Bureau of Budget surveys of 19 agency supply facilities, February 1947 through June 1948.

This situation arises from two primary causes; namely, (1) most agencies do not have satisfactory systems of stock control which permit the replenishment of stock to be related to agency needs, and (2) most agencies invest appropriation balances at the end of a fiscal year in supplies so as to avoid returning such funds to the Treasury.

3. Traffic Management

Annual charges paid by the Government for the transportation of property exceed 1 billion dollars, which is nearly one-tenth of the revenue of common carriers for the transportation of property. Government property and its channels of movement differ materially from the commercial traffic for which carrier tariffs have been constructed.

Most of the traffic personnel in the Federal Government are auditing transportation bills. Only a very few employees are engaged in activities aimed at improving traffic management and reducing costs. Agencies having well-developed traffic organizations have demonstrated that substantial savings can be achieved if attention is devoted to this problem. The Reconstruction Finance Corporation, for example, effected savings of 17 million dollars on its wartime traffic with an average annual salary expenditure of $200,000.

4. Specifications

If products purchased are to be of a satisfactory quality and are to meet the specific needs of the Federal Government, it is essential to establish standards which the products must meet.

There is considerable evidence that many commodities which should be covered by specifications are not so covered; that many existing specifications are out of date; and that valid specifications are not being enforced. Standards are described in terms of the physical characteristics or composition of the product rather than in terms of performance required. Much of the responsibility for these conditions rests upon the individual agencies, but a large part results from the fact that the machinery for developing and enforcing standard specifications of Government-wide application has not been functioning satisfactorily.

Specifications for common-use items are prepared under the Federal Specifications Board which is composed of the representatives of 11 agencies. Preparation or revision of a specification has become a very lengthy process, averaging over 2 years, largely because there is insufficient staff time devoted to this work.

93

5. Inspection

Inspection is an essential phase of supply, since it is the method of determining whether the quality of materials or equipment received meets the requirements stipulated in the specifications or purchase order.

In the civilian agencies there is no uniformity in quality of inspection, or in the basic concepts of what types of commodities should be inspected. Inspection service and testing laboratories are scattered throughout the country without any coordination.

In the military agencies, the quality of inspection was found to be reasonably good, but, in many large cities, each service department maintains a separate inspection office. There was also found to be a duplication of laboratory facilities.

6. Property Identification

It is impossible to provide economical management of personal property if its identity, classification, location, quantity, and physical characteristics are not known.

The Government agencies do not utilize a standard catalog or other system of identifying items regularly maintained in stock. In some agencies each supply point is permitted to devise its own catalog with the result that one part of an agency may be overstocked on a given item while another part is making additional purchases of the same item. There is no uniform system of cataloging which permits identification and classification of the materials used by all of the agencies. There have been 17 unrelated systems of property identification in use at one time. This situation has resulted in the development of costly duplicating inventories throughout the Government.

Since the recent war, the National Military Establishment has made some progress toward a coordinated system of property identification and the Bureau of Federal Supply is now cooperating in this endeavor. Nevertheless, a declaration of congressional policy insisting upon a Federal commodity catalog is necessary to insure conformity of some of the old-line civilian agencies and to insure continued military-civilian cooperation.

7. Property Utilization

Agencies have devoted far too little attention to effecting needed economies through maximum use of personal property. Some agencies maintain no property controls and numerous agencies have not inventoried their property in years. Other agencies have costly record systems which are not adapted to assisting management in obtaining full utilization.

The failure to provide adequate inventory procedures and property records has resulted in the accumulation of large inventories of surplus property. By continuing to store such property, these agencies are building up excess storage and handling costs as well as permitting the property to depreciate.

Chapter Three

BASIC CAUSES OF DEFICIENCIES IN
SUPPLY ADMINISTRATION

The deficiencies of Government supply operations spring from the following primary causes:

First: Supply is not fully recognized as an important executive function. At a time when personnel and budgeting have achieved status as vital staff functions, there has been a continued failure to appreciate fully the relationship of supply to Government efficiency. There is no comprehensive Government-wide system that gives adequate emphasis to the many phases of supply.

Second: This failure is reflected in an inadequate supply organization for the Government as a whole as well as for the various departments and agencies. The Bureau of Federal Supply, which is intended to be the supply organization for the Federal Government, is inappropriately located in the Treasury Department where is does not have adequate authority or facilities to do a satisfactory job. The departments and agencies do not have effective supply organizations. The result is a confused Federal supply system where agencies compete with one another for scarce commodities, maintain duplicating storage facilities in the same locality, and operate as many as 17 different systems of property identification at one time.

Third: This failure is reflected further in the personnel system which does not provide competent staff to fill supply positions. Although purchasing is a highly skilled profession that requires intimate knowledge of trade conditions and markets, salaries paid in Government agencies are inadequate to recruit and keep persons with the **required** professional competence. Personnel processes fail to make proper acknowledgment of the skills required.

Fourth: A maze of laws and regulations surrounds the whole process with unnecessary red tape. The emphasis of the laws is not on promoting efficiency and economy but upon preventing fraud. Overregulation encourages routine buying and prevents economy and the exercise of initiative. Purchasing is consumed in red tape. It is estimated that, on over half of the 3,000,000 purchase orders issued by civilian agencies, the cost of paper work exceeded the cost of the items purchased.

Fifth: The system of budgeting and appropriating funds fails to emphasize the need for advance planning of supply needs and fails to provide adequate control over supply expenditures. Budget officers must estimate their requirements nearly 2 years in advance and, as a result, most estimates are mere guesses. Funds remaining near the end of a fiscal year are frequently expended for supplies and equipment in order to avoid returning the money to the Treasury. Advance schedules of buying are inadequate. Purchasing officers do not participate to the necessary degree in budget and operational planning.

Sixth: Some phases of the supply operation are regulated by statute as well as by decisions of the Comptroller General; whereas other phases have neither legislative nor administrative sanction. Purchasing is regulated by both statutes and by detailed administrative rulings. Disposition of surplus property is governed by over 369 separate statutes. On the other hand, storage and issue, traffic management, standard specifications, inspection, and property identification have almost no legislative sanction and are governed by a very limited number of administrative regulations. The result is that some of the mutually dependent supply operations are so closely regulated as to stifle initiative and hamstring efforts to improve the supply system; whereas in other operations there is insufficient legislative sanction to support constructive administrative action.

Seventh: The Government has failed to compile adequate cost and statistical records which are needed for the efficient management of supply operations. Most agencies are overburdened with a surplus of complicated statistical and other records but few agencies have the type of data for making intelligent budget estimates and management decisions relating to manpower and supply requirements.

97

Chapter Four

PROGRAM FOR IMPROVING FEDERAL
SUPPLY OPERATIONS

It is impossible for this Commission to work out a completely detailed system of supply for the Government. Rather, we attempt in this report to outline such a system, and recommend an organization which can develop an effective mechanism.

The deficiencies of the Federal supply system stem in part from deficiencies in companion staff services, namely, the personnel and fiscal activities.

In our report on Personnel Management, we recommend a personnel organization and policies and practices which, if adopted, should contribute immeasurably to the solution of the problem of securing competent personnel to fill key supply positions. No other steps which the Government might take will contribute more to improved supply operations than the adoption of measures which will help insure the selection and retention of competent supply personnel.

Our report on Budgeting and Accounting recommends an improved system of appropriating funds and preparing agency budgets. The adoption of these recommendations will promote more realistic budgeting and accounting for supply activities and will eliminate detailed regulations which tend to hamstring the operations of imaginative supply officials.

In addition to these recommendations which are included in other reports, we outline below seven recommendations which, if adopted, will lay a sound basis for the development of an efficient system of supply in the Federal Government.

Recommendation No. 1

Enact legislation which will repeal the conglomeration of existing statutes, clear the books of present restrictive and often conflicting

decisions and regulations, and provide the basic principles for an effective supply system.

This legislation should be designed to provide a charter for the Bureau of Federal Supply in the Office of General Services (see recommendation No. 4 below) and to permit the development of effective and economical Federal supply practices.

Recommendation No. 2

Enact legislation to apply the principles of the Armed Services Procurement Act of 1947 to buying by all agencies.

This act permits contracts to be negotiated under specified circumstances and conditions, and raises from $100 to $1,000 the ceiling for purchases without competitive bids.

Such legislation is fundamental to achieving worth-while improvements in supply operations. This authority should be lodged in the President.

Recommendation No. 3

Establish a Supply Policy Committee composed of representatives of the Bureau of Federal Supply and the National Military Establishment to coordinate civilian and military supply operations.

Although the Commission recognizes that the wide differences in supply problems make it undesirable to unify civilian and military supply activities, there is a need for close coordination between the two systems. There are many items of common use, such as medical supplies, where purchase and storage by one or the other (but not both) would result in major savings. Our task force report on Medical Services recommends strongly a single agency to purchase all medical supplies, military and civilian. It is also desirable, as pointed out earlier, for civilian and military agencies to coordinate their activities as they relate to specifications, property identification, and traffic management.

It is for these reasons that the Commission recommends that a Supply Policy Committee be established. This Committee should not be formalized by statute but should serve at the pleasure of the President.

It would be the function of this Committee to develop policies and rules on supply operations common to both the military and civilian agencies and to make Government-wide purchase, stores, inspection, testing, and other assignments. It would assign responsibility for special programs such as stock piling and would settle disputes which might arise

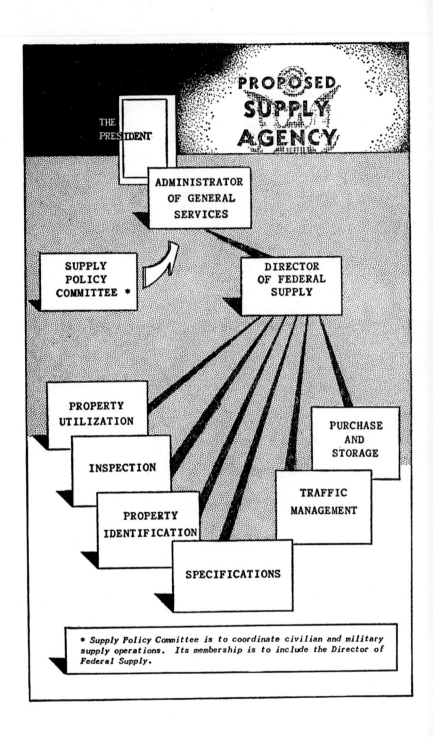

PROPOSED
SUPPLY
AGENCY

THE
PRESIDENT

ADMINISTRATOR
OF GENERAL
SERVICES

SUPPLY
POLICY
COMMITTEE *

DIRECTOR
OF FEDERAL
SUPPLY

PROPERTY
UTILIZATION

INSPECTION

PROPERTY
IDENTIFICATION

SPECIFICATIONS

PURCHASE
AND
STORAGE

TRAFFIC
MANAGEMENT

* Supply Policy Committee is to coordinate civilian and military
supply operations. Its membership is to include the Director of
Federal Supply.

in connection with the integration of civilian and military supply systems.

Coordination between civilian and military agencies is particularly important in the development of a standard property identification system and in the development of standard specifications for items of common use. For example, in purchasing such items as medical supplies and equipment which are used in large quantity by both military and civilian establishments, this Committee could assign the task of purchasing such items for the Government as a whole to the agencies which are best suited to make the purchases.

Recommendation No. 4

Establish a Bureau of Federal Supply in the Office of General Services with competent personnel and clothed with adequate authority to provide the leadership necessary to achieve in the executive branch an efficient supply organization which would also coordinate with the National Military Establishment.

A major function of this office should be the formulation of policies and regulations, on behalf of the President, to govern the supply operations of the executive branch. Its task would be to view the supply problems of the executive branch as a whole, and to adopt such policies and to provide such assistance to the agencies as will bring about a supply system which is effective and economical.

We do not recommend a specific internal structure for the Supply Bureau. We believe that its organization must be geared to existing circumstances and therefore must be decided upon by the Director of General Services and the Director of the Bureau of Supply. We do, however, outline the activities which should be assigned to the Bureau. (See chart, Proposed Supply Agency.)

A primary responsibility of the Bureau would be to assist the President in the formulation of policies, regulations, and practices which are to govern all phases of the supply function in the executive branch and to make administrative audits to determine compliance therewith. Through its membership on the Supply Policy Committee it should assist in the formulation of those policies, regulations, and practices which are to be common to both the civilian and military agencies. In addition it would carry out the following responsibilities:

Purchase and Storage Activities

Recommendation No. 5

We recommend that this unit:

a. Assign responsibility for the purchase or storage of commodities peculiar to the use of an agency to the agency best suited to make such purchases or to store such commodities.

b. Designate certain agencies to purchase specified supplies for all agencies.

c. Award contracts to vendors for common-use items, these contracts to be utilized by all agencies in the purchase of such items.

d. Handle the purchasing for small agencies whenever it is economical to do so.

e. Operate a Nation-wide system of storehouses to supply departmental and field services with those common-use items which can most advantageously and economically be distributed through such storehouses.

f. Purchase, through consolidated orders for all Government agencies, those items in which volume purchases result in appreciable savings.

g. Develop master forms of bid and contract documents, of which all suppliers should be informed and which can be incorporated by reference into each bid and contract.

Traffic Management Activities

Recommendation No. 6

We recommend that this unit:

h. Advise all Government agencies on traffic management problems.

i. Represent all agencies in negotiating rates with the carriers.

j. Represent all agencies in cases before the transportation regulatory bodies.

k. Advise agencies as to reasonableness of carriers' bills.

l. Prepare and maintain appropriate manuals and guides relating to traffic management activities of Government agencies.

Specifications Activities

Recommendation No. 7

We recommend that this unit:

m. Serve as a secretariat for a coordinating body of representatives of selected agencies including the National Military Establishment on Federal specifications. Such a board, if desired, would approve Federal specifications and recommend for the President policies and procedures governing their preparation.

n. Maintain a master list of qualified products, that is, products which meet Federal specifications.

Property Identification Activities

Recommendation No. 8

We recommend that this unit:

o. Serve as secretariat for a coordinating body made up of representatives of selected agencies including the National Military Establishment. Such a board would recommend to the President policies and procedures for developing a single commodity catalog for the Federal Government. It should also recommend rules and regulations for its mandatory use.

Inspection Activities

Recommendation No. 9

We recommend that this unit:

p. Determine what products should be inspected.

q. Make inspection assignments to specific agencies.

r. Make testing assignments.

s. Prepare inspection manuals.

t. Develop rules and regulations on inspection policies and methods.

Property Utilization Activities

Recommendation No. 10

We recommend that this unit:

u. Develop property use, maintenance, and replacement standards and rules and regulations, and determine the extent to which property disposal functions should be delegated to civilian agencies.

Recommendation No. 11

Strengthen the Authority of the Secretary of Defense so that he may provide the leadership necessary for improving the supply operations of the National Military Establishment.

The three military departments expend over 5 billion dollars annually for new supplies and equipment or 80 percent of the total amount so expended by the Government each year. Therefore, if substantial savings are to be realized in supply operations, improved practices must be adopted by the military departments as well as by the civilian agencies.

The Commission believes that the wider sphere of responsibility given to the Muntions Board under the National Security Act of 1947 is a step in the right direction. This charter should be expanded, however, to cover all phases of military supply including purchasing, storage and issue, traffic management, specification, inspection, property identification, and property utilization.

Recommendation No. 12

It is specifically recommended that the National Security Act of 1947 be amended so as to strengthen the authority of the Secretary of Defense in order that he may integrate the organization and procedures of the various phases of supply in the constituent departments of the National Military Establishment.

Recommendation No. 13

Remodel civilian agency supply organizations along the general lines proposed for the Bureau of Federal Supply.

It is not intended here to propose a rigid pattern which should govern the supply organizations of the civilian departments and agencies. The size and nature of agency supply organizations will vary with the type and quantity of supplies which the agency requires. The Supply Bureau, however, should have the responsibility of reporting to the President the provisions made by the various agencies for the adoption of policies outlined herein.

Recommendation No. 14

Eliminate the present surcharge levied on the price of commodities purchased through central supply organizations for the Govern-

ment as a whole and the departments and pay the administrative costs of such organizations through direct appropriations.

At the present time the Bureau of Federal Supply is required to levy a surcharge of 12 percent of the purchase price on commodities which agencies purchase through the Bureau. A similar practice exists in many of the departments which have central supply organizations handling purchasing on a department-wide basis. This practice has discouraged use of economical centralized facilities and fostered the growth of costly supply units throughout the Government. As long as the practice of levying surcharges exists, agency officials will persist in the impression that they are able to purchase more economically than the central organizations, since they do not take into account the overhead and operating costs of their own purchasing organizations.

*   *   *   *   *

The task force report of the Federal Supply Project makes detailed recommendation for the improvement of supply operations. These recommendations should be of inestimable assistance to Federal officials concerned with supply, and it is upon these officials that the primary burden for an improved system rests. In order to free these officials so that they may proceed with such a program, it will be necessary for the President and Congress to adopt the recommendations which the Commission has outlined in this report.

Savings

The task force reports that great savings will be realized if its recommendations are adopted.

The task force also estimates that it should be possible to reduce stores inventories, both military and civilian, by over 2,500 million dollars. This would permit a cut in personnel engaged in stores activities. The adoption of the recommendations relating to traffic management would produce additional savings. Adoption of the recommendations relating to inspection, specification, property identification, and property utilization would also achieve appreciable savings in personnel and operating costs.

VI
Personnel Management

Chapter One

INTRODUCTION

The Federal Government's total civilian employment in the fiscal year 1948 averaged 2,043,000. Twenty years ago it was 570,000. This tremendous expansion over the past two decades, representing an increase of over 300 percent, has thrust a problem upon the Government.

The administration of this vast personnel program is complicated by the very size and rapidity of growth. For example, the total annual salaries paid to civilian employees leaped in 20 years from approximately $1,000,000,000 to $5,650,000,000 per annum. The Government comprises over 60 great enterprises, each with its own problems and requirements. Personnel skills now number over 15,000, or two-thirds as many as the requirements of all private enterprises.

Inevitably an expansion of these proportions taxes the organization structure, the methods, and techniques of the Government. Furthermore, great expansions are likely to reveal organizational and procedural weaknesses which develop rapidly unless aggressive corrective action is applied. Expansion of the Government's civilian employment by millions has not been attended by necessary organizational adjustment, nor have the planning and administration of the personnel program kept abreast of the times and the needs of the Government.

This does not mean that substantial progress has not been made by the Federal Government in introducing and promoting modern personnel management practices. In fact, Presidents of the United States, the Congress, the Civil Service Commission, agency heads, and agency directors of personnel have evidenced keen interest in furthering sound and progressive personnel practices. As a result, considerable improvement has been made.

Nevertheless there are still outstanding deficiencies in the Government's vast personnel program—deficiencies which must be faced squarely and attacked vigorously. Only in this manner can we hope to achieve in the Federal Government a civilian career service which attracts and holds men and women of the highest intelligence and whose devotion to duty and whose competence is commensurate with the needs of our Government. Any personnel practices which do not attain this objective must be condemned. In their place we must substitute methods which will achieve such an objective. Unless the goal is attained we cannot expect sound, efficient, and economical Government.

What Is Wrong with the Career Civilian Service

A brief summary of the deficiencies of the present personnel practices follows:

Centralization

1. Centralization of personnel transactions in the Civil Service Commission and in the central personnel offices of the departments and agencies has resulted in unjustifiable delays and stands in the way of a satisfactory handling of the Government's personnel problems.

Recruiting and Examining

2. Machinery for recruiting is not adapted to the variety and numbers of workers required. It has proved to be too slow and cumbersome. As a result, there have been far too many temporary employees in jobs pending the establishment of regular civil-service lists.

3. The Government too often fails to get the right man for the job or the right job for the man.

4. Not enough time and effort are being spent on recruiting our best young men and women for junior professional, scientific, technical, and administrative posts.

Rates of Pay

5. A comprehensive pay administration policy for the entire executive branch is long overdue. The four policies now in force lead to situations where pay varies not only from agency to agency but also within agencies. Furthermore, the fact that until recent years the Civil Service Commission has not developed standards for classifying jobs under the Classification Act of 1923 and, in some instances, the complexity of present standards have at times resulted in an unsatisfactory handling of salaries for workers in the "white collar" class.

6. Too many supervisors believe that action to reduce the number of persons in their units will result in their salaries being reduced, while increases in the number of persons in their units will lead to their salaries being increased. This makes supervisors believe that they will be rewarded for inefficiency, and encourages "empire building."

7. Salary ceilings for professional, scientific, technical, and administrative personnel are so low that many of the best men and women in these fields are forced to leave the Government service for private enterprise. Pay raises in recent years have not been proportional. The lowest pay grades have been increased between 43 and 56 percent; the highest grade has been increased only 15 percent.

Obstacles to Career Service

8. Departments and agencies have failed to develop adequate programs for promoting career employees from one level of responsibility to the next.

9. Inadequate opportunities are provided employees for the presentation of suggestions designed to improve the Government's practices and procedures in the personnel field.

10. The efficiency rating system is too complicated and the legal requirements that the system be used as a basis for both rewards and penalties stand in the way of its contributing to sound supervisor-employee relationships.

11. Reduction-in-force regulations do not retain the best qualified persons when it becomes necessary for the Government to reduce the number of persons on the pay roll.

12. In view of the relative security offered by Government employment, the recruitment of 500,000 persons a year to fill vacancies caused by turnover is an indication of the existence of low morale, due, in part, to poor supervisory practices.

13. The separation of inefficient and unnecessary employees has been surrounded with so much red tape as to inhibit action.

14. There is little desire upon the part of some of the best talent in the country to enter civil service as a career.

Other Weaknesses

15. Personnel offices in many instances are overstaffed. A recent survey of major agencies employing 1,800,000 showed that in those agencies there are now over 23,000 employees in personnel offices earning a total of $76,000,000 a year—one personnel worker for every 78 employees. We have found that, in some instances, there is one personnel worker for every 38 employees.

16. The Civil Service Commission is not organized to handle personnel problems as quickly as they should be handled, not to render effective over-all leadership in the personnel field.

Chapter Two

WHAT MUST BE DONE

This Commission proposes a far-reaching revision in structure and methods in order to build a career service which will select the best of our citizens on merit, free of political influence, with incentives in the form of genuine opportunities for promotion in the service, and which will eliminate the unnecessary and inefficient employees. To do this we must, among other things, establish sufficient confidence in the service to attract the best of our youth, and we must provide for their adequate training after they have entered the service.

Top policy-making officials must and should be appointed by the President. But all employment activities below these levels, including some positions now in the exempt category, should be carried on within the framework of the decentralized civil-service system recommended in this report.

In order to achieve the objectives stated in the previous chapter and to correct many of the unsatisfactory conditions which now exist in the Federal service, the Commission makes the recommendations in the following section.

Reorganization of the Civil Service Commission

Recommendation No. 1

a. **The Civil Service Commission should place primary emphasis on staff functions, rather than upon processing a multitude of personnel transactions. (See chart, Proposed Basic Structure for Personnel Management.)**

The Commission's responsibility should be to furnish leadership for personnel administration in the Government by (i) setting standards for

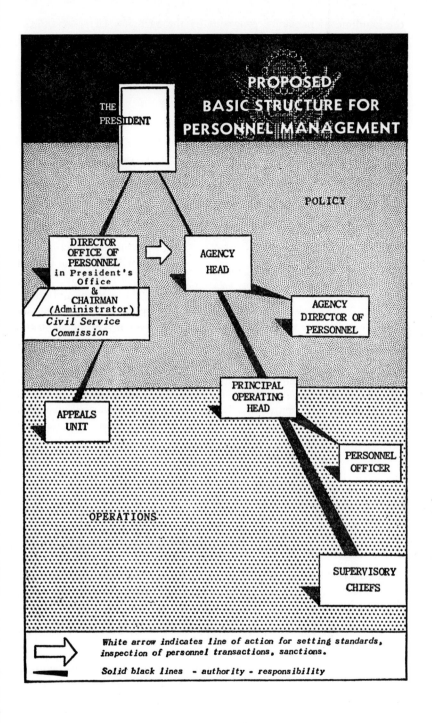

PROPOSED BASIC STRUCTURE FOR PERSONNEL MANAGEMENT

THE PRESIDENT

POLICY

DIRECTOR
OFFICE OF
PERSONNEL
in President's
Office
&
CHAIRMAN
(Administrator)
Civil Service
Commission

AGENCY
HEAD

AGENCY
DIRECTOR OF
PERSONNEL

PRINCIPAL
OPERATING
HEAD

APPEALS
UNIT

PERSONNEL
OFFICER

OPERATIONS

SUPERVISORY
CHIEFS

White arrow indicates line of action for setting standards,
inspection of personnel transactions, sanctions.

Solid black lines - authority - responsibility

the handling of personnel programs by the agencies, (ii) post-auditing personnel programs to determine that there has been adherence to standards, (iii) applying appropriate sanctions whenever there has not been adherence to standards, and (iv) considering appeals from the public or employees which are filed with it in accordance with pertinent laws and executive orders.

b. **The Civil Service Commission should be reorganized to vest in its chairman the responsibility for the administrative direction of its work.**

The chairman of the Commission should also perform the functions outlined in our first report.

c. **Heads of all departments and agencies should be required to have on their top management staffs a director of personnel.**

He should be their principal staff adviser in helping to make sure that their agencies secure an efficient staff and that inefficiency and unnecessary employees are constantly weeded out.

d. **The Civil Service Commission should be required to develop standards for the operation of personnel offices in the departments and agencies.**

These standards should place primary emphasis on delegating personnel functions to administrative and supervisory personnel with work in the personnel offices confined to rendering assistance requested by operating officials. There are, at present, in our judgment, too many persons engaged in personnel work. The acceptance of this recommendation should result in a reduction in the number so engaged.

Recruiting and Examining

Recommendation No. 2

a. **Primary responsibility for recruiting and examining Federal employees should be placed on the departments and agencies.**

This should be done with the understanding that recruiting and examining programs must be approved by the Civil Service Commission before they are put into effect, and with the further understanding that the actual conduct of the programs will be subject to inspection by the Commission in order to determine that there has been adherence to the Civil Service Act and the Veterans Preference Act.

The provision of the statute establishing the Tennessee Valley Authority, which makes mandatory the removal of appointing officers exercising political favoritism in making appointments, would be extended to the entire Federal service.

b. Appointing officers should be given more leeway than the present "rule of three" permits in the selection of personnel from among qualified applicants.

c. Far greater emphasis should be placed on the development and execution of programs designed to attract first-rate young men and women for subordinate (junior) professional, scientific, technical, and administrative posts.

A plan designed to implement the above recommendation should be worked out by an unpaid commission appointed by the President.

Rates of Pay

Recommendation No. 3

a. The Congress should enact a law which would embody a comprehensive pay policy for the entire executive branch.

b. Authority to evaluate jobs for pay purposes should be delegated to the departments and agencies under standards established and enforced by the Commission.

c. In granting authority to the executive branch, the Congress should make it possible for the President to issue and enforce rules which will reward administrators and supervisors for actions which reduce the number of persons on the Federal pay roll.

d. Rates of compensation for postal, clerical, subprofessional, and "blue collar" jobs should be fixed and adjusted in relation to prevailing locality, area, or industry pay differentials.

e. In view of the fact that pay in the lowest grades has been increased between 43 and 56 percent, while pay in the highest grade has been increased only 15 percent, immediate consideration should be given to providing adequate salaries for top civil-service employees with exceptional professional, scientific, technical, and administrative qualifications.

This action is imperative in the interest of sound management of the Federal Government.

Similar action is considered essential for other top positions throughout all branches of the Government. Salaries for Cabinet officers have not, for example, been changed since 1925. This is indefensible. Government can never compete on a dollar-for-dollar basis with private industry for persons for its top positions. It can and should, however, treat such persons in an equitable manner. This it is not now doing.

Developing a Sound Career Service

Recommendation No. 4

a. Departments and agencies should be required, under the direction of the Civil Service Commission, to work out specific programs for promoting career employees.

b. The Civil Service Commission should be given the authority and resources for developing a program which will open up promotion opportunities across agency lines.

c. Congress should make it possible for the executive branch to provide for the training of its most promising career employees.

d. The heads of departments and agencies should be required to provide for the positive participation of employees in the formulation and improvement of Federal personnel policies and practices.

e. The efficiency rating system should be simplified and should be used solely to develop a better understanding between supervisors and employees.

Separation of Employees

Recommendation No. 5

a. Congress should amend the law dealing with reductions in force to permit regulations to insure the retention in the Federal service of men and women who are best qualified to perform the duties of their jobs, irrespective of other considerations.

b. Existing directives dealing with dismissals should be amended so as to provide a more workable method for separating inefficient employees.

Chapter Three

PROBLEMS AND PROPOSED REMEDIES

A more complete discussion of the present situation in the personnel field, the recommendations of the Commission, and the reasons for the recommendations follow.

First. Recruitment and Placement

PROBLEMS

1. As a result of the Executive order issued by the President of the United States immediately following VJ-day, and as a result of regulations issued by the Civil Service Commission, considerable progress has been made toward decentralizing to the departments and agencies responsibility for recruiting and examining Federal employees.

Nevertheless, under present conditions, 4 to 8 months often elapse between the time when an examination is announced and the time when persons are appointed to Federal jobs. Consequently, many temporary appointments are made pending the results of an examination. Those who receive temporary appointments are at times of inferior ability. But about the time these temporary employees are giving reasonably satisfactory service, they must be replaced if they fail to score as well as new applicants when an examination is held. It should be noted in this connection that the examination score is not always a fully reliable index of an individual's suitability for, and performance on, a specific job.

The whole process contributes to inefficiency, delay, and excessive cost in carrying forward the Government's work.

2. Under the merit system as it operates in the Federal Government, appointing officers are generally required to select persons for jobs from among no more than three names of qualified applicants. This rule is,

in our judgment, unnecessary from the standpoint of insuring that selections will be made on the basis of merit and, at the same time, it often operates so as to keep the Government from getting the right man for the job.

3. Preference for veterans in the filling of Federal jobs is an integral part of our civil-service system. Too much reliance has been placed upon a rigid system to increase the number of veterans in Federal positions. As a result, there are not as many veterans serving in Federal jobs as might otherwise be the case and in many instances veterans are not serving in the types of jobs for which they are best qualified.

4. A great deal of lip service has been paid to the idea of recruiting outstanding young men and women for professional, scientific, administrative, and technical jobs. Actually, the Federal Government has not made nearly as much progress in this direction as must be made if capable young men and women are to be recruited and retained.

RECOMMENDATIONS

Recommendation No. 6

The President, by Executive order, should require all major departments and agencies to conduct vigorous recruiting programs for, and to examine and make final appointments to:

a. **All high-level administrative, professional, and technical positions.**

b. **All positions peculiar to the agency.**

c. **Any other classes of positions which, in the judgment of the Civil Service Commission, can be filled more effectively by the agencies.**

The agencies should be required to submit their proposed recruiting and examining programs to the Civil Service Commission for approval with the further understanding that the actual conduct of the programs will be subject to inspection by the Commission to enforce adherence to the Civil Service Act and the Veterans Preference Act. It should be clearly understood that, in carrying forward recruiting programs, except where the supply of qualified personnel is considerably in excess of the demand, agencies will receive applications on a continuous basis.

Personnel procurement offices, under the direction of the Civil Service Commission, should handle recruiting and examining activities for lower grade positions whenever it is more feasible than for them to be handled by the departments and agencies. Centralized recruiting should, however, always be regarded as the exception and subject to negotiation of suitable arrangements between the Commission and the agencies concerned in each locality.

In carrying out their responsibilities under this program of decentralization, all appointing officers in the Federal service should be subject to the provisions of a statute such as that establishing the Tennessee Valley Authority which calls for the removal of persons who permit political considerations to govern appointments.

Furthermore, it should be clearly understood that the departments and agencies will be bound by the laws and regulations governing the apportionment of positions in the District of Columbia among the residents of the various States.

Recommendation No. 7

All applicants for civil-service posts should be grouped into categories such as "outstanding," "well qualified," "qualified," and "unqualified."

Appointing officers should, with due regard to the provisions for veteran preference, start with the highest category of qualified applicants and select anyone in that category for vacancies.

Selections would still be made on the basis of merit but a much better job could be done in fitting people into those jobs for which they are best qualified.

Recommendation No. 8

Within each quality category referred to in Recommendation No. 7, veterans should be considered ahead of nonveterans.

No nonveteran should be selected for a position unless adequate reasons are given for failing to appoint any veterans in the category in question.

Veterans with a disability of 10 percent or more, and all other persons now entitled to a 10-point preference, and who have been placed in the "qualified" category, should be considered ahead of veterans and non-veterans in the "outstanding" category, except for professional, scientific, and technical positions paying $3,000 or more a year.

Recommendation No. 9

A Nation-wide recruiting system to place veterans in Federal positions should be operated through selected Government agencies for the next 3 or 4 years in principal communities.

Recommendation No. 10

Departments and agencies should be required, consistent with funds available for such purposes, to recruit each year a specified number of young men and women for junior professional, scientific, technical, and administrative posts.

This group should be chosen from among those who have prepared themselves for such services and have passed competitive examinations, and in accordance with a quota system to insure adequate representation from the various States.

A plan designed to implement the above recommendation should be worked out by an unpaid commission appointed by the President.

Second. Development of a Career Service

PROBLEMS

1. Unrealistic levels of compensation for technical, scientific, and executive personnel receiving more than $5,000 a year constitute one of the principal reasons for the Government's poor "holding power" as an employer.

While the pay of Federal employees in the various grades under $5,000 has been advanced 38 to 56 percent since 1939, those in the highest pay grade either have not been advanced at all or, where any increase occurred, have been advanced a maximum of 15 percent. Considering increased costs and increased income taxes, the actual "take-home" salaries of employees in the upper grades are substantially less than in 1939. As a result, the Government is losing some of its ablest men to private employment.

The responsibilities of management in the various departments of the executive branch are today so great that danger to the welfare and security of the country, as well as immense financial losses, can result from incompetence on the top executive level. High-caliber executives can eliminate cumbersome and wasteful forms of management.

Many able men, while willing to give patriotic service to their Government at lower salaries than are available to them in private employment, cannot be obtained for, or retained in, public service at present levels.

Government salaries in the higher levels do not have to be fully comparable with those in private life, but they do have to go considerably further than at present in relieving able men from financial worries if the Government is to maintain or improve the quality of its executives.

2. The executive branch has not done an adequate job in developing career promotion programs within the departments and agencies.

It has not, as an example, clearly identified the opportunities which exist for persons who are interested in pursuing an administrative career in the Federal Government. In addition, it has not developed adequate programs for insuring that career personnel are moved into administrative positions at various levels on the basis of merit.

3. The executive branch recognizes, but is not dealing adequately with, the problem of transferring competent personnel, particularly in the technical, scientific, and executive areas, from one agency to another.

Unless this situation is corrected the Government will continue to lose some of its ablest personnel in these areas. They will conclude that they are in "dead-end" jobs when their services may be desperately needed in more important jobs in another agency.

4. Both the legislative and executive branches of the Government have failed to develop a clear-cut statement of policy under which adequate training programs can be worked out for career employees.

RECOMMENDATIONS

Recommendation No. 11

Congress should raise the present salary ceiling of $10,330 for career employees. At the same time, it should increase legislative, judicial, and executive salaries at the level of assistant secretary, or its equivalent, and above.

The Commission had considered confining these recommendations to the executive branch alone. Although aware that it is exceeding its charter, the Commission has concluded that to recommend any increase in salary without taking the total picture into consideration, would confuse rather than clarify an action that is essential in strengthening our whole Government structure.

Recommendation No. 12

The President should direct the departments and agencies to work out practical programs designed to facilitate the promotion of career employees, and the Civil Service Commission should enforce the President's directive.

Recommendation No. 13

The Civil Service Commission should be required to identify the jobs which could be appropriately classified as administrative.

Young men and women entering junior administrative posts thus will have a clear understanding of the opportunities for promotion, as well as of the qualification requirements for higher positions.

Recommendation No. 14

The President and the Congress should place the Civil Service Commission in a position where it can spend more of its time and resources on developing a program to facilitate transfer of competent career personnel—particularly in the technical, scientific, and executive areas—from one agency to another.

Recommendation No. 15

Congress should enact legislation which will clearly set forth the policy of the Federal Government on the conduct of training programs for civilian employees.

Third. Need for a Comprehensive Pay Administration Policy

PROBLEMS

1. In addition to the inadequate level of compensation for top technical, scientific, and executive positions, the Government pay administration practices today are inequitable and complex.

While 92 percent of all Federal positions are subject to the same employment regulations, only 42 percent are subject to any single set of pay policies, of which there are four principal ones:

a. Under the Classification Act of 1923 are grouped about 850,000 employees, most of whom can be classified as "white collar" workers.

b. Wages are fixed by individual agencies for another large group—some 600,000—most of whom are "blue collar" workers. The bulk of these employees work as civilians for the various branches of the Armed Services, but they are also found in 17 other agencies.

c. Special and detailed laws passed by the Congress fix the compensation for 480,000 postal workers.

d. Finally, a group of 70,000 workers scattered in 16 agencies, including the Foreign Service, are compensated under special laws passed by the Congress.

As a result, the Federal Government has a system for compensating its employees which varies not only from agency to agency but also within individual agencies.

FEDERAL PAY
INCREASES LAG BEHIND

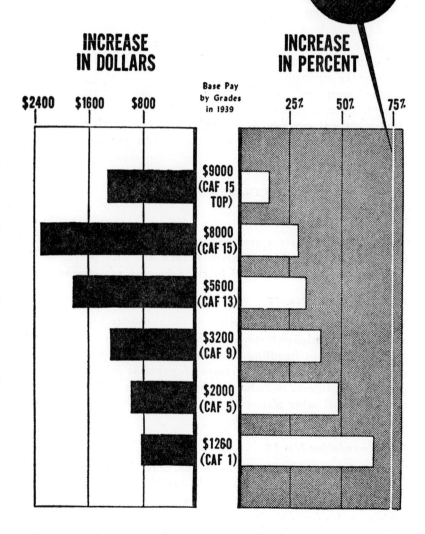

RISE IN COST OF LIVING 1939-48

INCREASE IN DOLLARS

INCREASE IN PERCENT

$2400 $1600 $800

Base Pay by Grades in 1939

25%   50%   75%

$9000 (CAF 15 TOP)

$8000 (CAF 15)

$5600 (CAF 13)

$3200 (CAF 9)

$2000 (CAF 5)

$1260 (CAF 1)

2. Pay adjustments for "white collar" workers and postal workers have tended, particularly from the point of view of timing, to lag behind similar adjustments in industry.

The tendency has been to handle these adjustments by either flat increases, or percentage increases, reduced in the higher brackets. This gives persons in the middle and upper brackets a much smaller percentage increase than those in the lower brackets and tends to destroy the proper relationship between various types of jobs. (See chart.)

3. Too many administrators act on the belief that increasing the number of persons in a supervisory unit will result automatically in an increase in salary for the supervisor, while reducing the number of persons in a supervisory unit will result automatically in a reduction in salary for the supervisor.

Both Congress and the Civil Service Commission have endeavored to correct this situation. The measures taken, however, must be made more effective if the Government is to provide supervisors with adequate incentives for getting jobs done with the smallest possible number of people.

RECOMMENDATIONS

Recommendation No. 16

Congress should enact a comprehensive pay administration policy applicable to the entire executive branch and incorporate in the policy the principles indicated in the following recommendations.

Recommendation No. 17

The Congress should be the source of the authority for all matters of Federal pay administration but should, in the interest of expeditious and efficient handling, limit its participation to establishing the minimum and maximum rates of payment within which all general adjustments in Federal compensation are to be made. Authority for all other phases of pay administration should be delegated to the executive branch.

Recommendation No. 18

The Civil Service Commission, as the central personnel agency, should, subject to the approval of the President, have responsibility for (*a*) the establishment of individual pay scales, including raises within grades for seniority and meritorious performance, and (*b*) fixing the standards which should govern the administration of the job evaluation plans in all departments and agencies.

However, the actual administration of these plans should be delegated to the heads of departments and agencies, subject to a post-audit to determine that there has been adherence to the standards.

In delegating this authority, the Congress should make it possible for the President to issue and enforce rules which will result in administrators and supervisors being rewarded for actions which have the effect of reducing the number of persons on the Federal pay roll.

Recommendation No. 19

In order to maintain a realistic pay relationship between comparable positions within Federal and private employment, differentials in pay for locality, area, and industry should be a primary consideration in fixing and adjusting pay scales for clerical, subprofessional, postal, and "blue collar" jobs.

Recommendation No. 20

For all other employees whose rates of pay are fixed on a Nationwide basis, the President should be authorized to direct the Civil Service Commission to review annually the Federal compensation levels and to make appropriate recommendations within the salary floor and the salary ceiling set by the Congress.

Upon receipt of these recommendations, the President should have the authority to decide what changes should be made in compensation levels and his decisions should become effective 60 days after their promulgation.

Such a procedure would enable the Government, as an employer, to adapt its pay structures to changed conditions much more expeditiously and effectively. It would also make it easier to work out adjustments which would maintain the proper relationships between jobs.

Fourth. Provision for Improving Efficiency and for Participation of Supervisors and Employees In Personnel Management

PROBLEMS

1. The Government has lagged behind American industry in improving employer-employee relations.

2. Federal employees, while given some degree of protection against abuse, discrimination, and unjust treatment, are not provided a positive

opportunity to participate in the formulation of policies and practices which affect their welfare.

3. Our Personnel Policy Committee has concluded that the present efficiency-rating procedures in the Federal Government have the effect of undermining supervisor-employee relationships.

It bases its conclusions on the fact that the system, under certain circumstances, makes mandatory either a public reward or a public penalty; that the supervisor's determination is subject to challenge and revision at three higher levels; that the efficiency-rating process is based upon contradictory and unvalidated assumptions; and that the system is not used to the extent that it should be as an aid in the development of the employee and for the purposes of measuring the employee's potential usefulness to the organization.

We concur in this analysis of the present situation.

4. The present reduction-in-force regulations require complex and cumbersome methods.

The Commission on Organization recognizes that never before in history has any employer found it necessary to reduce the number of his employees from 3,700,000 to approximately 2,000,000 as has the Federal Government. It feels that, on the whole, those who have carried the heavy work-load connected with this operation are to be commended for the conscientious job they have done.

Nevertheless, we feel that the system which has been followed can be improved when it is realized, for example, that in connection with the reduction of one agency from 7,000 to 5,000 a personnel office spent 14 man-years in processing the reduction at an estimated cost of $50,000.

There is a maze of personnel laws, rules, and regulations. Officials even with long periods of service are unable to interpret and administer them. This is undoubtedly one of the principal reasons for an unjustifiable expenditure of time and funds.

Also, the present reduction-in-force regulations provide another example of failure upon the part of the Federal Government to give adequate weight to the judgment of the supervisor. Efficiency ratings which do not effectively measure an employee's future usefulness to the organization, are a factor in determining who is to stay on the pay roll. Veterans with a rating of "Good" or better—regardless of experience— take precedence over all other employees, and length of service often, as a practical matter, becomes the sole factor in determining who is not to be laid off.

5. This Commission believes that the failure to take prompt and vigorous action to remove inefficient employees or deadwood from the

Government service is a source of discouragement and despair to the great majority of able and efficient public servants.

Red tape without end has accumulated in the separation of such employees from the Government. Yet this red tape is not required by the laws governing the civil-service system.

While such red tape does not always result in Federal employees being given life tenure in their jobs, and while some career employees are fired for both misconduct and incompetence, it must be recognized that the red tape does stand in the way of competent administration of Government.

One reason for its existence is the part which efficiency ratings play in the dismissal process.

When an employee receives an efficiency rating of "unsatisfactory" and his discharge is proposed, he often has three appeals: first, to the personnel office; second, to a representative of the head of the agency; and third, to an independent board of review, the chairman of which is provided by the Civil Service Commission.

Supervising officials are compelled to produce a documented bill of particulars at great trouble and loss of time. In consequence, there are very few ratings less than "fair," and there is a resulting general apathy in connection with weeding out the inefficient. In two agencies examined, fewer than 3 in 1,000 employees were marked "unsatisfactory" over a year.

Examination of 25 discharges in three agencies showed the time required to process the actions averaged 7 months. In one instance, a stenographer proved wholly unsatisfactory, but because of failure to present documentary evidence, the supervisory official was unable initially to bring about her dismissal. Finally, the employee resigned when faced with 45 exhibits collected over a period of 17 months. Steps must be taken to cut out the red tape surrounding removal procedures and to provide administrators with a simple, clear-cut procedure which can be understood by them and by the employees and which will be fair to both the Government as an employer, and the employees.

ESTABLISHMENT OF SUPERVISOR-EMPLOYEE COUNCILS

Recommendation No. 21

The President should require the heads of departments and agencies to provide for employee participation in the formulation and improvement of Federal personnel policies and practices.

One possible method would be to establish within each agency a council composed of both supervisor and employee representatives.

Such a program would result in suggestions which would materially reduce the time, money, and personnel used in perpetuating the red tape which exists in the personnel field.

"ABILITY AND SERVICE RECORD" RATINGS

Recommendation No. 22

a. **The present efficiency-rating system should be replaced by "ability and service record" ratings which would incorporate the following principles:**

(i) The supervisor would be required to evaluate, at least annually, each employee's ability, past performance, progress, and potential usefulness to the organization on specific factors, indicating for each factor whether the employee is superior, satisfactory, or weak.

(ii) Upon completion of the evaluation, the supervisor would be required to have a personal conference with each employee. This discussion would consist of a review of the employee's strengths and weaknesses and the development of concrete objectives for correcting these deficiencies and facilitating the employee's future progress.

b. **"Ability and service record" ratings should not be used as a basis for determining whether employees are to receive periodic salary increases, as a basis for determining the order of layoffs in connection with reduction in force, or as a basis for instituting dismissal actions.**

CHANGES IN REDUCTION-IN-FORCE REGULATIONS

Recommendation No. 23

a. **The statutory basis for and regulations governing reductions in force should be changed so that . . .**

(i) There will be a more realistic ranking of employees from the standpoint of their over-all usefulness to the agency in question.

(ii) The procedures will not be as complex as they are at the present time.

(iii) Veterans will be given additional credit in reductions in force for each 6 months of service with the Armed Forces but, except for those with disability preference, will not be accorded the absolute preference retention which they now receive under the law.

b. With respect to the problem of securing a more realistic ranking of employees for retention purposes, it is felt that such ranking should be approached from the point of view of "which employees should be retained" rather than which should be eliminated.

In effect, the organization which will result from the reduction in force should be conceived as a new, unstaffed organization and all present employees considered as qualified applicants with reemployment rights. Using this approach, the following rating principles are suggested:

(i) The jobs to be filled should be selected and their requirements defined.

(ii) All eligible employees should be placed on registers and rated according to their qualifications, past performance, and future potential (the same employee may be placed on several registers depending upon his qualifications). The rating should result in grouping eligibles into quality categories, such as "outstanding," "well-qualified," and "qualified," based upon standards developed by the agency and approved by the Civil Service Commission. (Separate registers would be established for permanent and temporary employees as at present.)

(iii) Within each quality category, eligibles should be ranked on the basis of length of service. Veterans should be given credit for one additional year of service for each 6 months of service with the Armed Forces. However, in selecting those to be retained, the incumbent of a given job should be given preference whenever he is in competition with another employee of equal qualifications and length of service.

(iv) The rating process should be conducted by "committees of examiners" composed of supervisors in the organizational units affected by the reduction in force, and a placement officer from the personnel division. This device should provide greater objectivity in rating the "eligibles" than would be obtained if the immediate supervisor alone rated the employees.

(v) Agencies should be required to establish a suitable review committee or officer to which employees may appeal their rating on reduction-in-force registers. Appeals to the Civil Service Commission should be permitted.

Under this plan the present basic procedures for determining the areas and levels of competition would be retained. The principal revision made is the substitution of a new method of rating and ranking "eligibles" for the present efficiency-rating, seniority formula. An important feature of the revisions is to attach greater weight to qualifications than at present, a principle in keeping with current private practice. A recent survey of lay-off policies among 89 companies revealed that over two-thirds consider seniority a secondary factor.

The Commission desires to emphasize that it believes veterans should be given preference for retention in reductions in force. It also believes, however, that a system is indefensible when it results in a nonveteran with 20 or 25 years of service and with an outstanding record being displaced by a veteran with only 1 or 2 years of service and a "good" record. The program outlined in the report of the Personnel Policy Committee provides substantial preference to veterans and, at the same time, insures the retention in the Federal service of the men and women who are best qualified to perform the duties of their jobs.

c. **Career employees who are laid off as a result of reduction in force should be given special consideration for other Federal jobs.**

(i) They should be referred to the Civil Service Commission for a determination as to where their services can be used most effectively.

(ii) They should be given a top priority for consideration for any vacancy in the Government for which the Commission considers them to be qualified.

(iii) Until such time as they are placed in a new job, or for a period not to exceed 3 months, they should be entitled to draw the same compensation they were drawing at the time the reduction in force took place.

During the period it takes to find new jobs for these employees, they should be regarded as a "reserve," subject to assignment by the Civil Service Commission to temporary service in departments and agencies.

SEPARATION FOR INCOMPETENCE

Recommendation No. 24

The President should direct the heads of all departments and agencies to put into effect a simple, clear-cut, and intelligent procedure for discharge of incompetent employees.

The procedure recommended below would be fair both to the employees and to the Government as an employer, and readily understood by employees and their supervisors:

Whenever a supervisory official decides that an employee should be discharged as incompetent, he should present the facts to the under secretary (or comparable official) or to the under secretary's designee, through the director of personnel, with the understanding that after such a presentation had been made the following steps would be taken:

(i) A designated official would make a preliminary confidential investigation. If he determined that there was no basis for the complaint, no further action would be taken.

(ii) If the investigation revealed that the employee should be dismissed, and he had not completed his probationary year's service, the employee would be dismissed without further formalities.

(iii) If the investigation revealed that an employee, who had completed his probationary period, was not performing satisfactorily but could qualify adequately for another job, efforts would be made to arrange for his transfer.

(iv) If the investigation revealed that a prima facie case of incompetence had been made out against an employee whose probationary period was completed, written charges would be presented to the employee and a hearing provided.

If the hearing determined that the employee should be removed, a certificate of dismissal would be issued in the name of the under secretary to be effective at the end of 30 days.

During the 30-day period, the employee could request the Civil Service Commission to review his case. If the Civil Service Commission decided to review the case, the employee would continue to draw pay pending the Commission's final decision. If the appeal was disallowed, the employee would be separated from the service. The Commission might, however, certify him as qualified for work in another agency.

If the Commission decided the appeal in his favor, the employee would have priority for reemployment in the agency in which he had been employed, for any appropriate vacancy for which he was considered qualified by the Commission. He would continue to draw his salary pending such reemployment. The employee should not, however, under ordinary circumstances, be returned to the actual position formerly held by him.

This suggested procedure should not replace present procedures which permit the immediate suspension and prompt discharge of an employee who is obviously unfit to perform the duties of his job or who is guilty of wilful misconduct. It should be regarded as an optional procedure designed to bring about a prompt disposition of cases involving incompetence. Such a procedure would, in the judgment of the Commission, have the following results:

It would speed action since it would provide just one appeal within the agency, and thus shorten present procedures which call for numerous appeals within the agency.

It would protect the employee from injustice.

It would make it possible for the Civil Service Commission, working with the agency, to see to it that square pegs in round holes are readjusted to proper jobs.

Supervisory officials would not be required to spend an exorbitant amount of time in removing employees who are inefficient or have become incompatible with their surroundings.

PERIODIC SALARY INCREASE

Recommendation No. 25

Employees should receive periodic salary increases within their job-grade only when the supervisor will certify, at the time the increase is due, that the employee's performance and conduct warrant the increase.

This procedure would be substituted for the present practice of using efficiency ratings as a basis for such increases and would, in the judgment of the Commission, help to strengthen the relationships between supervisors and employees.

Fifth. Revision of Personnel Organizations to Implement Decentralized Administration under Centralized Control

PROBLEMS

1. One reason for inefficient and slow handling of personnel matters in the executive branch has been the tendency to centralize the handling of personnel transactions in the Civil Service Commission and, within the agencies, to centralize these transactions in departmental personnel offices.

2. The utilization of the Commission form of organization for handling the administrative work of the central personnel agency has had the effect of slowing down the administrative work of the Commission and, as a result, the handling of personnel transactions in the departments and agencies.

3. The Commission believes that the ratio of personnel workers to total employees, in some instances as high as one personnel worker for about every 38 employees, is too high and should be substantially reduced.

RECOMMENDATIONS

Recommendation No. 26

Full responsibility for the administrative direction of the work of the Civil Service Commission should be vested in the chairman of the Commission.

The chairman of the Commission should serve in the President's Office in a coordinate capacity with such officials as the Director of the Office of the Budget. He should be the President's principal staff adviser on all matters dealing with the career civilian service as set forth in our first report.

The "full Commission" should be responsible for making recommendations to the President about civil-service rules and for the issuance of regulations and standards. It should take whatever steps may be necessary to insure compliance with rules, regulations, and standards, and should act as an appellate body in connection with the appeal functions vested in the Commission.

Recommendation No. 27

The Civil Service Commission should be given the responsibility for developing a pattern of personnel office operation which will give each head of an agency a clear picture of whether his personnel office or offices are now overstaffed.

Recommendation No. 28

Agency heads should be directed by the President to make sure that their personnel offices place primary emphasis on advising operating officials, and that most personnel activities are carried on by operating officials.

Recommendation No. 29

Heads of departments and agencies should recognize to an even greater extent than in the past the importance of enabling their personnel directors to advise on personnel matters whenever top management policies are being developed.

If competent advice is given on personnel matters while policies are being formulated, it will result in the saving of time, money, and personnel and in the rendering of more effective service upon the part of the Government.

Chapter Four

CONCLUSION

The Commission has been greatly aided in its consideration of this very important field by a Personnel Policy Committee which has functioned under the leadership of John A. Stevenson, president of the Penn Mutual Life Insurance Co. The Committee's entire report constitutes a landmark of constructive recommendations, and we suggest its thorough study.

To bring about the reforms set forth in this report, certain changes must be made in personnel laws.

Once again, however, we desire to emphasize that the recommendations in this report, and the actions which may be taken as a result of the recommendations, are to be subjected to just one test; namely, their ability to provide the United States Government, particularly in our scientific, administrative, technical, and professional jobs, with men and women of unquestioned ability, integrity, and devotion to the common good. We cannot entrust the Government of today to second-rate men and women.

Savings

This is, of course, an area in which it is difficult to develop estimates of savings. After a careful consideration, however, of the various factors involved, the Commission does believe that great savings can be achieved if the Commission's recommendations are put into effect.

VII
Foreign Affairs

Chapter One

THE APPROACH TO THE PROBLEM

The Commission on Organization of the Executive Branch of the Government has received from its task force on foreign affairs a report which is outstanding for its analysis of the present-day problems confronting the Government in the conduct of foreign affairs. The report brings out clearly the complex character of modern United States international relations. By giving attention not only to the State Department but also to the Congress, the President and his executive office, and the foreign affairs aspects of the work of departments and agencies other than the State Department, the report affords a sound perspective through which to ascertain the organizational requirements in this field of governmental activity.

In seeking solutions for organizational problems, the task force report properly places major emphasis on definition of principles and procedures upon which organizational reforms can be predicated. In addition, the report makes various suggestions for specific application of these principles and procedures. In so doing, however, it recognizes that these detailed applications generally can be made most effectively by the President, the heads of the various departments and agencies, and other individuals in the executive branch who have the actual responsibility for organization and administration. This general approach has the approval of the Commission, and it is desirable to underline the necessity for permitting the heads of the various units of the executive branch the maximum freedom to organize and administer their respective units to meet the various needs which exist.

The concepts on which the task force report is based and the recommendations of organizational principles and procedures derived therefrom are believed by the Commission to be sound. The Commission likewise is in agreement in the main with the recommendations of the report which involve application of these principles and procedures. The instances in which the conclusions of the Commission modify or differ from those set forth in the task force report will appear hereinafter.

Chapter Two

THE COMPLEXITIES OF THE PRESENT SITUATION

The time is particularly appropriate to appraise the machinery of the Government for the conduct of foreign affairs. The United States emerged from the recent World War with a radically new role in world affairs. As a result, today's organizational requirements are drastically different from those of the prewar era. The executive branch today finds itself forced to develop positive foreign policies and programs, involving not merely the State Department but many other departments and agencies as well, and to deal cooperatively with other nations on a multilateral as well as a bilateral basis. The Congress, in addition, finds that the exercise of its traditional powers in the domestic as well as in the international field has made it a participant in the conduct of foreign affairs on an unprecedented scale.

The problems of Government organization for the conduct of foreign affairs are, therefore, not confined to the State Department alone but involve the organization of the Presidency, the State Department and the Foreign Service, the departments and agencies other than the State Department, the interdepartmental relationships, and the relationships between the executive and legislative branches. The special problems in each of these cases will be discussed separately at a subsequent point. Accompanying the involvement of all these elements and contributing to the complexities of the situation is the increased size of the Government as a whole and of the State Department in particular.

Tangible manifestations of the foregoing are found on all sides. In the Presidency new factors affecting the conduct of foreign affairs include the Chief of Staff to the President and statutory interdepartmental bodies such as the National Security Council. The State Department itself in terms of appropriations is 12 times larger and in terms of personnel almost 5 times larger in 1948 than it was in 1938. In the inter-departmental field there are more than 30 committees concerned with economic, social, military, and other aspects of foreign affairs. Of 59 major departments and agencies in the executive branch,[1] at least 46 are drawn into foreign affairs to a greater or lesser extent. Certain units are deeply involved, such as the National Military Establishment in connection with the administration of occupied areas abroad, the Economic Cooperation Administration in connection with financial assistance overseas, the Treasury Department in international financial matters, and the Commerce Department in connection with export control. Finally, Congressional participation in the conduct of foreign affairs has become particularly evident in the enhancement of the role of the House of Representatives in connection with appropriations for foreign programs.

A. The Executive-Legislative Relationship under the Constitution in the Conduct of Foreign Affairs

The organization of the executive branch for the conduct of foreign affairs must necessarily be shaped to accord with the over-all governmental framework provided by the Constitution. The constitutional doctrine of separation of powers between the executive and legislative branches results in a duality of authority over foreign affairs which complicates the machinery of Government in that area, especially in contrast with the machinery of countries operating under the parliamentary system of government.

The difficulty caused by this duality of authority has been sharpened by the new position of the United States in world affairs. Prior to the recent World War, the Congress at times had considerable influence, of course, on foreign relations, but not on any continuous basis. The President, on the other hand, possessing relatively greater powers than in domestic affairs, largely controlled foreign affairs with only occasional reference to the Congress. Recent events have changed the situation and made the Congress a much more significant and regular participant in foreign affairs. As a consequence, the solutions of today's problems require joint legislative-executive cooperation on a scale heretofore unknown in American history.

---

[1] These 59 departments and agencies are exclusive of nonstatutory interdepartmental committees and certain temporary bodies which, if included, would raise the total to 74.

The Constitution is not at all precise in its allocation of foreign affairs powers between the two branches. The President has the power to negotiate treaties, but only subject to confirmation by two-thirds vote of the Senate. The Constitution gives the President the power to appoint ambassadors and ministers, again subject to Senate confirmation. In addition, he is specifically empowered to receive ambassadors and ministers of other nations. Except for such powers, however, the executive authority must be derived from general constitutional provisions.

On the other hand, the Constitution gives the Congress certain explicit authority in the international field, including the powers to regulate foreign commerce, to fix import duties, and to declare war. Most important of all is its control over appropriation of funds. As the United States has assumed its new role in world affairs, and as domestic and foreign problems have involved more and more the same or closely related issues, all these Congressional powers have assumed greater significance than in the prewar era.

It is one thing to suggest the need for the executive and legislative branches to cooperate in the conduct of foreign affairs and another to achieve such cooperation. One particular obstacle which should be frankly faced is the traditionally suspicious attitude of the Congress toward foreign affairs and toward the segment of the executive branch concerned with it.

This attitude appears to stem from three principal sources:

1. The fact that the State Department is the channel of communications between the United States and foreign nations. In that sense, the State Department represents foreigners. Furthermore, foreign affairs problems are usually troublesome and irritating, and they involve dollars or other commitments to other than the American electorate. In seeking to solve these problems the State Department is handicapped by the lack of any domestic constituency which will give the Congress credit for action taken or which will rise to the State Department's defense against Congressional criticism.

2. The fact that the conduct of foreign affairs of necessity must frequently be on a secret and confidential basis. This is particularly true in the preliminary stages of a given matter where announcement of the intentions of the United States prior to consultation with other nations would result in embarrassments which would make it impossible to deal with those nations. This secrecy is resented by the Congress, which feels that secrecy is too often used to avoid congressional interference and control. The result is to afford a breeding ground for constant conflict.

3. The fact that up to about 1924 social prestige and protocol considerations were paramount in the minds and actions of the bulk of Americans concerned with foreign affairs. From this grew the conception of State Department and Foreign Service personnel as being primarily concerned with tea parties and striped pants. Today, as a result of the Rogers Act of 1924 and the Foreign Service Act of 1946, and as a result of foreign affairs being injected as never before into the main stream of American life, this fact is no longer true, but the memory lingers on and will persist for at least another generation.

Given the present constitutional framework and the attitude of the legislative branch toward foreign affairs, the situation calls for mutual cooperation and restraint. The executive branch must appreciate the role of the Congress and the propriety of its participation in foreign affairs where *legislative* decisions are required. Similarly, the Congress should appreciate that leadership in the conduct of foreign affairs can come only from the executive side of the Government and that the Congress should not attempt to participate in *executive* decisions in the international field.

One serious procedural impediment to achieving satisfactory legislative-executive cooperation is the constitutional requirement of a two-thirds Senate vote for the confirmation of treaties. No thoughtful student of the conduct of foreign affairs can ignore the consequences of this provision. It is a serious trouble breeder between the executive branch and the Senate in that such an inherently rigid rule encourages circumvention by the executive by resort to the procedures of executive agreements and joint resolutions. Attempts to use these procedures, in turn, involve friction between the Senate and the House of Representatives. An especially bad result is that the emphasis is directed to the question of whether the proper procedure is being employed, instead of to the substance of the issues before the Congress. The question of a change in the present requirement of a two-thirds Senate vote is deemed, however, to be outside the province of this Commission.

B. The Organization within the Executive Branch for the Conduct of Foreign Affairs

The problem of organization within the executive branch for the conduct of foreign affairs is, in the final analysis, the same problem as in the Government as a whole. First, despite the relatively greater authority assigned by the Constitution to the President in the foreign affairs field, authority or the power of command over the foreign affairs activities of the entire executive branch is not satisfactorily vested in the President. Similarly, at the departmental level, including the State Department, full authority is not placed in the departmental or agency heads. Second, the line of command and supervision over foreign affairs activities from the President to the department and agency heads, and through them to their subordinate units, is far from clear. Third, the staff services for foreign affairs activities of the President, the Secretary of State, and the other department and agency heads are utterly inadequate. The present difficulties will be outlined in relation to:

1. The Presidency.

2. The interdepartmental relationships of the State Department and the other departments and agencies.

3. The internal organization of the State Department and the Foreign Service.

1. THE PRESIDENCY

The President, as the single member of the executive branch answerable to the electorate, is ultimately responsible to the American people for the formulation, execution, and coordination of foreign policies. The emphasis is on "ultimately," because the President, either personally or institutionally, can attempt to control only the very top and crucial problems of foreign policy formulation, execution, and co-ordination.

Today the authority of the President over the foreign affairs activities of the executive branch is seriously hampered by both legal and practical impediments. The legislative creation of new agencies and specific coordinative bodies with foreign affairs powers, the existence of independent regulatory agencies with executive functions, and the grant of foreign affairs authority and funds to bureaus and offices below the level of the department or agency head, all serve to lessen the efficiency of the executive branch as a whole. Likewise these factors detract from the President's ability to correct administrative weaknesses. They lessen the capabilities of the departments and agencies to provide "self-coordination" and correspondingly throw a greater burden on the executive office of the President. They also prevent the establishment of a direct and effective chain of command from the Chief Executive down through the numerous segments of the executive branch.

The Presidency, furthermore, is only casually organized to furnish staff assistance to the President in the conduct of foreign affairs. Better machinery is badly needed to bring competent and better rounded foreign affairs advice to the President and to force prompt resolution of interdepartmental disputes which, if left unsettled at lower levels, may impair the foreign relations of the United States. The Cabinet, moreover, it must be recognized, is not and cannot become an effective deliberative council of advisers to the President.

2. THE RELATIONSHIP OF THE STATE DEPARTMENT TO THE OTHER DEPARTMENTS AND AGENCIES

Active participation of the departments and agencies other than the State Department in all phases of present-day foreign affairs imposes severe strains on the organizational structure of the Government. These other departments and agencies display an increasing tendency to establish policies or to make policy interpretations which are not coordinated with the foreign policies and interpretations of the State Department. The State Department, in turn, does not always coordinate its policies with over-all United States national policies. With the conduct of foreign affairs no longer the exclusive province of the State Department, coordinated action by the State Department and some 45 other units with foreign affairs activities is a sine qua non for efficient and effective dispatch of business. Until such action is achieved, the line of command and supervision from the President down through the department heads to subordinate levels will remain unclear, indecisive, and ineffective.

This new situation in the foreign affairs field does not mean, however, that the State Department has become just another executive department. Its statutory authority, basically unchanged since 1789, definitely fixes its role as a staff specialist and arm of the President in the conduct of foreign affairs and leaves its duties flexible and elastic. The other departments and agencies, in contrast, derive their foreign affairs authority through direct grants from the Congress which spell out the substantive tasks to be accomplished, usually in considerable detail. In essence, the State Department functions can be described as relating to the means or procedures of conducting foreign relations, whereas the organic statutes of the other departments and agencies pertain more to stubstantive matters, e.g. powers over fissionable materials, loans, communications, aviation, exports, imports, and the like. Coordination of all these varied activities obviously cannot be directed from the Presidential level. A large part must be delegated by the President to the State Department as his staff agency.

On certain crucial issues, however, coordination of foreign policy formulation and execution must come from the President or his executive office. To date the principal response to this need for high-level integration has been the development of specialized interdepartmental bodies at the Cabinet level to advise the President on certain aspects of foreign affairs, such as national security and international finance. The absence of similar mechanisms in other important areas, particularly where foreign affairs touch upon domestic affairs, tends to give the President a partial and limited perspective in reaching decisions and to leave a substantial amount of policy execution to be coordinated on a "hit or miss" basis.

A final complicating factor in present-day governmental organization for the conduct of foreign affairs is the looseness and variation in organization of foreign affairs activities in the other departments and agencies. Some important departments have more than one bureau or office involved in foreign affairs but have no mechanism whereby the department head is able to coordinate the international activities of his own department. This results not only in confusion within a particular department but also places an added administrative burden upon the State Department which must seek not only to coordinate interdepartmental activity but activity within another department as well. Thus once again an important requirement of clear power of command and a clear chain of command is reemphasized.

3. THE INTERNAL ORGANIZATION OF THE STATE DEPARTMENT

The organizational difficulties of the State Department and the Foreign Service stem more from practical than legal sources. By and large the Secretary of State in legal theory is in command of the Department itself. In the case of the Foreign Service the Secretary's theoretical power in substantive matters is also clear. On the administrative side, however, ambiguous language in the Foreign Service Act of 1946 has tended to strengthen the traditional status of the career service as a semi-independent organization.

The practical difficulties in the main relate to impediments in the Secretary's chain of command and to his need for more adequate staff assistance and procedures. As a result, the Secretary and the Under Secretary have an intolerable burden and little time for thoughtful and considered reflection on foreign affairs problems. The frequent and continued absences of the Secretary from the Department since the end of World War II, moreover, set apart the job of head of the State Department from that of the usual department chief.

Numerous factors contribute to the existence of the present impediments in the Secretary's chain of command. One major factor is the existence of two personnel systems, one for the Foreign Service and the other for the Department, each separately administered. Serious unrest and bad feeling exist between the members of these two services and make effective administration an impossible job.

A second major impediment is the system whereby coordinate authority at the substantive policy action level is vested in two different types of units, geographic and economic, each of which reports to different heads who, in turn, report only to the Secretary and Under Secretary. This coordinate authority arrangement necessitates an elaborate and time-consuming system of lateral clearance (in part through excessive use of the committee device), prevents the fixing of responsibility, and tends to foster undesirable duplication of work.

Other significant and disturbing factors, less comprehensive in character, which tend to fragmentize the Department and thereby weaken the internal chain of command, include the following:

a. The Lack of Adequate Utilization of Staff Aids and Procedures

The heavy demands on the time of the Secretary and Under Secretary make it particularly essential that smooth working procedures exist for assembling and correlating staff advice on important policy matters and, conversely, for keeping the heads of action and other units informed of top-level decisions and the reasons therefor. The postwar establishment of the Executive Secretariat and the Policy Planning Staff represents steps in the right direction, and both should be strengthened and more effective use made of their resources.

b. The Need at the Top Command Level for Better Public Relations and Utilization of Public Opinion

Today, American and foreign public opinion are both vital factors in the conduct of foreign affairs. At present the Assistant Secretary, Public Affairs, is burdened with operational duties of the foreign information and educational exchange programs and is not a participant in high-level policy formulation. Furthermore, the State Department's relationships with the press and other media of public information are extremely weak.

c. The Need for an Effective Intelligence Organization in the State Department

The weakest and least effective unit in the State Department today is the one known as Research and Intelligence. This situation arises largely because of nonacceptance of the intelligence personnel by certain influential segments of the Department, particularly the geographic offices, and from a basic misconception on all sides, including the intelligence unit itself, of the intelligence needs of the State Department. At present there appears to be an overemphasis on pure research, the bulk of which is not utilized within the Department. The relationships with the Central Intelligence Agency, moreover, which at present partake of rivalry rather than cooperation, require correction.

d. The Imposition on the State Department of Program Operational Responsibility

In the years since the recent World War the State Department has tended more and more to assume responsibility for program operations, either as the direct operator or as an active coordinator. In some instances these responsibilities have been given the State Department because of the absence of any other agency in the Government to do the job. This situation throws needless burdens on the Secretary and Under Secretary. The regular units of the State Department, however, are not presently equipped or oriented to handle such programs. Finally, the creation of new and separate units inside the State Department to operate these programs increases the difficulties of internal and interdepartmental coordination.

All these factors, taken together, contribute to the low esteem in which the State Department is held in the eyes of the Congress, the press, the general public, and, indeed, of many of its own personnel. Organizational reforms, while not a panacea for the State Department's ills, can as a minimum, chart for it a truer course in these difficult times.

Chapter Three

ORGANIZATIONAL CONCEPTS

The conduct of foreign affairs today involves almost the entire executive branch—the President, the President's executive offices, the State Department, numerous other departments and agencies, and intricate interdepartmental machinery. In addition, it involves constant cooperation between the executive branch and the Congress. As a consequence the problems of organization are equally Government-wide in scope, and organization reforms must be based on definite concepts of the part to be played by each segment of the Government.

The concepts for organization within the executive branch are, in summary, the following:

1. The decisions within the executive branch on the objectives of the United States in world affairs are ultimately decisions for the President only to make. He may, of course, delegate this power, but, as the sole elected member of the executive branch, he cannot divest himself of his final responsibility. When the President does delegate the power to make decisions, it must be recognized that it is impractical to make a blanket delegation to the State Department alone or to any other single department or agency.

2. The executive responsibility for the formulation and carrying out of foreign policies to achieve objectives is today that of the President with staff assistance from his executive office and the State Department. Under the President this responsibility is shared in various degrees by numerous departments and agencies throughout the executive establishment.

3. The responsibility for coordinating all the foreign affairs activities of the State Department and other departments and agencies, whether in the decision-making process or in the processes of policy formulation

and execution, ultimately is also that of the President. In delegating this responsibility the President may turn to the State Department, which is the specialist in foreign affairs, as, for example, to provide chairmen for interdepartmental committees, or he may turn elsewhere, depending on the balance of foreign and domestic implications in a particular problem.

4. The conduct of foreign affairs today involves the use of many means and instruments. Financial assistance, force or potential force, and propaganda are a few of the major ones. The utilization of these instruments similarly involves the performance of numerous supporting functions. A few examples are collection of information, evaluation of information through analysis and research, dissemination of information, employment of personnel, disbursement of funds, making of contracts, issuance of rules and regulations, and drafting of legislation.

5. The responsibility today for a decision as to which of several instruments to employ in the conduct of foreign affairs, together with the accompanying decisions as to when to employ them and as to the purposes to be accomplished thereby, carries with it two additional responsibilities. The first is for coordination throughout the executive branch in the choice of the instrument, the time of its use, and the purposes to be accomplished thereby. The second is for loyal teamwork between the State Department and the other departments and agencies instead of the evasion and backbiting that characterized these relationships during the recent war.

It is essential to recognize that in the discharge of this multifold responsibility, two different segments of the executive branch may perform functions which appear similar, but there should not and need not be duplication in the performance of identical functions in two parts of the Government. For example, if it is deemed to be of advantage to the United States that a democratic rather than a communistic government be in power in a foreign country, it may be found desirable to employ many instruments, including those of public information or propaganda, financial assistance, or other aids against outside interference. The medium of information may be in the State Department, the financial assistance instrument in the Economic Cooperation Administration, the Export-Import Bank and elsewhere, and other instruments may be in other branches of the Government.

All of these instruments, for example, involve the function of research and analysis of information. The State Department's research and analysis would relate to the state of public opinion of the country in question and the factors influential in forming public opinion; the Economic Cooperation Administration's research and analysis would be directed to the economic condition of the foreign country and the balance of international trade; and the Military Establishment's research and analysis would pertain to the status of communist military power on the borders of the country in question and the strategic disposition of United States forces in occupied areas nearby to strengthen the democratic elements in power in the country in question. Yet the performance of these functions involves no inevitable duplication of effort. For example, no duplication would occur in the case of financial assistance so long as the State Department economic and research units do not go over the same economic ground as those of Economic Cooperation Administration.

6. The effective discharge of the executive responsibilities in the conduct of foreign affairs (including the formulation of policies, employment of instruments to carry out policies, and coordination in both the formulation and execution stages) requires that authority be vested in the President and descend from him through a clear line of command to responsible department and agency heads with subordinate authority over cohesive executive agencies.

7. Decisions as to the conduct of foreign affairs today inevitably are decisions affecting our whole political, economic, and social life. The problem of organization for the conduct of foreign affairs is, therefore, but a segment of the larger problem of organization for the conduct of national affairs. Hence, governmental organization for the conduct of foreign affairs cannot be treated as a separate mechanism but must be regarded as an integral part of a larger mechanism.

These general concepts provide the foundation for the recommendations which follow. In some measure these recommendations are geared to the immediate future. Times change, however, and organizational forms must be adjusted accordingly. Organization cannot be immutable and the recommendations herein cannot be regarded as having indefinite validity.

Chapter Four

RECOMMENDATIONS

The recommendations which follow are essentially recommendations of principles. Neither this report, nor that of the supporting task force, purports to be a complete "blueprint" covering the many possible applications of these principles. Certain specific suggestions for organizational changes in the State Department will, of course, be set forth, but the details of these reforms will generally have to be worked out by the men in charge of the various organizational segments.

A. Recommendations Concerning the Congress

Recommendation No. 1

Legislation which grants new foreign affairs powers of an executive nature otherwise than to the President or to an established executive department or agency will normally cause serious difficulty in efficient administration. Such legislation should not be adopted unless there are overwhelming advantages in creating a new agency.

Each time the Congress creates a new agency with the power to employ a specified instrument of foreign policy, it weakens the executive establishment as a whole. Jurisdictional conflicts are immediately set in motion which increase the possibility of duplication and the burden of coordination. The latter is already so heavy on the President that many problems of coordination must be left untouched.

By giving the new powers to the President, the Congress would strengthen his executive power to integrate this new authority with already existing authority. By giving it to an existing department or agency, the burden of coordination would be transferred in large measure from the President to the head of the department or agency. Particular care, moreover, should be taken not to confer executive powers on independent commissions which are not responsible to the President. While the creation of independent bodies to discharge quasi-judicial and quasi-legislative functions will always be necessary, the grant to them of executive powers is contrary to the principles of sound organization and impedes the efficient conduct of foreign affairs.

Recommendation No. 2

Effective administration is not achieved by establishing by legislation the precise functions and membership of coordinating and advisory bodies within the executive branch.

The recent legislative practice of establishing interdepartmental bodies with defined responsibilities over foreign affairs—e.g. National Security Council or National Advisory Council—tends to obscure the responsibility for making executive decisions, to make each of the bodies acquire the aspects of a new agency, and to encourage other interdepartmental groups to seek formal Congressional sanction. All of these tendencies add up to weakening the power of the Chief Executive, a circumstance which in turn reduces his responsibility and complicates the administration of the executive branch. Such legislation does not assure better coordination in the executive branch, nor can it require the President to use the advice received. The Congress can, however, facilitate executive creation of coordinating and advisory bodies by enactment of general enabling legislation which will provide a flexible framework within which the President can act.

Recommendation No. 3

Legislation making specific grants of foreign affairs powers and of supporting funds below the level of the appropriate department or agency head should be avoided.

In the past the Congress on occasion has granted specific power and appropriated specific funds below the department or agency head level, as in the cases of the foreign affairs activities of the Civil Aeronautics Administration and the Bureau of Labor Statistics. This practice tends to free the grantee from executive control and encourages him to establish independent channels of communication with the Congress. It aggravates the problem of coordinating foreign relations activities both within individual departments and agencies and between different units of the executive branch.

The practice of appropriating funds directly to a constituent unit of a department or agency further limits the ability of the department or agency head to adjust the foreign affairs programs of his several bureaus or offices to meet changing international conditions and to reduce internal overlapping or duplication of effort.

B. Recommendations Concerning the President

Recommendation No. 4

Cabinet-level committees, with their memberships and assignments fixed by the President, are necessary in crucial areas in the conduct of foreign affairs where the issues transcend the responsibility of any single department and where Presidential consideration or decision is necessary.

The foreign affairs requirements are but a part of the national requirements of the United States. In the formulation, execution, and coordination of the policies to meet these requirements, the ultimate responsibility lies with the President. In the main, this process takes place at the department and agency level, but on certain crucial problems Presidential consideration and often Presidential decision will be necessary.

In our first report, Chapter Two, the Executive Office of the President, attention is called to the desirability of the establishment of Cabinet-level national policy committees to advise the President in the instances where his consideration or decision is necessary. These committees, on a regular or ad hoc basis as required, will serve as a systematic means of providing the President with balanced advice on the critical international problems of the day which transcend the responsibilities of the State Department or any other single department.

Likewise, as recommended in our first report, the President should be free to select the membership of the Cabinet-level committees dealing with foreign affairs, and to determine their assignments and the scope of their authority. Since the President cannot be compelled to follow, or even listen to the advice of any particular body, no attempt should be made to legislate specifically on this subject. Instead, general enabling legislation should provide a flexible framework within which the President may act.

The need for Cabinet-level committees on the conduct of foreign affairs, as emphasized above, exists only where Presidential consideration or decision is required on matters transcending the responsibilities of a single department. In a great number of foreign affairs matters this requirement will not be present. The Cabinet-level committees should not, therefore, supplant the State Department as a staff arm of the President, and the State Department in this role should be the major coordinating force within the executive branch on foreign affairs matters. Likewise, the Cabinet-level committee device must be carefully controlled so that the committees confine themselves to producing integrated advice to the President and do not become additional foreign affairs agencies in the executive branch which themselves have to be coordinated.

Recommendation No. 5

The successful functioning of Cabinet-level and other interdepartmental committees in the foreign affairs area should be facilitated by the assistance of specific institutional aids in the Executive Office and the State Department.

The Cabinet-level and interdepartmental committees cannot function successfully without specific institutional aids. The staff secretary to the President, whose appointment is recommended in our report, General Management of the Executive Branch, should keep the President advised of policy issues being considered by the principal Cabinet-level committees, and of any overlapping of assignments or conflicts which may exist. Each permanent or semi-permanent Cabinet-level committee, moreover, such as the present National Security Council and National Advisory Council, will ordinarily require a full-time executive secretary, and a small nucleus of staff supplemented by additional staff drawn from the regular policy units of the departments and agencies participating in the work of the various committees. By this means the essential secretariat service and staff work will be furnished. Through these institutional aids coordination of high-level foreign affairs matters should be greatly facilitated and, indeed, the issues for Presidential consideration should be so narrowed as to relieve the President in practice of what would otherwise be a heavy burden.

Similarly, staff and secretariat assistance should be provided for interdepartmental committees below the Cabinet level. In most instances this assistance should be provided by the State Department, which at present is doing considerable work of this kind. In special cases, however, other departments or agencies may furnish these aids. The activities of these interdepartmental committees should also be subject to scrutiny by the President's staff secretary.

C. Recommendations Relating to the State Department and the Foreign Service

These recommendations, based on the organizational concepts previously set forth, fall into two general categories. First, general recommendations defining the role of the State Department in the conduct of foreign affairs and, second, specific recommendations of internal organizational reforms.

1. RECOMMENDATIONS RELATING TO THE ROLE OF THE STATE DEPARTMENT

Recommendation No. 6

The State Department should concentrate on obtaining definition of proposed objectives for the United States in foreign affairs, on formulating proposed policies in conjunction with other departments and agencies to achieve those objectives, and on recommending the choice and timing of the use of various instruments to carry out foreign policies so formulated.

The ultimate responsibility within the executive branch in the determination of United States objectives and in formulating, executing, and coordinating foreign policies lies with the President. Under him, the State Department is cast in the role of the staff specialist in foreign affairs, and, pursuant to Presidential delegation, its role will involve leadership in defining and developing United States foreign policies, in determining the means and timing of their accomplishment through employment of the available instruments, in the recording of such policies, and in seeing to it that such policies are explained at home and abroad. These responsibilities necessarily will mean that, except for coordination in crucial areas where Cabinet-level committees are involved, the State Department will be the focal point for coordination of foreign affairs activities throughout the Government.

The State Department is not, however, the sole unit of the executive branch for determination of the objectives of the United States in world affairs or for formulating and executing foreign policies to achieve those objectives. Many other governmental departments and agencies, by reason of the present-day blending of the domestic and foreign aspects of national problems and by reason of operations abroad, are sources of policy considerations in the conduct of foreign affairs. The State Department should consult with and advise these other departments and agencies for the purpose of bringing their experience to bear in the formulation of foreign policies and of assisting them in administering particular instruments of foreign policy so as to achieve desired objectives in a consistent manner. The agency charged with responsibility for action should not, however, be required to obtain the concurrence of other agencies prior to taking action.

It is sound to adopt the principle that the department or agency with the power to exercise an instrument of foreign policy should be looked to, and relied upon, by the State Department to gather the necessary facts within the special competence of the particular department or agency on a world-wide basis; to evaluate those facts; to propose policies or programs within its power to execute; and to execute the programs agreed upon in accordance with established policy. These other departments and agencies must be organized internally so as to be able to meet the State Department's requests promptly and, if they are still unable to render these services adequately, the President should take measures to ensure the correction of their shortcomings. The State Department then would be free to concentrate on coordination within the executive branch, particularly on seeing that conflicts are resolved, making sure for the President that other departments and agencies do not, as in the past, slide out of their responsibilities, and exercising general guidance so that all the Government's foreign affairs activities are conducted in consonance.

In this manner, the State Department will be able to discontinue the bulk of the specialized functions it has recently been, or now is, performing in the fields of foodstuffs, petroleum and other fuels, aviation, shipping, labor, welfare, and the like. It will, however, have to retain a small group of specialists in these fields as expert advisers and as the focal point for consultation and coordination with other agencies. Furthermore, insofar as certain other departments and agencies are oriented to act only in terms of domestic interests and pressures, the State Department on occasion may still have to assume more positive leadership, but it should do so only after the particular failure has been brought to the Chief Executive's attention.

Recommendation No. 7

The State Department as a general rule should not be given responsibility for the operation of specific programs, whether overseas or at home.

This proposition as a general rule is desirable. Difficulties in application, however, exist, especially in that the sudden thrusting on the executive branch of responsibility for new world-wide programs found it with little or nothing in the way of machinery to carry out such programs. As a consequence the State Department has had to assume responsibility for activities such as liquidation of surplus property abroad, the foreign information program, and the educational exchange program.

The recent creation of the Economic Cooperation Administration to handle the economic assistance program in Europe and in the Far East prevented the placing of this additional program burden on the State Department. In this instance the advantages in creating a new agency appear to have been overwhelming and the solution is in accord with the principle of this recommendation.

The Government's responsibilities for occupied areas in Germany, Austria, and the Far East are divided, with the State Department being assigned responsibility for formulation of policy and the Army Department for execution and administration of policy. From the outset, serious frictions have existed in this arrangement. The basic difficulty has been the uncertainty and delay in the preparation and enunciation of policy and the consequent tendency of the administrative agency, through its daily decisions, to make its own policy. Other factors have been the attempt to handle occupied-areas problems below the secretarial level, without clear definition of responsibility and without clear channels for the transmission of policy guidance from the State Department to the theater commanders.

The transfer of responsibility for the civil or non-military aspects of administration of occupied areas from the Army Department to the State Department, leaving the garrison or other military functions to the Army Department, has been under frequent consideration during recent years. In the instant recommendation, it is proposed that the State Department not undertake operational programs unless unusual circumstances exist. The present circumstances do not appear to be sufficiently unusual to call for an assumption of occupied-areas responsibility by the State Department.

The machinery for administration of occupied areas, as well as that of logistical support, is presently supplied by the Military Establishment. It is wholly consistent with the concepts underlying this report that this administrative machinery be located outside the State Department, as, for example, in the Military Establishment or in a new administration of overseas affairs, but that it receive its instructions from, and report to, the Secretary of State. Thus a direct channel of communication would exist between the theater commanders, as high commissioners or otherwise, and the Secretary of State, who in turn is directly under the President, who is the Commander in Chief. Likewise, the State Department would not have to build up, by transfer from the Army Department or otherwise, a self-sufficient group within its own organization responsible for the nonmilitary administrative phases of occupied areas.

In certain other areas, governmental agencies are now in existence to which the State Department's present operational responsibilities for engineering, rehabilitation, and like programs could be transferred. Likewise, the functions of visa control and munitions export control should be transferred from the State Department to the Justice and Commerce Departments, respectively.

In two instances it appears that operational responsibility, for the present at least, must remain in the State Department in default of any other satisfactory location in the executive branch. The one is the educational exchange program which the task force report recommended be transferred to the Federal Security Agency. The Federal Security Agency does not have the orientation, experience, or skills to carry on work in this broad cultural field, and therefore the State Department should continue to administer this program.

The second instance is the foreign information program with its heavy load of operational and technical duties in connection with the radio broadcasting activities of the "Voice of America." Here, the task force recommended transfer to a Government corporation which would make it possible to keep the operation responsive to State Department policy guidance. A strong motivation behind this suggestion is the urgent need for freeing the Assistant Secretary, Public Affairs, from devoting his personal attention to details of an operational nature and for making him available as a high-level staff adviser and chief of press and other public relations for the Secretary of State. This end can be equally well attained, however, by reorganization within the public affairs area. One possibility is the creation of a new post under the Assistant Secretary of a "general manager" to whom would be assigned full operational authority and responsibility for the "Voice of America" and such other portions of the foreign information program as are primarily operational in character.

Recommendation No. 8

The State Department should continue to discharge its traditional responsibilities of representation, reporting, and negotiation.

The State Department's principal duties under Presidential direction should be:

a. To establish, man, maintain, and conduct the machinery of diplomatic relations, correspondence, conversations, negotiation, and agreement with other governments except where, in technical or special cases, parts of these activities are assigned to other departments or agencies, and even then the State Department should observe and counsel their conduct.

b. To recruit and maintain personnel adequate for its tasks at home and abroad, protected as a career service by tradition as well as law from invasion by political or other demoralizing influence.

c. To give guidance and direction to our diplomatic missions and delegations abroad, to review and distribute to other interested agencies the intelligence gathered by the State Department, to see to it that the recommendations of the missions are acknowledged and considered but leaving to them, wherever possible, ways and means of accomplishment.

d. To aid the President in the selection of qualified persons other than career servants whenever he or the Congress determines they should be drawn from the public at large for particular purposes or particular missions.

e. To assume primary responsibility for foreign relations aspects of general policies followed by all peacetime missions overseas, including occupation forces and special missions and programs, and to this end to see that the activities of all American officers abroad are reported to, and are observed and counseled by, the chief of the American diplomatic mission if such officers are temporary, and if permanent and not involving operational programs, that such officers are made part of the diplomatic mission itself.

f. To recommend to the President any participation and the extent of our participation in international bodies and conferences and to supervise our delegations when established except as the President or Congress otherwise determines in special cases. This involves consultation and coordination with other departments and agencies.

g. To preserve with the Senate and House a continuous working system of liaison and intercommunication on all matters affecting foreign affairs, in order to reach mutual comprehension, confidence, and agreement.

2. RECOMMENDATIONS RELATING TO INTERNAL ORGANIZATION

Recommendation No. 9

The State Department should be organized so that the Secretary of State, legally and practically, is in command of the Department

and the Foreign Service, so that the line of command from the Secretary of State through the Under and Assistant Secretaries to the lowest level is clear and unencumbered, and so that the Secretary of State is provided with adequate staff services at the top level. The Department should also have authority and funds to equip itself with persons of the highest capacity to represent this country at international organizations and conferences.

This recommendation is fundamental. Its objectives, in terms of the internal organization of the State Department, are to simplify the structure, clarify the Secretary's authority, make his lines of command clear and free from interference, separate staff responsibility from action or line responsibility, and relieve the Secretary and Under Secretary from the burdensome details which now come to them, and thereby afford them an opportunity for thoughtful study of major policy problems.

Representation of the United States at international organizations and conferences by individuals with special abilities for the peculiar type of task involved will relieve the Secretary and other top departmental officials from the additional heavy burdens which have been imposed on them since the end of the recent war. While the United Nations Participation Act—with the amendments currently proposed—equips the Government with permanent representatives and staff at the United Nations headquarters, problems still remain in regard to departmental assistance at meetings of the General Assembly. Similar problems arise in connection with the greatly increased need for representation at such meetings as the Council of Foreign Ministers, Council of Foreign Ministers of the American Republics, and the like. Furthermore, a need exists for providing State Department representation at conferences dealing with telecommunications, aviation, shipping, agriculture, labor, and many other matters.

The only present means of providing representatives is to tear the Department apart to meet each individual situation. At one time in the past year, for example, the Secretary of State and all but one of the Assistant Secretaries were absent from the Department on missions to nternational meetings. The burden on those left behind was excessive and the functioning of the Department was seriously impaired.

The Secretary of State and his principal assistants are needed in Washington. The Government should be able to send high-level officials, with adequate staffs, to represent the United States at international organizations and conferences. When not so engaged, these men should, in part at least, be able to spend their time in the Department advising and aiding the Secretary in the formation of the policies which they may have to handle. In this way they can be fully informed of all facets of United States policies.

This over-all recommendation will be amplified in various respects by the recommendations which follow. In reaching these conclusions the Commission and its task force have kept in close touch with the organizational plans for the State Department developed under Secretary Marshall and Under Secretary Lovett. The Commission is happy to say that its thinking and that of the State Department are in complete accord on principles, and, except for certain particulars in which the Commission's recommendations are more far-reaching than those of the State Department, the conclusions of both on specific changes are in agreement.

By way of preface to these recommendations it is first desirable to outline the general pattern of internal organization which will facilitate achievement of the objectives of the over-all recommendation. This pattern, shown graphically on pages 162 and 163 together with the present top-level organization, is as follows:

1. The strengthening of the Secretary and Under Secretary level by the addition of two Deputy Under Secretaries, the one to act in matters of substance, and the other, as "general manager," to administer the Department and the overseas service.

2. The fixing of responsibility for action in five line units under five Assistant Secretaries. Four of these Assistant Secretaries would head up regional units, with the responsibility for the four traditional geographic segments of the world. A fifth would be in charge of relationships with international organizations, including the United Nations and its affiliated organizations.

Both the regional and international organization Assistant Secretaries would *at the action level* be responsible for and be equipped, in terms of personnel, to deal with not solely "political" aspects of foreign affairs, as is the basic conception of the duties of the existing geographic office directors, but for all aspects, whether they be political, economic, public opinion, intelligence, or administration.

The Assistant Secretary, Public Affairs, would also have top, but not immediate, responsibility for action in connection with the operations of the foreign information programs and of the educational exchange programs. Action in these public affairs fields, however, is not of the same character as that required of the regional and international organization Assistant Secretaries, and, moreover, the Assistant Secretary,

161

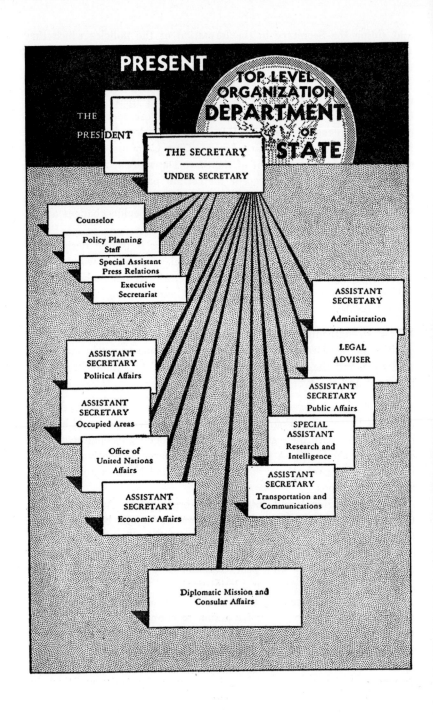

PRESENT

TOP LEVEL
ORGANIZATION
DEPARTMENT
OF
STATE

THE
PRESIDENT

THE SECRETARY
─────────
UNDER SECRETARY

Counselor

Policy Planning
Staff

Special Assistant
Press Relations

Executive
Secretariat

ASSISTANT
SECRETARY
Administration

LEGAL
ADVISER

ASSISTANT
SECRETARY
Political Affairs

ASSISTANT
SECRETARY
Public Affairs

ASSISTANT
SECRETARY
Occupied Areas

SPECIAL
ASSISTANT
Research and
Intelligence

Office of
United Nations
Affairs

ASSISTANT
SECRETARY
Transportation and
Communications

ASSISTANT
SECRETARY
Economic Affairs

Diplomatic Mission and
Consular Affairs

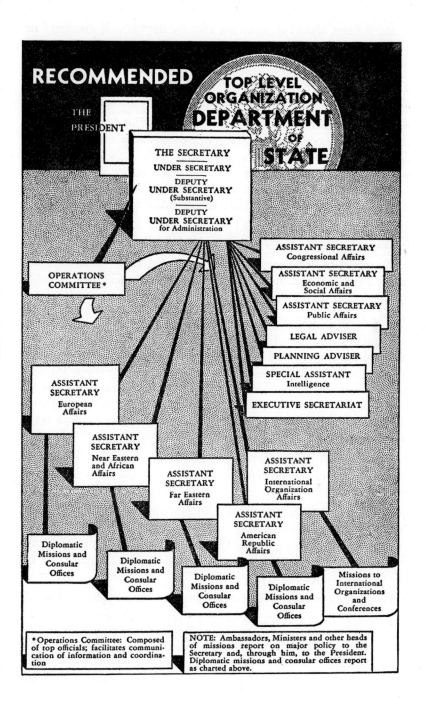

RECOMMENDED TOP LEVEL ORGANIZATION DEPARTMENT OF STATE

THE PRESIDENT

THE SECRETARY
UNDER SECRETARY
DEPUTY
UNDER SECRETARY
(Substantive)
DEPUTY
UNDER SECRETARY
for Administration

OPERATIONS COMMITTEE *

ASSISTANT SECRETARY
Congressional Affairs

ASSISTANT SECRETARY
Economic and
Social Affairs

ASSISTANT SECRETARY
Public Affairs

LEGAL ADVISER

PLANNING ADVISER

SPECIAL ASSISTANT
Intelligence

EXECUTIVE SECRETARIAT

ASSISTANT
SECRETARY
European
Affairs

ASSISTANT
SECRETARY
Near Eastern
and African
Affairs

ASSISTANT
SECRETARY
Far Eastern
Affairs

ASSISTANT
SECRETARY
International
Organization
Affairs

ASSISTANT
SECRETARY
American
Republic
Affairs

Diplomatic
Missions and
Consular
Offices

Diplomatic
Missions and
Consular
Offices

Diplomatic
Missions and
Consular
Offices

Diplomatic
Missions and
Consular
Offices

Missions to
International
Organizations
and
Conferences

*Operations Committee: Composed of top officials; facilitates communication of information and coordination

NOTE: Ambassadors, Ministers and other heads of missions report on major policy to the Secretary and, through him, to the President. Diplomatic missions and consular offices report as charted above.

Public Affairs, should organize his unit, by the "general manager" device referred to earlier, or otherwise, so that he can devote the bulk of his own time to his staff duties at the top level of the State Department.

3. The provision of adequate *staff* services to the Secretary and Under Secretary and to the line units consisting of:

a. An Assistant Secretary, Economic and Social Affairs, with the dual function of supervising a staff group who would afford a source of expert advice from a global instead of a regional point of view on economic, social, and other specialized aspects of foreign affairs and who would be the channel of communication and the point of coordination on interdepartmental relations within the executive branch in the foreign affairs field.

b. An Assistant Secretary for Congressional relations on a full-time basis.

c. An Assistant Secretary, Public Affairs, referred to previously, who would serve as the high-level adviser on domestic and foreign public opinion and as the chief of press and other media of public relations.

d. The Legal Adviser as at present.

e. An active high-level Operations Committee, under the direct supervision of the Deputy Under Secretary for substantive matters, assisted by the Executive Secretariat to insure coordination between the staff and action levels. This Committee is not be an additional layer in the line of command but a device to facilitate communication of information, coordination of related activities, and generally to promote teamwork between the action and staff units.

f. A Planning Adviser supported by a broad-gauge staff to function as an anticipator of the problems which will arise tomorrow because of today's policies.

g. A Special Assistant, Intelligence, who, as chief of intelligence, would supervise the centralized intelligence activities of the Department, serve as a source of guidance to the decentralized intelligence arms of the regional units, and provide the focal point for coordination with the Central Intelligence Agency.

This pattern of organization means that the State Department would have a Secretary, Under Secretary, two Deputy Under Secretaries, eight Assistant Secretaries, and three senior officials of rank equivalent to that of Assistant Secretary. It contemplates abolition of the posts of Counselor, Assistant Secretary, Occupied Areas, and Assistant Secretary, Transportation and Communications. The net increase in senior officials over the present scheme of organization is three, namely the two Deputy Under Secretaries and one additional Assistant Secretary. It will further have the effect of eliminating the Director General of the Foreign Service and the Special Assistant, Press Relations.

The office level as an additional "layer" in the Department's structure will also disappear except possibly on the administrative side, thus removing a blockage point in the Secretary's line of command. Deputies to the various Assistant Secretaries on the substantive side, equivalent in experience and stature to the present office directors, will, of course, still be required.

Finally, the pattern of organization set forth above can succeed only on the fundamental premise, set forth in Recommendation No. 20 hereinafter, that the two personnel services—the Foreign Service and the Department Service—be amalgamated into a single service responsive to the Secretary.

a. Recommendations Pertaining to Action Responsibilities

Recommendation No. 10

The fundamental world objectives and foreign policies of the United States should be continuously defined so as to permit delegation of authority to the line units to take action within the objectives and policies so defined.

The State Department, since the war, has at all levels been too much concerned with "details" and not enough with "policy." The Secretary-Under Secretary top command is overburdened by being drawn down into participation in too many daily decisions with the consequence that the entire Department lives day-to-day, and policies tend to be determined in terms of short-range decisions.

The State Department began in recent years to endeavor to reduce the United States objectives and foreign policies to writing. Continued emphasis on this admittedly difficult task, and on making such written statements available to all concerned, will provide the means by which the regional Assistant Secretaries and the international organization Assistant Secretary may assume responsibility for all but the most crucial decisions and afford the top command time for reflection and long-range thinking. Furthermore, this process will make possible the relation of objectives within and between countries and regions and between regions and international organizations, thereby leading to greater consistency of policy. Likewise, it will furnish a means for more

165

intelligent guidance to chiefs of missions abroad and relieve them of the necessity of referring all details to Washington.

Recommendation No. 11

Within the action units responsibility for decisions should be clearly fixed with adequate machinery by which the decision-maker can consult but never be required to obtain the concurrence of staff advisory units or other action units.

The responsibility for the formulation of foreign policy proposals and for action in line with approved policies should be placed on the four regional Assistant Secretaries and the international organization Assistant Secretary. Instances of unclear jurisdiction should be resolved at the top level through the Deputy Under Secretary on the substantive side, particularly through the Operations Committee, of which he would be deputy chairman. Each Assistant Secretary will have, as an integral part of his line operation, the functional advisers on economic and social problems, who are now under the Assistant Secretary, Economic Affairs. Likewise, each Assistant Secretary should have a very small group of intelligence personnel and information specialists.

Within the regional and the international organization systems the responsibility for recommending action in a given case should be assigned to a single officer below the Assistant Secretary level. The present intolerable system of coordinate authority whereby concurrences in different chains of command within the Department are required should be eliminated. The action officer should, however, consult staff advisory groups or other action units and report the results of such recommendations with his recommended action. Adequate machinery to enforce this consultation process should be developed through the Executive Secretariat. Every consultant should be allowed to attach to any document his comment or protest if he dissents, after his views have been considered. The action on such recommendations should be restricted to the five Assistant Secretaries concerned, the Deputy Under Secretaries, the Under Secretary, and the Secretary. By this means the present evils of the geographic-functional conflict can be materially reduced.

The role of the Assistant Secretary, International Organizations, is different from that of the four regional Assistant Secretaries in one important respect. While participating in the formulation of foreign policy he should not be an additional agent in this field, but should, so far as possible, obtain his policy guidance from the various regional units, the Planning Adviser, and from other staff advisers, probably largely through the Operations Committee. This difference lends emphasis to the conclusion that a properly conceived and executed regional scheme of organization can operate adequately to arrive at policies for multilateral dealings.

Recommendation No. 12

The five Assistant Secretaries with action responsibilities should serve as the focal points of contact between the Department and the overseas and international organization missions in both substantive and administrative matters.

The delegation of substantive authority to the four regional Assistant Secretaries and to one international organization Assistant Secretary should result in their being able to handle the bulk of substantive matters coming into the Department from missions at overseas points and at international organizations without reference to the top command of the Department. Concurrently, the Deputy Under Secretary for Administration should delegate to them adequate tools of administration with which to meet the needs of these missions. While the Deputy Under Secretary on the administrative side must at all times retain firm control over the determination and carrying out of administrative policies, particularly with respect to inspections, much of the day-to-day work in connection with personnel administration, organizational planning, budgetary and other matters with respect to overseas and other missions can be more efficiently performed on a decentralized basis in the action units. Within the State Department, however, the administrative aspects of the action units should be decentralized only to the extent the Secretary, acting through the Deputy Under Secretary for Administration, deems it advisable.

The delegation of authority to act and the decentralization of tools of administration to the line Assistant Secretaries can, moreover, be advantageously carried one step further by giving greater authority (but not autonomy) to the missions abroad and at international organizations, both in regard to substantive action and administration. This further delegation and decentralization must, of course, be a matter of secretarial policy and must depend upon the capacity of the various chiefs of missions. Progress in this direction is essential, however, because at the present time the officers in the Department in Washington tend to ride the field missions with much too tight a rein and endeavor to give them much too meticulous guidance.

Recommendation No. 13

The chief of each United States foreign mission should be the responsible American spokesman for the area or country to which he is assigned. He should observe and counsel all United States activities therein, and he should be responsible for administration of his mission.

In its new role in the conduct of foreign affairs, the United States frequently engages in two general types of activity in foreign countries. The one is the traditional representation and reporting activities of the diplomatic missions; the other, the special operational activities of various economic, social, and other programs.

As to the traditional representation and reporting activities, it is desirable not only to have all personnel responsible to the chief of the mission but also part of the mission. There has been less serious question of this proposition since the 1939 consolidation of the Commerce and Agriculture overseas services with the Foreign Service. In subsequent recommendations herein, however, it is proposed that a small number of specialist attachés who, as part of their work, fill the information needs of the other departments and agencies, be designated by those other departments and agencies. These specialists while on overseas service should, as temporary or reserve officers, be a part of the Foreign Affairs Service and should be responsible to the chief of the mission for their work, deportment, and for purposes of administration. They should, moreover, be an integral part of the mission to which they are assigned and their services would be utilized by the chief of mission and the State Department as well as by the department by which they are appointed. This line relationship to the chief of the mission is essential and his authority should include:

a. The power to return to the United States any specialist on duty for reasons related to improper deportment or for unsatisfactory work performance, subject always to final decision by the Secretary of State.

b. The right to object to assigning a given individual to the mission, subject always to the Secretary of State having the final word.

c. The right to express disagreement with (but not to prevent transmission of) reports of specialists designated by the other agencies.

d. The ultimate authority overseas with respect to foreign affairs aspects of program operations, such as those currently being performed by the Economic Cooperation Administration.

In the case of operational activities abroad, where they are directly under the State Department, the personnel involved should also be part of the mission. Where such tasks are assigned to other departments or agencies, whether they be economic, social, technical, or otherwise, they may be separately headed and administered at home. It is unworkable and dangerous, however, to have American spokesmen and operators abroad dealing with foreign nations who are independent of the ambassadors or ministers and who are not responsible to them for supervision and coordination.

b. Recommendations Pertaining to Staff Responsibilities

Recommendation No. 14

The Assistant Secretary, Economic and Social Affairs, should concentrate on providing a source of economic, social, and other advice from a global standpoint and upon serving as a channel of communication and focal point of coordination with the other departments and agencies in the executive branch.

The staff advisers under the Assistant Secretary, Economic and Social Affairs, must be *consulted* by the action units, but their *concurrence* in proposed action should *not* be required. A very small group of functional advisers should suffice for these purposes and they should not seek to duplicate as at present the staffs of other departments and agencies or the functional specialists assigned to the State Department's regional action units. The other departments and agencies should, in the main, be relied upon for information within their special competences, both domestic and foreign.

At the same time, it must be recognized that the division between the action and staff units heretofore drawn has in certain respects a delusive simplicity. There are limited occasions when the action requirements of the Department will transcend the four regional and the one international organization units and where action with respect to individual countries must be taken on a global basis. An example is the handling of trade agreements. To this limited extent this staff unit is a hybrid organization with some action responsibilities. The top command of the State Department must take particular care that this limited action responsibility does not afford an "empire-building" device whereby the unit headed by the Assistant Secretary, Economic and Social Affairs, again seeks to have coordinate authority with the action units, and that the geographic versus functional conflict does not again cripple the Department. The overseeing of this particular problem is one which

169

the Deputy Under Secretary on the substantive side must keep under his direct and continuous surveillance.

Recommendation No. 15

The Assistant Secretary, Congressional Affairs, should be responsible on a full-time basis for establishing a coordinated program of two-way liaison with the Congress.

The recent experience of endeavoring to take care of Congressional relations on a part-time basis has demonstrated the need for full-time, high-level direction in this field. The Assistant Secretary, Congressional Relations, should participate actively in top-level policy formulation in the State Department He should be able to marshal personnel from anywhere within the Department to present to the Congress special phases of foreign affairs problems. Conversely, he should be able to arrange to bring to the Department the views of Congressional leaders on international matters.

It is not intended that this Assistant Secretary should serve as the exclusive channel of communication between the State Department and the Congress. On frequent occasions the Secretary and the Under Secretary will be called upon to consult with Congressional leaders. In addition, the Assistant Secretary will have to be able to call upon various specialists within the Department to provide information on technical phases of foreign affairs activities. He will also have to work with the budget officers of the State Department in connection with appropriation matters. Where Congressional contacts are made directly by other departmental officials, the Assistant Secretary should be kept informed. Finally, as a minor but significant part of his work, the Assistant Secretary should be the medium whereby the State Department provides helpful services to the members of Congress. In all these duties the Assistant Secretary must have adequate staff to aid in the preparation of material, in following important issues, and in performing various services.

Recommendation No. 16

The Assistant Secretary, Public Affairs, should concentrate on serving as a high-level staff adviser on domestic and foreign public opinion, and as chief of press relations and other media of public relations for the State Department.

Today American public opinion is a vital factor in the conduct of foreign affairs, and the State Department must not only estimate and evaluate the views of the American public in foreign affairs matters but also must win its acceptance and support on the paramount issues. Furthermore, the opinions of the peoples of foreign countries, as contrasted with their governments, also bear upon the conduct of American foreign relations.

The weakest link with the American public is the absence in the State Department of a single high official responsible for the vital contacts with the press and other media of public information. The Assistant Secretary, Public Affairs, should fill this void. Furthermore, he should be the staff officer advising the Secretary and Under Secretary, and also the action units, on the public opinion aspects of any problem. Finally, he should observe and give policy guidance to foreign information and educational exchange programs, the operational responsibility for which should be in a "general manager" reporting to the Assistant Secretary. A precedent for the relationship envisaged between the Assistant Secretary and the "general manager" is that which recently existed between the Under Secretary and the Coordinator for Aid to Greece and Turkey where the latter, with effective backing from the Under Secretary, ran the operational program without interference from other segments of the Department.

Recommendation No. 17

The Secretary of State should continue the present high-level planning activity under a Planning Adviser, with special emphasis on freeing him and his staff of current problems, upon providing him with a broad-gauge staff, and upon utilization by him of competent advice from inside and outside the Government.

The present Policy Planning Staff has been a valuable aid to the top command of the State Department, especially as an "anticipator" of problems. At present, however, its effectiveness appears to have been lessened by a tendency of the top command to utilize it on day-to-day problems, by its almost exclusive reliance for its staff on individuals with Foreign Service backgrounds, and by its reluctance to draw sufficiently upon the resources of other departments and agencies except possibly those of the National Military Establishment. These weaknesses should be corrected.

In addition, the Secretary of State should endeavor to bring together a small group of highly competent and reliable individuals from outside the Government to counsel the Planning Adviser. This group should not, either on request or on its own initiative, give affirmative advice as to what the world objectives and foreign policies of the United States should be, but it should concentrate on problems submitted to it by the Planning Adviser and on advising him on the probable consequences of various proposed courses of action. This group might include former ambassadors, other former Government officials, leaders from business, commerce and labor, and educators.

Recommendation No. 18

The centralized intelligence unit in the State Department should be reorganized and reoriented, and intelligence advisers should be assigned to the regional action units.

The present misconception of the intelligence needs of the State Department must be eradicated. The creation of revitalized regional units on the action side should tend to correct the current deplorable attitude of the existing geographic offices toward intelligence. The reorientation of the centralized intelligence activities by de-emphasis of academic research and increased attention on current estimates and evaluations and to serving and making use of the Central Intelligence Agency is required. At present, except for the Special Projects Staff, the Biographic Information Division, and the routine library reference and collection functions, the existing intelligence unit appears to expend too much of its energies on projects which do not contribute sufficiently to the main work of the State Department.

The task force report contemplates the decentralization of the present area research personnel as intact units to the four new regional action units. This move would involve almost 5 percent of the personnel of the entire Department.

The Commission is not in favor of this step.

It is recognized, however, that the new regional units, as self-contained line organizations, will need intelligence advisers just as they also need economic and social advisers. These regional intelligence advisers should perform staff functions within the action units and should not themselves engage in research work. Their responsibilities should be to understand the foreign policy problems of the action units, to recommend particular intelligence research projects to the central intelligence unit, and to follow up on the performance of such research by the central unit. In addition, they should assist the central unit in the preparation of "political" estimates for the Central Intelligence Agency and for other departments. It is recommended that these regional intelligence advisers be assigned to the regional units from the present research divisions.

The really significant intelligence needs of the Department must be met on a centralized basis. This central unit, under a Special Assistant to the Secretary as at present, should occupy a dual position. In relation to the intelligence advisers in the regional units, the central unit should be both a source of general intelligence guidance and a channel of communication with the Central Intelligence Agency and the intelligence organizations of other departments. As an intelligence unit itself it should be a device by which the Secretary and Under Secretary can obtain expert evaluations and check on information coming from the action units.

The Planning Adviser in particular should make full use of the Special Assistant and of his central staff in connection with his planning activities. For this task the Special Assistant should build up a group of mature individuals with high talent in analysis and evaluation, who should have full access to all information coming into the Department. This group must be supported by a body of skilled researchers.

The central unit should not, however, seek to monitor all information coming into the State Department from abroad, but should concentrate on tasks assigned to it by the Secretary, the Under Secretary, and the Planning Adviser, and on issues raised through its relations with the Central Intelligence Agency. It should continue to include, of course, the library, reference and collection functions, but should be organized internally so that the Special Assistant does not have to devote the bulk of his time to administrative and supervisory duties.

A prime responsibility of the chief of the intelligence unit is in relation to the Central Intelligence Agency and the intelligence units of other departments. He should be responsible for setting up effective machinery by which the Central Intelligence Agency and the other departments can obtain "political" estimates from the State Department. Conversely, he must see to it that the State Department gets evaluations and other data from the Central Intelligence Agency and the other departments which are useful to the State Department in formulating its policies and programs. In part he should be able to do this through membership on the Intelligence Advisory Committee. In these various ways he will be better able to make evaluations for the top command of the State Department and, in particular, to check on the recommendations of the regional units.

Recommendation No. 19

The Operations Committee, with the Under Secretary or Deputy Under Secretary for substantive matters as chairman, and staffed by the Executive Secretariat, should be made the coordinating link between the action and staff segments and between the various units within each segment.

Serious present weaknesses are the lack of any systematic means of bringing problems to the top command level and, conversely, of ensuring that the various Assistant Secretaries are advised of what takes place at the top level. High-level committees have been suggested on past occasions, but the efforts to place them in operation have proved abortive largely because of inadequate top-level support, the absence of any secretariat and staff assistance, and the inclusion of too many individuals as participants in the meetings. Failure to overcome the individualistic tradition of the Department whereby senior career officers insist upon direct access to the Secretary and Under Secretary has also been a factor.

The Operations Committee should meet frequently, perhaps daily. The Under Secretary, when present, should preside, although as a general rule the Deputy Under Secretary on the substantive side, as a kind of combined deputy chairman and executive secretary, would probably carry the bulk of the responsibility. The present Executive Secretariat should provide "secretarial" and "staff assistance." This assistance would include maintenance of a file on pending problems, preparation of agenda and organization of documentation for meetings, preparation of post-meeting reports and transmission of decisions to the heads of action units, and following up to make sure that action is actually taken.

The provision of a top-level head for the Operations Committee, particularly by making it the primary responsibility of the Deputy Under Secretary, plus the selection of a man for that post with the will to make the Committee work, and the provision of staff assistance by the Executive Secretariat, should meet two of the past difficulties which defeated less ambitious attempts. Confining the participants to Assistant Secretaries and other senior officials of equivalent rank, moreover, would reduce the membership of the Committee to workable size (approximately 12), thereby removing another objectionable feature. Finally, other recommendations, particularly the delineation of line and staff responsibilities and the amalgamation of the Foreign Service and Department personnel systems, should in time help break down the individualistic tradition and the atmosphere of distrust which have prevented similar committees from functioning successfully in the past.

174

c. Recommendations Relating to Personnel

Recommendation No. 20

The personnel in the permanent State Department establishment in Washington and the personnel of the Foreign Service above certain levels should be amalgamated over a short period of years into a single Foreign Affairs Service obligated to serve at home or overseas and constituting a safeguarded career group administered separately from the general Civil Service.

The State Department and the American embassies, legations, and consulates abroad, which together make up the diplomatic and consular machinery of the Nation, are now served by two separate groups of men and women, one "The Foreign Service of the United States" and the other enrolled under the ordinary Civil Service system. The two groups, in terms of American citizens, are approximately equal in size. This division of forces between a Foreign Service centering on a separate corps of officers, mostly stationed abroad but partly in key positions in Washington, and a group of employees who work chiefly at home is a source of serious friction and increasing inefficiency. Such a division of personnel in foreign affairs has been abandoned in all but a handful of countries. Among those in which it still exists, the United States is the only great power.

The division leads to jealousies and to inequality of compensation among people doing much the same work. The Foreign Service, through long periods of service abroad, undoubtedly loses contact with American domestic conditions. The Civil Service employees, who seldom or never serve abroad for any long period, fail often to understand other nations and appreciate foreign conditions.

The present conditions also lead to the existence of two administrative offices, one for each body of public servants, but both in the same household and dealing frequently with the same personnel questions. The Foreign Service is in law and practice largely self-administered, and is to some degree even independent of the Secretary of State.

In recommending the consolidation of the Foreign Service and the State Department Service into a single new Foreign Affairs Service, it is believed that for the present the consolidated service should be separate from the general Civil Service. The Commission's recommendations on the general Civil Service, in our report on Personnel Management, contemplate sweeping changes in the entire Civil Service personnel system. These changes will necessarily involve adjustments and experimentation extending over a period of years. Similarly, the consolidation of the Foreign Service and the State Department Service will also require the gradual solution of numerous problems in terms of practical circumstances. Consequently it is believed that the two reorganizations should for the present proceed on separate bases but that the top officials in both systems should keep in close touch with each other so that the guiding principles in both readjustments are not at variance.

Certain general principles for carrying out this consolidation are set forth in the task force report, not included here. The Commission is generally in accord with those principles. The list below reiterates some of those principles which warrant special emphasis, and restates others with certain modifications:

a. The members of the single new Foreign Affairs Service should all be pledged to serve at home or abroad.

b. The consolidation should be *mandatory* but should be carried out *gradually* over a short period of years.

c. The consolidated service should include all personnel except (1) at the top level, the Secretary, the Under Secretary, the Deputy Under Secretaries, the Assistant Secretaries, and others of comparable rank, and ambassadors and ministers; (11) certain technical personnel in programs such as foreign information, for whom the existence of comparable overseas assignments seems improbable; (111) at the lower levels, mechanical or subsidiary employees such as janitors, engineers, guards, and messengers, and all alien employees of whatever rank.

d. The consolidation should receive the continuous attention and support of the Secretary and the Under Secretary, with the direct execution being entrusted to the Deputy Under Secretary for Administration. Over-all policies and standards governing entrance, transfer, classification, examination, promotion, and retirement should be established by the Secretary, perhaps after consultation with a temporary advisory board with a membership such as that suggested by the task force report. Particular attention should be given to equalizing the time spent in the field with that at home.

e. The assignment of personnel within the consolidated system requires a flexible system of personnel administration so that the Secretary is free to draw upon not only the various talents within the service as he needs them, but also on qualified personnel from elsewhere in the executive branch and from outside the Government. This flexible system should also make it possible for members of the Foreign Affairs Service to transfer to positions elsewhere in the executive branch for which they have the necessary qualifications. Under this principle the general, special, and staff personnel categories suggested in the task force report should be utilized as tools in personnel administration and not as rigid compartments to which considerations of caste and perquisites become attached.

f. The present Civil Service personnel of the State Department should enter the consolidated service on application and oral examination. This process must take into account the needs of the single service for personnel with special as well as general aptitudes, including certain aptitudes of primary importance in the Department at home as contrasted with the missions overseas. Departmental personnel who are unwilling to enter the new service but who are qualified for their present duties might be continued in their present posts on some special "limited service" basis or be given opportunities elsewhere in the government.

g. All members of the consolidated service of the same grade should have equal status in every respect, including compensation and retirement rights.

h. Recruitment and promotion policies should be varied and flexible so as to obtain and keep individuals with the different required qualifications, including especially resourcefulness and executive ability. Administration should be geared so as to place more responsibility on young men in the first 15 years of service. In the case of members with special aptitudes, they should be enlisted and promoted without reference to the versatility and elasticity expected of others with more general talents. This will necessarily involve recruitment of personnel at all levels and not merely at the bottom or present Class 6 level.

i. A temporary or reserve officer classification should be continued and should be open to (1) representatives of other departments and agencies nominated by them and acceptable to the State Department on personal and similar grounds who will serve abroad as technical reporters and attachés in the small number of cases where this service cannot be adequately performed by the new corps; (11) personnel to implement special programs such as the European Recovery Program or in other temporary capacities; and (111) applicants for admission to the general or special officer classifications who have passed the necessary examinations but who are awaiting appointment. These temporary or reserve officers should have status identical with the general and special officers of corresponding grade and should be paid and supported like other members of the corps, the funds, in the case of representatives of other departments and agencies, to come from grants to the single service from appropriations of the other departments and agencies.

j. The consolidated service should not be self-administered but subject to direction and inspection of the Secretary. For purposes of recruitment, examination, promotion, retirement, and inspection, the Secretary should have authority to set up special boards to assist him in an advisory capacity.

The departments and agencies other than the State Department will continue to have heavy requirements for information from overseas points. In the main these needs should be filled by the single Foreign Affairs Service which should take active measures to recruit specialists from the other segments of the executive branch and from business, labor, and other sources. The Secretary of State should obtain advice from the other departments and agencies through interdepartmental consultation, but the existing Board of the Foreign Service, which represents the undesirable practice of administration by a committee, should be abolished.

In the limited number of cases where specialized technical reporting, or an unusual quantity of reporting or other special requirements exist, the other departments and agencies should designate and obtain appropriations for personnel for their overseas work. These individuals would be sent abroad as temporary or reserve officers in the single service (see subparagraph (*i*) above). While on such assignments they should constitute an integral part of the missions to which they are assigned and should serve the chiefs of mission and the State Department as well as the department or agency by which they are appointed and in which their career lies.

D. Recommendations for the Other Departments and Agencies

Recommendation No. 21

The other departments and agencies should consider the possible foreign impact of all proposed major policies and programs, and consult with the State Department in regard thereto.

The present attitude of the other agencies is that they do not want the State Department to formulate foreign policies or programs without consulting with them. Although the State Department has made sincere efforts to do this, the other agencies feel it is their sole prerogative to initiate a domestic policy or program and that the State Department need not be consulted. It seems needless to labor the point that in a world as economically and socially interdependent as ours, an agricultural price-support program, for instance, is not without consequence to foreign states.

Each agency should, moreover, constantly bear in mind that the instruments of foreign policy should always be used to achieve objectives of foreign policy and not as methods of determining foreign policy.

Recommendation No. 22

The other departments and agencies which have important duties in foreign affairs should each establish an officer or office directly responsible to the department or agency head for coordinating its foreign affairs activities.

Few departments and agencies have recast their organizations to meet effectively their increased responsibilities in foreign affairs. Some of the bureaus or offices within the major executive establishments have had to operate largely without benefit of top-side direction. This situation has placed an added administrative burden upon the State Department as it often has had to try to coordinate constituent parts of a department, or to sit silently in interdepartmental committees, while contending bureaus of one agency resolve their internal differences. Likewise, the other departments and agencies must be geared to provide prompt and reliable information to the State Department so that in urgent matters the State Department is not forced to set up its own specialist units in order to get the job done. This also would be the responsibility of the single officer or official acting under the department head.

Important tasks for such a department or agency coordinating officer to perform would include supervision and improvement in its committee participation; assurance of the development of a department or agency viewpoint before its representative speaks in an interdepartmental conference; follow-up on departmental or agency committee and international conference commitments; functioning as the department's or agency's focal point for liaison on foreign affairs matters; fostering of required cooperation and working relationships; review of departmental or agency legislative proposals to determine impact on foreign affairs; overcoming of insular or domestic perspective of departmental or agency personnel performing substantive work involving foreign and domestic considerations; avoidance of departmental or agency attempts to separate domestic and foreign aspects of work; and coordination of all departmental and agency report requests to overseas missions.

Chapter Five

ECONOMY AND THE CONDUCT OF
FOREIGN AFFAIRS

The task force report does not attempt to calculate the amount of immediate savings if all of its recommendations are accepted. The reason lies in the fact that the present-day requirements for the effective conduct of foreign affairs by the United States are on a scale unprecedented in American history. The accompanying expenditures are necessarily large but they do not in the main represent costs of administration. The total estimated appropriations for international affairs and finance for fiscal year 1949 are approximately $7 billion, including $4.4 billion for recovery programs such as the European Recovery Program and $1.25 billion for occupation responsibilities in Germany, Austria, Japan, and Korea. Of this $7 billion, the State Department and Foreign Service appropriations are only $120 million or less than 2 percent of the total.

The estimated 1949 military appropriations other than those for occupied areas are, in large measure as a result of the international situation, in the neighborhood of over $12 billion. Coupling this amount with the above amounts for economic assistance and occupation activities makes it evident that the only real prospect of economy lies in making progress toward world peace and stability. Wars and threats of wars and their drain on men and resources occur because diplomacy and other peaceful instruments fail or threaten to fail. The organizational segments of the Government in the foreign affairs field must be equipped to play their vital part in seeking to attain this ultimate goal. By recruitment of high-quality personnel to man these units and by increased efficiency in their performance, both contemplated by the recommendations heretofore, stated savings in manpower and dollars will inevitably result.

For the present the functions being performed by the State Department and the other departments and agencies in the foreign affairs field are crucial and necessary governmental functions and, except for minor readjustments, cannot be curtailed. In the particular case of the State Department it should be noted that readjustments have been going on ever since 1945 when it was first saddled with wartime programs and personnel for the want of better locations elsewhere. This readjustment process, accomplished in part by transfer of personnel, has reduced the total personnel in the State Department from a peak of 7,623 in 1946 to 5,652 on September 1, 1948, or a reduction of 26 percent.

An admonition should also be expressed as to organizational arrangements for participation by the United States in international organizations and conferences. For fiscal year 1949, the appropriations for this purpose are $160 million or $40 million more than the combined appropriations for the State Department and Foreign Service. With responsibilities for this participation spread throughout the Government and with the unfamiliar nature of the task, the Bureau of the Budget and the State Department must take aggressive leadership in promoting efficient arrangements and procedures for participation in international organizations so that the United States gets value received for its expenditures.

VIII

The National Security
Organization

Chapter One

NEED FOR THE NATIONAL SECURITY ORGANIZATION

World conditions demand that the United States maintain a strong National Security Organization.

This need results directly from the total disruption of the old balance of power among nations, and from new forms of communications and warfare which have impaired America's ocean-moated isolation. Ours is a need for defense and our military strength must be predicated upon the degree of menace which we face. At present outlook, the United States' need for a strong Military Establishment is obvious.

In the past, the United States has maintained merely a nominal Army and Air Force, and its Navy has been sharply limited. The assumption was that war, and international crises which could result in war, would be rare and that there would always be ample time to build a strong military force around this permanent cadre. Now the United States, in the forefront of world affairs, must continuously deal with political and economic pressures.

The maintenance of a huge military force and of enormous military budgets in peacetime poses a severe problem. It introduces a new element into our social and political life; this spending, both as a drain on the taxpayers and as purchasing power, can vitally affect our economy. The degree of our success in achieving efficiency of military operations and planning, economy in execution, and proper relationship of this new force to our political and economic fabric can make the difference between democracy and totalitarianism, both for our Nation, and for the whole world.

Military strength and efficiency is important, but it is only one element of national security. National strength depends upon economic, political, and human values. We must, therefore, assure ourselves that the military arm of Government, in its new strength, will not grow up as a thing apart. In particular, it must be unequivocally under the direction of the executive branch and fully accountable to the President, the Congress, and the people.

Throughout its history, the United States has been fearful of military cliques and has thrown up safeguards against this threat to democratic government. Under the Constitution, we have subordinated the military to civilian control by making the President Commander in Chief of the armed forces, and by installing civilian secretaries to direct the departments.

The pressure of events has resulted in a budget of approximately $15,000,000,000 in the current fiscal year, more than a third of all Federal appropriations, and large military budgets must be the expectation for the immediate future. Under these circumstances, the Nation must make very sure that means of exercising civilian control are strong and effective. We repeat, that under these circumstances, we must hold the military rigidly accountable to the President, the Congress, and the people. We must do this not only to safeguard our democratic traditions against militarism, but to insure that military policy shall be in close accord with national needs and national welfare; and also to insure that the huge military budget shall be used with efficiency, and that costs shall be commensurate with actual needs without damaging or destroying our national economy.

At present, we can be sure of none of these things.

Chapter Two

WHAT IS WRONG WITH THE PRESENT ORGANIZATION

The National Security Organization, as legislated in 1947 to establish unification of the armed services and unified national policy on security, has achieved gains. Further improvement may be expected since the organization is still young, but there is evidence that the utmost that can be accomplished under the present statute will fall far short of national needs.

The Commission on Organization of the Executive Branch has had the benefit of an investigation into the National Security Organization by a distinguished committee. The committee found continued disharmony and lack of unified planning. Extravagance in military budgets and waste in military expenditure show a serious lack of understanding of the effect of military costs and spending upon the total economy. True national security depends more upon economic stability and political strength than upon military power.

Interservice rivalries indicate a lack of understanding of the fact that military security depends upon cooperation and balance among the Army, Navy, and Air Force, and upon the creation of a genuinely unified military arm. There is a lack of close working relationships among such important elements as the Research and Development Board and the Joint Chiefs of Staff and the Central Intelligence Agency.

Some part of these weaknesses undoubtedly can be traced to the newness of the operation, but the Commission believes that they show serious organizational defects. The lack of central authority in the direction of the National Military Establishment, the rigid statutory structure established under the act, and divided responsibility have resulted in a failure to assert clear civilian control over the armed forces.

Over-all Department Management

In our first report we have urged that the foundation of good depart-mental administration requires that the Secretary have authority from the Congress to organize and control his organization, and that separate authorities to component subordinates be eliminated.

In our Report on the Budget we propose a new form of "perform-ance" budget for all departments. We also propose that each depart-ment or agency keep its own administrative accounts in the manner prescribed by an Accountant General in the Treasury and subject to the approval and audit of the Comptroller General.[1] The Commission also recommends that personnel recruitment be performed by the Department (except possibly in the lower grades), subject to standards and methods of merit selection to be proposed by the Department, but with the approval and enforcement of the Civil Service Commission.[2] The Commission likewise recommends elsewhere that the procurement of supplies peculiar to the Department be decentralized into the Depart-ment, under standards and methods established in the Office of General Services.[3] The items of common use would of course be handled by the latter office. Further, we propose that the Department should strengthen its management research unit, working in cooperation with a comparable staff unit under the Office of the Budget.[4]

Civilian Control and Accountability

In its study of the executive branch the Commission has established certain principles that must underlie systems of organization in order to assure the three essentials of good Government management: efficiency, economy, and clear accountability to the Congress and the people.

These principles call for centralization of authority and control in the President and the department heads, for clear lines of command and accountability, and for provision of adequate staffs for policy formula-tion and for supervision of operation. Without these, the President and the department heads cannot exercise positive control and hence cannot be held responsible by the Congress and the people for failures or deficiencies of performance.

[1] Report on Budgeting and Accounting.
[2] Report on Personnel Management.
[3] Report on the Office of General Services.
[4] Report on General Management of the Executive Branch.

In the establishment of the present organization for national security, these principles have been repeatedly violated.

a. **The President's authority has been curtailed by statutory stipulation of the membership and duties of both the National Security Council and the National Security Resources Board—the Cabinet committees concerned with vital defense policies.**

b. **The authority of the Secretary of Defense, and hence the control of the President, is weak and heavily qualified by the provisions of the act of 1947 which set up a rigid structure of federation rather than unification.**

c. **In direct proportion to the limitations and confusions of authority among their civilian superiors, the military are left free of civilian control.**

The Commission's report on departmental management [5] has pointed out the weaknesses and fallacies of a department in which statutory authority is delegated to subordinate units, and the department head is left with only the most general supervisory powers over policies, operations, and budgets. In such cases, the department head cannot enforce consistent policies and obtain the necessary efficiency and economy. Nor can he be held strictly accountable since he lacks authority to carry out the mandates of determined policy. The National Military Establishment as set up under the act of 1947 is perilously close to the weakest type of department.

The Secretary of Defense, at present, has only "general" authority over the service departments—the Army, Navy, and Air Force. He cannot hire and fire subordinates except on his immediate staff. Almost all appointive power not in the President's hands is in that of the subordinate service secretaries. The powers of the Secretary of Defense over the budget for the National Military Establishment, and over expenditures, are inadequate. He is inadequately provided with staff and has no authority to reorganize the Establishment, most of whose machinery is rigidly prescribed by statute.

The principle of federation, rather than firm unification, is implicit in the statutory provision that "all powers and duties relating to such departments (the Army, Navy, and Air Force) and not specifically conferred upon the Secretary of Defense" are reserved to the departments. The pattern does not cease at that point. Within the service departments, subordinate units—such as the Corps of Engineers in the Army

[5] See report on General Management of the Executive Branch.

insofar as its civilian functions are concerned—have direct authority from the Congress exclusive of control even by their own secretaries.

Moreover, the service secretaries are given specific authority to resist the supervision of the Secretary of Defense in budgetary matters by appealing over his head to the President or to the Director of the Budget. The service secretaries sit with the Secretary of Defense on the National Security Council and can "outvote" him in that body's deliberations. They have more staff for planning and execution and, in fact, operate as almost fully autonomous units.

Under these circumstances centralized civilian control scarcely exists. Each military branch follows its own purposes and, due both to the weakness of the Defense Secretary's powers and to the confusion of authority over them, has very much a free hand. In effect, divided responsibility means no responsibility. Civilian control thus depends directly upon the Congress whose chief mechanism is the tightening or loosening of the purse strings. In the present unsatisfactory state of military budget practices and procedure, the effectiveness of this mechanism in the hands of the Congress is highly attenuated.

In the period ahead when national security will demand a large military budget, this time-honored device for subordinating the military to civilian control will be ineffective. The remedy must be sought through organization of the executive branch to establish firm lines of authority and accountability. Otherwise, civilian control will continue to be a label instead of a reality.

What is true of the National Military Establishment is equally true of the operations of the Joint Chiefs of Staff. Three of the four members are spokesmen for separate service arms. The Secretary of Defense, and his viewpoint for the unified Establishment as a whole, is not represented in their deliberations. Thus, though the Secretary of Defense is, under the act, the principal assistant to the President, in military matters, he cannot, as a practical matter, maintain effective civilian control over this most powerful of military units. The Joint Chiefs of Staff, as a unit, report to two officials—the Secretary of Defense and the President. As individuals, they report to the President, the Secretary of Defense, and the service secretaries. Each will tend to answer much more to the service secretary who is his direct superior than to the single policies of a unified Establishment.

Here, too, it is clear that divided responsibility and allegiance are tantamount to an almost complete absence of control. Under this system, the Joint Chiefs of Staff are virtually a law unto themselves, as evidenced in the fact that their activities are not well coordinated with intra-Military Establishment operations, nor with the policy work of the Cabinet councils. The Joint Chiefs of Staff, like the rest of the National Military Establishment, are not firmly under civilian control.

Budget and Expenditure

The present budget of the armed forces represents about $100 per capita for the Nation, as contrasted with some $2.25 before the First World War. Our task force reports that the current preliminary budget estimates of the three military departments for the fiscal year 1950 were for more than $30,000,000,000.

Such a budget would be justifiable only if the Nation were actually involved in warfare. It would require a sharp reduction in production for civilian consumption, precipitate the need for controls over the economy, and enormously increase inflationary pressures. It reflects a lack of realistic understanding by the three military departments of the economic and social factors of national security.

Moreover, military budgets are not drawn with careful consciousness of cost factors. For example, an examination of the 1950 budget revealed estimates requesting modernization of 102 more tanks of a certain type than the Army actually possessed. In another case, a misplaced figure added some $30,000,000 to budget estimates.

The committee which examined into these matters for the Commission on Organization of the Executive Branch was unable to compare with any degree of accuracy the cost of similar functions in the three services because of varied organizational structures and differing budgetary and accounting classifications and procedures.

Firm control over the budget and over military expenditures, as authorized by the Congress, is of the utmost importance to the national economy. Full control in the hands of the Secretary of Defense, under the authority of the President, would accomplish three main purposes: (a) It would assure budgeting and spending from the standpoint of national welfare, rather than from the standpoint of service rivalries; (b) it would assure clear and direct accountability to the President, the Office of the Budget, and the Congress through a single official, and by these means would assure a budget that conformed to national policy; (c) it would provide the Secretary of Defense with a most effective mechanism for asserting civilian control over the military.

Recommendation No. 1

The Commission, therefore, recommends:

a. That full power over preparation of the budget and over expenditures as authorized by the Congress be vested in the Secretary of Defense, under the authority of the President.

b. That the Secretary of Defense direct and supervise a major overhaul of the entire budget system; that the budget be of a performance type with emphasis on the objectives and purposes to be accomplished rather than upon personnel, supplies, and similar classifications; [6] that uniform terminology, classifications, budgetary, and accounting practices be established throughout all the services along administrative lines of responsibility, so that fiscal and management responsibility go together.

Under the performance budget system, each major organizational unit with management responsibility would have to prepare, and defend before the Secretary of Defense, complete estimates for its activities on the basis of functions and performance, and therefore could be held responsible for any money it might spend. Accountability would extend to accounting for operating results and to the measurement of performance against standards set through budgetary planning and cost estimates.

Such a system would accomplish a great deal, not only for efficiency, but to establish the authority of the Secretary of Defense and hence to assure civilian control.

c. That the armed services be required, at least in peacetime, to keep complete, accurate, and current inventories.

[6] This system of budgeting is discussed in detail in the Commission's report on Budgeting and Accounting.

Chapter Three

WHAT SHOULD BE DONE TO IMPROVE ORGANIZATION

The Commission calls attention to the findings of its task force report submitted separately to the Congress. The Commission is in general agreement with the conclusions and recommendations of the task force. However, the Commission feels that certain of the measures suggested by the task force for carrying out the policies need strengthening from the broader standpoint of reorganization of the entire executive branch —particularly to insure firm civilian control.

The Commission, in its first report, has recommended that all statutory restrictions on the National Security Council and the National Security Resources Board which limit the authority of the President should be removed and that the President have entire discretion over their membership, assignments, and direction.

The Commission recommends that the post of Chief of Staff to the President be abolished.

Civilian Control

Singleness of control is the essence of efficiency. The present scattering of authority is expensive, promotes rather than curtails service rivalries, and destroys the very principle of unification. Accountability is most strongly enforced when the President and the Congress, in the people's name, can call a single official to book for his conduct of a Government operation.

Pecommendation No. 2

Therefore the Commission makes the following recommendations:

a. **That the principle of unified civilian control and accountability be the guiding rule for all legislation concerned with the National**

Military Establishment and that full authority and accountability be centered in the Secretary of Defense, subject only to the President and the Congress.

b. That all statutory authority now vested in the service departments, or their subordinate units, be granted directly to the Secretary of Defense, subject to the authority of the President, with further authority to delegate them as he sees fit and wise.

c. That the Secretary of Defense shall have full authority, subject only to the President and the Congress, to establish policies and programs.

d. That the service secretaries be deprived of their privilege of appeal over the head of the Secretary of Defense; that they be directly and exclusively responsible to him; that the Secretary of Defense be the sole agent reporting to the President; that the service secretaries, to clarify their positions, be designated the Under Secretaries for Army, Navy, and Air Force.

e. That specific provisions be made that the three military services shall be administered by the several under secretaries subject to the full direction and authority of the Secretary of Defense.

f. That there shall be Joint Chiefs of Staff representing the three services, appointed by the President and subject to confirmation by the Senate and that the Secretary of Defense, with the President's approval, shall appoint a chairman to preside over the Joint Chiefs of Staff and to represent, and report to, the Secretary of Defense.

g. That all administrative authority be centered in the Secretary of Defense, subject only to the authority of the President, including full and final authority over preparation of the military budget and over the expenditure of funds appropriated by the Congress.

h. That the Secretary be provided with an Under Secretary of Defense, who shall be his full deputy and act for him in his absence, and three assistant secretaries; and that the Secretary of Defense be empowered to set up such personal assistants to himself as he shall require to relieve him of day-to-day detail, to advise and assist him in planning and carrying out programs, and to organize this staff as he sees fit.

i. That full authority for the procurement and management of supplies and matériel be vested in the Secretary of Defense. The Secretary can delegate this authority to the Munitions Board (or to other officers or agencies as he may determine) with directions to expedite by all possible means the elimination of costly duplication in procurement and waste in utilization among the three services. Our further recommendations regarding the coordination of military with civilian supply management are contained in the Commission's report on the Offices of General Services.

Recommendation No. 3

The following recommendations are made regarding personnel:

a. That, in line with our recommendation below for an integrated system of military personnel administration, military education, training, recruitment, promotion, and transfers among the services be put under the central direction and control of the Secretary of Defense.

b. That the recruitment of civilian employees should be decentralized into the National Military Establishment under standards and procedures to be approved and enforced by the Civil Service Commission.[7]

c. That full authority be vested in the Secretary of Defense, subject only to policies established by the Congress and the President, to prescribe uniform personnel policies for civilian and military personnel throughout the several services.

Teamwork

Recommendation No. 4

Teamwork and coordination throughout the National Military Establishment should be improved. For these purposes, the Commission recommends:

a. That more adequate and effective relations be developed at the working level among the appropriate committees of the Joint Chiefs of Staff on the one hand and the National Security Council, Central Intelligence Agency, Research and Development Board, Munitions Board, and the National Security Resources Board on the other hand.

b. That the jurisdiction and activities of the National Security Resources Board be further defined and clarified by the President.

[7] See the Commission's report on Personnel Management.

c. **That vigorous steps be taken to improve the Central Intelligence Agency and its work.**

The present system of military administration does not allow for interchange of military and civilian personnel in administrative positions. Economy and efficiency would be fostered by a flexible system permitting the use of military or civilian skills in the higher posts of military administration and the Secretary should have authority to make such shifts as circumstances dictate.

Supervision over military personnel is now vested in the service department heads and in the President, not in the Secretary of Defense. There are, in addition, many statutory prescriptions of certain administrative services such as promotion boards, retirement boards, and others composed of military personnel, all of which serve to restrict the authority of the Secretary and his top civilian administrators. Moreover, statutory specifications of the numbers and grades of military personnel to be assigned to specific organizational units limit the most economical utilization of available military manpower when conditions require transfers and changes among organizational units.

The Secretary should have full authority to organize personnel management throughout the Military Establishment for greater efficiency and economy, and present hampering restrictions should be removed.

Medical Services

Recommendation No. 5

That steps be instituted to implement the recommendations which the Commission will file later concerning the medical departments of the three services, and their coordination with other medical programs of the Federal Government, as detailed in the Commission's separate report on medical services.

Civilian and Industrial Mobilization

For the security of the Nation, the formulation of plans for civilian and industrial mobilization should be completed at the earliest possible date.

Recommendation No. 6

The Commission therefore makes the following recommendations:

a. **That emergency plans for civilian and industrial mobilization be completed promptly and continuously revised.**

b. That use of civilian advisory boards should be continued.

c. That full responsibility and authority for formulating stock-pile policy and for its execution be clearly determined and centralized.

d. That further steps be taken immediately under the President's direction to prepare plans for civilian defense. Such an effort will require the participation of many agencies of Government. Similar action should be taken under the President's direction with respect to internal security. No clear allocation of responsibilities has been worked out among the agencies involved. The Commission believes that the problem in this area is one of determining what needs to be done and designating administrative responsibilities.

e. That defenses against unconventional methods of warfare be developed promptly and more vigorous and active attention be given to psychological warfare.

f. That the economic warfare section of the National Security Resources Board develop a comprehensive economic warfare program aimed at supporting national security both in peace and war.

Conclusions

These provisions should insure the full control and accountability of the National Military Establishment and the full subordination of the military to civilian control by establishing the Secretary of Defense as the principal assistant to the President in military matters, responsible to him and to the Congress for the conduct, efficiency, and economy of the National Military Establishment. Lines of command would be clear; interservice rivalries reduced by the fresh emphasis on the single-ness of purpose of the total military effort; efficiency promoted and economy achieved through consistent policy and program, and through centralized control.

IX

Treasury Department

Chapter One

REORGANIZATION OF THE TREASURY

The Treasury Department is one of the largest of the Executive departments. It now has about 90,000 employees. The Federal revenues, most of which it collects, have risen during the past 20 years from approximately $4 billion to over $40 billion. The Treasury also manages the national debt of some $252 billion with annual interest charges of $5.25 billion; in 1929 the national debt was only $17 billion.

Some 46,000,000 individuals pay personal income taxes annually, the collection of which is a responsibility of the Treasury Department. In addition to this, there are corporation and innumerable direct and indirect taxes levied on nearly every resident of the country. The activities of this Department, therefore, vitally affect the lives of all our countrymen. Our national finances are of major concern to every citizen.

The enormous expansion and far-reaching implications of Government finance make it imperative that the Treasury Department should be thoroughly reorganized. Its organization and methods have become obsolete. Some of its functions are not germane to its major purpose.

In order to fulfill its historic role, the Treasury Department should again be made the real fiscal center of the Government. Its responsibilities should include (a) the assessment and collection of revenues, (b) the custody and disbursement of public funds, (c) the maintenance of central and control accounts, (d) the preparation of financial reports, (e) the management of the national debt and currency, (f) the maintenance of the public credit, (g) advice in the conduct of credit institutions, and supervision of certain others, and (h) the periodic inspection of lending and other agencies in process of liquidation.

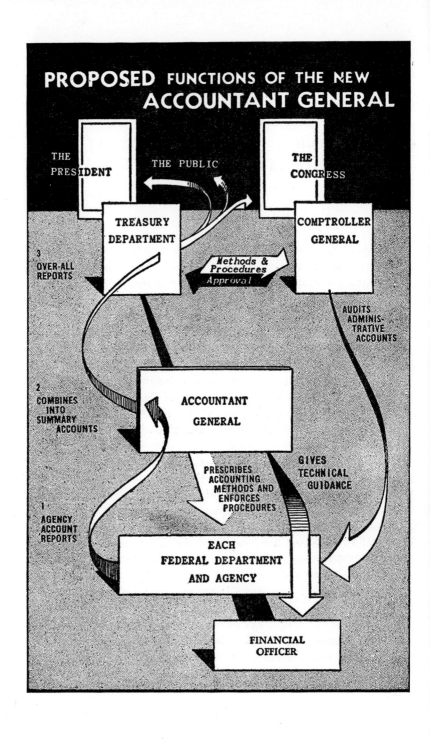

Chapter Two

OVER-ALL DEPARTMENTAL MANAGEMENT

In our first report we urged that good departmental administration requires that the Secretary have authority from the Congress to organize and control his organization, and that independent authority should not be granted directly to subordinates.

In our report on Budgeting and Accounting we proposed a new form of "performance" budget for all departments. We also proposed that each department or agency keep its own administrative accounts in the manner prescribed by an Accountant General in the Treasury and subject to the approval and audit of the Comptroller General.[1] The Commission also recommended that personnel recruitment be performed by the Department (except possibly for certain lower grade positions common to all departments and agencies) subject to standards and methods of merit selection to be proposed by the Department, approved and enforced by the Civil Service Commission.[2] The Commission likewise recommended elsewhere that the procurement of supplies peculiar to the Department be decentralized into the Department under standards and methods established by the proposed Office of General Services.[3] Items of common use would, of course, be handled by the latter office. Further, we proposed that the Department should strengthen its management research unit, working in cooperation with a comparable staff unit under the Office of the Budget.[1]

Recommendations on Accounting

Further, the Commission has recommended that:

a. An Accountant General should be established under the Secretary of the Treasury with authority to prescribe and inspect general accounting

[1] Report on Budgeting and Accounting.
[2] Report on Personnel Management.
[3] Report on the Office of General Services.

methods and procedures to be followed by all departments. These procedures and methods should be subject to the approval of the Comptroller General within the powers now conferred upon him by the Congress.

b. The Accountant General should, on a report basis, combine departmental accounts into the summary accounts and prepare financial reports for the information of the Chief Executive, the Congress, and the public.

c. Each department should be responsible for maintaining detailed accounting records under the direction of a chief departmental accountant who will be subject to the technical guidance of the Accountant General. (See chart on page 202.)

We give our reasons for the foregoing recommendations in our report on Budgeting and Accounting.

Transferring Nonfiscal Functions

Recommendation No. 1

We recommend that the Department should be thoroughly reorganized along functional lines contributing to its major purpose.

This will require the transfer of the nonfiscal activities from the Department and the incorporation of other appropriate agencies within it.

Recommendation No. 2

We recommend that the following agencies and activities of the Treasury should be transferred to other offices or departments to which they are functionally more closely related:

a. The functions of the Bureau of Federal Supply to be absorbed in the Office of General Services.

b. The United States Coast Guard, and probably certain of the marine functions of the Bureau of Customs, to the Department of Commerce.

c. The Bureau of Narcotics to the Department of Justice.

These agencies have a much closer relationship to the major purposes of other departments. The justification for the first recommendation is set forth in our report on the Office of General Services, wherein we

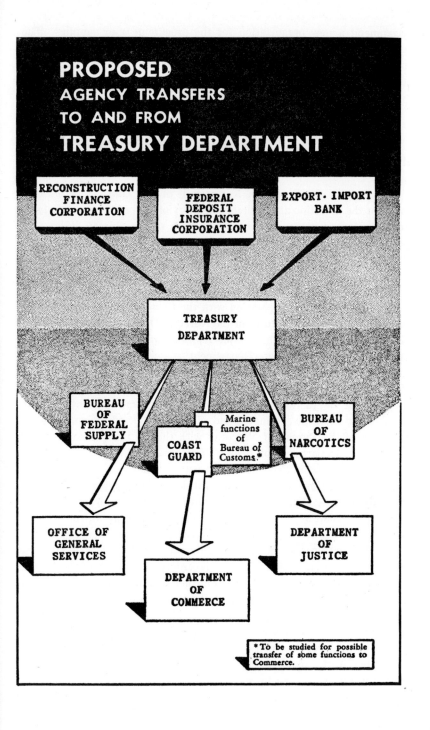

PROPOSED
AGENCY TRANSFERS
TO AND FROM
TREASURY DEPARTMENT

RECONSTRUCTION
FINANCE
CORPORATION

FEDERAL
DEPOSIT
INSURANCE
CORPORATION

EXPORT· IMPORT
BANK

TREASURY
DEPARTMENT

BUREAU
OF
FEDERAL
SUPPLY

COAST
GUARD

Marine
functions
of
Bureau of
Customs.*

BUREAU
OF
NARCOTICS

OFFICE OF
GENERAL
SERVICES

DEPARTMENT
OF
COMMERCE

DEPARTMENT
OF
JUSTICE

* To be studied for possible
transfer of some functions to
Commerce.

recommend a new organization for the procurement of supplies. The reasons for the second change are contained in our report on the Department of Commerce, wherein we recommend the grouping of marine services according to their major purpose.

Bureau of Narcotics

This Bureau is much less concerned with collecting revenue than with the enforcement of regulations to prevent the illegal sale and use of narcotics.

The work of the Bureau of Narcotics is of two kinds. Law enforcement, or the detection and apprehension of violators of the narcotic laws, accounts for about 80 percent of the work of the Bureau. About 20 percent of its work consists of regulating the flow and manufacture of drugs and preparations made from narcotics. This latter phase of its work is done primarily through licensing.

The relation of the Bureau to the rest of the Treasury Department is largely confined to cooperation with the Customs Bureau in administering the prohibitive features of the Narcotic Drugs Import and Export Act at the ports. Its other major relations are with the Federal Security Agency and the State Department.

The police work of the Bureau involves much the same kind of relationship with State and local police authorities as is maintained by the Department of Justice for other types of Federal law enforcement. Duplication could be eliminated and economy achieved by consolidating the work of the Bureau of Narcotics with that of the law enforcement work of the Department of Justice. The same working relations would of necessity be maintained with the Customs Bureau.

At the same time crime detection within the country would be facilitated by a single channel of contact with State and local authorities in the apprehension of violators who generally form a part of the criminal element shifting or combining their activities with other lawless acts.

The law enforcement work of the Bureau is police work to suppress illegal use of narcotics and is unlike the enforcement work of the Bureau of Internal Revenue with respect to income and alcohol taxes where the emphasis is on taxation of legitimate business. In transferring the functions of the Bureau, the Commission considered separating regulatory work and locating it elsewhere but the evidence is that no economies would be achieved by such a move inasmuch as the enforcement and regulatory work are so closely related that greater problems of coordination would be created by such a split.

New Functions

The major functions to be brought into the Department include those of the newly established Accountant General mentioned above, the examination and stimulation of the liquidations of Government lending agencies, and the coordination of policies governing domestic lending.

It should be emphasized in connection with the Accountant General that his duties with respect to the Treasury Department should be confined strictly to accounting matters in that Department. He should be in a position, for example, to see that independent and effective checks are established over tax accruals and collections in both Internal Revenue and Customs Bureaus. He should not be directly involved in the other fiscal operations of the Department which have to do with the assessment of taxes, collection, custody, and disbursement of public moneys.

Lending and Guarantee Agencies to Be Transferred to Treasury

The Reconstruction Finance Corporation, the Export-Import Bank, and the Federal Deposit Insurance Corporation are independent agencies reporting directly to the President. The President cannot give the time necessary for their supervision. Practically, they are accountable to nobody.

Reconstruction Finance Corporation. The Commission believes that the operations of this corporation, on which we make recommendations in our report on Federal Business Enterprises, should be placed in the Treasury Department with general responsibility for its supervision vested in the Secretary.

Federal Deposit Insurance Corporation. This corporation, which has responsibility for the examination of insured banks should also be under the general supervision of the Secretary. At present, bank examinations are conducted by three agencies, the Federal Deposit Insurance Corporation, an independent agency, the Comptroller of the Currency in the Treasury Department, and the Federal Reserve Board. While, as a practical matter, a more or less satisfactory modus vivendi has been reached for the elimination of major duplication among the functions, the placing of the Federal Deposit Insurance Corporation under the supervision of the Secretary would insure the continuation of such cooperative arrangements. Through the National Monetary and Credit

Council, which we discuss later, a coordination of policies in bank examinations with the Federal Reserve Board would also be achieved.

Export-Import Bank. The Treasury Department now has certain responsibilities in the foreign field. It operates the Stabilization Fund, including the loan made by the fund to the Republic of Mexico. It is the agency through which the British loan is administered. The Secretary of the Treasury is Chairman of the National Advisory Council on International Monetary and Financial Problems, the major policy body in this field. In the opinion of the Commission, he should also have general supervision over the operations of the Export-Import Bank.

Recommendation No. 3

We recommend, therefore, that the supervision of the operations of the Reconstruction Finance Corporation, the Federal Deposit Insurance Corporation, and the Export-Import Bank be vested in the Secretary of the Treasury.

Chapter Three

GROUPING OF AGENCIES BY MAJOR PURPOSES

Recommendation No. 4

We suggest that the Department should be divided, as listed below, into major purpose or functional groups.

We are, however, setting no hard and fast rule of organization. Some of this organization is already in effect.

The following services and major activities should be included in the Department, with an official in charge of each.

ADMINISTRATIVE SERVICES

BUDGETING AND ACCOUNTING (within the Treasury Department)
PERSONNEL
SUPPLY
MANAGEMENT RESEARCH
INFORMATION AND PUBLICATIONS
LIAISON WITH CONGRESS

CONSOLIDATED REVENUE SERVICE

BUREAU OF INTERNAL REVENUE
BUREAU OF CUSTOMS

FISCAL SERVICE

MANAGEMENT OF FEDERAL FINANCES
CUSTODY AND DISBURSEMENT OF FUNDS
MANAGEMENT OF DEBT
UNITED STATES SAVINGS BONDS DIVISION

BUREAU OF THE MINT
BUREAU OF ENGRAVING AND PRINTING
SECRET SERVICE

BANKING AND INTERNATIONAL FINANCE

OFFICE OF INTERNATIONAL FINANCE
COMPTROLLER OF THE CURRENCY
NATIONAL MONETARY AND CREDIT COUNCIL (new)

THE OFFICE OF LIQUIDATION

The Treasury already has many duties incident to the inactivation of several discontinued activities, as stated below. We suggest further additions.

ACCOUNTANT GENERAL (new)

The functions of the present Bureau of Accounts probably would be divided between the Accountant General and the reorganized Fiscal Service.

TRANSFERRED CORPORATIONS

RECONSTRUCTION FINANCE CORPORATION
FEDERAL DEPOSIT INSURANCE CORPORATION
EXPORT-IMPORT BANK

In consolidating the Bureau of Internal Revenue and the Bureau of Customs into a Revenue Service, advantage should be taken of the opportunity to integrate the overhead management, the administrative services, and the field offices of these agencies. These steps would greatly improve and expedite the administration of the Revenue Service. The replacement of obsolete equipment and methods by up-to-date machinery and procedures would also add immensely to the efficiency of the Service.

The supervision of the Reconstruction Finance Corporation, the Federal Deposit Insurance Corporation and the Export-Import Bank would be the responsibility of the Secretary unless he should decide to assign such supervision elsewhere.

We suggest that the reorganization of the Department should be made without regard for the retention of existing offices and units except as they conform to the new structure. Each new service should be a complete realignment and integration of the functions assigned to it, and not merely a corralling of old offices and agencies. Legislative action will be necessary in order to abolish obsolete offices and institute up-to-date procedures.

Administrative Staff

Recommendation No. 5

The top staff of the Department should consist of:

a. THE SECRETARY—and his personal assistants including the Tax Research Division and the Office of the Technical Staff

b. THE UNDER SECRETARY—and his personal assistants

c. THE GENERAL COUNSEL—including the Office of Tax Counsel

d. THE ACCOUNTANT GENERAL

e. THE ADMINISTRATIVE ASSISTANT SECRETARY in charge of Administrative Services

f. THE COMMISSIONER OF REVENUE, with the rank of Assistant Secretary

g. THE FISCAL ASSISTANT SECRETARY

h. AN ASSISTANT SECRETARY in charge of Banking and International Finance

i. A DIRECTOR OF THE OFFICE OF LIQUIDATION

Appointment of Officials

Recommendation No. 6

All officials of secretarial rank should be appointed by the President and confirmed by the Senate, except the Fiscal Assistant Secretary, who is now exempt from Senate confirmation. The Administrative Assistant Secretary, the Accountant General, the Commissioner of Revenue, the Assistant Secretary for Banking and International Finance should preferably be men with a background of long experience in the career service.

One of the chief handicaps to effective organization of the Department is the political appointment of Collectors of Internal Revenue and of Customs, and certain other officials. These appointments are regarded by some as sinecures. In any event, they form a bar to orderly development of an experienced staff.

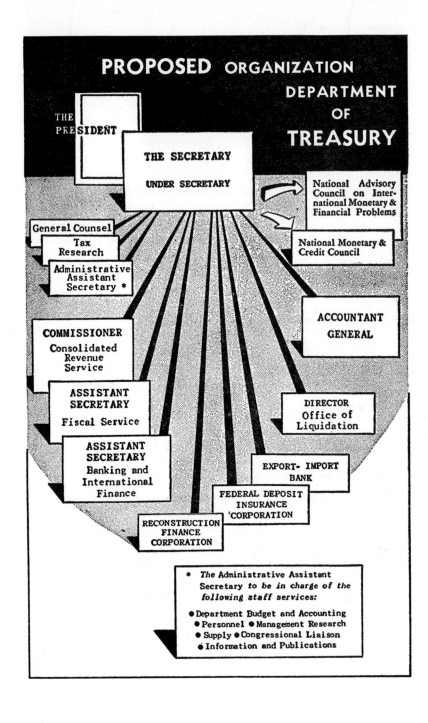

PROPOSED ORGANIZATION
DEPARTMENT OF TREASURY

THE PRESIDENT

THE SECRETARY

UNDER SECRETARY

National Advisory Council on International Monetary & Financial Problems

General Counsel

Tax Research

Administrative Assistant Secretary *

National Monetary & Credit Council

ACCOUNTANT GENERAL

COMMISSIONER
Consolidated Revenue Service

ASSISTANT SECRETARY
Fiscal Service

DIRECTOR
Office of Liquidation

ASSISTANT SECRETARY
Banking and International Finance

EXPORT- IMPORT BANK

FEDERAL DEPOSIT INSURANCE 'CORPORATION

RECONSTRUCTION FINANCE CORPORATION

* The Administrative Assistant Secretary to be in charge of the following staff services:

● Department Budget and Accounting
● Personnel ● Management Research
● Supply ● Congressional Liaison
● Information and Publications

Recommendation No. 7

The Commission recommends that all officials in the Department below the rank of Assistant Secretary should preferably be appointed from the career service without Senate confirmation.

The Office of Liquidation

In addition to various liquidation responsibilities already in the Department, there are now 10 lending agencies which have ceased active operations or are in the process of liquidation. The assets of these agencies are in excess of $1 billion. These liquidation operations are located in several different places.

For example, the Federal Farm Mortgage Corporation, with assets of about $127 million as of June 30, 1948, has been in liquidation by the Farm Credit Administration since its lending authority expired July 1, 1947.

The Home Owners Loan Corporation, with assets of $452 million as of June 30, 1948, has been in process of liquidation since June 12, 1936, under the supervision of the Home Loan Bank Board.

Defense Homes Corporation, with total assets of nearly $54 million as of June 30, 1948, has been in process of informal liquidation since December 1945, first by the Public Housing Administration and since June 30, 1948, by direction of Congress, by the Reconstruction Finance Corporation.

While some of these agencies are being expeditiously and efficiently liquidated, we suggest that there is a need for a central agency to inspect and stimulate the liquidation process.

Recommendation No. 8

We recommend that the Treasury Department examine and report to the President and the Congress semi-annually upon all these agencies in liquidation. The Commission also recommends that the President be given the authority to delegate the work of liquidation to such agencies as he may determine.

Domestic Lending Council

There are 30 agencies in the Government actively engaged in lending, guaranteeing, or insuring loans. They represent an investment of $12.5 billion; they have further commitments from the Government of $9 billion. In addition, there is $85 billion in loans or deposits guaranteed by the Federal Government and insurance outstanding for veterans and others in the amount of about $40 billion.

These agencies now report in whole or in part to seven different departments or administrations and seven report directly to the President, who has little time for their supervision.

Their conduct can have a profound effect upon both the fiscal and financial policies of the Government and upon the economic condition of the country. It is desirable for some of them to be tied into major Government departments, especially in the fields of housing and agriculture.

We do not at present favor proposals that they be placed in the Treasury Department. There should, however, be coordination of the credit policies of these activities.

Recommendation No. 9

We recommend that there be established a National Monetary and Credit Council of domestic financial agencies in connection with the Treasury to advise on policies and coordination of the operations of domestic lending and Government financial guarantees.

The National Advisory Council on International Monetary and Financial Problems under the chairmanship of the Secretary of the Treasury is already a successful council concerned with foreign lending. The new domestic council should also be under the chairmanship of the Secretary of the Treasury, with representatives appointed by the President from such agencies as the Federal Reserve Board, the Housing and Home Finance Agency, the Farm Credit Administration, the Reconstruction Finance Corporation, and others as the President may determine, having in mind the impact of their programs upon the economy of the country. Consideration should be given, in this connection, to joint meetings with the Council dealing with foreign credits, or to the merger of the two councils.

The purpose of this Council is to develop and recommend national policies in the domestic field which would promote coordination of purpose and avoid overlapping activities and inconsistent credit policies. By the creation of such a council, the home and housing lending and credit agencies can remain associated with the Housing and Home Finance Agency, and the agricultural credit agencies with the Department of Agriculture.

This new council should be housed in the Banking and International Finance Service of the Treasury, with the Assistant Secretary in charge of the Service as secretary of the Council.

Further Recommendation—Surety Bonding

Surety bonding methods, as at present practiced, add greatly to departmental red tape and cost, especially in the Treasury Department where lists of qualified and authorized bonding companies are maintained and where all surety bonds in force are required to be filed. Under the present procedure, about 558,000 accountable officers and employees are required to pay their own surety bonds obtained from private companies at an aggregate premium cost of about $2 million, with assessable recoveries averaging about $230,000 annually (the recent war period included).

Recommendation No. 10

The Commission recommends that the Congress should continue its study of the whole question of fidelity insurance for the accountable officers of the Government in order to arrive at a simpler and less expensive system. The problem, it seems, could be better solved by establishing a fidelity insurance fund in the Treasury to which accountable officers and employees would be required to contribute.

Savings

The consolidation and segregation of these services could do much to restore the intended role of the Treasury Department and, at the same time, effect substantial savings.

The union of revenue services would eliminate considerable overhead and several duplicating administrative and field services. The modernization of existing accounting and statistical methods would also effect large savings.

In the Fiscal Service additional savings will accrue as the result of unification.

Much of the routine accounting, filing, and record keeping in connection with Government bonds should be shifted to the Federal Reserve banks, where a substantial operating economy is possible.

Savings can be accomplished by the reorganization of the Treasury's field services and the elimination of political appointments among them. Our task force report on Field Services points out certain faults in the field services of the Treasury that require remedial action.

The savings to be made in the Treasury Department by such reorganization are considerable.

X
The Post Office

Chapter One

ROLE OF THE POST OFFICE

The Post Office Department operates one of the world's largest businesses.

From its first full year of operations in 1790, when revenue amounted to $38,000, it has grown to an enterprise with revenue above $1.3 billion a year. It employs more than 500,000 persons, operates a fleet of more than 10,000 trucks, and manages 24,000 buildings, of which about 3,200 are federally owned. During 1947 it transported and delivered more than 37 billion pieces of mail—including some 1.6 billion pieces of free mail—and handled more than 800 million transactions in such special services as money orders, collect-on-delivery mail, and postal savings. The establishment's 42,000 post offices range from fourth-class units, each with annual revenue below $1,500, to the establishment in New York City with 100 stations and an annual revenue, in 1947, of $132 million.

The Post Office Department contracts for tens of millions of dollars yearly for rail, ship, air-line, and trucking transportation. It sells money orders—284 million of them in 1947—and runs the Postal Savings System, whose 4 million depositors have total accounts of more than $3.4 billion.

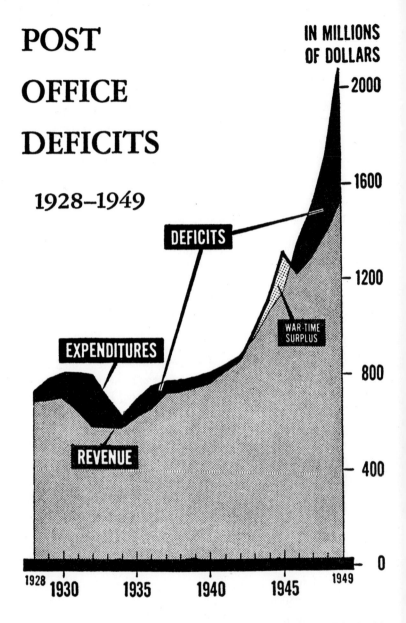

POST OFFICE DEFICITS

1928–1949

IN MILLIONS OF DOLLARS

DEFICITS

EXPENDITURES

WAR-TIME SURPLUS

REVENUE

2000
1600
1200
800
400
0

1928 1930 1935 1940 1945 1949

SOURCE: U.S. BUREAU OF THE BUDGET
1948 UNAUDITED; 1949 ESTIMATED

Chapter Two

WHAT IS WRONG WITH THE POST OFFICE

a. The administrative structure is obsolete and overcentralized.

b. A maze of outmoded laws, regulations and traditions freezes progress and stifles proper administration.

c. Although the Post Office is a business-type establishment, it lacks the freedom and flexibility essential to good business operation.

d. Rates have not kept pace with wages and other costs, and rate-making machinery is inadequate.

e. The service is used to hide subsidies.

f. Political appointment of first-, second-, and third-class Postmasters and certain other officials produces inefficiency and militates against the incentives of promotion.

g. Accounts are kept by the General Accounting Office outside the Department and are available to the Post Office for management purposes only after months of delay. Methods of budgeting and appropriation are entirely unsuited to a business of the size and character of the Post Office. The pressure of these forces in a rapidly growing business accumulates to make impossible the most economical and efficient conduct of the service.

h. In recent times, except for a few years, the Post Office Department has operated at a loss. In 1948, only the first-class mails, certain categories of foreign mails, and the Postal Savings System more than met their own expenses.

In 1947, the total deficit was $263 million, or 20 percent of the revenues.

In 1948, the total deficit was $310 million, or 22 percent of the revenues.

In 1949, the total defict will probably exceed $500 million, or more than 30 percent of the revenues. (See chart.)

There is as yet insufficient information to analyze the estimated deficit for the fiscal year 1949. The deficit of $310 million for the fiscal year 1948 resulted after deducting about $190 million from profitable services, leaving a loss on the other services for that year of over $500 million. The accompanying table shows the division of profit and loss for the major services during the year.

These deficits have been created by circumstances mostly beyond the control of officials in the Post Office Department, and can be remedied only by strong and courageous action.

Fiscal Year 1948*

MAIL

	Receipts	Cost	Gain or (loss)	Percent of total costs
First class	$669,003,080	$517,916,006	30.0	$151,087,074
Air mail, domestic	53,601,798	85,627,195	5.0	(32,025,397)
Second class, paid	41,201,211	196,379,109	11.4	(155,177,898)
Third class	111,528,491	199,202,180	11.6	(87,673,689)
Fourth class	272,602,334	343,170,345	19.9	(70,568,011)
Foreign, other than air mail..	71,894,438	72,104,394	4.2	(209,956)
Air mail, foreign	24,231,519	45,669,573	2.6	(21,438,054)

SPECIAL SERVICES

	Receipts	Cost	Gain or (loss)	Percent of total costs
Registry, paid	23,590,349	32,552,479	1.9	(8,962,130)
Insurance	14,967,377	16,634,807	1.0	(1,667,130)
Collect on delivery	16,883,757	23,363,960	1.4	(6,480,203)
Special delivery	17,977,912	30,153,613	1.7	(12,175,701)
Money order	34,149,826	64,982,570	3.8	(30,832,744)
Postal notes	3,711,050	7,602,003	0.4	(3,890,953)
Postal savings	27,381,460	8,297,888	0.5	19,083,572
Unassignable (including box rents)	28,294,686	6,704,802	0.4	21,589,884
Total revenue-producing mail and special services	1,411,019,288	1,650,360,924	95.7	(239,341,636)

FREE CATEGORIES

	Receipts	Cost	Gain or (loss)	Percent of total costs
Free in county (second class)	....	10,700,000	0.62	(10,700,000)
Penalty	....	31,630,000	1.8	(31,630,000)
Franked	....	955,573	0.06	(955,573)
Free for the blind	....	355,935	0.02	(355,935)
Registry, free	....	7,439,203	0.4	(7,439,203)

OTHER

	Receipts	Cost	Gain or (loss)	Percent of total costs
Nonpostal services	3,426,002	22,352,645	1.3	(18,926,643)
Grand total, all operations	1,414,445,290	1,723,795,153	100.0	(309,349,863)

* Preliminary figures, subject to adjustment.

Chapter Three

PROPOSED DEPARTMENTAL
ORGANIZATION

We have urged in our first report that the foundation of good departmental administration is authority from Congress for the Postmaster General to organize and control his Department. Separate authorities to his subordinates should be eliminated.

Under our recommendations made elsewhere, we propose a new form of "performance" budget.[1] We propose that the Department keep its own administrative accounts as prescribed by an Accountant General in the Treasury and subject to an approval of such system by the Comptroller General and audit by him.[1] The Commission also recommends that all personnel recruitment should be decentralized into the Department (except possibly in the lower grades), subject to standards and methods of merit selection to be proposed by the Department, but with the approval and enforcement of the Civil Service Commission.[2] The Commission likewise recommends elsewhere that procurement of supplies should be decentralized into the Department with the exception of items of common use to all Departments but under standards and methods established by the Office of General Services.[3] Further, we propose that the Department should strengthen its management research unit, working in cooperation with a comparable staff unit under the Office of the Budget.[4]

We have in addition a number of specific changes to be made in the Post Office Department.

Management Structure

Recommendation No. 1

We recommend that the Postmaster General should remain a

[1] Report on the Budgeting and Accounting.
[2] Report on Personnel Management.
[3] Report on the Office of General Services.
[4] Report on General Management of the Executive Branch.

Cabinet officer appointed by the President and confirmed by the Senate, but should not be an official of a political party, such as Chairman of a National Committee.

He should be relieved from the details of day-to-day operating duties and should be free to determine departmental and public policies.

Recommendation No. 2

We recommend that there should be a Director of Posts under the Postmaster General who should be appointed by the President without term and confirmed by the Senate.

He should be an experienced executive, preferably chosen from the service. He would be the operating head of the Post Office.

Recommendation No. 3

We recommend that the Postal Service should be decentralized into 15 regions under Regional Directors of Posts and District Superintendents.

Regional Directors would direct all transportation in the region and the activities of the District Superintendents who would have supervision over all post offices in a prescribed area.

The line of authority should run from the Postmaster General through the Director of Posts to the Regional Directors and thence to the District Superintendents.

Recommendation No. 4

We recommend that there should be appointed by the President a national board of seven advisors serving part time and representing the different elements of the public.

Their duties would be advisory as to methods and policies. They should be unpaid except for a fee for attendance. In addition, the Postmaster General should serve ex officio as Chairman of the Advisory Board and the Director of Posts ex officio as Vice Chairman.

Career Postmasters

The Post Office should be taken out of politics.

Of the 470,000 persons employed, over 22,000 are in fact politically appointed. They are the strategic positions of first-, second-, and third-class Postmasters and some top officials.

Under Presidential orders beginning in 1932, and now under a law passed in 1938, the selection of candidates for Postmasters has been limited to a list approved by the Civil Service Commission based upon merit examinations. This method has lessened the appointment of unqualified officials. However, the choice from the list usually results in appointments from the political party in power. A deleterious effect has been to create a political barrier to promotion within the service and thus deprive it of a great incentive to good work.

Recommendation No. 5

We recommend that the confirmation of Postmasters by the Senate should be abolished.

The primary responsibility for personnel selection and management other than the Postmaster General and the Director of Posts should rest in the service. The Post Office Department is alone able to determine and find the skills required. The selection of Postmasters should be, as far as possible, from the local community and in consultation with community leaders. We have stated above that all selections of personnel should be subject to merit standards set by the Post Office and approved by the Civil Service Commission and subject to enforcement by that body.[5]

And we have proposed a reorganization of the Civil Service Commission which would make practicable the establishment and enforcement of such standards.

Our purpose is a career service based upon merit selection with the widest opportunity for promotion as its objective.

Budget, Accounting, and Audit

The whole accounting and administrative problem of the Postal Service is confused by the present form of the budget. Currently the Service is operated under 58 separate appropriations, each of which must be independently justified by the Department, reviewed and approved by the Congress, and apportioned to individual post offices for each quarter by the Bureau of the Budget. Individual appropriations of 1948–49 ranged from $3,000 to over $500,000,000 in such vertical classifications as "clerks, first- second-class post offices," "village delivery service," and "carfare and bicycle allowance."

Every dollar spent must be charged against a specific appropriation, and transfers from one account to another—even in the case of exhaustion of funds—is permitted only within certain narrow limits. As a

[5] See our report on Personnel Management.

result, the postal management is unable, for example, to operate any post office as a fiscal unit, but must concern itself with the expense of separate activities within the office—clerks, vehicle hire, carriers—as though they were totally unrelated.

One effect of the present combined budget and accounting system is that it hampers a businesslike operation of the service.

For instance, cash books are kept in each post office, and each entry is covered by a voucher or similar document when turned in for quarterly settlement. Accounting units of the Post Office Department have only 30 days after the close of the quarter to review this mass of material from 42,000 post offices and to turn it over to the General Accounting Office, which performs the full audit, settles directly with individual Postmasters, and turns its report over to the Department some 8 months after the quarter's end—too late for effective use in day-to-day and month-to-month analysis and supervision. Consequently, the Post Office Department must depend, in fulfilling its operating responsibilities and budgeting, on its own partial duplication of certain accounts and estimates of others.

The inadequacy of such a structure of accounting and budgeting becomes more apparent when it is considered that the volume of business, and hence expenses, will fluctuate with changing economic conditions. Nor can the Post Office Department alter its services to fit its budget, since it must accept whatever volume of service the public requests. The only recourse today when expenses exceed estimates is to request a supplemental appropriation from the Congress.

The present system does not permit of competent cost accounting fundamental to efficient management of a business. It is outrageously cumbersome and results in a mass of unnecessary red tape and a host of employees.

It must be recognized that the Post Office is:

a. Predominantly of a business nature;

b. Revenue-producing and potentially self-sustaining;

c. Characterized by a large number of business-type transactions with the public; and

d. In need of greater flexibility than the customary type of appropriation budget ordinarily permits.

Such a reorganization is essential to provide:

a. Accounting, budgeting, and auditing procedures designed to improve management's control of the business.

b. Flexibility of expenditures to meet fluctuating demands for postal service and varying conditions of operation on a Nation-wide scale.

c. Reasonable freedom from restrictive laws and regulations governing contracts, purchases, and personnel practices.

d. Administrative authority commensurate with responsibility.

We wish to emphasize our recommendations elsewhere that the Department should keep its own accounts and make its own disbursements subject to audit by the Comptroller General and in accordance with procedures determined by the Accountant General, these procedures to be approved by the Comptroller General.

The experience of the Federal Government in many of its business enterprises has already pointed the way to the solution of these problems in the Post Office. The Government Corporation Control Act of 1945, as amended, provides for a "business form" of budget, accounting and audit, and gives modern business flexibility to the management of those concerns. Already several billion dollars annually of Government business is done under those provisions.

We do not recommend that the Post Office should be incorporated under that law, as we consider that to be unnecessary.

Recommendation No. 6

We do recommend that the provisions of the law in respect to business management, budgeting, accounting, and audit be applied to the Post Office.

Such a provision will bring the Department into step with modern business methods and will not lessen Executive or Congressional controls. At the same time it will provide flexibility in management, simplification of budgeting, accounting, and audit which will result in large economies.

Inflexibility of the Organization

There are over 900 pages in detailed laws and regulations which tend generally to favor operation of the Postal Service as an expensive service arm of the Government, rather than as the revolving-fund service which it actually is.

These provisions curtail the Department's authority over minor details, or place important powers in the hands of other agencies. They provide inadequate incentives for cost-conscious, economical operation. They limit the ability of the Department to adjust to changing commercial conditions by depriving it of flexibility, both in financial and operational activities.

Recommendation No. 7

We recommend that the laws, regulations, and other stipulations governing the service should be revised not only to bring about these structural changes but also to simplify the whole operation.

Postal Rates

Certain postal rates are fixed, not primarily to provide postal income, but as an element of public policy in the dissemination of information and in the provision of services not otherwise obtainable by the people.

It is our view, therefore, that the final determination of rates for first-class (including air mail), second-, third-, and fourth-class mail should be made by the Congress.

However, there are other services performed by the Post Office that are of primary interest to certain groups, the losses from which should not fall upon the general taxpayer.

Recommendation No. 8

We therefore recommend that the Congress should authorize and instruct the Postmaster General to make rates charged for registered mail, insured mail, money orders, postal notes, postal cards, special delivery, and collect-on-delivery mail which would make each of these services self-supporting.[6]

On the basis of the 1948 estimates this would increase postal revenues by $113,000,000 per annum.

A reorganized method of accounting, as mentioned later, would not only enable far more efficient conduct of the service, and afford more accurate budgeting and cost control systems, but also would form the basis upon which Congress could act with more assurance upon rates.

To provide such data to the Congress a small unit should be established in the Department to furnish Congress with information and estimates useful in rate making.

The Congress might consider the feasibility of securing recommendations on rates from, say, the Civil Aeronautics Board or the Interstate Commerce Commission.

[6] We are informed that this recommendation already has been partially carried out.

Subsidies

Payments to common carriers for transporting the domestic and foreign air mail are fixed by the Civil Aeronautics Board at a level to provide a subsidy to aviation. Contracts for overseas mail are also made on a subsidy basis. These subsidies may be most desirable.

Recommendation No. 9

We recommend, however, that the amounts of these subsidies should be paid to the Post Office by open appropriation from tax funds and not imposed upon the Post Office or the mail users in this hidden manner.

By such a course, the President, the Congress, and the public may know what the amounts of the subsidies are.

Chapter Four

RECOMMENDATIONS
AS TO ADMINISTRATIVE SAVINGS

The above recommendations of a major nature will require legislative action. After such a general structure is erected by statute, then a great number of administrative improvements and savings will be possible which do not require legislation.

The Commission has had the assistance in the investigation and development of recommendations of Robert Heller and Associates, Inc. Many administrative recommendations are given in detail in their report which also is transmitted to the Congress. They estimate, based on their broad experience in business and industry, that the eventual savings of such modernization will be considerable, although a substantial proportion will require capital investment for equipment. The improved business structures and increased rates on special services will do much to reduce the deficits.

There are other advantages accruing from this reorganization which cannot be measured in dollars. These advantages include increased incentives in the service, increased efficiency, and increased cooperation with the public.

XI

Department of Agriculture

Chapter One

ROLE OF DEPARTMENT OF AGRICULTURE

The Department of Agriculture has been a vital and effective agency of Government since its creation in 1862. In the last 20 years the Department has expanded from about 22,000 employees to over 82,000, and expenditures have increased from about $25,800,000 to $834,000,000 in fiscal year 1948.

The net expenditure is less than the previous year due to substantial receipts of the several corporations of the Department. The present outlook is that 1949 expenditures will be greater because of the drop in farm commodity prices which will probably result in increased cash outlays by the Commodity Credit Corporation.

Steady expansion of the functions of the Department has been influenced by a variety of changing conditions. War and depression profoundly affected agricultural activities as did shifts and increases in population and changing relations between Federal and State Governments. Scientific progress in new knowledge of plants and animals, mechanization of farms, more rapid communications, new processing and marketing methods have created new demands on the Department.

Other conditions which have had their effect are distress of individual farmers, new needs for agricultural credit, demand for food and processing inspection, and public interest in the enlarged welfare of the farmers. Expanded activities also include concern with wiser use and conservation of the soil. Changing international markets have been an influence in the widening of functions. This tremendous growth in Government agricultural activities demands administrative reorganization in order to obtain the most effective and economical service for the future.

The Department's function today, as stipulated in various Congressional acts, embraces broad activities. The Commission has directed its efforts not toward evaluating the policies behind these activities, but toward assuring their effective and economical organization.

The major objective of the Department is to promote the national welfare through an improved economic and social status for the farm home and the farm life:

a. By increasing agricultural productivity and improving marketing procedures through scientific research and experiment.

b. By aiding individual farmers with skilled scientific advice.

c. By conserving soil, forests, range, and water resources.

d. By supporting farm prices so that the efficient farmer's income maintains a parity in relation to other industries.

e. By protecting producers and consumers of agricultural and related products through regulation of markets and inspection of quality.

f. By giving credit assistance and protection to the farmers.

Chapter Two

THE BASIS OF REORGANIZATION

Deficiencies of the Department

Our task force on agricultural activities enumerates the following faults in the organization of the Department:

a. Its rapid growth has resulted in some 20 different offices reporting directly to the Secretary, causing an unnecessary diffusion of authority.

b. The Department has grown to its present size without sufficient integration of its parts and with considerable overlap and duplication. It is a loose confederation of independent bureaus and agencies.

c. There are agricultural activities in other parts of the Government which overlap and duplicate those of the Department of Agriculture.

d. The Cooperative Extension Service established by the Federal Government and the States for educational purposes is being increasingly bypassed by several of the bureaus and agencies of the Department.

e. With the rapid growth of new activities, many field organizations at State and county levels have developed. Their work results in duplications, overlappings, and often conflicting policies. They confuse and multiply the difficulties of the farmer in his relations to the Department.

f. The Department has organized a variety of local advisory committees at the county level, and their members tend to become local administrators of uncoordinated agencies instead of advisors.

g. The inspection of agricultural products for protection of the consumer and the farmer is scattered through many agencies of the Government, and the resulting confusion requires producers and manufacturers to comply with regulations issued by agencies of two or more departments or administrations.

b. The present systems of budgeting, treatment of intra-departmental funds, and earmarking of recurring funds have the cumulative effect of obscuring bureau expenditures and of promoting waste.

i. The services and policies of the several Farm Credit Agencies overlap. Their organization is contrary to sound banking principles. Some of them make loans which require costly individual supervision.

The Basis of Reorganization

Our task force on agricultural activities has given a number of important recommendations for reorganization of the Department. The problem of this Commission has been to fit their recommendations and our own views into a general pattern of the Government. In doing this we have at times departed from the views of the task force.

Recommendation No. 1

In general, we recommend an extension of the functional organization of the Department and a better grouping of activities related to the same major purpose.

The purpose is to secure more concentration in the responsibility of direction, elimination of overlap, conflict and waste, and further, to make possible the realization of broad policies in the Department.

The Commission believes this structure is sufficiently flexible to permit programs and activities to be added or dropped without requiring major reorganization. At the same time, with such an organization, the resources of the entire Department can readily and effectively be brought to bear on any problem.

Chapter Three

PROPOSED DEPARTMENTAL STRUCTURE

We have urged in our first report that the foundation of good departmental administration is that the Secretary shall have authority from the Congress to organize and control his organization, and that separate authorities to subordinates be eliminated.

Under our recommendations made elsewhere, we propose a new form of "performance" budget.[1] We propose that the Department will keep its own administrative accounts as prescribed by an Accountant General in the Treasury and subject to an approval of such systems by the Comptroller General and audit by him.[1] The Commission also recommends that personnel recruitment be performed by the Department (except possibly in the lower grades), subject to standards and methods of merit selection to be proposed by the Department, but with the approval and enforcement of the Civil Service Commission.[2] The Commission likewise recommends elsewhere that procurement of supplies should be decentralized into the Department with the exception of items of common use to all Departments, but under standards and methods established by the Office of General Services.[3] Further, we propose that the Department should strengthen its management research unit, working in cooperation with a comparable staff unit under the Office of the Budget.[4]

Recommendation No. 2

We recommend that the present positions of Under Secretary and two Assistant Secretaries be retained and that an additional

---

[1] Report on the Budgeting and Accounting.
[2] Report on Personnel Management.
[3] Report on the Office of General Services.
[4] Report on General Management of the Executive Branch.

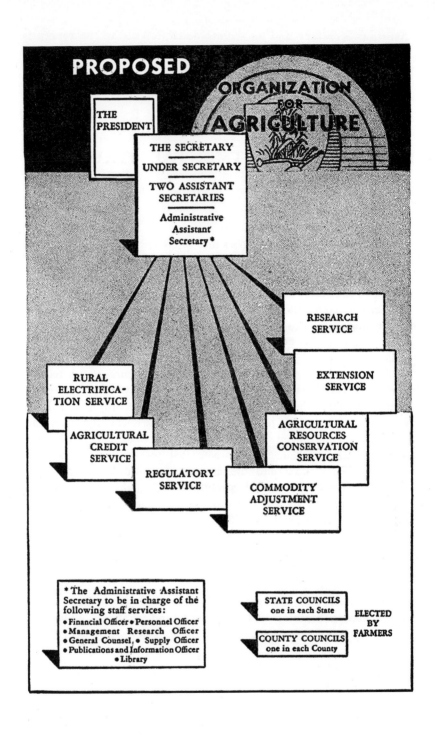

PROPOSED ORGANIZATION FOR AGRICULTURE

THE PRESIDENT

THE SECRETARY
UNDER SECRETARY
TWO ASSISTANT SECRETARIES
Administrative Assistant Secretary*

RESEARCH SERVICE

EXTENSION SERVICE

RURAL ELECTRIFICATION SERVICE

AGRICULTURAL CREDIT SERVICE

AGRICULTURAL RESOURCES CONSERVATION SERVICE

REGULATORY SERVICE

COMMODITY ADJUSTMENT SERVICE

* The Administrative Assistant Secretary to be in charge of the following staff services:
• Financial Officer • Personnel Officer
• Management Research Officer
• General Counsel, • Supply Officer
• Publications and Information Officer
• Library

STATE COUNCILS
one in each State

COUNTY COUNCILS
one in each County

ELECTED BY FARMERS

Assistant Secretary and an Administrative Assistant Secretary be added. These officials should be appointed by the President, by and with the advice and consent of the Senate, with the possible exception of the Administrative Assistant Secretary. The duties of these officials in supervision of Departmental activities should be assigned by the Secretary. All officials below the Under Secretary and the Assistant Secretaries should, where possible, be appointed from the career service.

It is intended that the Administrative Assistant Secretary should have charge of staff services and should, if possible, be selected from the career service.

The following would, therefore, be top structure of the Department. (See chart.) Part of the structure is already established. We are not, however, recommending a hard and fast rule. The Secretary would determine the organization, be free to amend it and assign the duties of the Assistant Secretaries.

THE SECRETARY OF AGRICULTURE, with his own office staff
THE UNDER SECRETARY OF AGRICULTURE, and his office staff
TWO ASSISTANT SECRETARIES
ADMINISTRATIVE ASSISTANT SECRETARY in charge of staff

The Commission recommends that operational functions of the Department in Washington be grouped into eight major units:

1. STAFF SERVICES
2. RESEARCH SERVICE
3. EXTENSION SERVICE
4. AGRICULTURAL RESOURCES CONSERVATION SERVICE
5. COMMODITY ADJUSTMENT SERVICE
6. REGULATORY SERVICE
7. AGRICULTURAL CREDIT SERVICE
8. RURAL ELECTRIFICATION SERVICE

1. Staff Services

FINANCIAL OFFICER (budgeting, accounting, and disbursements)
PERSONNEL OFFICER
MANAGEMENT RESEARCH OFFICER
GENERAL COUNSEL for legal work outside the Regulatory Service
SUPPLY OFFICER
PUBLICATIONS OFFICER
LIBRARIAN

241

2. Research Service

It is proposed that the basic scientific, economic, and social research activities be brought into a Research Service, and divided into appropriate bureaus, i. e., Crops, Forest and Range, Animals, Structures and Machines, Soil and Water, Human Nutrition and Home Economics, Marketing and Utilization, and Agricultural Economics. It is understood that management and operational research should be conducted by the respective services.

3. Extension Service

This would be a newly constituted Extension Service and not the present Cooperative Extension Service, although it would include the present activities of the latter. It is proposed that the major Federal educational and joint Federal-State educational, demonstrational, and informational activities of the Department be brought into this Service. The Service would cooperate directly with other services of the Department in promoting those phases of their work requiring demonstrational and informational activities.

4. Agricultural Resources Conservation Service

It is proposed that all major soil, range, and forest conservation agencies be brought into an Agricultural Resources Conservation Service.

5. Commodity Adjustment Service

It is proposed that all major agencies having to do with formulation of plans and control of production, together with activities for price support and allocation of quotas, be brought into a Commodity Adjustment Service.

6. Regulatory Service

It is proposed that all regulatory agencies in the Department be brought into a central Regulatory Service.

7. Agricultural Credit Service

Under this division, the Farm Credit Administration as reorganized would be administered, including the functions of the present Farmers Home Administration.

8. Rural Electrification

This would be the present Rural Electrification Administration.

Chapter Four

FIELD ORGANIZATION

Recommendation No. 3

We recommend a thorough overhaul of the organization of the Department, at State, county, and farmer levels.

At the State Level

The State governments operate effective agricultural departments. They have in the past engaged in effective cooperative activities with the Department at State, county, and farmer levels. In recent years, the Department has not taken full advantage of the established and effective State organizations in performing many agricultural programs and has thereby produced some duplication of national and State effort at local levels.

At the County Level

This Commission was unable to conduct a detailed survey of activities at the county level. Sampling inquiries, however, revealed that considerable duplication has developed. For example, 47 employees attached to 7 districts and separate field services of the Department of Agriculture in 1 cotton-producing county in Georgia were working with 1,500 farmers; a fruit and grazing county in the State of Washington has 184 employees of separate field services working with some 6,700 farmers; a dairy county in Maryland had 88 employees attached to these field services working with less than 3,400 farmers. In these and other counties, representatives of each agency frequently advise the same farmers on the same problems. Farmers are confused and irritated, as climaxed in one Missouri county, where a farmer recently received from five different agencies varying advice on the application of fertilizer on his farm. There are many separate field services at the county level. These include the Soil Conservation Service; Extension Service; Farmers Home Administration; Production and Marketing Administration with its conservation payment program and school-lunch program; Farm Credit Administration through its Production Credit Associations and National Farm Loan Associations; and the Rural Electrification Administration. In addition, the Forest Service may be represented by Federal-State farm forest management advisers; the Bureau of Animal Industry by Specialists on animal disease eradication programs; and the Bureau of Entomology and Plant Quarantine by others who work on plant disease eradication and insect control.

Separate from those of the Department of Agriculture, representatives of the Veterans' Administration are usually present to administer the on-farm industrial training program for veterans. The farm labor representatives of the Federal-State Employment Service and Federal-State Department of Agriculture representatives may also be in the field at the county level.

A multitude of county advisory committees of farmers has been created and employed by these various activities at a cost exceeding 5 million dollars a year. These local committees have been given administrative functions. The task force on agricultural activities believes that the local committees should be purely advisory on program formulation and operation. All administrative work should be done by departmental or State employees.

Our task force recommends that only one committee be set up in each county. It estimates their annual cost for the entire Nation need not exceed $700,000.

At the Farmer Level

Recommendation No. 4

We recommend that Department of Agriculture Councils comprising representatives of the several departmental services in each county be organized to exchange information on their programs.

This alone, however, is not sufficient to meet the local problem. As presently administered, each agency representative finds himself more responsible to authority at State or national levels than to the local people. This results in continued independent rather than coordinated action. Furthermore, present fragmentary agricultural services at county level which too often reflect the highly specialized divisions within the existing departmental organizations, can be partly corrected by the functional reorganization proposed herein.

The first step toward unified national and State agricultural cooperation is to prepare a unified program in the Department of Agriculture; and this unity may best be achieved by reorganization of the Department along functional lines.

Recommendation No. 5

In view of the widespread activities of the State governments in agriculture, the Commission recommends that, except in the most unusual circumstances, activities that are services to individual farmers should be administered in the field by departmental employees through offices based on the States as units. The services at county levels and to farmer units should be so merged as to reduce the number of duplicating and unnecessary employees, with due regard to avoiding divided authority.

Recommendation No. 6

We recommend the establishment of one State Council in each State, and one County Council in each agricultural county, as aids to orderly operations in the field.

Replacing all present Federal committees and boards, these councils should be elected by the farmers of the counties and States through properly prescribed procedures. The members of these councils should receive no compensation, but should be reimbursed for out-of-pocket expenses when properly authorized.

All programs of the Department to be carried out at State and county levels should be cleared through the appropriate councils. These councils should be advisory. All programs should be presented to, and considered by, them, but it is not the sense of this recommendation that they should have "veto power."

Chapter Five

FURTHER RECOMMENDATIONS

Federal Research Stations

There are numerous and effectively administered joint Federal-State research stations now in existence. Efforts of the Department should be directed toward strengthening this existing system in lieu of diffusing and dissipating its efforts in erecting duplicate or overlapping stations.

Where the work of stations or substations has been completed or is being duplicated elsewhere, careful study should be made to determine the manner of their disposal. Any station listed by the Department for disposal, but deemed essential by a State, should be transferred to the State under terms deemed mutually fair.

Recommendation No. 7

In the future, new Federal agricultural research stations should generally be established only where existing joint Federal-State facilities cannot be developed to fill the need.

Conservation Payments

Recommendation No. 8

We recommend that Conservation payments to a farmer should be restricted to those which will bring about the adoption of complete and balanced conservation programs on his farm.

They should not be used as income supplements in disguise. When the conservation plan on any farm has been completed, such payments to the owner should stop.

Adjustment Programs

Conditions of imbalance in agricultural production are present in varying degrees and to varying extents in the Nation. Adjustment programs should be ready to operate in the event of imbalance in either domestic or foreign demand for specific agricultural products. This should apply to surpluses as well as shortages.

Recommendation No. 9

We recommend that adjustment programs with respect to commodities and commodity groups should be operated on a stand-by, rather than a continuous basis.

Inspection Costs

Recommendation No. 10

To obtain economy and efficiency, this Commission recommends that inspection costs on farm products, when imposed for the benefit and protection of the general public, be paid by the Federal Government. Inspection and grading services primarily for the benefit or protection of producers or processors should be paid for by the producers or processors.

Customs Receipts

Some years ago the Congress granted to the Department of Agriculture the use of 30 percent of certain customs receipts for various purposes. Under this arrangement both the responsibility of Congress for appropriations and Government accounting are obscured. This Commission believes it critical that the Congress reestablish its obligation to appropriate all public moneys.

Recommendation No. 11

We recommend that customs receipts now allotted directly to the Department be paid into the Treasury and that direct annual appropriations be made by the Congress for specified purposes.

Agricultural Credit Activities

Many problems arise from the maze of agricultural credit agencies. Our task force on agricultural activities has made several constructive recommendations with respect to their organization and administration.

The agricultural credit agencies here concerned are:

THE FEDERAL LAND BANKS
THE PRODUCTION CREDIT CORPORATION
THE BANKS FOR COOPERATIVES
THE FEDERAL INTERMEDIATE CREDIT BANKS
THE FARMERS HOME ADMINISTRATION
THE RURAL ELECTRIFICATION ADMINISTRATION
THE FEDERAL CROP INSURANCE CORPORATION
AGRICULTURE DEPARTMENT DISASTER LOANS
COMMODITY CREDIT CORPORATION

In Liquidation:

THE REGIONAL AGRICULTURAL CREDIT CORPORATIONS
THE AGRICULTURAL MARKET ACT REVOLVING FUND
THE JOINT STOCK-LAND BANKS
THE FEDERAL FARM MORTGAGE CORPORATION

The Government has an investment of about 2 billion dollars in these agencies. Current loans approximate 3,500 million dollars as compared with lending authorizations of nearly 7 billion dollars. Borrowings from private sources included in the above total authorization have been utilized to the extent of approximately 1,200 million dollars.

The Commission recommends in its report on Business Enterprises of the Government a number of requirements which apply in part to the above agencies.

These recommendations are designed to strengthen and simplify the agriculture credit structure and to bring about savings of capital and expenditures. The administration cost to the Federal Government of these agencies might be reduced by more than 36 million dollars and much larger sums can be saved by better organized lending activities.

Irrigation Projects

Long-continued friction between the Bureau of Reclamation in the Department of the Interior and the Department of Agriculture has marked the planning and operation of irrigation projects. At times, as in 1945, proposed programs have gone to Congress before the Department of Agriculture knew about them. The Department should have an opportunity to comment on all irrigation projects from the point of view of agricultural needs.

Recommendation No. 12

We recommend that the Department of Agriculture be required to report to the President and the Congress on all irrigation or reclamation projects about their use or timeliness.

Regulation of Food Products to Protect Consumer

There are some 21 legislative acts bearing on the purity of food and drugs, standards and grades of products, etc.:

The Department is vested with regulatory authority to grade various agricultural products. It is directed to inspect meat, animal virus serum, toxins, insectides, and seeds. It also supervises the standardization of containers.

The Federal Security Agency, under the Food and Drug Acts, regulates the branding of wool and fibre products.
poisonous ingredients of foods, and various milk requirements. In addition, it regulates drugs, virus serum, and toxins for human use.

The Federal Trade Commission administers regulations against false advertising of foods, drugs, therapeutic devices, and cosmetics. It regulates the adulteration of foods, standards of containers, tolerances of

The Bureau of Internal Revenue in the Treasury administers the taxes on oleomargarine for food purposes, the prohibitory taxes on renovated butter, and on filled cheese.

Many of these authorities were once in the Department of Agriculture. Their separation from other departmental activities in these fields creates great overlap and also confuses the public. The Department is much better equipped for research on these matters.

A few random examples of confusion are :

Requirements for labeling and advertising of foods and drugs should be substantially identical; the same misrepresentations are likely to occur in both labeling and advertising and should be dealt with at the same time. Labeling is handled by the Federal Security Agency and advertising by the Federal Trade Commission with diverse requirements enforced through diverse procedures.

Many chemicals have multiple uses. Insectides or rodenticides are regulated under the Federal Security Agency, while insectides, fungicides, and rodenticides are inspected also by the Department of Agriculture. Likewise, single-use products such as disinfectants, mold preventives, or products for treatment of fungicidal skin diseases, may fall within both departments.

Viruses, serums, and toxins for human use are regulated by the Federal Security Agency, while their animal uses are regulated by Agriculture.

Voluntary standards for grading fruits, vegetables, and other agricultural products to facilitate trade transactions are extended by the Department through educational processes to the consumer, and yet are at variance with standards for foods developed for consumer protection by the Federal Security Agency.

Adulteration of meat and other food products falls under the Meat Inspection Act administered by the Department of Agriculture and also under the Food and Drug laws administered by the Federal Security Agency.

There are innumerable illustrations of what happens to the producer. As a result, a manufacturer of a rat poison containing strychnine must comply with regulations of the Department of Agriculture, while the same or another manufacturer of a pharmaceutical product using strychnine as a drug must comply with regulations administered by the Federal Security Agency.

Recommendation No. 13

This Commission recommends that all regulatory functions above relating to food products be transferred to the Department of Agriculture and that those relating to other products be placed under a reorganized Drug Bureau administered by the public health agency.

We believe, as does our task force, that the Department of Agriculture will be vigorous in the protection of consumer interest.

A summary of the laws dealing with these subjects is attached in Annex II.

Transfer of Bureaus from Other Departments

Certain major questions of functions to be included in this Department, or removed to other departments of the Government, have necessitated major conclusions by this Commission.

There has been a long and wasteful conflict and overlap between certain soil conservation, range, forest, and allied services due to the division of their functions between the Department of Agriculture and the Department of Interior.

One of the important areas of duplication relates to the management of the forest and range lands of the public domain. The Forest Service, the Bureau of Land Management, and, in some areas, the Soil Conservation Service operate on adjacent or intermingled Federal land areas under different statutory and administrative policies. Many ranchers run their livestock on both the national forest pastures and lands in public grazing districts. They must obtain separate permits with different terms and conditions from the different Federal agencies, and their grazing resources and livestock plans must be reviewed by each agency.

A similar situation prevails on Federal forest lands. The Forest Service and the Bureau of Land Management administer these lands under different policies. The most striking case is the intermingled or adjacent timber on some 2½ million acres, scattered in checkerboard fashion along both sides of the Willamette Valley in the heart of the Douglas fir region of western Oregon. On these revested Oregon and California railroad company lands, the Bureau of Land Management conducts a program of forest management which parallels, but differs in important details from the one long in force on the intermingled national forests. Two sets of regional and local forest officers carry on these duplicating programs.

The conflict extends to payments made to local governments in lieu of taxes normally collectible on privately owned lands. The Bureau of Land Management at present must return 50 percent, and ultimately 75 percent of gross revenues from the "O and C Lands" to local governments, while the Forest Service is required to return only 25 percent of the gross revenues from the national forest lands.

Those conflicting, confusing and duplicating activities of the two agencies concerned present problems which call for basic organizational changes.

Recommendation No. 14

Our three task forces on Agriculture, Natural Resources, and Public Works all urgently recommend the consolidation of these agencies. It has been urged for many years by students of government. The Commission agrees with this recommendation.

The task force on agricultural activities urgently recommends that these consolidated activities be placed in the Department of Agriculture. Our task force on natural resources urgently recommends that they be transferred to the Department of the Interior or its successor.

Recommendation No. 15

This Commission believes that logic and public policy require that

major land agencies be grouped in the Department of Agriculture. It recommends that the land activities of the Department of the Interior, chiefly the public domain (except mineral questions) and the Oregon and California revested lands be transferred to the Department of Agriculture and that the water-development activities (except the local farm supply of water) be transferred to the Department of the Interior.

Management Survey

Recommendation No. 16

We recommend that on completion of the organization of the Department, as contemplated in this report, the Secretary of Agriculture institute immediately a comprehensive management survey to determine further savings, and to eliminate facilities, stations, and offices that duplicate facilities and work otherwise conducted by the Department or the States.

Recommendations resulting from such a survey should be made prior to submission of the budget estimate for the fiscal year 1951.

Chapter Six

CONCLUSIONS

These recommendations, if accepted, would result in the elimination of overlap and conflict. They are designed to give greater efficiency and economy to the administration of the Department. Estimates, which are admittedly approximations, have been made of the amounts which might be saved by taking the actions recommended. The tabulation of our task force on agricultural activities reveals that the total specific annual savings in operating expenses by functional reorganization, as estimated by the task force, amount to over 44 million dollars.

Further, by adoption of our recommendations as to credit agencies an annual saving of more than 36 million dollars can be made to the Government, the Government losses on loans can be lessened, and the Government capital now employed by lending agencies can be reduced.

Consequential returns can be made to the Treasury of funds now in the hands of agricultural credit agencies, and by the reduction of borrowing authorities.

This Commission believes useless duplication to the citizen will be eliminated, and economy to both the Government and the citizen will result from these recommendations.

Annex I

STATEMENT OF VIEWS
SUPPORTING THE CONSOLIDATION OF
LAND MANAGEMENT FUNCTIONS

For many years the Department of the Interior has administered certain portions of the public domain and related activities whereas the national forests have been the responsibility of the Department of Agriculture. This division of responsibility for closely allied activities between two departments has resulted in long and wasteful conflict and, at times, outright duplication of functions.

After careful study of this problem our task force on agriculture activities and our task force on natural resources have concluded that these land management functions of the Federal Government should be united in a single agency if the present wasteful competition is to be eliminated. In support of this conclusion our committee on natural resources states:

. . . The committee feels that one of the important areas of duplication in Government organization relates to management of the forest and range lands of the public domain. The Forest Service, the Bureau of Land Management and, in some areas of the West, the Soil Conservation Service, operate adjacent or intermingled Federal land areas under differing statutory and administrative policies, despite the frequent similarity of the adjacent grazing resources. Many ranchers run their livestock on both the national forest pastures and the grazing districts. They must obtain separate permits with differing terms and conditions from the Federal agencies each of which must review their grazing resources and livestock plans. In the intermountain region centered in Ogden County, Utah, there are many areas where ranchers own the

255

valley lands and the Forest Service manages the high altitude forests and grazing lands, while the Bureau of Land Management administers the area of land lying in between the two. All are used for grazing livestock at certain periods of the year. Each agency establishes its own fees, and different standards are used to determine the number of livestock that can be fed on a given area.

A similar situation applies in the handling of Federal forest lands. The Forest Service and the Bureau of Land Management administer these lands under differing policies. The most striking case is the intermingled or adjacent timber on some $2\frac{1}{2}$ million acres, scattered in checkerboard fashion along both sides of the Willamette Valley in the heart of the Douglas fir region of western Oregon. On these O and C lands the Bureau of Land Management conducts a program of forest management which parallels that long in force on the intermingled national forests. Two sets of regional and local forest officers carry on these duplicating programs.

The conflict extends to payments made in lieu of taxes normally collectible on privately owned lands. The Bureau of Land Management at present must return 50 percent, and ultimately 75 percent of gross revenues from O and C lands to local governments, while the Forest Service is required to return only 25 percent of the gross revenues from national forest lands.

These problems of conflicting, confusing, and duplicating activities of the bureaus concerned call for basic organizational changes. . . .

The committee firmly believes that in the interest of good stewardship, the forests and range lands of the public domain, for the most part adjacent or intermingled, should be under the jurisdiction of one agency which can be charged with responsibility for developing a consistent over-all program of administration. . . .

The views of the committee on agriculture activities have been summarized by Dean Rusk, chairman of the committee, as follows:

The responsibilities of the Government for diverse land management functions on the same land or in similar areas cannot be successfully discharged unless a high degree of coordination and integration of policies, personnel, and action are maintained. The intelligent use and conservation of our vital land resources, whether for the production of grass, trees, or other crops, or used by cattle, sheep, or wildlife, involve overlapping and interdependent management procedures which cannot be separated and successfully carried out by unrelated administrative departments of Government.

These views have been shared by many others who have been well acquainted with the problem. For example, the Secretary of Agriculture in his report for 1938 states:

. . . There are no separate problems of forestry, of wildlife conservation, of grazing, of soil conservation, or of rational crop adjustment. There is one unified land-use problem, of which forestry, grazing, crop adjustment, and so forth are merely aspects. This problem involves the institutions; it has to do with social and economic conditions, as well as with the physical problems of crop, livestock, and timber production, and of soil and water conservation. Research and action programs must fit together, and come into a dynamic focus on the farm and on the watershed. Equally important, they must mesh with urban policy. Not otherwise can we attain the full efficient use in town and country of all our human and material resources.

Dr. Milton Eisenhower, president of Kansas State College of Agriculture and Applied Science, has summarized the argument for consolidation as follows:

. . . The Natural Resources report properly stresses the interdependence in use of the checkerboard forest and range lands of the West and properly advises unified administration. The agriculture report will . . . agree with this. But the agriculture report will surely go on to say with equal validity that publicly owned forest and range lands are checkerboarded with privately owned and operated ranch lands; that the private operator uses all three classes of land as a unit in managing his livestock operations; and that, if sound results are to be obtained . . . all Federal policies and programs bearing upon the user's business must be consistent. This argues for a unification of Federal services to land users, whether the lands be publicly or privately owned.

Annex II

LEGISLATION ON REGULATION OF FOOD PRODUCTS AND DRUGS

DEPARTMENT OF AGRICULTURE

The Department of Agriculture administers the following acts:

1. *Meat Inspection Act of 1907:* Sanitary requirements for slaughtering, packing, meat-canning, and similar plants; ante mortem inspection of live animals and post mortem inspection of carcasses at such plants for fitness for food; use of dyes and preservatives in meats; labeling of canned meat and meat food products.

2. *Horse Meat Act of 1919:* Requirement that horse meat and horse meat products be so labeled.

3. *Imported Meat Act* (sec. 306, Tariff Act of 1930): Prohibition against importation of meat unfit for food or from countries with rinderpest or foot-and-mouth diseases.

4. *Animal Virus, Serum, and Toxin Act of 1913:* Licensing and regulation of establishments for preparation of animal viruses, serums, and toxins, and of the importation of such products.

5. *Federal Insecticide, Fungicide, and Rodenticide Act of 1947:* Adulteration, misbranding, and informative labeling of economic poisons for control of weeds, insects, rodents, fungi, and other pests except viruses on man or animals; registration of economic poisons. Farmers are probably the largest group of consumers interested.

6. *Federal Seed Act of 1939:* Adulteration, unfitness, misbranding, informative labeling, and false advertising of agricultural and vegetable seeds for seeding purposes; staining seeds for place of origin. Farmers are the primary group of consumers interested.

7. *Standard Containers Acts of 1916 and 1928:* Standard climax

baskets, hampers, round-stave baskets, splint baskets, and half-pint, pint, and quart, and multiple-quart baskets for fruits and vegetables and mushrooms; approval of manufacturers' specifications for hampers, round-stave and splint baskets.

FOOD AND DRUG ADMINISTRATION

The Food and Drug Administration of the Federal Security Agency administers the following acts:

8. *Food, Drug and Cosmetic Act of 1938:* Adulteration, misbranding, and informative labeling of foods, beverages, compendia drugs, other drugs, therapeutic devices, and cosmetics; a definition and standard of identity, a standard of quality, and standards of fill of containers for any food; tolerances for added poisonous ingredients to foods; certification of coal-tar colors for foods, drugs, and cosmetics; emergency permit control of producers of contaminated foods; inspection of sea-food plants; permits for new drugs; and certification of strength, quality, and purity of insulin, penicillin, and streptomycin. "Food" includes beverages, and "food" and "drug" include those for animals as well as for man.

9. *Caustic Poison Act of 1927:* "Poison" and antidote statements on consumer packages of caustic poisons.

10. *Imported Milk Act of 1927:* Sanitary requirements for fluid milk imported from Canada.

11. *Filled Milk Act of 1923:* Prohibition against combining fats or oils with milk, cream, or skimmed milk so that resulting product is an imitation.

12. *Tea Importation Act of 1883:* Prohibition of importation of tea below established standards of quality.

FEDERAL TRADE COMMISSION

The Federal Trade Commission administers the following acts:

13. *Wheeler-Lea Amendment, Federal Trade Commission Act:* False advertising of foods, drugs, therapeutic devices, and cosmetics.

14. *Wool Products Labeling Act of 1939:* Misbranding of wool and specialty fiber products.

PUBLIC HEALTH SERVICE

The Public Health Service of the Federal Security Agency administers the following acts:

15. *Human Virus, Serum, and Toxin* (*Biologics*) *Act of 1944:* Licensing of manufacturers of viruses, serums, toxins, antitoxins, and analogous products for treatment of man; misbranding and informative labeling of such products.

BUREAU OF INTERNAL REVENUE

The Bureau of Internal Revenue of the Treasury Department administers the following acts:

16. *Oleomargarine Act of 1886:* Tax on oleomargarine and prohibitory tax on yellow oleomargarine.

17. *Adulterated and Process or Renovated Butter Act of 1886:* Prohibitory tax on adulterated and process or renovated butter. Also the Secretary of Agriculture administers provisions for the sanitary inspection of renovated butter factories and for the labeling of process or renovated butter and for the confiscation of such butter found to contain materials deleterious to health or unwholesome.

18. *Filled Cheese Act of 1896:* Tax on filled cheese and labeling requirements.

19 and 20. *Harrison Antinarcotic Act and Marijuana Act:* Taxes on various narcotics and control of distribution.

21. *Section 5* (*2*) *and* (*f*) *of Federal Alcohol Administration Act:* Labeling and advertising and standards of fill of containers for alcoholic beverages.

XII
Department of the Interior

Chapter One

ROLE OF DEPARTMENT OF THE INTERIOR

We propose that the Department of the Interior be given more clearly the mission of development of subsoil and water resources. As these activities require large public works, we recommend that other major public works also be managed by this Department.

The organization of a department somewhat along the lines we recommend, and in which would be concentrated the major construction activities of the Federal Government, was proposed by the Joint Congressional and Presidential Committee on Reorganization of 1924, again in a Presidential message during 1932, and again by the President's Committee on Administrative Management of 1937. A partial accomplishment was represented in the Federal Works Agency, established in 1939 and embracing a number of these activities. Had such a department been created 25 years ago, hundreds of millions of dollars would have been saved to the public over these years. Today it is a complete necessity.

The magnitude of the problem is indicated by the fact that 1949 appropriations, for the agencies which we propose to bring together, exceed $1.3 billion. To complete the works now in construction will call for over $5.5 billion, and projects authorized by the Congress but not yet started will call for $7.3 billion more. In addition to these totals of over $15 billion, there are projects contemplated which exceed $30 billion. Approximately 100,000 persons are now employed in these agencies, plus other thousands by the contractors. (See chart.)

Phases of this problem have been investigated for this Commission by our task forces on Public Works, Natural Resources, and Agricultural Activities.

The Commission has the duty of assessing the weight of the recommendations of these able men, reconciling their differences and working out a pattern of action.

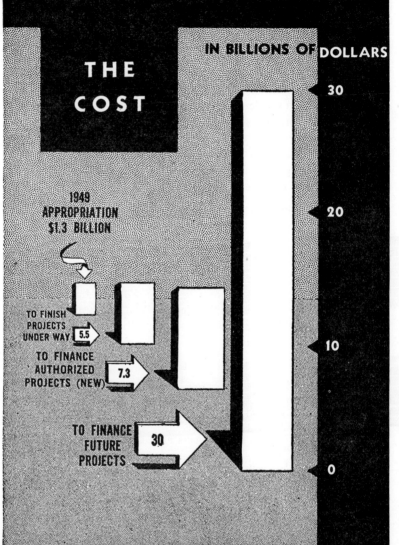

FEDERAL CONSTRUCTION

THE
COST

IN BILLIONS OF DOLLARS

30

1949
APPROPRIATION
$1.3 BILLION

20

TO FINISH
PROJECTS
UNDER WAY   5.5

TO FINANCE
AUTHORIZED
PROJECTS (NEW)   7.3

10

TO FINANCE
FUTURE
PROJECTS   30

0

Board of Impartial Analysis

There is no adequate check in the Government upon the validity or timing of development projects and their relation to the economy of the country.

Recommendation No. 1

We therefore recommend the creation of a Board of Impartial Analysis for Engineering and Architectural Projects which shall review and report to the President and the Congress on the public and economic value of project proposals by the Department. The Board should also periodically review authorized projects and advise as to progress or discontinuance. The Board should comprise five members of outstanding abilities in this field and should be appointed by the President and included in the President's office.

This board should review projects not only from a technical point of view but also in their relation to the economy of the country.

Some effort has been made by the Office of the Budget to review projects but it has been without adequate staff and support. Forty-two projects objected to by the Office were nonetheless presented to Congress by the sponsoring agencies and 36 were authorized. The need for more exhaustive investigation and report than that provided by the Office of the Budget is indicated by the statement of our task force on Natural Resources, quoted below:

. . . this clearance procedure has not been as effective as it ought to be . . . project reports are submitted for review only after they are completed and long after plans have been publicized. It is then too late for effective coordination, and generally even too late to prevent authorization by Congress of projects found not feasible or not fully reconciled. The Corps of Engineers generally makes no effort to change a completed report when informed by the Budget Bureau that the report is not in accord with the President's program. The Corps submits the report to Congress with its favorable recommendation, but accompanied by a statement as to the advice received from the Budget Bureau. Furthermore, the Budget Bureau does not have the staff to make a thorough review of all projects. . . . Finally, the task of review is vastly complicated by the presentation of conflicting plans or views by the Corps of Engineers and the Bureau of Reclamation. Confronted with the completed, conflicting plans of two development agencies, working from the vaguest sort of statutory and administrative standards of feasibility and of benefit-cost evaluation, and operating with two professional staff members, the Budget Bureau as now staffed obviously cannot provide a fully adequate review . . .

To the end that only economically feasible projects shall be instituted by the resource agencies and especially by the Water Development Service, the establishment . . . of a Board of Coordination and Review with responsibility for reviewing and coordinating plans for each major project from the time it is first proposed; for making certain that only projects which are economically and socially justifiable are recommended for approval; and for assuring effective participation by all Federal and State agencies concerned during the formative stage . . .

In the past, projects have been carried through which should never have been undertaken at all. Others have been wastefully constructed, and without regard to important potential uses. Still others have been premature. Bad accounting methods have consistently underestimated costs. Inadequate basic data, interagency competition, and local political pressures bear the primary responsibility for this extravagance and waste . . .

Corrections are relatively easy when plans are gestating, but when they have been perfected by an agency . . . it is often impossible to obtain the revisions which joint investigation or early review could achieve . . .

One result of inadequate evaluation of projects is illustrated by under-estimation of cost when presented to the Congress. Some part of under-estimation is no doubt due to subsequent increase of costs of labor and materials. But some underestimates by the Bureau of Reclamation—such as, for example, the Colorado-Big Thompson Project which increased from $44 million to $131.8 million; the Hungry Horse Project in Montana from $6.3 million to $93.5 million; the Central Valley of California from $170 million to probably over several hundred million—hardly can be explained by increases in labor and material costs.

Our task force on Public Works strongly supports these views:

. . . It would be worth a great deal to the country to have a thorough, factual, unbiased report by the seagreen incorruptibles of the engineering profession on all major construction projects, especially if such a report were couched in plain, ordinary Anglo-Saxon English, understandable by the average layman. We have therefore recommended, as a most important feature of the . . . new Department, a board of three experts to be known as the Board of Impartial Analysis.

Chapter Two

BASIC STRUCTURE OF
THE DEPARTMENT

It has been recommended by some of our task forces that the Department of the Interior be abolished and replaced by a new department. The Interior Department is a century old in national life and has served in many of these fields. Aside from sentiment, the cost of merely changing its name would be considerable. The laws and authorizations under which it acts would require much disentanglement. And there is conflict as to what a new name should be, i. e., "Natural Resources," "Works and Resources," or "Public Works." Altogether it seems to the Commission that a reorganization of the present Department would be preferable.

Recommendation No. 2

We recommend that the Department of the Interior should be thoroughly reorganized along more functional and major purpose lines.

This involves the transfer of certain agencies from the Department and the incorporation of certain agencies within it.

Recommendation No. 3

We recommend that the agencies listed below should be transferred to other offices or Departments, to which they are functionally more closely related:

a. **The Bureau of Indian Affairs to a new department for social security, education, and Indian affairs.**[1]

[1] The reasons are discussed in our report on Social Security, Education, and Indian Affairs.

b. The Bureau of Land Management (except minerals) to the Department of Agriculture.[2]

c. The Commercial Fisheries from the Fish and Wildlife Service to the Department of Commerce.[3]

Recommendation No. 4

We recommend that the following agencies related to the major purposes of the Department be transferred to it:

a. Flood Control and Rivers and Harbors Improvement from the Department of the Army.

b. Public Building Construction from the Federal Works Agency.

c. Community Services from the Federal Works Agency.

d. Certain major construction to be assigned on behalf of other agencies of the Government, except where carried on by grants-in-aid programs.

Over-all Departmental Management

We have urged in our first report [4] that the foundation of good departmental administration is that the Secretary shall have authority from the Congress to organize and control his organization, and that Congressional grants of independent authority to subordinates be eliminated.

Under our recommendations made elsewhere, we propose a new form of "performance" budget for all departments.[5] We also propose that the Department keep its own administrative accounts as prescribed by an Accountant General in the Treasury and subject to an approval of such system by the Comptroller General and audit by him.[5] The Commission also recommends that all personnel recruitment should be decentralized into the Department (except possibly in some lower grade positions common to all departments and agencies), subject to standards and methods of merit selection to be proposed by the Department, but with the approval and enforcement of the Civil Service Commission.[6] The Commission likewise recommends elsewhere that the procurement of supplies peculiar to the Department should be decentralized into the Department under standards and methods established by the proposed Office of General Services. Items of common use will of course be

[2] The reasons are discussed in our report on Agriculture.
[3] The reasons are discussed in our report on the Department of Commerce.
[4] Report on General Management of the Executive Branch.
[5] Report on Budgeting and Accounting.
[6] Report on Personnel Management.

PROPOSED
AGENCY TRANSFERS
TO AND FROM
INTERIOR DEPARTMENT

INDIAN AFFAIRS
to (new)
department
for education and
social security

**LAND
MANAGEMENT**
(Except Minerals)
TO
AGRICULTURE
DEPARTMENT

**COMMERCIAL
FISHERIES**
TO
COMMERCE
DEPARTMENT

**INTERIOR
DEPARTMENT**

**FLOOD CONTROL,
RIVERS & HARBORS**
FROM ● ARMY CORPS
OF ENGINEERS

**GOVERNMENT
TIN SMELTER**
TEXAS CITY, TEXAS
FROM ● RFC

**INVESTIGATIONS OF
NATURAL GAS RESOURCES**
FROM ● FEDERAL POWER
COMMISSION

**COMMUNITY
SERVICES**
FROM ● FEDERAL
WORKS AGENCY

**LEASING OF
MINERAL LANDS**
FROM ● AGRICULTURE
DEPARTMENT

**PUBLIC BUILDING
CONSTRUCTION**
FROM ● FEDERAL
WORKS AGENCY

**CERTAIN MAJOR
CONSTRUCTION
PROJECTS***

*Major land construction work for Coast Guard;
Hospital construction (except projects under grants-in-aid program).
Civilian Airport construction for the proposed Bureau of Civil Aviation in the Department
of Commerce (except projects under grants-in-aid program).

handled by the latter office.[7] Further, we propose that the Department should strengthen its management research unit, working in cooperation with a comparable staff unit under the Office of the Budget.[7]

Departmental Staff

In making the following recommendations as to the assignment of officials and the service grouping of agencies, we are proposing no inflexible rules. The responsibility for these assignments should lie with the Secretary. Parts of such organization are already in force.

Recommendation No. 5

We recommend that the top officials of the Department in addition to the Secretary and his personal assistants should be:

a. UNDER SECRETARY and his personal assistants

b. TWO ASSISTANT SECRETARIES, as at present

c. ADDITIONAL ASSISTANT SECRETARY

d. ADMINISTRATIVE ASSISTANT SECRETARY

e. SOLICITOR

The purpose of creating an Administrative Assistant Secretary is to provide more effective direction of the following departmental staff services:

a. FINANCIAL OFFICE (accounting and budgeting)

b. PERSONNEL

c. SUPPLY

d. MANAGEMENT RESEARCH

e. PUBLICATIONS

f. LIAISON WITH CONGRESS

The officials in charge of these services should not have operational duties. Those duties must lie with the Divisional or Bureau Administrators. These staff officers must needs be linked in their work with the similar officials upon the President's staff. In the case, however, of the Financial Officer, he must coordinate his work with that of the Accountant General in the Treasury and with the Office of the Budget.

[7] Report on an Office of General Services; Supply Activities.

APPOINTMENTS

Recommendation No. 6

We recommend that all officials of the rank of Assistant Secretary and above be appointed by the President and confirmed by the Senate.

We recommend, however, that the Administrative Assistant Secretary preferably be appointed from the career service.

It is essential in building up capable administrative staff in all departments that opportunities for promotion of capable administrative career employees be made as wide as possible.

Recommendation No. 7

The Commission therefore recommends that all officials below the rank of Assistant Secretary be appointed by the Secretary, preferably from the career service.

Major-purpose Grouping of Agencies Proposed for Department

Recommendation No. 8

We recommend as logical and practical the following major-purpose assignments of the reorganized department functions:

WATER DEVELOPMENT AND USE SERVICES

RECLAMATION
RIVERS AND HARBORS IMPROVEMENT
FLOOD CONTROL
BONNEVILLE POWER ADMINISTRATION
SOUTHWESTERN POWER ADMINISTRATION
DIVISION OF POWER

A study should be made as to separation of certain general survey activities from the Federal Power Commission and their inclusion in this department.

BUILDING CONSTRUCTION SERVICES

PUBLIC BUILDING CONSTRUCTION
COMMUNITY SERVICES

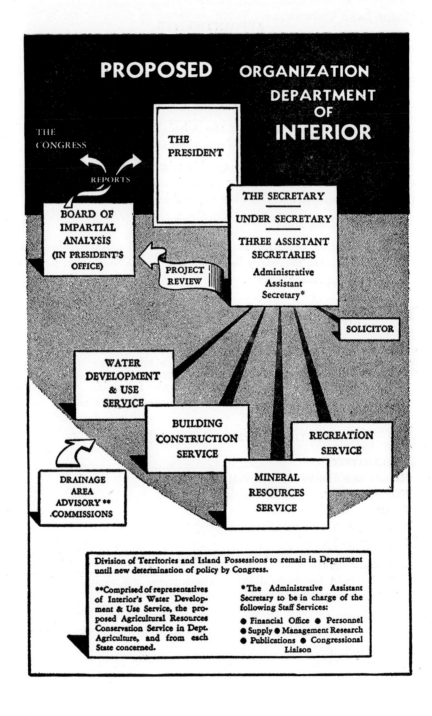

PROPOSED ORGANIZATION
DEPARTMENT OF INTERIOR

THE CONGRESS

REPORTS

THE PRESIDENT

THE SECRETARY
___
UNDER SECRETARY
___
THREE ASSISTANT SECRETARIES

Administrative Assistant Secretary*

BOARD OF IMPARTIAL ANALYSIS
(IN PRESIDENT'S OFFICE)

PROJECT REVIEW

SOLICITOR

WATER DEVELOPMENT & USE SERVICE

BUILDING CONSTRUCTION SERVICE

RECREATION SERVICE

MINERAL RESOURCES SERVICE

DRAINAGE AREA ADVISORY ** COMMISSIONS

Division of Territories and Island Possessions to remain in Department until new determination of policy by Congress.

**Comprised of representatives of Interior's Water Development & Use Service, the proposed Agricultural Resources Conservation Service in Dept. Agriculture, and from each State concerned.

*The Administrative Assistant Secretary to be in charge of the following Staff Services:

● Financial Office ● Personnel
● Supply ● Management Research
● Publications ● Congressional Liaison

MAJOR LAND CONSTRUCTION WORK on behalf of Coast Guard in the Department of Commerce

HOSPITAL CONSTRUCTION on behalf of other departments, except in cases where carried on by grants-in-aid programs

CIVILIAN AIRPORT CONSTRUCTION on behalf of the proposed Bureau of Civil Aviation of the Department of Commerce, except in cases where carried on by grants-in-aid programs

In none of these fields would the Department operate after construction is completed. Moreover, it is not proposed to absorb all construction into the Department solely because it is technical work. Many other agencies will need routine engineering and architectural staffs. We propose for the Department of the Interior only the preparation of plans, awarding of contracts, and supervision and inspection of major construction.

MINERAL RESOURCES SERVICES

GEOLOGICAL SURVEY

BUREAU OF MINES

DIVISION OF OIL AND GAS

ADMINISTRATION OF MINERAL LEASES, TITLE RECORDS, AND RESERVATIONS

LEASING OF MINERAL LANDS (those functions now in the Department of Agriculture)

INVESTIGATIONS INTO NATURAL GAS RESOURCES, from the Federal Power Commission

GOVERNMENT TIN SMELTER at Texas City, Texas, from the Reconstruction Finance Corporation

AN ADVISORY FUNCTION to a score of Federal agencies dealing with minerals, to be established, for better information and elimination of duplicate staffs

RECREATION SERVICES

PUBLIC PARKS AND MONUMENTS

WILDLIFE AND GAME FISHING

TERRITORIES AND POSSESSIONS

It is proposed that the Division of Territories and Island Possessions remain in the Department until some policy is determined by the Congress on the question of our administration of overseas areas. This problem will be treated in our report on the Administration of Overseas Affairs.

Chapter Three

OUR REASONS FOR THESE PROPOSALS

The over-all reasons for these recommendations are:

a. The grouping of those agencies related to the development of natural resources and construction, according to their major purposes, to secure coordinated policies in these fields.

b. Elimination of disastrous conflicts and overlaps which cost the tax-payers enormous sums annually.

c. Provision of a center for more energetic development in water and mineral resources.

d. Establishment of a center for collection of fundamental data upon which water conservation works should be based.

e. Provision of a center for coordination of State and Federal action in these fields.

f. Provision for a center in the Government where engineering advice can be obtained by other agencies of Government.

g. Provision for the Congress of an over-all view of the major construction activities of the Government.

h. Elimination of competition for construction labor and materials.

i. Provision of a center for planning and action of Federal construction to be coordinated with the ebb and flow of employment.

Amplification of these major proposals is given in the following sections of this report.

Planning and Administering Construction to Aid in Preventing Unemployment

A further reason for these proposals lies in the need for long-view planning to meet the ebb and flow of employment.

In times of great employment in private construction, the Government should reduce its work (except for emergency needs) so as not to inflate costs and should save its construction for times of unemployment. Our task force on Public Works states:

. . . The advance planning and promotion of public works for such periods of slack employment should be recognized as a continued responsibility of the Federal Government, working in cooperation with States and municipalities. It is senseless to proceed on the theory that every major slump in business and employment is an unexpected Divine visitation not to be anticipated and to be dealt with only on the basis of ineffective, wasteful, and hastily improvised emergency measures . . .

Public works admittedly can take care of only a fraction of the depression employment problem, but it is an exceedingly important fraction; it is the marginal area in which men out of work will stew around helplessly unless the Government is ready to meet their problem . . .

At the present time there is a short supply of construction labor and materials. They are urgently needed for national defense, for housing, and for current construction in private industry. In these circumstances the agencies enumerated here should carry on the minimum nonpostponable work, should undertake no new projects, but should have blueprints ready for use when unemployment creates a need.

Better Organization in Water Development and Use

The Federal Government's interest in the development of our water resources has been constant since the foundation of the Republic.

At its beginnings, practically all transport was by water. River and canal improvement loomed large in Government interest. With the growth of the railways, the shallow draft channels on canals and rivers became less important.

The development, in modern terms, of our water resources begins with the present century. The systematic deepening of river and lake channels, and the expansion of intercoastal canals, show an increase in annual traffic carried over them to some 22 billion ton miles at the present time. Destructive floods have been lessened by great levee systems, alternate channels, and headwater storage.

The systematic development of irrigation and reclamation began with the Reclamation Act of 1902. Up to 1930 these works were primarily comprised of the easier or less complex types of projects, furnishing water to some 2,790,000 acres of land. Up to that time, some 17 small hydroelectric plants had been built by the Government as an adjunct to irrigation dams with a total installed electrical generating capacity of about 226,000 kilowatts. All of these electrical byproduct enterprises were operated by irrigation districts or under lease.

CHANGED PATTERN OF DEVELOPMENT

With the Hoover Dam in 1930, there began an enlargement of the water development concept. This new concept entailed the storage of water by large dams which would serve the multiple purposes of navigation, flood control, irrigation, and byproduct hydroelectric power.

In setting up the financial organization of these multiple-purpose projects, the Federal Government has established certain policies. Because flood control and navigation do not produce revenues, the portion of the capital cost attributable to them has been set aside as irrecoverable. Because other features, including irrigation, power, and domestic water, do produce revenue, a portion of the outlay is allocated in various amounts as recoverable by the Government.

The following are the active agencies engaged in this field:

BUREAU OF RECLAMATION
THE ARMY CORPS OF ENGINEERS
THE BONNEVILLE POWER ADMINISTRATION
THE SOUTHWESTERN POWER ADMINISTRATION

SCOPE OF ELECTRIC OPERATIONS

These operations by the Government, including those also of the Tennessee Valley Authority, have attained great magnitude.

By June 30, 1947, there had been constructed or purchased 46 hydroelectric and 10 steam power plants of an installed generating capacity of 4,909,582 kilowatts. There were 37 additional plants in construction with a capacity of 8,481,400 kilowatts.

Construction authorized by the Congress contemplates 79 more plants of a capacity of about 6,842,655 kilowatts. Thus, in, say, 1960 when these 172 plants are in full operation, they will have a capacity of about 20,233,637 kilowatts.

The transmission lines now exceed 14,000 miles.

The total installed electrical generating capacity in the Nation in June 1947, owned by private enterprise, municipalities, and the Federal Government, was about 52,000,000 kilowatts. Allowing for increased installation of private and municipal plants during the next 5 years, plants of the Federal Government will be producing probably 15 or 20 percent of the power supply of the whole country by that time.

The total expenditure of the Federal Government on these multiple-purpose projects is roughly estimated at $3.7 billion as of June 30, 1948. Probably $4 billion will be required for completion of those in construction and authorized. Beyond the above-mentioned plants already authorized, there are several hundred other possible plants listed as feasible. They may or may not be constructed. The further plants thus listed, if constructed, would involve an expenditure of over $35 billion and would have an installed generating capacity about equal to the whole of the actual capacity of the country in June 1947.

The multiple-purpose dams constructed or planned are situated in many States. Those of the Corps of Engineers are in 37 States, in every part of the country—New England, the Middle West, the South, and the Mountain and Western States. The Bureau of Reclamation projects lie in 17 States, in the Western, Mountain, and Southwestern areas. These services have projects in 14 of the same States. Other Government agencies, such as the Tennessee Valley Authority or Bonneville Power Administration, have projects which will produce or distribute hydroelectric power in many of the same States in which either the Bureau of Reclamation or the Corps of Engineers, or both, operate.

The Bureau of Reclamation

The Bureau of Reclamation has constructed, or now has under construction, and operates or manages multiple-purpose projects directed mainly to electric power and irrigation purposes. These projects have supplementary effects upon flood control and navigation.

The installed capacity of electric power in these projects is at present about 1,465,400 kilowatts and projects in construction or authorized, 4,181,837 kilowatts.

The Bureau of Reclamation, which employs about 17,000 persons, was created in June 1902. Its original financial support was derived from the disposal of public lands in 16 Western States and Territories (and, after 1906, Texas), and was to be used for irrigation and reclamation of arid lands in those States. In 1920, Congress added the royalties and other income received by the Government from certain minerals, including oil, on the public domain. In the same year Congress provided that 65 percent of the Government receipts from water-power licenses for use of public lands should be added to the Reclamation Fund.

Our task forces estimate that, from the inception of the fund until June 30, 1949, the Fund will have received from the United States Treasury a total of over $1,234,000,000, and from sales of public lands and its hydroelectric power, irrigation, and other revenues, a total of over $546,000,000, or an aggregate sum of over $1,777,000,000. The financial statements of the fund do not permit full analysis, but it appears that, by June 30, 1949, the Reclamation Fund will have expended on construction of projects up to date over $1,530,000,000; and further great sums are required to complete works already under construction.

Irrigation

As we have said, at the time the great multiple-purpose projects were inaugurated the easier projects of irrigation had been largely completed and were furnishing water to about 2,790,000 acres. In the 18 years since that time, about 1,500,000 acres of additional soil have been brought under irrigation with perhaps 550,000 acres more benefiting indirectly from the water supplied by the multiple-purpose projects.

The Congress, in setting up the irrigation system, provided that the farmers should repay the costs of the system without interest added to the cost during construction, or subsequent interest on the cost. Experience has shown, however, that even with this indirect subsidy of interest, these projects, on the average, do not pay off, as the capital cost is too great (with a few exceptions) for the farmers to bear. It is simply accepted that the national advantage of more farm homes and more national productivity are advantages which will offset Government losses.

U. S. Army Corps of Engineers

This agency engages in flood control and river and harbor improvements. Since 1902, the Government has appropriated over $6 billion and actually expended over $5 billion on these projects. The recommended appropriation for fiscal year 1950 is $754,423,700. The estimated cost of completion of authorized projects is about $3.2 billion. The staff for civilian functions consists of some 200 Regular Army

ARMY STAFF FOR RIVER PROJECTS

● 200 ARMY ENGINEERS
● 50,000 CIVILIANS

41,000
OTHER
CIVILIAN
EMPLOYEES

9,000
CIVILIAN
ENGINEERS

200
ARMY
ENGINEERS

engineers, about 9,000 civilian engineers, and some 41,000 other employess.

In improvement of flood control and navigation the Corps of Engineers has constructed, and is engaged in constructing, numbers of multiple-purpose dams of which electrical power is one important byproduct. These installations thus become Government business enterprises of importance. The business of marketing the power from Engineer Corps installations in certain instances is managed by the Department of the Interior, as in the cases of Bonneville Power Administration and Southwestern Power Administration. Generally this is the case in the Western and Southwestern States.

Outside these areas, the Engineers have under construction or authorized about 20 hydroelectric power plants of a total installed capacity of over 1,400,000 kilowatts and a total cost of over $500 million, a portion of which costs will be assigned to power.

Defects in Organization of Water Development and Use

There are glaring defects in the organization of these services in the Government.

a. There is no effective agency for the screening and review of proposed projects to determine their economic and social worth. There is no effective review of the timing of the undertaking of these projects in relation to the economic need or financial ability of the Nation to build them. We have dealt with this subject earlier.

b. There is duplication and overlap of effort, and policy conflicts exist between the Army Engineers and the Bureau of Reclamation in construction of, and jurisdiction over, projects.

c. There is an inherent conflict between the most efficient operation of storage dams for the purpose of flood control and of dams used for the generation of hydroelectric power. Flood control requires empty storage space prior to the high-water season, the storage of water during the flood season, and the emptying of the dams during dry spells. The generation of hydroelectric power needs as nearly an even flow of water as is possible the year around. And the irrigation cycle, which requires storage of water in the winter months and its release in the summer, conflicts with the continuous flow of water required for electrical operation. As flood-control concepts are in the hands of one agency of the Government and power concepts in another, there is inevitable conflict

280

of the highest importance in design and operation, which can be solved only by a consolidated administration.

d. There is considerable doubt as to the proper assignment of capital costs as between irrecoverable costs attributable to flood control and navigation, on the one hand; and recoverable capital to be reimbursed from reclamation and sale of water and power, on the other.

e. The Federal laws in respect to the Bureau of Reclamation, embracing some 803 pages, are indefinite, complex, and contradictory.

f. There is no uniformity of principles guiding Congressional authorization of these projects. Some are authorized under the Reclamation Acts, some under the Flood Control Acts, and some projects have been created by individual legislation.

g. In their hydroelectric power and irrigation aspects, these agencies are essentially Government business enterprises. They are subject to many deficiencies and they lack flexibility of management, budgeting, accounting, and audit which successful business enterprises require.

Elimination of Disastrous Conflicts and Overlaps

One of the major reasons for grouping these agencies into the Department of the Interior is the elimination of disastrously wasteful conflict. Our task force on Natural Resources discusses the conflicts on water development and use as follows:

. . . The function of river development is a multiple-purpose one, cutting across many of the unifunctional agencies. Experience has shown that parceling out river-development responsibilities among these functional agencies produces endless confusion and conflict. A plan for the development of a river basin cannot be devised by adding together the special studies and the separate recommendations of unifunctional agencies concerned respectively with navigation, flood control, irrigation, land drainage, pollution abatement, power development, domestic and industrial water supply, fishing, and recreation. These varied and sometimes conflicting purposes must be put together and integrated in a single plan of development . . .

Under conflicting laws, rival Federal agencies compete for taxpayer money in what often appear to be premature and unsound river development projects, duplicating each other's surveys and bidding against each other for local support at national expense . . .

The Corps of Engineers and the Federal Power Commission have broad and overlapping survey authority, on a Nation-wide basis, while a third agency, the Bureau of Reclamation, was having its survey authority extended in scope in the Western States where the public domain was concentrated . . .

Enactment of the Flood Control Act of 1936 marked the beginning of a new era of administrative confusion. In that act primary responsibility for flood protection on the main streams was assigned to the Corps of Engineers, and in the upper watersheds to the Department of Agriculture. The most serious consequence from the standpoint of organization was not the division of flood-control responsibility between the Corps of Engineers and the Department of Agriculture, but the effect on relations between the Corps and the Bureau of Reclamation. As the Corps' original responsibility for navigational improvements was expanded to cover flood control and other purposes incidental or related to flood protective works, and the Bureau's original responsibility for irrigation was expanded to include other potential byproducts of irrigation structure, the one agency working upstream met the other coming down. Now we are witnessing the spectacle of both agencies contending for the authorization, construction, and operation of projects in the same river basins, for example, in the Central Valley, Columbia, and Missouri Basins . . .

Division of responsibility means duplication of surveys and investigations. Elaborate basin-wide surveys and plans have been made in several instances by the Corps of Engineers and the Bureau of Reclamation, in addition to the comprehensive basin surveys made by the Federal Power Commission and the watershed surveys of the Department of Agriculture . . .

Jurisdictional jealousy is inevitable, and costly as well, so long as such organization separation is practiced. Friction therefrom operates as a perpetual drag on efficiency and as a stimulator of group and sectional competition for favoi and undue influence. Without more inclusive operating units, plans are made which see only parts of the whole situation, and wasteful expenditure of funds results, while the total objective which might have been attained is only partly realized . . .

Attempts have been made to secure coordination through interdepartmental committees, but the Natural Resources task force states:

. . . no effective method has been found for reconciling conflicting opinions and programs . . .

The [interagency] committees have failed to solve any important aspects of the problem . . . because the dominant members, the Corps and the Bureau, have been unwilling to permit interagency committees to settle their differences. The result has been neglect or avoidance by the committees of virtually all major areas of interagency conflict, and concentration instead on technical studies and publicity . . .

The development agencies sometimes compromise their differences. After sharp clashes over plans for the development of the Missouri Basin, the Corps and the Bureau announced complete agreement on the Pick-Sloan plan. Analysis of that plan reveals the fact that it contains many projects which previously had been subjected to devastating criticism by one or the other agency. The "compromise" consisted for the most part in a division of projects, each agency agreeing to forego the privilege of criticizing projects assigned by the agreement to the other. The result is in no sense an integrated development plan for the Basin, and there is serious question in this case whether agreement between the two agencies is not more costly to the public than disagreement . . .

Each of the two major development agencies, the Corps and the Bureau, not unnaturally tries to stake out claims in advance of the other. Each completes its basin surveys as quickly as possible, and proposes its development plans for authorization. The Executive and the Congress are presented with conflicting proposals prepared by agencies with different water-use philosophies. The plans of the Corps of Engineers are built around navigation and flood-protection features, those of the Bureau of Reclamation around irrigation, with power development and other allied purposes given some consideration by both. Desirable though it would be, it is difficult to forestall authorization until thorough analysis has been made . . . once project plans are announced and publicized such powerful local pressures are usually generated that development cannot be postponed. Occasionally, however, interagency disputes have the opposite effect of retarding worthwhile developments for many years, as in the case of the Kings River project in the Central Valley of California . . .

The existence of a number of survey and development agencies has encouraged the perpetuation of special-purpose policies and has accentuated statutory inconsistencies. Varying administrative standards of feasibility, benefit-cost evaluation, and cost allocation have added to the confusion in these areas. Interagency rivalry has fostered a sort of Gresham's law with respect to Federal financial policies, the tendency being for higher standards of repayment by State, local, and private beneficiaries to be replaced by lower . . .

This particular overlap of authority exists not only in the 17 Western States, but the situation for the Nation as a whole is also highly confused. The Corps of Engineers is the principal survey and development agency, but has only minor authority in the Tennessee River Basin, where the Tennessee Valley Authority experiment was set up. Elsewhere the Corps must share its authority (1) on installation of power-generating equipment with the Federal Power Commission; (2) on disposal of all surplus power generated at its projects, with the Secretary of the Interior; (3) on fish and wildlife conservation, with the Fish and Wildlife Service; (4) on pollution abatement, with the Public Health Service . . .

In addition to creating inequities among beneficiaries and a drain on the Federal Treasury, inconsistencies regarding repayment policies also are a source of friction between the Corps of Engineers and the Bureau of Reclamation. The Corps, emphasizing its primary responsibility for navigation and flood control, can offer more "free" improvements than the Bureau, whose projects are primarily for the purpose of irrigation. This difference is intensified by antispeculation provisions and acreage limitations that are established features of projects built under reclamation laws and that have no counterpart in projects built by the Corps of Engineers under flood control and navigation laws . . .

There is simply no escaping the fact that so long as the present overlapping of functions exists with respect to the Corps of Engineers, the Bureau of Reclamation, and the Federal Power Commission, costly duplication, confusion, and competition are bound to result. It has been demonstrated time and again that neither by voluntary cooperation nor by executive coordination can the major conflicts be ironed out . . .

An example of duplication and conflict may be found in the plans for a project at Hell's Canyon, Idaho. These were duplicated at a cost very roughly estimated at about $250,000 each by the Corps of Engineers and the Bureau of Reclamation.

They differed in essential particulars of construction and by over $75 million in cost of erection.

We have pointed out the inherent conflict in use of reservoirs for flood control and their use for power or irrigation. The greatest power development requires the most even flow of water possible. The greatest flood prevention use is to empty reservoirs prior to the flood season and soon thereafter. With the Reclamation Service in control of one function of some reservoirs and the Army Corps of Engineers in charge of others, there can be only continued friction. The consolidation of these agencies is the only remedy. An inquiry into the disastrous flood at Portland, Oreg., in 1948, might show the nature of this conflict in the use of reservoirs.

The Question of Employment of Military Engineers

It is contended that the conduct of Rivers, Harbors, and Flood Control by the Army Engineers has a value in their military training or an economy in Government. Upon this subject our task force on Public Works, which weighed it carefully, says:

The argument that river and harbor work can be directed only by the Army Engineers becomes even more absurd when it is realized that less than 200 Army Engineers are involved and that the remainder of the personnel under their control . . . are civilians who supply most of the detailed knowledge and continuing direction. If the Army Engineers supply unusual ability and obtain invaluable training by contact with this responsibility, there is no reason why the same and even better results cannot be obtained by assigning them and corresponding officers of the Navy and Air Forces, on a proper, dignified, and respected basis, to a central consolidated Works Department.

The Secretary of Defense temporarily should assign to the Secretary of the Interior engineer officers of the Army, Navy, and Air Force who would direct and be engaged in public works tasks commensurate with their rank and experience. In this way, particularly, junior officers would obtain varied training and experience. The Secretary of Defense would continue, as he does now, to prescribe regulations relating to service, rotation of duties, and promotion of these engineer officers, with full power to withdraw them from the Department of the Interior during times of emergency. The Corps of Engineers of the Army would continue in close contact with the best civilian engineering brains in the country to perform functions of a military engineering nature under the Secretary of Defense. Only the civil functions of the Corps would be transferred to the Works Department under the proposed plan.

This subject is far too important to be approached from the point of view of old school-tie tradition. A detached and scientific spirit is required.

Our task force on Natural Resources supports these views:

. . . Painful as the operation may be, the case for a unification of functions of the Corps of Engineers and the Bureau of Reclamation is so overwhelming that it ought to be effected without further delay. The training provided in peacetime for . . . Army engineers at present utilized on this civilian program can surely be secured in some far less costly fashion—perhaps by arrangement with the new Water Development Service or in various installations of the Armed Services themselves. There is a real question in any event as to how far these water resource activities are useful in training for wartime problems.

Lack of Hydrologic Data

This division of agencies in the area of water development between different departments has resulted in no adequate provision of hydrologic data. There are great deficiencies in the fundamental data which have resulted, and are resulting, in great losses to the country. The consolidation of water services is essential to remedy this grievous situation.

Our task force on Natural Resources states:

The really disturbing thing is that so little progress has been made in obtaining reliable hydrologic data in advance of project planning and construction. Though the necessity for more adequate data has long been recognized, we find ourselves embarking on the most gigantic water projects ever devised with alarming gaps in our knowledge of the probable behavior of the waters we are trying to control and utilize. So serious are these deficiencies that it is estimated on the basis of experience that the limit of error or ignorance in present water developments is rarely less than 25 percent, and is frequently greater than that.

Present knowledge of the relationships among precipitation, run-off, evaporation, ground-water movement, soil condition, vegetal cover, transpiration, etc., is far from complete, but our greatest shortcoming has been the failure to provide sufficient funds for the utilization of rain gauges, snow surveys, stream-flow measurements, evaporation stations, run-off and erosion studies, ground-water observation wells, water-quality analyses, and other established methods of obtaining data essential to the planning and construction of.river development projects. Continuous application of these techniques over a period of years is required to furnish reliable data, yet not infrequently the first intensive efforts to apply them are coincident with the commencement of a project study. Few areas are even adequately mapped for water development purposes. In the Columbia Basin, for example, less than half of the watershed has been topographically mapped or has had ground control lines established. Stream survey and stream gauging programs have lagged far behind project planning, notwithstanding the fact that development agencies have transferred considerable funds to data collecting agencies and have frequently undertaken surveys themselves. Conditions in the Missouri Basin are equally unsatisfactory.

Losses due to lack of adequate hydrologic data have always been heavy and may reach staggering figures during the next few years. The most spectacular form which such losses take is the failure of dams as a result of overtopping by floods. In a large proportion of the important dam failures of this kind structures were built too weak or too small because of lack of sufficient information as to precipitation, 'run-off, stream flow, etc. Made cautious by the number of such catastrophes in the past, engineers now tend to overbuild where adequate data are lacking, and as a result we have an increasing number of overelaborate spillways, power plants, and water-supply systems. Losses from overbuilding of structures are less spectacular than those that occur from underbuilding but may turn out to be even more costly.

Siltation of reservoirs due to absence of sufficient data concerning sedimentation is another common form of loss. Many river development works have failed to function as expected or are doomed to early failure due to loss of storage capacity for power production and other purposes. In some cases siltation has necessitated the raising of dams at considerable expense . . .

Overextension of irrigation systems, arising from lack of dependable data as to amounts of available water, has resulted in many costly failures . . .

Recommendation No. 9

For the many reasons above, we recommend that the Rivers and Harbors and Flood Control activities of the Corps of Engineers be transferred to the Department of the Interior and that any Army engineers who can be spared from military duties be detailed to the Department in positions similar to those which they now hold in the Corps of Engineers.

Business Aspects of Multiple-purpose Projects

There are many reforms in finance, budgeting, accounting, and business management which are urgently needed in the conduct of the electrical and irrigation aspects of Water Development. The responsible officials cannot effect these reforms under the present laws.

The subjects are dealt with in reports of the Commission on Budgeting and Accounting, and on Government Business Enterprises, where we make specific recommendations.

There is great confusion in the laws governing the Bureau of Reclamation generally.

Recommendation No. 10

We recommend a clarification and codification of the laws pertaining to the Bureau of Reclamation.

Organization and Planning upon a Drainage Basin Basis

A further reason for unified organization of water development agencies is to permit the determination of policies upon a watershed basis.

Our task force on Natural Resources says:

In the management of our great rivers, the coordinated development of whole river basins with their watershed tributaries is peculiarly essential . . .

The (Water Development) Service would have a clear responsibility to devise for each river basin a plan of development designed to achieve the maximum benefits, after weighing all uses and interests. It would be charged with the responsibility for the Federal part in planning, constructing, and operating river development projects . . .

There should be regional decentralization of the Water Development Service and the Forest and Range Service, by river basins where practicable, to facilitate "grass roots" decisions, interservice cooperation, and local participation in planning . . .

In addition to unification of Federal Water Development agencies, the relation to, and participation of, the States in water development needs enlargement. As said, the unit of water development is the drainage area. Within it are the multiple purposes of navigation, flood control, irrigation, hydroelectric power, municipal and industrial water supply, and the problems of pollution. The governments of the States involved not only are interested, but also, for some purposes, should be called upon for contribution to expenditure. Nor can too much emphasis be laid upon any one of these multiple uses of water to the prejudice of other States. Moreover, State laws govern water rights.

Prior to 1936 the States were required to contribute to flood control, but the removal of this condition in 1938 in respect to reservoir projects has, in effect, imposed the whole burden on the Federal Government and at the same time removed effective restraints on projects of doubtful feasibility.

In order to bring about coordination of State interest and the different Federal agencies as well, the following recommendation is made:

Recommendation No. 11

The Commission recommends that a Drainage Area Advisory Commission be created for each major drainage area, comprising representatives of the proposed Water Development and Use Service of the Department of the Interior, the proposed Agricultural Resources Conservation Service in the Department of Agriculture, and that each State concerned should be asked to appoint a representative. The purpose of these Drainage Boards should be coordinating and advisory, not administrative.

International Boundary Streams

With respect to international boundary streams, our task force on Natural Resources states:

. . . There may be instances in which it will be desirable to have joint action by the Water Development Service and the State Department in view of the latter's responsibility for negotiating agreements. Insofar as the State Department is necessarily involved in planning and operation, it should utilize the facilities of the Water Development Service wherever practicable and should effect careful coordination with the Service so that the plans for the development of the national and international sections of streams are not in conflict. The Water Development Service, in turn, should clear all construction and operation plans for international streams with the State Department for conformity with international agreements.

Recommendation No. 12

The Commission shares these views and recommends that the responsibility for negotiating international agreements continue with the State Department, but that all construction be made a function of the Water Development and Use Service.

Review of Irrigation Projects by the Department of Agriculture

Our task force on Natural Resources recommends:

Serious friction can be avoided, it is believed, if the following general principles are adopted: (*a*) the Water Development Service should not engage in basic agricultural research; (*b*) the Water Development Service should not provide irrigation farmers with the type of services ordinarily furnished by the Department of Agriculture; (*c*) the Water Development Service should be required by statute to obtain and consider the views of the Department of Agriculture with respect to the agricultural feasibility of water projects before making its own determination . . .

The Commission is convinced that the Department of Agriculture should play a more significant role with respect to irrigation than has been the case in the past.

Recommendation No. 13

Therefore, we recommend that no irrigation or reclamation project be undertaken without a report to the Board of Impartial Analysis by the Department of Agriculture.

Chapter Four

BETTER ORGANIZATION IN BUILDNG CONSTRUCTION

Major public building construction is now carried on by many departments or agencies involving an expenditure, recommended in the 1950 budget, of some $1.2 billion. As stated above, our reasons for placing this work in one Department are (*a*) to secure more adequate technical supervision; (*b*) to link such work with other major construction; (*c*) to eliminate competition for labor and materials within the Government; and (*d*) to plan construction work to meet the economic situation.

Our task force on Public Works recommends that all Government housing agencies be brought into this Department. We do not approve of including housing activities as they involve mostly lending operations and are, in part, of an emergency nature. These housing agencies are not directly engaged in major construction activities. However, if any of the housing agencies should undertake actual extensive construction for the Federal Government, this construction should be the responsibility of the Department of the Interior.

Chapter Five

BETTER ORGANIZATION IN MINERAL RESOURCES SERVICES

Our task force on Natural Resources states:

Consumption of minerals in the United States has been steadily on the upgrade. The total value of domestic mineral products was $367,-000,000 in 1880 and $8,143,000,000 in 1945. The fuel minerals, coal, natural gas, petroleum and its products increased in value from $120,-000,000 in 1880 to $5,212,000,000 in 1945. The advent of the automobile brought in a remarkable increase in the consumption of petroleum the total value of which was $32,000 in 1859, $120,000,000 in 1907, and $2,033,000,000 in 1944.

National industry in the past has been securely based on large and companion iron and coal deposits. The production of iron ore was only 15 million long tons in 1889. It rose to 52 millions in 1907 and over 100 million tons in 1947. Likewise the production of bituminous coal rose from 80,725 tons in 1824 to a peak of 620 million tons in 1944.

Cutting across minerals, water, and even some organic resources is the need for unified attention to the energy resources base of our economy. There is at present no department assigned to watch out for the consistent conservation and development of water power, oil, gas, and coal. No one is advising Congress, the President, and the operating agencies on changes in Federal policy required to conserve the more valuable or nonreplaceable energy substances and to increase the availability of the perpetual or more plentiful and cheaper forms of energy.

We have need for more extensive geological explorations, for more research into improved methods of mining and recovery, for more adequate management of the Government relations to title leases, royalties, reservations, etc.

We have need for study leading to revision of our mining laws, some particulars of which are outlined in the report of our task force on Natural Resources.

There is grave need for a center of mineral services in order to develop mineral resources, to advise on broad national policies, to administer the Government leases and mineral reservations, to recommend revision of mineral laws, and to advise other agencies of the Government.

There are some 25 agencies in the Government which have to do with mineral resources. They involve extensive duplication, much of which could be avoided by a consolidation and a more systematic source of information and advice. The Reconstruction Finance Corporation and the National Security Resources Board are important cases in point.

The Reconstruction Finance Corporation has large powers to make loans to organizations engaged in mining, milling, and smelting of ore, and to make loans for the development of lodge, ledge, or veins.

Recommendation No. 14

We recommend that, in connection with its financing, the Reconstruction Finance Corporation should secure reports from the proposed Mineral Resources Services of the Department of the Interior.

The Tin Smelter at Texas City, Tex., is a Government enterprise now conducted by the Reconstruction Finance Corporation. This is an intensely technical operation which should be allied with the research and technical services of the Bureau of Mines in the Mineral Resources Services.

Recommendation No. 15

We recommend that this enterprise should be operated by the Bureau of Mines.

The National Security Resources Board is engaged in stock-piling and development of mineral production. They should avail themselves at all times of the advice of the Minerals Service.

Chapter Six

RECREATION SERVICES

Bureau of National Parks

As to the National Parks, our task force on Natural Resources states:

On the whole, there has been little duplication in the administration of recreational resources. However, much remains to be done in integrating recreational policies relating to the national forests and national parks, and in integrating national recreational policies with State park and forest programs. There has been some conflict between the Forest Service and the National Park Service over boundaries. There could be closer cooperation between the National Park Service and the Forest Service in custodial supervision of monuments within the national forests. There could likewise be more consistency in operational policies concerning camp sites, tourist cabins, commercial enterprises, and other public facilities.

Bureau of Fish and Wildlife

We have recommended elsewhere the transfer of Commercial Fisheries to the Department of Commerce and given our reasons in the report on that Department. Other functions of this Bureau remain in Interior.

Chapter Seven

CONCLUSIONS AND SAVINGS

The Commission believes that the foremost obstacles to consistent Government policies and efficient functioning of these agencies will be removed by their unification as proposed above.

We can present no accurate estimate of the savings to be made by this reorganization of functions. In preventing unwise projects and disastrous conflicts and by securing coordinated policies, they should amount to large sums.

XIII

Department of Commerce

Chapter One

ROLE OF DEPARTMENT OF COMMERCE

The act of 1903, which originally established the Department of Commerce, provided that its major purpose should be ". . . to foster, promote, and develop the foreign and domestic commerce; the mining, manufacturing, shipping, fishery industry; and the transportation facilities of the United States."

Thus, the major purpose of the Department, as originally established by the Congress, was to embrace the activities of the Government in the development of industry, transportation, and commerce. However, a number of these functions have been placed elsewhere in the Government structure and the transportation activities have been scattered over many parts of the executive branch.

In this report on the Department of Commerce, the Commission is mainly concerned with problems that involve:

a. Remedying the Department's present defective administrative and organizational structure.

b. Grouping in the Department major transportation activities of the Government, except the regulatory functions of the independent commissions and boards.

c. Restoring the commercial fisheries activities to the Department.

d. Strengthening the commodity divisions of the Bureau of Foreign and Domestic Commerce so as to enable them to serve other Government agencies.

e. Determining the responsibility for overseas reporting activities.

Chapter Two

BASIS OF REORGANIZATION

We propose that certain agencies be brought into the Department from other parts of the executive branch. The purpose is two-fold (*a*) to group activities according to their major purpose, thereby saving overlap, conflict, and waste; and (*b*) to make possible the constructive development of policies impossible of realization when these agencies are scattered over 11 other departments and executive agencies. The following table shows the changes proposed. Later we give our reasons for recommending these changes.

Transportation Services

ACTIVITIES NOW IN DEPARTMENT

THE CIVIL AERONAUTICS ADMINISTRATION
THE COAST AND GEODETIC SURVEY
THE WEATHER BUREAU
THE INLAND WATERWAYS CORPORATION

ACTIVITIES TO BE ADDED

THE MARITIME COMMISSION (Independent)—Except for regulatory functions, which would continue independent
NATIONAL ADVISORY COMMITTEE FOR AERONAUTICS (Independent)
CIVIL AERONAUTICS BOARD (Independent)—Certain safety activities only; other functions to continue as at present
INTERSTATE COMMERCE COMMISSION (Independent)—Railway and motor carriers safety and car service activities only; other functions to continue as at present

THE PUBLIC ROADS ADMINISTRATION (Federal Works Agency)
THE OFFICE OF DEFENSE TRANSPORTATION (Executive Office of the President)
THE COAST GUARD (Treasury Department)
THE BUREAU OF CUSTOMS (Treasury Department)—Certain activities only; a study should be made of the marine functions of the Bureau of Customs to determine whether some of them should be shifted to the Coast Guard or some other part of the proposed Transportation Service

Industrial and Commercial Services

ACTIVITIES NOW IN DEPARTMENT

THE NATIONAL BUREAU OF STANDARDS
THE BUREAU OF THE CENSUS
THE PATENT OFFICE
THE BUREAU OF FOREIGN AND DOMESTIC COMMERCE
BUSINESS ADVISORY COUNCIL
FOREIGN TRADE ZONES BOARD
OFFICE OF INDUSTRY COOPERATION
NATIONAL INVENTORS' COUNCIL
OFFICE OF TECHNICAL SERVICES
TEXTILE FOUNDATION

ACTIVITIES TO BE ADDED

DIVISION OF COMMERCIAL FISHERIES (from Fish and Wildlife Service, Department of the Interior)

Chapter Three

PROPOSED DEPARTMENTAL ORGANIZATION

We have urged in our first report that the foundation of good departmental administration is that the Secretary shall have authority from the Congress to organize and control his organization, and that separate authority to subordinates be eliminated.

We recommend that the present positions of Under Secretary and two Assistant Secretaries be retained in the Department of Commerce and that an Administrative Assistant Secretary be added. These officials should be appointed by the President, by and with the advice and consent of the Senate, with the possible exception of the Administrative Assistant Secretary.

The duties of these officials should be assigned by the Secretary. However, it is intended that the Administrative Assistant Secretary should have charge of administrative staff services, and he should, where possible, be appointed from the career service. All officials below the Under Secretary and the Assistant Secretaries should preferably be appointed from the career service.

Under our recommendations made elsewhere, we propose a new form of "performance" budget.[1] We propose that the Department will keep its own administrative accounts as prescribed by an Accountant General in the Treasury and subject to an approval of the system by the Comptroller General and an audit by him.[1] The Commission also recommends that all personnel recruitment should be decentralized into the Department (except possibly in lower grades common to all departments and agencies), subject to standards and methods of merit selection to be proposed by the Department, but with the approval and enforcement

[1] Report on Budgeting and Accounting.

of the Civil Service Commission.[2] The Commission likewise recommends elsewhere that procurement of supplies peculiar to the Department should be decentralized into the Department but under standards and methods established by the Office of General Services.[3] The latter will, of course, handle items of common use. Further, we propose that the Department should strengthen its management research unit, working in cooperation with a comparable staff unit under the Office of the Budget.[4]

The following will indicate the opinion of the Commission concerning the arrangement of the Department. Part of this structure is already established. We do not, however, recommend a hard and fast rule. The Secretary should determine the organization and be free to amend it.

a. THE SECRETARY OF COMMERCE (with his own office assistance)

THE UNDER SECRETARY OF COMMERCE (with his own office assistance)
TWO ASSISTANT SECRETARIES
AN ADMINISTRATIVE ASSISTANT SECRETARY
THE BUSINESS ADVISORY COUNCIL

b. STAFF SERVICES, to include (i) the Solicitor; (ii) Chief Financial Officer for accounting and budgeting; (iii) Personnel Officer; (iv) Information and Publications Officer; (v) Management Research Officer; (vi) Foreign Affairs Activities Coordination Officer; (vii) Congressional Liaison Officer.

c. TRANSPORTATION SERVICE to include (i) Merchant Marine Activities; (ii) Civil Aviation activities; (iii) Highway Transportation activities; (iv) Rail Carriers activities; (v) Aids to Navigation, Coast Guard, Coast and Geodetic Survey, Weather Bureau; (vi) Bureau of Custom's marine functions, if deemed advantageous.

d. INDUSTRIAL AND COMMERCIAL SERVICE to include (i) the Bureau of Foreign and Domestic Commerce; (ii) the Bureau of Standards; (iii) the Bureau of the Census; (iv) the Patent Office; (v) the Bureau of Commercial Fisheries; (vi) the Office of Industry Cooperation; (vii) the National Inventors' Council; (viii) Office of Technical Services; (ix) the Textile Foundation; (x) the Foreign Trade Zones Board.

[2] Report on Personnel and Management.
[3] Report on the Office of General Services.
[4] Report on General Management of the Executive Branch.

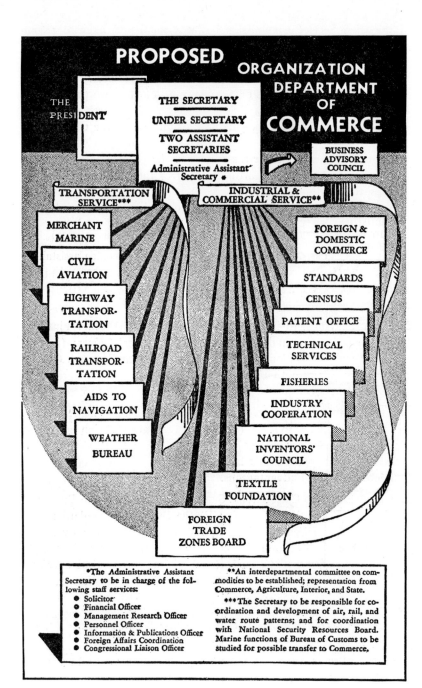

PROPOSED ORGANIZATION DEPARTMENT OF COMMERCE

THE PRESIDENT

THE SECRETARY
UNDER SECRETARY
TWO ASSISTANT SECRETARIES
Administrative Assistant
Secretary *

BUSINESS ADVISORY COUNCIL

TRANSPORTATION SERVICE***

INDUSTRIAL & COMMERCIAL SERVICE**

MERCHANT MARINE

CIVIL AVIATION

HIGHWAY TRANSPORTATION

RAILROAD TRANSPORTATION

AIDS TO NAVIGATION

WEATHER BUREAU

FOREIGN & DOMESTIC COMMERCE

STANDARDS

CENSUS

PATENT OFFICE

TECHNICAL SERVICES

FISHERIES

INDUSTRY COOPERATION

NATIONAL INVENTORS' COUNCIL

TEXTILE FOUNDATION

FOREIGN TRADE ZONES BOARD

*The Administrative Assistant Secretary to be in charge of the following staff services:
● Solicitor
● Financial Officer
● Management Research Officer
● Personnel Officer
● Information & Publications Officer
● Foreign Affairs Coordination
● Congressional Liaison Officer

**An interdepartmental committee on commodities to be established; representation from Commerce, Agriculture, Interior, and State.

***The Secretary to be responsible for coordination and development of air, rail, and water route patterns; and for coordination with National Security Resources Board. Marine functions of Bureau of Customs to be studied for possible transfer to Commerce.

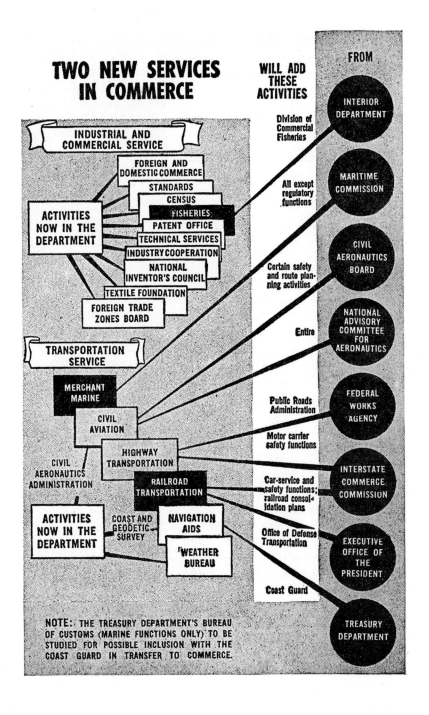

TWO NEW SERVICES IN COMMERCE

WILL ADD THESE ACTIVITIES

FROM

INDUSTRIAL AND COMMERCIAL SERVICE

ACTIVITIES NOW IN THE DEPARTMENT

- FOREIGN AND DOMESTIC COMMERCE
- STANDARDS
- CENSUS
- FISHERIES
- PATENT OFFICE
- TECHNICAL SERVICES
- INDUSTRY COOPERATION
- NATIONAL INVENTOR'S COUNCIL
- TEXTILE FOUNDATION
- FOREIGN TRADE ZONES BOARD

TRANSPORTATION SERVICE

- MERCHANT MARINE
- CIVIL AVIATION
- HIGHWAY TRANSPORTATION
- RAILROAD TRANSPORTATION
- CIVIL AERONAUTICS ADMINISTRATION

ACTIVITIES NOW IN THE DEPARTMENT

- COAST AND GEODETIC SURVEY
- NAVIGATION AIDS
- WEATHER BUREAU

Division of Commercial Fisheries — INTERIOR DEPARTMENT

All except regulatory functions — MARITIME COMMISSION

Certain safety and route planning activities — CIVIL AERONAUTICS BOARD

Entire — NATIONAL ADVISORY COMMITTEE FOR AERONAUTICS

Public Roads Administration — FEDERAL WORKS AGENCY

Motor carrier safety functions

Car-service and safety functions; railroad consolidation plans — INTERSTATE COMMERCE COMMISSION

Office of Defense Transportation — EXECUTIVE OFFICE OF THE PRESIDENT

Coast Guard — TREASURY DEPARTMENT

NOTE: THE TREASURY DEPARTMENT'S BUREAU OF CUSTOMS (MARINE FUNCTIONS ONLY) TO BE STUDIED FOR POSSIBLE INCLUSION WITH THE COAST GUARD IN TRANSFER TO COMMERCE.

Chapter Four

ESTABLISHMENT OF
TRANSPORTATION SERVICE

It is hardly necessary to emphasize the importance of the transportation activities of the Government. The United States has more than 227,000 miles of railways which annually haul over 600 billion ton-miles of freight and operate 70 billion passenger-miles. There are about 1,500,000 miles of surfaced roads for our approximately 40 million vehicles. Our air services operate more than 7,000,000 passenger-miles annually and haul cargo and mail over 100,000 miles of domestic routes and 179,000 miles of international routes with a total of more than 6,000 airports. We have 27,000 miles of improved inland waterways, carrying over 22 billion ton-miles of freight annually. We have nearly 5,000 ocean-going vessels. There are also 142,000 miles of pipe lines for gas and oil in operation.

It was the original intent of the Congress, in creating the Department of Commerce, that it should embrace the Government's interest in the development and safeguarding of transportation. Our recommendations are directed toward accomplishing this end.

The Commission, however, does not recommend that the Department include the regulatory responsibilities of the Interstate Commerce Commission, the Maritime Commission, and the Civil Aeronautics Board. These duties should not be assigned to the Department, for, in our opinion, operation and development activities should be entirely divorced from major regulatory functions.

The major forces in the development of our transportation system—greater in service than that of any other country—have been the private enterprise of our citizens and the existence of competition between the different systems of transportation. The role of Government must be to aid private enterprises in operating the systems, and to regulate rates and services in protection of the public.

The relation of the Government to transportation is indicated by the fact that, within the last 30 years, the Federal Government has spent more than 30 billion dollars on the development of transportation facilities, and in the fiscal year 1949 it will spend at least an additional 1.2 billion dollars. Our task force, which studied transportation, estimates that there are 89,000 Federal employees in a great many agencies engaged in this work.

Government aids to transportation have taken a multitude of forms, including:

a. Subsidies for early railway construction and, later, loans to railroads when in financial distress, and guidance in reorganization.

b. Dredging and canalization of rivers and harbors and construction of canals.

c. Subsidies tc, and actual operation of, a large portion of our international merchant marine, with a multitude of aids to navigation.

d. Subsidies to aviation, and provisions of airways, air fields, and other aids.

e. Grants-in-aid for highway construction.

f. Research in these fields.

What Is Wrong with the Federal Transportation Organization

a. Transportation activities are scattered over many separate agencies, with consequent waste and overlap.

b. There is no coordination of policies in the transportation field.

c. The scattering of functions makes intelligent budgeting difficult, and policies or programs cannot be considered for transportation as a whole.

d. Research activities are carried on in narrow segments of certain areas of transportation, and these segments are not coordinated. In some areas, they overlap; in others, they are deficient.

e. The amount of subsidies to carriers included in mail contracts is not clear under the present system of appropriations and accounting.

f. In operating the Government, or subsidized, merchant marine busi-

ness, activities are directed by a full-time board, whereas good administration requires a single executive.

g. Safety requirements are too often administered by regulatory groups,
rather than by executive agencies.

h. Transportation planning for national defense is inadequately
centralized.

What Should Be Done about Transportation

It is not the purpose of the commission to outline detailed remedies
for all these faults but rather to establish such an organization as will
be able to evolve remedies. In many cases, the mere statement of the
deficiencies indicates what steps should be taken to accomplish reform.

The major weaknesses in Federal transportation policy clearly arise
from a failure, in practice, to recognize that the primary objective must
be to assure the Nation the best possible transportation system for the
movement of persons and goods. There has been a failure to think, or
act, in terms of total transportation requirements.

This is manifested in the preoccupation, in Federal transportation
agencies, with the regulation of rates and services, and with isolated
problems in individual fields of transportation. The Government, in
attempting to determine the volume and character of transportation
services, divides responsibility between promotional and regulatory
agencies in such a way that there is no possibility of effective development or coordination. No single Government agency is in a position to
evaluate the total needs in transportation, the total service provided, or
the net results of all Federal transportation undertakings.

These facts, revealed by a study of the organization and methods of
operation of our existing transportation agencies, point unmistakably
to the one major step that must be taken to bring order to this chaos.
A close grouping of the major transportation activities is essential to the
development of intelligent, total transportation policy, and to the efficient administration of transportation activities.

The Commission, however, disagrees with the suggestion of its task
force that such unification should be provided through the establishment of a new Department of Transportation. The Commission recognizes that transportation is only one industry among many with which
the Federal Government is concerned. It would be quite inadvisable
for the Federal Government to set up a department which would be
devoted entirely to the problems of one industry. Moreover, since

transportation is an element in the costs of practically every other industry, Government policies on transportation should be coordinated with Government policies toward industry in general.

Recommendation No. 1

The Commission recommends, therefore, that there be established in the Department of Commerce a grouping of all major nonregulatory transportation activities of the Federal Government.

Such a transportation service would study:

a. Physical needs of transportation.

b. Priority among these needs.

c. Costs of meeting these needs and methods of defraying them.

d. Governmental promotional programs directed toward achieving the most effective system at the lowest cost.

e. Military transportation requirements and their integration with civilian needs.

f. Most advantageous route patterns for extension of transportation services. Provision of new services in any given case should be weighed against all types of transportation service already provided, as, for example, a proposed new air route should be weighed not only against other air routes, but against all other types of transportation.

We add the following in explanation of these proposed recommendations:

The Merchant Marine

Aside from the primary necessity to group the Government's activities in transportation for coordination of policies, and for economy, there is a still further impelling reason for bringing merchant marine activities into the Department of Commerce.

The U. S. Maritime Commission, made up of full-time members, has a dual function. It exercises regulatory functions affecting the whole merchant marine and, at the same time, buys, sells, and subsidizes shipping and makes loans on ships on a huge scale.

It is an anomaly that a regulatory commission should also conduct the executive function of managing a huge business; that executive functions should be carried on by an agency that is not subject to Presidential direction; that executive functions should be carried on by a full-time board of which all members have equal responsibility and authority, instead of by a single administrator.

Recommendation No. 2

The Commission recommends that the business operations of the Maritime Commission be placed within the Department of Commerce. Although no new corporation need be set up to handle these operations, the agency in charge should be given the flexibility of business-type management in budgeting, accounting, and auditing, which are established for Government corporations by the Government Corporation Control Act of 1945, as amended.

We make separate recommendations on the Inland Waterways Corporation in our report on Business Enterprises of the Government.

Coast Guard and Coast and Geodetic Survey

The Coast Guard is obviously misplaced in the Treasury Department at the present time. The principal functions of the Coast Guard relate to provision of coastal and interior aids and services to air and water navigation. It regulates and inspects provisions for marine safety. Considering the general nature of the work it performs, its location in the Treasury has no reasonable basis. On the other hand, there is need to coordinate its activities with those of the Civil Aeronautics Administration, the Maritime Commission, and with the work of the transportation agencies. Its functions are more closely related to transportation than to the activities of any other major department of the Government.

The major functions of the Coast and Geodetic Survey is to provide aids for water and air transportation.

Marine Functions of the Customs Bureau

The Bureau of Customs of the Treasury Department performs certain marine functions which have to do largely with transportation. They include such responsibilities as the filing with the Collector of Customs of evidence of registry, crew lists, shipping articles and the collection of tonnage taxes. If the ship carries steerage passengers, the space allotted, menus served, sanitary facilities, and the like are checked to see that adequate provision was made for such passengers. When the ship departs, clearance papers, such as manifests of cargo, export declarations, export licenses, and the like are checked and clearance authorized.

Recommendation No. 3

The Commission recommends that a study be made of these marine functions of the Bureau of Customs to determine whether some of them can advantageously be transferred to the Commerce Department.

Civil Aviation

Recommendation No. 4

The Commission recommends that there be established in the Department of Commerce a Bureau of Civil Aviation which would administer the functions listed below, in addition to the present functions of the Civil Aeronautics Administration.

Recommendation No. 5

The Bureau also would have the responsibility for promulgating air safety rules, with a right of review to the Civil Aeronautics Board from the promulgation, or refusal to promulgate specific rules. Enforcement of these rules should be in this Bureau as successor to the Civil Aeronautics Administration.[5] Investigation of major aircraft accidents should remain with the Civil Aeronautics Board.

Recommendation No. 6

The National Advisory Committee for Aeronautics should be incorporated into this Bureau.

The National Advisory Committee for Aeronautics is directed by an independent committee consisting primarily of officials of the National Military Establishment and of the Department of Commerce, with some members from private life. It supervises and directs scientific studies for civil and military aviation. This agency is not directly in the basic line of Presidential authority, and it is unsound organization for it to be governed by a committee. We doubt whether it is sufficiently important, despite its size, to warrant independent status.[6] Its work is closely related to that of the Bureau of Standards, the U. S. Weather Bureau, and the Civil Aeronautics Authority, and it also works closely with the commercial aircraft and aircraft component industries. The logical solution,

[5] See our report on Regulatory Commissions.
[6] It has 6,876 employees as of Jan. 31, 1949.

therefore, is that it be placed under the Bureau of Civil Aviation in the reconstituted Department of Commerce.

Highway Transportation

This Bureau would have responsibility for all Federal activities involving the promotion of better highway transportation. To facilitate this, we make the recommendations below.

Recommendation No. 7

The Public Roads Administration should be transferred from the Federal Works Agency to the Department.

Recommendation No. 8

The motor-carrier safety functions should be transferred here from the Interstate Commerce Commission.

Motor-carrier safety functions of the Interstate Commerce Commission are highly technical in nature and are an executive function. In addition, they involve continuing cooperation with State agencies, a field in which the Public Roads Administration is active and for which it has set up machinery. On the basis of technical studies, safety regulations can be developed.

Railroad Transportation

This Bureau would have the duty of promoting railroad transportation. To facilitate this, the steps recommended below should be taken.

Recommendation No. 9

Two functions of the Interstate Commerce Commission should be transferred to this Bureau: (*a*) that of formulating railroad-consolidation plans and (*b*) that dealing with car service and safety.

Railroad safety regulation enforcement and railroad car service activities add to the already heavy administrative burden of the Interstate Commerce Commission and divert its attention from its primary regulatory responsibilities. A board is not a satisfactory administrative device for executive functions.

Moreover, experience in car service matters has demonstrated that the regulatory mechanism is inadequate to deal with the problems of railroad car supply in critical and prolonged periods of shortage. Thus, during the war, this responsibility was vested in the Office of Defense Transportation.

Recommendation No. 10

The Office of Defense Transportation should be transferred here from the Office for Emergency Management in the Executive Office of the President. Under present legislation, Office of Defense Transportation goes out of existence June 30, 1949. Its functions should be made permanent in this new location.

The Weather Bureau

The Weather Bureau serves both aviation and merchant marine. It also conducts services to the farmers and the public generally.

Recommendation No. 11

We recommend that the Weather Bureau's coordination in the departmental structure be established by the Secretary.

Route Patterns

One of the uncoordinated activities of Government is that dealing with planning and authorizing route patterns for transportation. It should be recognized that through the application of direct or indirect subsidies to shipping, highways, and aviation, together with the certificates of convenience and necessity in railway expansion, the Government is, in fact, determining route patterns in transportation.

Hitherto, route patterns have been determined haphazardly upon a case-by-case basis by regulatory commissions. Routes should be planned with careful consideration for the total transportation needs of the country and the areas to be served, and for the services already available by all means of transportation. Aviation-route planning particularly is a highly important promotional tool. Air-route planning should be coordinated with airway and airport development programs.

A regulatory body which operates on a case-by-case basis is inherently unable to engage in the long-range research and planning which air-route planning requires. Some agency is urgently needed in the Government for study, development, and preparation of systematic route plans for all land, air, and water transportation.

Recommendation No. 12

The Commission recommends that the Secretary of Commerce be assigned the duty of making over-all route programs for air, land, and water transportation. He should also initiate action before the regulatory agencies when such action appears to him to be appropriate.

When individual carriers or groups of carriers make recommendations to the regulatory agencies at variance with his over-all programs, the Secretary of Commerce should appear before such boards or commissions to present his views.

Relation of National Security and Transportation

War conditions may place new burdens upon individual carriers and upon the transportation system as a whole. This happened in the recent war and might well occur again if the Nation should unfortunately become involved in another conflict. Wartime transportation requirements must be carefully calculated and arrangements made for handling the most essential types of traffic. It should be the responsibility of the Secretary of Commerce, who should, of course, coordinate his work with the National Security Resources Board, to insure the preparation of plans for the mobilization of the Nation's transportation resources in the event of a national emergency.

Chapter Five

INDUSTRIAL AND COMMERCIAL
SERVICE

With one exception, all of the functions and activities of the Government that would comprise the Industrial and Commercial Service in the enlarged Department of Commerce are already located there. That exception is the activities of Government dealing with commercial fisheries. Certain other improvements in Commerce activities are, however, recommended.

Fishery Activities

At one time, the commercial fishery functions of the Federal Government were handled by a Bureau of Fisheries which was located in the Department of Commerce. In 1940, this Bureau was consolidated with the Biological Survey of the Department of Agriculture, and transferred to a new organization, called the Fish and Wildlife Service, was located in the Department of the Interior. A Bureau of Fisheries can be one of the most important industrial and commercial agencies in the Government. It is related to industry, to commerce, and to the merchant marine at many points.

Our committee on natural resources, whose report is submitted separately, recommends that this essential industry, commercial fisheries, should be more actively developed as an important contributor to the Nation's food supply. However, the committee recommended that this activity be grouped with those agencies dealing with natural resources.

Recommendation No. 13

The Commission recommends that all commercial fishery activities of the Department of the Interior be transferred to a Bureau of Commercial Fisheries in the Department of Commerce.

Commodity Research

In its commerce activities, the Department is concerned with commodities after they enter trade, whereas the Department of the Interior and the Department of Agriculture are mainly concerned with raw materials up to the time of initial processing.

It is impossible to draw a hard and fast line as to where the activities of other departments should cease, and the activities of the Department of Commerce should begin. It would seem appropriate that, when an article becomes a commodity in trade, studies of its distribution, consumption, and marketing should be handled by the Department of Commerce. At the same time, it is necessary to recognize that the farmer, for example, is interested in what is happening to his products after they become commodities in trade, as well as before that time. Therefore, the Commission recognizes that commodity studies may legitimately be made not only by the Department of Commerce, but also by the Bureau of Mines, the Department of Agriculture, etc.

It is, however, essential that major duplication between departments be eliminated.

To accomplish this, it is important that informed and competent major commodity divisions be located in certain places in the Government. In many instances, the logical place is the Department of Commerce. The present duplicate commodity divisions in the Department, one for domestic trade, and one for foreign trade, should be consolidated and strengthened. By such emphasis, for instance, the Departments of State, the National Military Establishment, and the National Security Resources Board can obtain adequate technical aid without the present duplication of effort and expenditure.

There should be one individual in charge of the activities of the Bureau of Foreign and Domestic Commerce.

Recommendation No. 14

We recommend that an interdepartmental committee be established between the Departments of Commerce, Agriculture, Interior, and State to determine the fields of the different departments.

Foreign Affairs Activities of the Department

The foreign affairs activities of Commerce are treated more completely in the Commission's Report on Foreign Affairs. That report recommends, in general, that the Department of State should divest itself of large staffs of specialists to perform functions in the economic field and, in lieu thereof, should depend upon the facilities of existing agencies for information within the latter's special competences. At the same time, the Department of State will continue to need a small group of technical advisory specialists in various fields who would serve as a channel of communication and as a point of coordination between the Department of State and other agencies.

Foreign Affairs Recommendations

Our report on Foreign Affairs also recommends:

1. That Department of State personnel, in the main, meet the overseas reporting requirements of the Department of Commerce.

2. That in a limited number of cases which involve highly specialized technical reporting, or an unusual amount of commercial reporting, the Department of Commerce obtain its own appropriation and designate officials to fill such overseas posts.

The Department would then make a grant of funds to the Department of State and its appointees would be temporarily enrolled as Department of State employees. The Department of State would have the right to reject any individual so designated and, while overseas, such persons would be an integral part of the missions to which they were assigned. In addition to their work as Commerce reporters, their services would be available to the ambassador, or minister.

3. That impediments in the Department of State which delay the flow of commercial information from abroad be removed.

Field Organization

There is some indication that the field organization of the Bureau of Foreign and Domestic Commerce may be overly elaborate. Sufficient attention does not seem to have been given to the possible use of private and State agencies—chambers of commerce, for example, and State commerce departments—to disseminate information. This situation should be given early attention by the Department with a view to closing down some of the field offices, and reducing the size of others.

Conclusion

It is the opinion of the Commission that this proposed arrangement will permit the Department of Commerce to do a better job in serving the transportation, industry, and commerce of the country, and that great savings by elimination of overlaps and by better administration can be made.

XIV
Department of Labor

Chapter One

INTRODUCTION

The labor functions of the Federal Government received recognition at the Cabinet level in 1903 with the establishment of the Department of Commerce and Labor. In 1913 the Department of Labor was created as a separate department.

The Department has been steadily denuded of functions at one time established within it. With the widening of Federal policy in the field of labor, there has been a growing tendency to set up specialized labor services outside of the Department, either as independent establishments or as subordinate units of other related agencies, thus causing a diffusion of labor functions throughout the Government.

a. The United States Employment Service was transferred in 1939 to the Federal Security Agency, where it has remained, except for the period from 1945 to 1948.

b. The Immigration and Naturalization Service was transferred to the Justice Department in 1940.

c. Except for its labor functions, the Children's Bureau was transferred to the Federal Security Agency in 1946.

d. The Labor-Management Relations Act of 1947 transferred the conciliation activities of the Department to an independent Federal Mediation and Conciliation Service.

Chapter Two

OVER-ALL DEPARTMENTAL
MANAGEMENT

The Present Department

The top management positions in the Department are:

SECRETARY OF LABOR (with staff assistants)
UNDER SECRETARY OF LABOR (with staff assistants)
THE SOLICITOR
THREE ASSISTANT SECRETARIES
THREE ADMINISTRATIVE OFFICERS .

The department is subdivided into the following functional units:

BUREAU OF LABOR STANDARDS
BUREAU OF LABOR STATISTICS
WOMEN'S BUREAU
WAGE AND HOUR AND PUBLIC CONTRACTS DIVISION
BUREAU OF APPRENTICESHIP
BUREAU OF VETERANS' REEMPLOYMENT RIGHTS

The total annual administrative expenditure of the Department is about $16,000,000 and it employs about 3,400 persons. The Department has about the same number of top officials as certain other departments with 100 times the expenditures and number of employees.

In general, it may be said that the Department is now overmanned at the top levels for the functions which remain. The Department has lost much of its significance. It should be given more essential work to do if it is to maintain a significance comparable to the other great executive departments.

We propose later in this report that several agencies closely related to the work and purpose of the Department be transferred to it.

Proposed Departmental Organization

We have urged in our first report that the foundation of good departmental administration is authority from the Congress for the Secretary to organize and control his Department. The granting by the Congress of independent authority to subordinates, of which there are several instances in the Department, should be eliminated.

Under our recommendations, made elsewhere, we propose a new form of "performance" budget.[1] We propose that the Department keep its own administrative accounts as prescribed by an Accountant General in the Treasury and subject to approval and audit by the Comptroller General.[1] The Commission also recommends that all personnel recruitment should be decentralized into the Department (except possibly some positions in the lower grades), subject to standards and methods of merit selection to be proposed by the Department, but with the approval and enforcement of the Civil Service Commission.[2] The Commission likewise recommends elsewhere that procurement of supplies peculiar to the Department should be decentralized into the Department under standards and methods established by the Office of General Services. Items of common use would, of course, be handled by the Office of General Services.[3] Further, we propose that the Department should strengthen its management research unit, working in cooperation with a comparable staff unit in the Office of the Budget.[1]

Recommendation No. 1

We recommend that officials of secretarial rank be appointed by the President and confirmed by the Senate, and that all officials in the Department below the rank of Assistant Secretary be appointed by the Secretary.

In conformity with our conclusions on departmental organization, we recommend that one of the Assistant Secretaries be designated as Administrative Assistant Secretary; that he be chosen preferably from the career service and be assigned to the direction of the departmental staff which would comprise officials in charge of:

BUDGETING AND ACCOUNTING
PERSONNEL
PROCUREMENT OF SUPPLIES

[1] Report on Budgeting and Accounting.
[2] Report on Personnel Management.
[3] Report on the Office of General Services.

MANAGEMENT RESEARCH
INFORMATION AND PUBLICATIONS
LIAISON WITH CONGRESS

This staff should have no operational duties, those being the functions of bureau and division heads.

The agencies in the Department should be organized on a functional basis. We make no suggestions about their organization as it can not be determined until, or unless, decision is taken as to the agencies to be brought into the Department. In any event this Commission recommends no hard and fast forms; the Secretary should determine those questions.

Chapter Three

AGENCIES AND FUNCTIONS TO BE TRANSFERRED TO THE DEPARTMENT

a. BUREAU OF EMPLOYEES' COMPENSATION (from the Federal Security Agency)

b. EMPLOYEES' COMPENSATION APPEALS BOARD (from the Federal Security Agency)

c. BUREAU OF EMPLOYMENT SECURITY (from the Federal Security Agency. Placement service and unemployment compensation) [4]

d. SELECTIVE SERVICE SYSTEM, including the Appeals Board (independent)

e. ENFORCEMENT OF LABOR STANDARDS in government contracts (from contracting departments and agencies)

f. DETERMINATION OF MINIMUM WAGES FOR SEAMEN (from U. S. Maritime Commission)

g. "PREVAILING WAGE" RESEARCH to be conducted by the Bureau of Labor Statistics

h. DIVISION OF INDUSTRIAL HYGIENE—Certain components only (from the Bureau of State Services of the Public Health Service in the Federal Security Agency)

There are cogent reasons why these agencies and functions should be transferred to the Department of Labor. They are more nearly related to the problems of labor than those with which they are now

---

[4] Including Veterans' Employment Service.

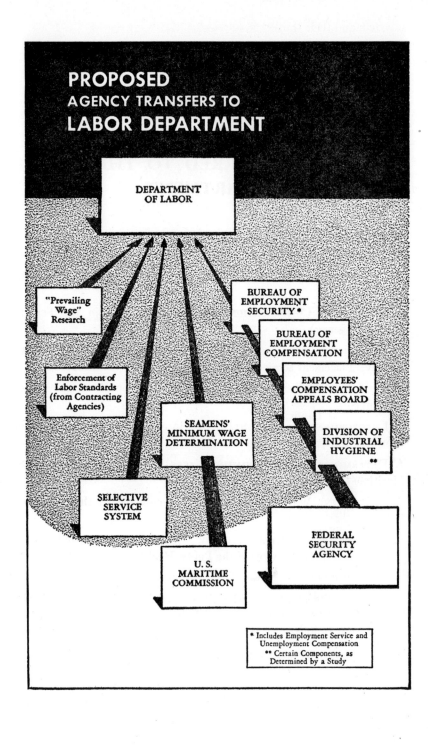

PROPOSED
AGENCY TRANSFERS TO
LABOR DEPARTMENT

DEPARTMENT
OF LABOR

"Prevailing
Wage"
Research

BUREAU OF
EMPLOYMENT
SECURITY *

BUREAU OF
EMPLOYMENT
COMPENSATION

Enforcement of
Labor Standards
(from Contracting
Agencies)

EMPLOYEES'
COMPENSATION
APPEALS BOARD

SEAMENS'
MINIMUM WAGE
DETERMINATION

DIVISION OF
INDUSTRIAL
HYGIENE
**

SELECTIVE
SERVICE
SYSTEM

FEDERAL
SECURITY
AGENCY

U. S.
MARITIME
COMMISSION

* Includes Employment Service and
Unemployment Compensation
** Certain Components, as
Determined by a Study

associated, and their transfer accords with the Commission's first report which recommended that agencies be grouped according to their major purpose.

Bureau of Employees' Compensation

This Bureau administers the Federal laws establishing workmen's compensation for certain employments within Federal jurisdiction. Besides specified Federal employees, the laws cover certain maritime and dock workers in private employment and private employees within the District of Columbia to whom the laws are applicable.

The Bureau employs about 375 persons and has 15 district offices which could well be housed with other agencies of the Department of Labor. The administrative expenses of the Bureau are about $1,500,000 per annum and the estimated expenditures for compensation in fiscal year 1950 are about $23,000,000.

Its work in safety, statistics, and industrial standards is allied with other Department of Labor functions.

The functions of Employees' Compensation Appeals Board are closely related to those of the Bureau.

Recommendation No. 2

We recommend that the Bureau of Employees' Compensation and the Employees' Compensation Appeals Board be transferred to the Department of Labor.

Bureau of Employment Security

This Bureau administers the employment service and unemployment compensation. It employs some 1,030 persons and spends about $6 million per annum in administration. Unemployment insurance is collected by the Treasury from employers and is available, under certain laws, to the States who administer the funds under varying State requirements. The unemployment tax is generally 3 percent, of which money the Treasury retains for the account of the Federal Government up to 10 percent, or roughly 0.3 percent of the total taxable pay rolls. The totals collected by the Treasury for the account of the Federal Government were $207,920,000 for fiscal year 1948.

From the money so collected for the account of the Federal Government, the Bureau pays its administrative expenses and remits certain money to the States for administrative purposes. The amounts so remitted to the States for the fiscal year 1948 were approximately $130 million. The accumulated amount held in trust in the Treasury now amounts to more than $6 billion for all the States in the aggregate.

The Wagner-Peyser Act of 1933 authorized Federal grants for the operation of public employment offices by the States. Originally Wagner-Peyser funds were made available on a 50–50 matching basis. Under Title III of the Social Security Act, tax offsets and administrative grants for unemployment compensation are made to the States for administration of unemployment compensation through public employment offices. The employment service and unemployment compensation were placed within the Federal Security Agency in order to avoid two systems of financing, two sets of conditional requirements, and two different supervisory agencies at the national level. Operationally, the two programs are closely linked through the same facility—State employment offices.

It is now generally agreed by both Federal and State officials that it is desirable to integrate fiscal and administrative review of the two State programs under the supervision of the same Federal department. The placement operations are the primary objectives of this dual arrangement. The paying of unemployment compensation claims is a temporary expedient until the eligible worker can be brought back into the productive labor force. Occupational analysis, testing, reporting, counseling, and placement standards and procedures are the principal functions involved. These are employment functions.

Employment offices and unemployment compensation are more closely related to each other than to retirement or old-age assistance or educational programs. Both are Federal-State programs dealing with labor conditions and labor-management relations. These programs have close operating relationships with other employment and labor functions in the Department of Labor—with the Bureau of Labor Statistics, Women's Bureau, the Bureau of Apprenticeship, Wage and Hour Division, the Bureau of Labor Standards and the Bureau of Veterans' Reemployment Rights. Personnel for these functions all acquire the same basic training in labor and employee relations problems.

The States themselves either place employment security in an industrial commission or labor department, in a department with other labor functions, or organize them independently. In no State are they merged with health, education, or welfare. In addition, more and more States are rewarding employers with good "experience" ratings in providing stable employment. This type of activity ties in directly with the kind of research and planning performed by the State labor agencies and by the Department of Labor, particularly that of its Bureau of Labor Statistics.

The only real relationship between unemployment compensation and other functions in the Federal Security Agency is that it is a social insurance. This is only a theoretical relationship. Pay-roll deductions for unemployment compensation and old-age and survivors' insurance are enforced by the Bureau of Internal Revenue. Beyond the collection of pay-roll taxes there is no common point of administration. Old-age and survivors' insurance is Federal, unemployment compensation is State. The employment function, and with it the administration of unemployment compensation, is part of the complex of functions dealing with the labor force.

Recommendation No. 3

The Commission recommends the transfer of the Bureau of Employment Security to the Department of Labor.

Selective Service System

This System functions essentially for the purpose of mobilizing the manpower of the country for military service. The system is now an independent agency reporting to the President, yet the President cannot give it over-all supervision. Its personnel, except in top positions, is entirely civilian. To place it under the Secretary of Defense would raise the most serious objections, since its operation involves many considerations which require that its supervision be objective and not be biased in favor of the military. On the other hand, the effect of conscription on the labor force must receive the continual examination which can be provided by the Labor Department.

Recommendation No. 4

We recommend that the Selective Service System be placed under the Secretary of Labor.

Bureau of Veterans' Reemployment Rights

This Bureau should be administered in conjunction with the placement service program. The removal of this program from the Labor Department has left this Bureau isolated. It would be restored to proper functioning by the relocation of the Employment Service in the Department.

Determination of Minimum Wages for Seamen

As seamen's wages have become increasingly a matter of international negotiation, and as the managerial responsibilities of the Maritime Commission over the shipping industry are reduced by transfer of its executive functions to the Department of Commerce, it becomes appropriate for these determinations to be made by the Department of Labor where their relation to wages in other industries can be evaluated.

Recommendation No. 5

We recommend that the determinations of minimum wages for seamen on privately operated vessels should be transferred from the Maritime Commission to the Secretary of Labor.

Veterans' Employment Service

At present, the Veterans' Employment Service is nominally a part of the Bureau of Employment Security, but its chief is appointed by the Chairman of the Veterans' Placement Service Board, who is the Administrator of Veterans' Affairs. The need for correction of this anomalous administrative arrangement is evident.

Recommendation No. 6

The functions of the Veterans' Employment Service in the Bureau of Employment Security should be merged with the employment service of the Bureau of Employment Security.

Statistics Relating to Labor

"Prevailing Wage" inquiries incident to determining wages for "blue collar" Federal employees are now conducted by the several agencies and should be centered in the Bureau of Labor Statistics. Some overlaps with the Census Bureau, the Bureau of Mines, and the Bureau of Employment Security exist. These should be corrected as recommended by our task force on Statistical Activities.

Recommendation No. 7

The Division of Statistical Standards in the Office of the Budget, in its efforts to coordinate statistical activities,[5] should focus responsibility in the Bureau of Labor Statistics for collection of

[5] Report on Budgeting and Accounting.

data, research, and analysis relating to wholesale prices and living costs, employment and unemployment, working hours, wages and pay rolls, and productivity.

Industrial Hygiene

The recent Federal policy in grants to the States for industrial hygiene work has created serious imbalance in State programs and is closely related to established Department of Labor functions and programs. The Public Health Service's administration of grants to State health departments on a two-for-one basis has led the States to build up their health departments and to let the industrial hygiene work of their labor agencies atrophy. This is a serious situation inasmuch as the actual inspection and administration of industrial hygiene and labor standards generally is traditionally part of the State labor agencies' factory inspection and general labor work.

At the Federal level, the centering of grants for industrial hygiene in the Public Health Service overlaps the responsibility of the Bureau of Labor Standards and the Wage and Hour Division in the Department of Labor. The former is responsible for working with State labor agencies, trade unions, and others in developing and promoting standards of safety and health. It assists in the preparation, among other labor laws, of State industrial safety codes. The Wage and Hour and Public Contracts Divisions have a field service including a factory inspection service to administer the Fair Labor Standards Act and the Walsh-Healey Act (public contracts).

The imbalance between State labor and health agencies would be corrected by a better allocation of functions on the Federal level.

Recommendation No. 8

The Commission recommends that a detailed study be made of industrial hygiene functions to work out a logical division of functions between labor and health agencies.

Other Agencies

The question has been raised as to the restoration of the Federal Mediation and Conciliation Service to the Department, and placing in the Department, for housekeeping purposes, the National Mediation Board, which deals with labor disputes involving rail and air carriers, and the National Labor Relations Board.

331

The Congress is engaged in revising labor policies which will affect some of these agencies. The Commission can make no recommendations as to their organization until these questions are settled.

General Comment

In general, it can be said that the Department of Labor has lost much of its significance and should have restored to it the many agencies we have here recommended. This would make for greater efficiency in the Government.

XV
Medical Activities

Chapter One

REORGANIZATION OF FEDERAL MEDICAL ACTIVITIES

The immediate purpose of the Commission, in recommending reorganization of Federal medical activities, is to unite the functions now in five major agencies so as to eliminate overlap, waste, and inefficiency. The proposed form of organization is a unification in which each of the major agencies will have an advisory voice in management.

However, the much wider and critically necessary objectives are:

First: To provide better medical care for the beneficiaries of the Federal Government's medical programs.

Second: To create a better foundation for training and medical service in the Federal agencies.

Third: To reduce the drain of doctors away from private practice. The country is now dreadfully short of doctors.

Fourth: To provide better organization for medical research.

Fifth: To promote a better state of medical preparedness for war.

Recommendation No. 1

To accomplish these purposes, the Commission recommends the establishment of a United Medical Administration into which would be consolidated most of the large-scale activities of the Federal Government in the fields of medical care, medical research, and public health (in which we include preventive medicine).

It should be said at once that, under this plan, the military medical services would remain intact, except for hospitalization within the United States. Each of the three services would retain one major teaching and

335

research center (such as the Naval Medical Center at Bethesda, Md., and the Walter Reed General Hospital, Washington, D. C.). The professional personnel of the services may be assigned to the new Administration for duty, research, and training. The proposed United Medical Administration would provide the major part of all hospital care required by the military forces in the continental United States.

The Veterans' Administration would continue to certify patients for treatment and would determine disability, ratings, etc., but the United Medical Administration would look after veterans' medical care.

The recommendation of our task force that medical supply be centralized in a single agency, preferably in one of the Armed Forces or in the United Medical Administration, merits favorable consideration.

In reaching the conclusion that medical services should be unified, the Commission had the aid of extensive surveys by its distinguished task forces on Medical Services and on the National Security Organization. The recommendations set forth in our report are generally in accord with those submitted by these two task forces.

The task force on Medical Services was instructed to base its original report on the premise that "the Commission will recommend a Cabinet Department embracing health, education, and security." However, in view of the size of the medical operations of the Federal Government and the extreme dissimilarities among the activities which would have composed such a department, the task force was later requested to consider the advisability of placing medical service functions in a single agency. Its supplementary report favors very strongly a separate United Medical Administration.

Medical Obligations of Government

The Federal Government is attempting to give varying degrees of direct medical care to 24,000,000 beneficiaries—about one-sixth of the Nation. Veterans estimated to number over 18,500,000 constitute the bulk of this large segment of our population. Present and future personnel of the Military Establishment will increase this number as they become eligible for veterans' benefits upon discharge from service.

At one extreme of those receiving medical care are members of the armed forces, their dependents, merchant seamen, and other lesser groups totaling upwards of 3,000,000 persons. They are eligible for almost complete medical care.[1] At the other extreme are about 2,000,000

[1] Dependents of members of the armed forces receive full medical care only under certain circumstances.

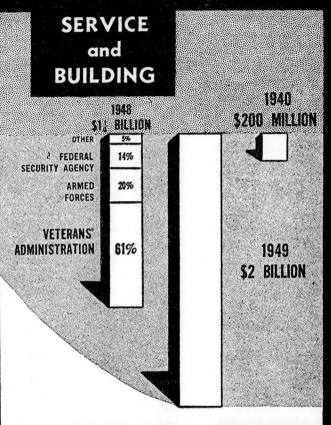

FEDERAL MEDICAL EXPENDITURES

SERVICE and BUILDING

1948
$1½ BILLION

OTHER	5%
FEDERAL SECURITY AGENCY	14%
ARMED FORCES	20%
VETERANS' ADMINISTRATION	61%

1940
$200 MILLION

1949
$2 BILLION

PROPOSED HOSPITAL CONSTRUCTION TOTAL: $1¼ BILLION

HILL-BURTON PROGRAM	$225 MILLION
VARIOUS AGENCIES	$200 MILLION
VETERANS' ADMINISTRATION	$820 MILLION

employees of the Federal Government. They are eligible for medical care only for industrial accidents and outpatient service of the industrial hygiene type.

Over 40 Government agencies render Federal medical service. In this fiscal year they plan to spend nearly $2 billion, about 10 times the amount spent in 1940. Last fiscal year's expenditures were about one and a quarter billion dollars. Most of this money (61 percent) was spent by the Veterans' Administration. The armed forces expended more than half of the remainder and the balance represented costs in the Federal Security Agency, the Department of Agriculture, the Atomic Energy Commission, the Department of the Interior, the Department of Justice, and many other agencies. (See chart, Federal Medical Expenditures.)

Over 85 percent of the total expenditures during the last fiscal year was for direct medical care. The rest went for public health, research activities, training, and administration. Expenditures for research were less than 4 percent of the total.

Almost one-half of the estimated cost of the Veterans' Administration medical program for this fiscal year will be for construction of hospitals. Its hospital building program, until recently, contemplated a total expenditure of $1.1 billion. Projects for the construction of new hospitals by other agencies total another $200,000,000. At the same time, the Government is planning to spend $225,000,000 over the next 3 years to aid non-Federal hospital construction under the Hill-Burton Act. Thus the plans for hospital construction totaled around $1.5 billion.

However, after our task force's report was made public, the President altered the Veterans' Administration construction program by canceling authorizations for 24 hospitals with an aggregate capacity of 11,000 beds, and reduced the size of 14 additional hospitals by an aggregate of about 5,000 beds. The Veterans' Administration estimates that this action will result in a saving of $280,000,000 in construction costs alone, thus reducing its projected $1.1 billion program by that amount. This will be done without reducing the quality and extent of medical service to the veterans.

Chapter Two

DEFICIENCIES IN PRESENT CONDUCT
OF MEDICAL ACTIVITIES

1. General

More than half of the departments and agencies of the Federal Government conduct medical or health activities. These agencies compete for doctors and other technical personnel, and for funds. There is no central supervision of their activities; and they operate under diverse policies with respect to quality of treatment, types of beneficiaries served, types of research, and areas of authority.

The enormous and expanding Federal medical activities are devoid of any central plan. Four large, and many smaller Government agencies, obtain funds and build hospitals with little knowledge of, and no regard for, the needs of the others. They compete with each other for scarce personnel. No one has responsibility for an over-all plan. There is not even a clear definition of the classes of beneficiaries for whom care is to be planned. The Government is moving into uncalculated obligations without an understanding of their ultimate costs, of the lack of professional manpower available to discharge them, or of the adverse effect upon the hospital system of the country.

It is fundamental that whatever care the Government provides must be of the highest quality. The health of the Nation demands the maximum employment of present scientific knowledge to control disease, and of research to find new means for the prevention of disease. Such research must be stimulated and supported to the maximum limits of available manpower. The Nation's future can best be protected by using every means to prevent disease, rather than by providing unlimited hospitalization to treat it. Medical care offered by the Federal Government should be a model for the Nation.

339

The present methods being employed by the Federal Government make it impossible to achieve these objectives. It is essential that Federal medical services be so organized as to provide for over-all planning and for execution of these plans.

2. Dissimilarities in Construction Costs

The per bed construction cost varies from $20,000 in the larger hospitals to from $30,000 to $51,000 in the small ones. This compares with an estimated cost of $16,000 per bed in voluntary hospitals.

3. Failure to Utilize Capacity

While these great new construction programs are going forward, there is a large unused capacity in existing Federal hospitals. On June 30, 1948, there were only 155,000 patients in Government hospitals having a capacity of 255,000. (See chart.) Yet, despite the President's recent action reducing its building program by 16,000 beds, the Veterans' Administration alone is planning or has already contracted for 38,000 additional beds, of which 15,000 are under contract. Continuation of present policies may lead to a hospital system in 1980 of 300,000 beds for the Veterans' Administration alone. The armed forces plan an additional 5,000.

4. Lack of Trained Manpower

There is insufficient medical manpower to staff existing facilities. In the Veterans' Administration, 5,600 beds are now closed because of inability to service them. The best opinion is that staff personnel is available for only about 120,000 Veterans' Administration beds. Construction is far outrunning available manpower.

None of the Federal agencies has the manpower resources in sight to meet its responsibilities. This shortage is particularly acute in the armed forces, where the lack of medical specialists is critical. The situation is neither temporary nor self-correcting. Federal agencies, as presently organized, compete with each other and civilian institutions, thereby aggravating conditions. They do not make proper utilization of their physician personnel. There is no planning by the Federal organizations in relation to the medical and hospital resources of the country as a whole.

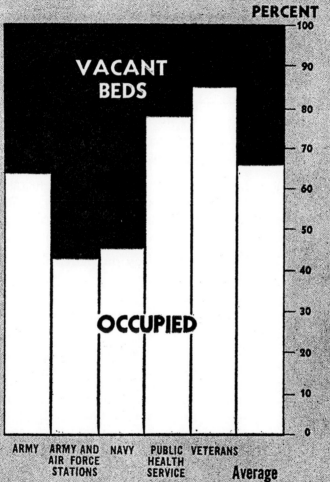

USE OF FEDERAL HOSPITALS
(GENERAL HOSPITALS, AS OF JUNE 30, 1948)

PERCENT

VACANT
BEDS

OCCUPIED

100

90

80

70

60

50

40

30

20

10

0

ARMY   ARMY AND   NAVY   PUBLIC   VETERANS
        AIR FORCE   HEALTH
        STATIONS   SERVICE   Average

5. A Medical Draft

This summer, the tour of duty of some 1,700 medical officers in our armed forces, trained under the wartime V-12 program and the Army Special Training Program (ASTP) will expire. Most of these young physicians have indicated their desire to enter private practice.

Great difficulty is being encountered by the armed forces in voluntary recruitment of medical personnel. It has been suggested that it will be necessary to draft certain medical personnel to replace the young physicians who are leaving the service. This is a policy matter for the Congress to determine.

Even if Congress should enact a draft law for medical personnel, it would still be improbable that the armed forces could obtain sufficient numbers of medical and surgical specialists. This is absolutely essential if the men in the armed forces are to get adequate medical care.

6. The Varied Quality of Service

The most important result of this situation is its effect on the quality of medical care which is available to the beneficiaries of this system. This is inadequate as far as military personnel are concerned.

7. Lack of Clear Policy on Beneficiaries

An enormous plant is being built for groups of beneficiaries, to many of whom the Federal Government has no clearly defined obligation. Veterans with nonservice-connected disabilities are receiving care in Veterans' Administration hospital beds, under an authorization to hospitalize them only if beds are "available." Yet about 100,000 Veterans' Administration hospital beds have been built or authorized which serve no purpose except to make beds available for nonservice-connected cases. It may be presumed that Congress must have expected that care to this extent would be given; otherwise it would not have made appropriations for the beds. But the fiction of limiting the right to such care only if a bed is "available" leads to the construction of a Federal hospital plant at staggering costs, although much of the hospitalization might be more economically provided in community hospitals on a reimbursable basis.

Because veterans with nonservice-connected disabilities are authorized to receive only hospital care, it has not been possible to give them outpatient care, nor effectively to employ the kind of preventive measures that might avert long, chronic hospitalization. The present eligibility provision for such cases is highly uncertain in operation, giving the veteran no assurance of hospital care when he needs it. The fact that hospital care can be obtained merely by signing a statement indicating inability to pay has the effect of giving care to some who are in much less financial need of this assistance than are others who do not apply for it.

Over 60 years ago an appropriation act authorized medical officers to care for dependents of Army personnel "whenever practicable." On the basis of this act, some 900,000 dependents of Army and Air Force personnel are receiving, or are considered eligible for, substantially free medical care. Congress has supported this practice by appropriations year after year.

8. Failure to Make Best Use of Highly Skilled Private and University Physicians

There are not enough highly skilled specialists in the Federal service. In an effort to remedy this situation, the Veterans' Administration established in 1946 a program for utilizing the best skilled physicians and surgeons in the Nation, both in private practice and in universities. (Other agencies have not followed this lead as effectively or extensively.) The hospitals so staffed would become part of a United Medical Administration which would thereby be in position to give a far better caliber medical care to all services. This not only would benefit those receiving care, but it also would be invaluable in improving the training opportunities for medical personnel within the Federal Government.

For the physicians and other skilled medical personnel in the armed forces, this would offer a great opportunity. It would be possible, for instance, for the Surgeons General and the Air Surgeon to detail military personnel to hospitals having superior facilities, a more varied clinical load, and more expert instruction.

Chapter Three

THE PROPOSED UNITED MEDICAL
ADMINISTRATION

Only the creation of a new United Medical Administration can remedy the weaknesses of the present organization and give the leadership, direction and planning urgently needed. To it would be transferred the Government's major services in the field of medical care, public health, and medical research.

The Nation's vast medical services, which we have noted lack any central plan of operation, require unified responsibility. The Government must have a central plan if waste and inefficiency are to be avoided. The advantages of unification of Federal medical services include the following:

a. The general standard of Federal medical care would be improved.

b. There would be central supervision of the major Federal medical care, public health, and medical research activities. Unified responsibility is the key to good management. The President, the Congress, and the public could look to one man for results.

c. Construction costs could be standardized and reduced.

d. Federal hospitals could be utilized to the fullest extent by eliminating present distinctions as to the particular types of beneficiaries for which each can care. After all, a patient is a patient whether he is a veteran, a merchant seaman, or in the Army, Navy, or Air Force.

e. The medical manpower at the call of the Federal Government could be used to the fullest extent, and present deficits in skilled personnel could be greatly reduced.

f. The need for any draft of medical manpower in time of peace would be greatly lessened.

g. The cost of health and medical services would be clearly identified and known to Congress.

h. The facilities of private hospitals and the skills of physicians in private life and in the universities could be utilized far more effectively than they are now.

Organization

This unification does not contemplate the creation of an additional Government agency in the usual sense. It proposes uniting the facilities and resources of existing agencies.

The Administration should be headed by an outstanding Administrator. He should report directly to the President. He should be the ablest medical and health administrator whose services can be obtained by the Government. The Administration should be manned by career personnel drawn initially from the various agencies whose functions are recommended for transfer to the new United Medical Administration, supplemented by medical officers whom the armed services would have the right to detail for training and rotation.

This practice of detailing medical officers from the armed services would offer marked advantages. It would make possible far better training for these medical officers and they would be given more interesting, and broader, opportunities in the field of medicine. The result would be far better care for the military personnel for whose health they are responsible.

In addition, the Administration should utilize to the full medical personnel of proved competence in private practice and in the universities.

Advisory Board

Recommendation No. 2

Therefore, the Commission recommends that the Administrator of the United Medical Administration should be assisted by an advisory board, consisting of the Surgeons General of the Army and Navy, the Air Surgeon, and the Administrator of Veterans' Affairs or his representative. This board should advise the Administrator on policies. Thus, we propose a unity of services in the national interest, rather than separate services to special groups.

Over-all Management

In our first report, we recommended that all departments and agencies should have adequate direction at the highest level. In the case of the United Medical Administration, there should be three Assistant Administrators who might be either professional men or general executives of wide experience.

Particularly in the hospitalization field, the function of management research should be emphasized. Furthermore, arrangements should be made for adequate liaison with Congress. One of the Assistant Administrators should be assigned to the supervision of the following officials:

a. GENERAL COUNSEL
b. FINANCIAL OFFICER (budgeting and accounting)
c. SUPPLY OFFICER
d. MANAGEMENT RESEARCH OFFICER
e. PUBLICATIONS AND INFORMATION OFFICER
f. DIRECTOR OF PERSONNEL

Recommendation No. 3

We recommend that the Adminstrator and three Assistant Administrators be appointed by the President with the advice and consent of the Senate. All other officials in the Administration should be appointed by the Administrator and due consideration should be given to the promotion of properly qualified personnel in the career service.

Components of Medical Administration

Recommendation No. 4

We recommend that the functions, facilities, and the personnel for medical care of the following activities should be transferred to the United Medical Administration.

a. The general hospitals of the armed forces in the continental United States (except a medical center for each of the three services), and station hospitals (certain of which the Navy calls "dispensaries") in the continental United States except those at outlying posts so located that other hospitals of the United Medical Administration would not be near enough to provide the care required.

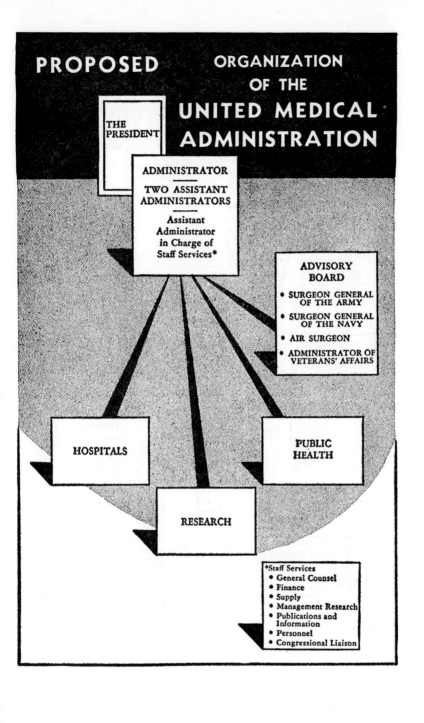

PROPOSED ORGANIZATION OF THE UNITED MEDICAL ADMINISTRATION

THE PRESIDENT

ADMINISTRATOR
———
TWO ASSISTANT ADMINISTRATORS
———
Assistant Administrator in Charge of Staff Services*

ADVISORY BOARD

• SURGEON GENERAL OF THE ARMY
• SURGEON GENERAL OF THE NAVY
• AIR SURGEON
• ADMINISTRATOR OF VETERANS' AFFAIRS

HOSPITALS

PUBLIC HEALTH

RESEARCH

*Staff Services
• General Counsel
• Finance
• Supply
• Management Research
• Publications and Information
• Personnel
• Congressional Liaison

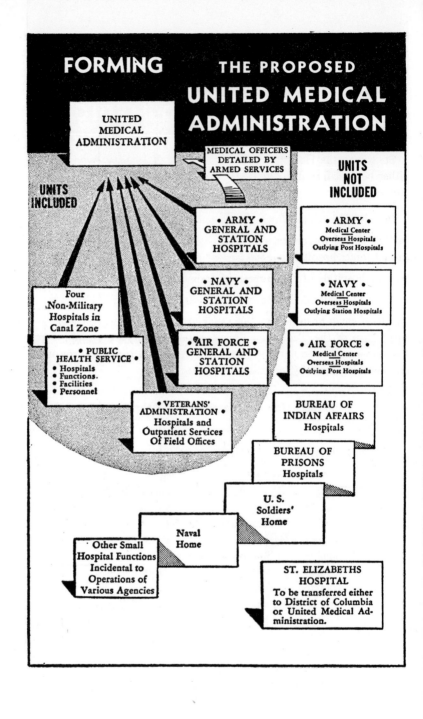

FORMING THE PROPOSED UNITED MEDICAL ADMINISTRATION

UNITED MEDICAL ADMINISTRATION

MEDICAL OFFICERS DETAILED BY ARMED SERVICES

UNITS NOT INCLUDED

UNITS INCLUDED

• ARMY •
GENERAL AND STATION HOSPITALS

• ARMY •
Medical Center
Overseas Hospitals
Outlying Post Hospitals

Four Non-Military Hospitals in Canal Zone

• NAVY •
GENERAL AND STATION HOSPITALS

• NAVY •
Medical Center
Overseas Hospitals
Outlying Station Hospitals

• PUBLIC HEALTH SERVICE •
• Hospitals
• Functions.
• Facilities
• Personnel

• AIR FORCE •
GENERAL AND STATION HOSPITALS

• AIR FORCE •
Medical Center
Overseas Hospitals
Outlying Post Hospitals

• VETERANS' ADMINISTRATION •
Hospitals and Outpatient Services Of Field Offices

BUREAU OF INDIAN AFFAIRS Hospitals

BUREAU OF PRISONS Hospitals

U. S. Soldiers' Home

Naval Home

Other Small Hospital Functions Incidental to Operations of Various Agencies

ST. ELIZABETHS HOSPITAL
To be transferred either to District of Columbia or United Medical Administration.

b. The hospital functions of the Veterans' Administration in toto, including the outpatient services in the field offices of the Veterans' Administration.

c. The four nonmilitary hospitals in the Canal Zone.

d. The hospitals of the Public Health Service.

e. The functions, facilities, and personnel of the Public Health Service.

St. Elizabeths Hospital, now in the Federal Security Agency, should either be transferred to the District of Columbia or included in the new Administration.

Hospital functions which should not be transferred include:

a. The armed forces station hospitals above excepted, together with all armed forces hospitals overseas.

b. The hospitals of the Bureau of Indian Affairs.

c. The hospitals of the Bureau of Prisons.

d. Other small hospital functions such as those which are incident to the operations of the Tennessee Valley Authority and the Atomic Energy Commission. The Indian and prison hospitals should, however, be assisted in procuring staff by professional personnel from the United Medical Administration.

e. The U. S. Soldiers Home in Washington and the U. S. Naval Home in Philadelphia.

Our task force states in substance as follows:

. . . 1. As to armed forces' general hospitals: These general hospitals cannot maintain quality staffs because they lack specialists. High quality care should be given in a unified system; many Veterans' Administration and some Public Health Service hospitals, which would be transferred to such a system, are already well staffed with specialists because of their association with teaching medical centers. We have found no other way to give high quality care to the armed forces.

2. As to transfer of Veterans' Administration hospitals to the new Administration: If they were to remain separate, the new United Medical Administration would be a central health agency in name only. Only by incorporating the Veterans' Administration hospitals can an integration be achieved which will provide equally high-grade specialist care for the armed forces and the veterans. Only by this means can scarce medical manpower be efficiently utilized.

Congressional Policies

For this plan to function, it must be accompanied by a clear definition by the Congress of the rights and priorities to medical care of all the various classes of beneficiaries. Based upon such a new definition, this plan presupposes that the resources in medical manpower and the facilities of community hospitals—where these are of satisfactory quality—will be utilized for care of Federal beneficiaries to the maximum extent possible.

The principle should be that hospital care for Federal beneficiaries be planned in relation to the hospital resources of the country as a whole, not merely through construction of Federal hospitals as a class apart.

It must be constantly borne in mind that assumption of Federal financial responsibility is an entirely distinct question from provision of such medical care directly in Federal hospitals.

Beneficiaries

The basic question as to what the Government owes to its veterans and the dependents of members of the armed forces is a policy matter which must be determined by the Congress. The decision as to what financial burden for medical care is to be assumed is separate and distinct from the question as to whether such care should be given in Federal hospitals. But such a decision is essential for sound planning.

A single policy for dependents of armed forces personnel should apply to all three services. The right to medical care for dependents is an inducement to remain in the armed services, and is a morale factor. The question is really one of pay of the armed forces, except overseas and in posts in this country remote from adequate community facilities and professional personnel. In such areas, care by military doctors is essential.

Recommendation No. 5

Congress should define the beneficiaries entitled to medical care from the Government and prescribe how this care should be given.

Chapter Four

FURTHER RECOMMENDATIONS

Integration with Non-Federal Hospital System

Inadequacies exist in the Nation's hospital plant. The Federal Government has recognized the need for aid in remedying them and is now giving such assistance. This effort would be furthered by hospitalizing Federal patients in non-Federal hospitals on a reimbursable basis wherever it is efficient to do so, instead of further enlarging the Federal hospital plant. In that way, many such patients could be cared for near home in their community hospitals. (See chart, Care of Federal Patients under Proposed System.)

This step is further indicated because the Federal Government is dependent upon voluntary and other community teaching hospitals for undergraduate and postgraduate training of medical personnel, and for the advancement of medical science by joint efforts with the medical schools affiliated with them.

Recommendation No. 6

The present inconsistency in policy between the Federal hospital construction program and Federal aid to non-Federal hospitals under the Hill-Burton Act should be ended.

The Armed Services

It is basic that the armed forces must have supporting medical service subject to military control.

The proposal to transfer general hospitals and most station hospitals in the continental United States to a single national hospital system will

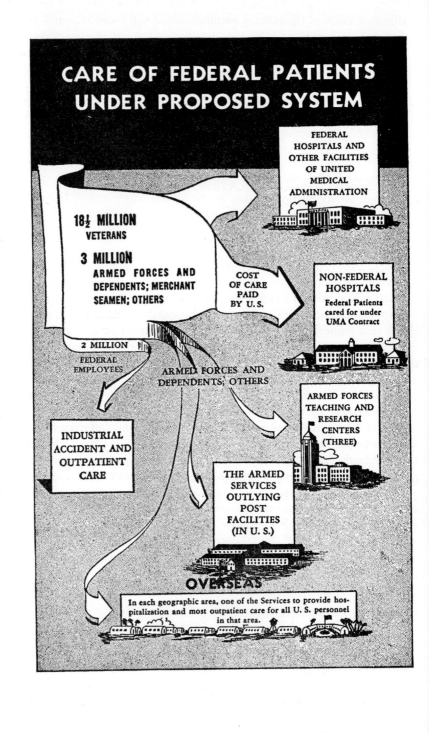

CARE OF FEDERAL PATIENTS UNDER PROPOSED SYSTEM

FEDERAL HOSPITALS AND OTHER FACILITIES OF UNITED MEDICAL ADMINISTRATION

18½ MILLION
VETERANS

3 MILLION
ARMED FORCES AND DEPENDENTS; MERCHANT SEAMEN; OTHERS

COST OF CARE PAID BY U.S.

NON-FEDERAL HOSPITALS
Federal Patients cared for under UMA Contract

2 MILLION
FEDERAL EMPLOYEES

ARMED FORCES AND DEPENDENTS; OTHERS

ARMED FORCES TEACHING AND RESEARCH CENTERS (THREE)

INDUSTRIAL ACCIDENT AND OUTPATIENT CARE

THE ARMED SERVICES OUTLYING POST FACILITIES (IN U. S.)

OVERSEAS

In each geographic area, one of the Services to provide hospitalization and most outpatient care for all U. S. personnel in that area.

eliminate much of the existing duplication and will conserve scarce professional manpower.

Overseas, the Secretary of Defense should assign to one of the services full responsibility for the hospitalization, and much of the outpatient care, of all United States personnel in each geographic area. This proved successful during the war; it should be done now in an even more systematic manner. This step would conserve scarce medical personnel and effect optimum use of facilities. The service having greatest responsibilities in an area would be the natural choice for the task there.

Recommendation No. 7

The control of medical policy in the armed services should be exercised by the Secretary of Defense.

National Defense

These recommendations, it is believed, are calculated to provide a sound organization, not only for our peacetime requirements, but also for war emergency needs. The United Medical Administration should give continuing attention to the wartime medical needs of the country, including the status and availability of medical personnel and the relative facilities of Government and civilian hospitals. The overwhelming shortage of doctors which war would create could thereby be met by optimum utilization of those we have. Not only would the proposed single Federal hospital system reduce the need for full-time Federal doctors by making more care of Federal beneficiaries possible without withdrawing physicians from their communities, but it would also assist in saving doctors because it could be fully integrated with non-Federal hospitals. The problems of another war would mean that not as many physicians as in the last war could be taken from their communities. To do so would destroy essential civil defense.

Recommendation No. 8

The United Medical Administration should give constant attention to necessary measures for national defense.

Personnel Policies in Medical Services

The United Medical Administration should have full responsibility for recruiting, selecting, assigning, training, and otherwise handling its own professional and technical civilian personnel on the basis of standards determined by it but approved and enforced by the Civil Service Commission. It should make greater use of ancillary technical personnel.

Recommendation No. 9

Medical and other technical personnel in the Administration should be on a career service basis.

Aid to Medical Education

Many schools are in serious condition. Adequate facts on which to base the extent of, or to determine intelligently, the aid required are not now available. There should be a short-range survey immediately made by an independent commission appointed by the President to determine the real needs for emergency aid, amplified later by a longer range study. Any aid must be given in a manner to maintain the professional independence and the initiative of the schools, and in a way which will increase the output and result, partially at least, in meeting especially acute current deficiencies.

Recommendation No. 10

A survey should be made to determine the needs for emergency aid to medical schools.

Control of Disease

The necessity for medical care, which requires heavy expenditures and much personnel, must not be permitted to result in minimizing the even greater importance of controlling disease. Research must be stimulated, and supported to the extent which may prove necessary, to the maximum potential of the skilled manpower available to conduct it.

Since the Federal Government now gives varying degrees of medical care to one-sixth of the Nation and since it may very well face expansion in veterans' hospitalization as veterans grow older and as their numbers increase, the Government can protect its financial position best by using every means to prevent disease rather than to treat it by unlimited hospitalization. This will also promote both the national welfare in peace and a stronger manpower to preserve our security in war. The highest priority in Federal medical expenditures should, therefore, go to the research and public health fields. We must, and to a large degree we can, if we will, control disease.

Recommendation No. 11

The highest priority in importance should be given to research, preventive medicine, public health, and education.

XVI
Veterans' Affairs

Chapter One

REORGANIZATION OF THE VETERANS' ADMINISTRATION

The Veterans' Administration, according to budget estimates, will spend more money in fiscal year 1950 than any other Federal agency except the National Military Establishment and the Treasury Department. Its expenditures for that year will amount to an estimated 5.3 billion dollars, which is about 11 percent of the total national budget.

Some of the major services which the Veterans' Administration is expected to provide for veterans are:

	Number of Veterans Assisted
EDUCATION AND TRAINING PROGRAMS	1,575,000
COMPENSATION AND PENSION ROLLS	3,002,042
(as of June 30, 1950)	
VOCATIONAL REHABILITATION ALLOWANCES	157,000
AVERAGE DAILY PATIENT LOAD	119,586
(veterans' hospitals)	
READJUSTMENT ALLOWANCES	74,000
HOME LOAN GUARANTEES	275,000
OTHER LOAN GUARANTEES	18,000
(farm and business)	

The cost of these services is estimated as follows:

Program	Cost
READJUSTMENT BENEFITS (including education and training programs)	$2,118,000,000
PENSIONS	2,111,000,000
MISCELLANEOUS BENEFITS	82,000,000
HOSPITAL FACILITIES (new construction)	81,000,000
SALARIES AND EXPENSES (including operation of hospitals)	859,000,000
TOTAL	$5,251,000,000

The totals of guarantees of loans to veterans exceeds $3.5 billion; veterans' life insurance serves nearly 7 million veterans, with insurance outstanding of over $2.2 billion. The total number of employees of the Veterans' Administration on July 1, 1948, was 186,000 persons, distributed as follows:

Place	Number of Employees
WASHINGTON OFFICE	11,732
BRANCH OFFICES (13)	20,809
REGIONAL OFFICES (60)	61,556
HOSPITAL FACILITIES	90,583
SUPPLY DEPOTS (4)	905
PHILIPPINE ISLANDS OFFICES	532

Defects in the Structure of the Veterans' Administration

In pointing out the defects in the Veterans' Administration, we wish to emphasize that this Commission is cognizant of the tremendous and sudden burden thrown upon the organization by the last world war. Services to an additional 14,900,000 veterans were authorized by various acts of Congress. Experience under this heavy work load has dictated certain changes in organization that represent real progress.

While the Administrator of Veterans' Affairs enjoys broader administrative discretion in organizing his agency than most important governmental officials, serious internal organizational defects still exist.

a. There are conflicting lines of authority between the officials in Washington and the line officers in the field, which result in divided responsibility for a given program.

b. There are too many organizational units within the Veterans' Administration, many of which are based on a process rather than a program. In addition to the Executive Assistant Administrator, there are nine Assistant Administrators and a Chief Medical Director in the Washington office. The number of employees supervised by each of these ranges from 70 to 2,991.

c. There is an excessive number of staff officers for major programs, causing confusion of responsibility within the headquarters in Washington.

d. The entire structure has become too complicated, and there is an excess of voluminous written instructions on internal methods and procedures which defy intelligent execution. For example, there are 88 different manuals, 665 varieties of technical bulletins, and over 400 circulars of various kinds.

e. Administrative difficulties have arisen out of conditions over which the Administrator of Veterans' Affairs has had little control. For example, the armed forces have not fully advised military personnel, upon separation, about their insurance rights. There has been trouble in obtaining full cooperation from policyholders on premium payments.

f. A high employee turnover within the Administration has militated against efficient operation.

Proposed Management Reforms

In our first report we urged that good departmental administration requires that the head of a department or agency have authority from the Congress to organize and control his organization, and that independent authority to subordinates be eliminated.

In our report on the budget, we proposed a new form of "performance" budget for all departments. We also proposed that each department or agency keep its own administrative accounts in the manner prescribed by an Accountant General in the Treasury and subject to the approval and audit of the Comptroller General.[1] We also recommended that personnel recruitment be performed by the department (except possibly in the lower grades), subject to standards and methods

[1] Report on Budgeting and Accounting.

361

of merit selection to be proposed by the department, but with the approval and enforcement of the Civil Service Commission.[2] Likewise the Commission recommended elsewhere that the procurement of supplies peculiar to a department be decentralized into the department, under standards and methods established by the Office of General Services. The items of common use would of course be handled by the latter office.[3] Further, we proposed that the department should strengthen its management research unit, working in cooperation with a comparable staff unit under the Office of the Budget.[4]

Proposed Organization

The Veterans' Administrator, in a recent directive, abolished the thirteen branch offices, which were supervised by Deputy Administrators. This directive requires the 70 regional offices and 12 centers to report directly to the Administrator and calls for the liquidation of all branch office operations except those relating to insurance. The burden of close and unified supervision over field installations, which has heretofore been provided by the branch offices, will require major improvements in the structure of the central office. A clear separation of staff and line operations must be made and each program must be supervised by a single official, acting as an agent of the Administrator.

Recommendation No. 1

The Commission recommends:

a. **That the Administrator of Veterans' Affairs reorganize his office in Washington in accordance with the general principles suggested in our first report.[5]**

b. **That the title of the Executive Assistant Administrator be changed to Deputy Administrator, and that there be three or more Assistant Administrators, whose functions will be assigned by the Administrator.**

c. **That all management services be consolidated under an Assistant Administrator for Administrative Services.[6]**

d. **That the Coordination Service become an Office of Management**

[2] Report on Personnel Management.
[3] Report on The Office of General Services.
[4] Report on General Management of the Executive Branch.
[5] See Report on General Management of the Executive Branch.
[6] See Report on Medical Services.

Research under an Assistant Administrator, and that it include the present inspection and investigation research service.

e. That all functions relating to insurance be consolidated and incorporated into a Veterans' Life Insurance Corporation.

f. That the administration of pensions, retirement benefits, disability compensation, and guardianships be consolidated in a Veterans' Benefit Service.

g. That administration of the vocational rehabilitation, education and readjustment allowance programs, as well as the certification of veterans for loan guaranties, be consolidated in a Readjustment Service.

h. That the Office of Legislation be consolidated with that of the General Counsel.

The resulting top organization of the Veterans' Administration except for the Department of Medicine and Surgery and the Office of Special Services,[7] would then be:

a. THE ADMINISTRATOR
b. THE DEPUTY ADMINISTRATOR
c. ASSISTANT ADMINISTRATORS, three or more
d. THE BOARD OF VETERANS' APPEALS
e. THE GENERAL COUNSEL
f. THE OFFICE OF FOREIGN RELATIONS
g. THE OFFICE OF INFORMATION
h. THE ASSISTANT ADMINISTRATOR FOR ADMINISTRATIVE SERVICES
    including:
                         Finance
                         Personnel
                         Supply and Real Estate
                         Management Research
i. THE VETERANS' LIFE INSURANCE CORPORATION
j. THE VETERANS' BENEFIT SERVICE, under a director
k. THE READJUSTMENT SERVICE, under a director

Recommendation No. 2

The Commission recommends that all directives from the Central Office be promulgated by the Administrator.

[7] See Report on Medical Services.

363

Chapter Two

LIFE INSURANCE

As of June 30, 1948, the Veterans' Administration was handling nearly 7 million life insurance policies with a face value of nearly 40 billion dollars.

The insurance in force was divided as follows

	No. of Policies	Value of Policies
U. S. GOVERNMENT LIFE INSURANCE (World War I Veterans)	514,000	$2,242,000,000
NATIONAL SERVICE LIFE INSURANCE (World War II Veterans)	6,437,000	37,676,000,000
TOTAL INSURANCE in force	6,951,000	39,918,000,000

Some 1,800,000 policies, or 26 percent of the total on June 30, 1948, were held by persons still in the military service. Premium payments on these policies are deducted from military pay by the armed forces and transmitted to the Veterans' Administration. On all the remaining insurance policies the Veterans' Administration collects premium payments directly from the insured individual.

Comparison With Private Firms

In order to perform its insurance activities, the Veterans' Administration on June 30, 1948, had a total of 15,432 employees engaged in these operations. The average work load, therefore, was 450 policies per employee.

Our task force on Veterans' Affairs has reported that the private company providing the best basis of comparison has a work load per employee of 1,762 policies. This is about four times that of the Veterans' Administration. The Metropolitan Life Insurance Co. has a work load per employee in its "ordinary life" department of 1,706 policies.

SIMPLER OPERATIONS

Our task force points out that there are certain differences between the insurance operations of the Veterans' Administration and those of a private life insurance company which make the work of the Veterans' Administration simpler:

First: Because National Service Life Insurance is so new, and because many of its policies are on a term plan, cash surrenders and policy loans are very few. Seventy-seven percent of national insurance in force is still in term policy form.

Second: There are no agents selling life insurance or collecting premiums for the Veterans' Administration, and hence there are no "new business" or "agency" departments in the Administration and no accounting system is required to take care of commission payments.

Third: There is no investment department, since premium receipts are turned over to the Treasury Department and invested in Government bonds.

MORE COMPLICATED

On the other hand, the following aspects of the insurance operations of the Veterans' Administration are somewhat more complicated than those of a private insurance company:

First: A much larger proportion of the premium payments to the Veterans' Administration are made monthly.

Second: Since National Service Life Insurance issued to members of the armed forces during the war was term insurance, it must be converted to other forms of insurance in order to be continued indefinitely. This may mean a large volume of conversion operations.

Third: The Veterans' Administration deals directly with all policyholders, while private companies have the benefit of screening their work through local agency offices.

Our task force in evaluating the advantages and disadvantages under which the Veterans' Administration operates as compared to private life insurance companies states: "It would seem that if the monthly payment of premiums is allowed for, the necessary clerical operations per policy are at least no greater than those in the commercial companies."

The work load per employee is far less than the number of premium payments, conversions, and individual contacts should warrant. This is illustrated by the comparison made by our task force between an agency branch office and a company of similar size. With about the same number of employees, the company handled five times as many policies as the branch office, sent out more premium postings and letters, and indeed exceeded the performance of the branch office on all of 10 types of operation.

Deficiencies in Insurance Operations

A number of deficiencies exist in the present handling of insurance operations.

a. The issuance of converted insurance policies has lagged, and the calculation of insurance dividends owed to policyholders has been long delayed.

b. The separation of the handling of death claims from insurance operations has created some inefficiency.

c. Machines for premium billing and accounting have not been utilized to the fullest.

d. Private inspection services have not been adequately utilized to corroborate claims.

e. Work measurement standards have not been adopted to the fullest extent possible.

f. The premium record card has often been inefficiently kept and policies sometimes lapse because of a failure to keep addressograph plates for premium billing in agreement with payment records.

g. Supervision of insurance operations has not been adequate, and employees have lacked sufficient training for performance of the more difficult tasks.

h. Service on death claims has been very slow and has been a cause of great irritation. The average time required to process death claims on an insurance contract is much longer for government insurance than for insurance in private companies. On converted Veterans' Administration insurance policies the average time required to process death claims is 80 days. Too many claims remain unpaid for as long as a year. Private companies pay from 71 to 82 percent of their death claims within 15 days after receipt of notice of death.

What Should Be Done for Better Insurance Operations

Recommendation No. 3

The Commission recommends that the insurance operations of the Veterans' Administration, including the processing of death claims from beneficiaries, be separated from all other programs of the Administration and be organized as a Government corporation, under the Government Corporation Act of 1945. The Administrator should be President, with authority for day-by-day operations vested in an Executive Vice President and General Manager, appointed by the Administrator. The Administrator should also be given authority to appoint a part-time advisory board.

The incorporation of all the insurance activities would provide a freedom of action which would allow the corporation to employ the practices of private insurance companies. In accordance with the findings of our task force, we recommend the transfer of the death claims work from the present Office of Claims to the Insurance Corporation. This would eliminate the necessity for checking information outside the corporation and would lessen the amount of paper work which is responsible for much of the present delay and confusion in the handling of death claims.

The insurance activities of the Veterans' Administration generally meet the criteria for a Government corporation. These activities are predominantly of a business nature. The revenues are derived from the sale of insurance service and the whole operation should be self-sustaining, except perhaps for administrative costs. The insurance operation involves a large number of business-type transactions with the public. Moreover, it requires greater flexibility than the customary type of appropriation budget ordinarily permits, and accounting procedures would benefit from the provisions of the Government Corporation Control Act of 1945.

As a Government corporation, the insurance activities would continue to be performed by an administrative agency of the executive branch. The entire financial program would henceforth be shown in a business-type budget submitted annually to the President and the Congress. Congressional action would perhaps be required to provide administrative expenses. Under corporation accounting practice, business-type accounts would be kept on an accrual basis reflecting charges by major types of activity. The corporate type of accounts would be far more useful in reflecting the actual financial condition of operations. The Veterans' Administration has maintained business-type accounts for the insurance funds of the First World War veterans and is contemplating their extension to the accounts of veterans of the recent war. This step would be hastened by incorporation of the Administration's insurance activities.

The commercial-type audit prescribed by the Government Corporation Control Act would provide a more useful tool for management, Presidential, and Congressional review than the existing voucher type of settlement of accounts and claims. This commercial-type audit would include a complete analysis of the financial condition and operations of the insurance program.

Under present practices, the cost of administering the Veterans' Administration insurance program is met from appropriations and is not charged against premium receipts. If organized as a Government corporation, the insurance operations could continue to receive a direct appropriation for all administrative costs. But under corporate financial accounting, the entire and exact amount of this cost would be indicated.

The personnel practices of the Veterans' Administration would not be particularly affected by the incorporation of insurance activities, since most Government corporations are already subject to the personnel laws and rules applicable to other departments and agencies.

Under Government corporation practice, a corporation may arrange compromise claims. While the Administrator of Veterans' Affairs can be sued under the present law, the incorporation of the insurance program would provide some advantages and economies over the established procedures in handling insurance claims.

Government corporations, moreover, ordinarily handle their own disbursement of funds. The incorporation of the insurance program would mean a reduction in paper flow between the Veterans' Administration and the Treasury Department. Moreover, within the Veterans' Administration the insurance corporation could arrange its own separate financial machinery apart from that handling ordinary veterans' benefits.

The incorporation of insurance activities, furthermore, would make it easier to establish a field structure for insurance activities apart from the field organization for other veterans' programs. This field organization could then be based upon that most appropriate to provide economical and efficient administration of the insurance program alone. In addition, such incorporation would more readily permit of comparisons of its operating efficiency with that of private insurance companies.

The corporate form of management for insurance activities could accomplish no miracles overnight in improving the operation of insurance programs. It would provide an opportunity for a fresh start. It would make possible a whole new emphasis upon the economical and efficient performance of the insurance program.

Chapter Three

VOCATIONAL REHABILITATION AND EDUCATION PROGRAMS

The Veterans' Administration manages two broad programs, the one for the vocational rehabilitation and the other for the education of veterans.

For the fiscal year 1948, an estimated average of 235,000 persons each month received vocational rehabilitation training. This program cost 287 million dollars, which is about 5 percent of total agency expenditures during the year.

Under the general education program the average monthly numbei of persons assisted during the fiscal year 1948 came to an estimated 2,218,000. This program accounted for 2,743 million dollars in fiscal year 1949, exclusive of administrative costs, which is 36 percent of total agency obligations during the year.

Deficiencies in the Programs

Our task force has pointed to a number of administrative problems which have arisen in the operation of these programs:

a. The legislation provides the Administrator with very limited authority over education and training. The Federal Government has insufficient control over the quality or the utility of the training provided veterans in many schools.

b. In some instances the Federal Government pays the highest possible tuition and equipment charges to schools where such charges are difficult, if not impossible, to justify.

The Veterans' Administration has been somewhat slow to recognize these problems as they emerged and then to recommend changes in the law where necessary to correct deficiencies in the program. For example, only after a long period of time did it recommend even a partial elimination of avocational and recreational courses. The Administration has also been slow in urging the enactment of standards for on-the-job training. And only at a late date did it decide that the so-called "institutional on-farm" training program had developed on an unsound basis.

c. The Veterans' Administration needs to give immediate attention to the possible use of grants to States to promote better job training and to prevent abuses in related school training.

d. It should also consider cooperation with the Federal apprentice training program in the Department of Labor to prevent the lowering of apprentice training standards through the use of veterans' training funds.

e. The Administration should analyze the justification for the present 10 percent book-handling service charge made by universities and other schools.

f. The major problems in this field arise in connection with "non-accredited" educational institutions or those not recognized by the State departments of education.

It seems doubtful, too, whether the State universities' practice of charging nonresident tuition fees for veterans residing within the State is justifiable. Certain schools are also charging general or miscellaneous fees in addition to the amount agreed upon in a contract as the estimated cost of instruction and supplies.

What Should Be Done

Recommendation No. 4

We recommend that the Veterans' Administration be given authority to establish a system of certification for all educational institutions which are not "accredited institutions" in that they have not been approved by recognized accrediting organizations, or by the appropriate State department of education; and that no payments be made to any institution, or student of it, which has failed to receive this certification.

Our task force has reported that in the field of vocational rehabilitation, and education and training particularly, there has been a lack of "management consciousness" in the Veterans' Administration. There has also been a subdivision of authority and responsibility for processing subsistence allowance for veterans. Unsatisfactory handling of subsistence allowances has been one of the major criticisms by veterans in the last three years. The Administration should give increased attention to work simplification methods, particularly to the plans which have been developed for more efficient and economical processing of education and training subsistence allowances. More attention should also be given to the possibility of greater use of machine methods in this program.

Where certain difficulties in the administration of the program have arisen out of provisions specified in Public Law 346 of the Seventy-Eighth Congress, the Administrator of Veterans' Affairs should take a more active responsibility for recommending changes to the Congress.

Chapter Four

FURTHER RECOMMENDATIONS

Compensation and Pensions

The disability compensation and pension programs of the Veterans' Administration are currently costing about 2 billion dollars per year, exclusive of administrative costs, and, according to a projection made by our task force, this amount, under present law, will increase in ten years to 2.7 billion dollars. These programs present a tremendous management and clerical operation, and yet they are not organized in such a way as to fix responsibility and promote efficiency. The result has been to inflict undue delays on veterans and their dependents in the processing of claims.

Recommendation No. 5

It is recommended that the records of pension payments and compensation for individual veterans now kept by the Office of Contact and Administrative Services be transferred to the new Veterans' Benefit Service; that the active records kept in branch offices be transferred, during the liquidation of those offices, to regional offices; and that these records be kept separately from those of the readjustment and education programs, as well as from insurance accounts.

Loan Guarantees

The Veterans' Administration guarantees loans to veterans up to 50 percent of the loan, not to exceed $4,000 on real property, and $2,000 on personal property. It also guarantees up to 20 percent of loans partially insured by the Federal Housing Administration.

The provision that the Veterans' Administration will pay the first year's interest on the guaranteed portions of loans involved an expense of 60 million dollars in fiscal year 1948. The Veterans' Administration is inexperienced in the lending field and foreclosures will add a burden of real-estate management. Standards which the Federal Housing Administration appropriately requires for the mortgaged property do not apply to veteran loans. In addition, the program is conducted without reference to its effect on the economy.

The Congressional Joint Committee on Housing, in its Final Majority Report of 1948, has said . . .

. . . The committee also is of the opinion that consideration should be given to the relationship between the Housing and Home Finance Agency and the Veterans' Administration with respect to the program of home-loan guarantees for veterans administered by the latter agency. The committee has been in receipt of numerous complaints as to inconsistencies and duplications in appraisals as between the Veterans' Administration and the Federal Housing Administration. While the committee understands that these agencies are working in close consultation to eliminate such inconsistencies and duplication to the extent possible under their respective statutes, the committee feels that further study is needed to determine whether it will be necessary to enact legislation to assure the elimination of such inconsistencies and duplications.

Recommendation No. 6

The Commission recommends that the veterans' housing loan guaranty program be transferred to the Housing and Home Finance Agency, except that the Veterans' Administration should continue to certify the eligibility of a veteran for these guaranties.

Other Programs

Of the remaining activities of the Veterans' Administration, we have already proposed that the administration of unemployment readjustment allowances be placed in the new Readjustment Service, and that the guardianship service for minor dependents of deceased military personnel and veterans be placed in the new Veterans' Benefit Service.

Savings

Our task force estimates that there is room for considerable savings in operations of the Veterans' Administration, if its recommendations are carried out. Particularly is this true in the insurance field.

XVII
Federal Business
Enterprises

Introduction

There are about 100 important business enterprises which the Federal Government owns or in which it is financially interested. These concerns engage directly or indirectly in lending money; guaranteeing loans and deposits; writing life insurance; the producing, distributing, and selling of electric power and fertilizers; the operation of railways and ships; the purchasing and selling of farm products; and the smelting and sale of metals.

The Government's direct investment in these enterprises is in excess of $20 billion, and there are further authorized commitments to supply about $14 billion to them. In addition, the Government guarantees directly and indirectly about $90 billion of deposits or mortgages, and the life insurance written by Government agencies approaches $40 billion. In this report we discuss these agencies under four headings:

Chapter One.   GENERAL OBSERVATIONS AND RECOMMENDATIONS

Chapter Two.   LENDING, GUARANTEEING, AND INSURANCE ENTER-
                PRISES

Chapter Three. ELECTRIC POWER AND IRRIGATION ENTERPRISES

Chapter Four.   MISCELLANEOUS BUSINESS ENTERPRISES

The Commission had the assistance of a task force on Lending Agencies with a distinguished advisory committee, and a task force on Revolving Funds and certain other business enterprises and independent engineering assistance. Other aspects of Government business enterprises were also considered in the reports of our task forces on Agriculture, Natural Resources, and Public Works.

Chapter One

GENERAL OBSERVATIONS AND RECOMMENDATIONS

There are two major organizational forms of Government business enterprises: those which are incorporated under special charter or in accordance with the Government Corporation Control Act of 1945; and unincorporated enterprises which are administered under the older departmental forms.

Government Corporations

To make possible more effective management of business enterprises, the executive branch and the Congress over the years have turned more and more to a corporate form similar to that developed in the business world.

One of the first of the present Government corporations was the Panama Railroad Company, purchased in 1903. This was followed by the establishment of the Federal Land Banks in 1916, although the latter were so incorporated that the borrowers ultimately absorbed the Government's investment.

The corporate form was used extensively in World War I. Most of those war agencies were largely liquidated during the period from 1919 to 1930. The corporate form was again extensively used in the depression emergency from 1931 to 1940. The number of these organizations increased during World War II. In addition to its use in emergencies, the corporate form has been widely adopted for permanent Government agencies; particularly among those active in the field of Government financing.

Originally many of these enterprises were incorporated under State laws. The looseness in administrative, financial, and accounting procedures permitted by State incorporation laws led the Congress to enact stricter controls.

The Government Corporation Control Act of December 6, 1945 (31 U. S. C. 841 et seq.), declares that it is the policy of Congress to scrutinize annually and to control the finances of Government corporations. In short the Act provides that:

a. No corporation shall be created, organized, or acquired by an officer or agency of the Government except by act of Congress or "pursuant to an act of Congress authorizing such action."

b. Federal reincorporation of all State corporations with Federal ownership was required prior to June 30, 1948, except for those in process of liquidation.

c. Each corporation was obliged to present "a business-type budget" through the Bureau of the Budget to the President and the Congress, setting forth its plan of operations with due allowance given to the need for flexibility.

d. Estimates were required of the amount of Government capital which might be returned to the Treasury, or which might be required for restoration of capital impairment.

e. The General Accounting Office was commissioned to audit the accounts annually in accordance with the customary commercial corporation auditing practices.

f. The Comptroller General was required to report on the expenses of each, the origin of its funds, and its financial status, with comments on irregularities.

g. All banking and checking accounts of more than $50,000 were to be kept with the Treasury.

h. Purchases or sales of United States obligations in amounts exceeding $100,000 were prohibited unless approved by the Secretary of the Treasury.

To provide a further review of these activities, the Committees on Appropriations of the Senate and of the House of Representatives established special subcommittees to consider appropriations for, and to report on, most of the Government corporations.

379

Government Corporation Charters

The charters of incorporated enterprises often vary as shown by the following examples:

a. Some corporations have part-time boards of directors; others have full-time boards. Some boards set corporate policies, others do not. The number of directors varies from 3 to 13. The tenures of board members vary widely.

b. In some cases there are statutory prohibitions against guarantees by the Government to make good any losses incurred by private investors in securities of partially or wholly owned Government-controlled corporations. In most cases this is not mentioned.

c. Borrowing powers differ. Nearly all may borrow, but the limitations vary widely.

d. In the case of only one corporation are expenditures for any one year limited to those provided in the annual budget.

e. In some corporations, there is no clear evidence of ownership.

Defects in Organization of Government Corporate Enterprises

a. There is confusion and duplication in the functions of these enterprises. Unnecessary multiplication has occurred, particularly in the agricultural field.

b. Some are making what amount to grants or subsidies by charging less interest on their loans than the Treasury must pay for the money loaned. Some are subsidizing their clientele by incurring losses of capital. In some cases, Congressional appropriations are granted to cover corporation administrative expenses—also a form of subsidy. Often these subsidies may be justifiable, but proper information about them is not plainly shown in annual budgets.

c. Most of these agencies are within executive departments, but some have independent status and their activities are not adequately coordinated with those of the executive branch.

d. Some of these enterprises receive funds from sources other than Congressional appropriations. The appropriations granted by the Congress do not of themselves make clear the financial effectiveness of ineffectiveness of the agency.

e. Confusion exists between the Congressional appropriations granted to these concerns, and Congressional authorizations for them to receive loans from the Treasury. In some cases, the appropriations are in reality loans but carry no interest. The Treasury loans usually bear interest, but do not always do so. These distinctions are not always clear.

f. Local tax exemptions for Government corporations vary. Some have no exemptions; some have complete exemptions. In other cases, only the real property is subject to taxation.

g. Some of the agencies invest their surplus cash in Government securities, thus compelling the Government to pay interest on its own investment.

h. Some agencies have accumulated excessive surpluses.

Recommendations on Corporation Charters

To correct the defects in corporation charters, we recommend that the Congress should, by new enactment, or by amendment to the Government Corporation Control Act of 1945, provide:

a. That borrowing powers, Government liability for their obligations, and budgetary presentation be made uniform for like classes of loans and like securities.

b. That the Government stock in these corporations be held by the President or by the head of such agency as he may direct.

c. That the Congress determine what disposition should be made of surpluses already earned by partly owned Government corporations. Policies as to distribution of future surplus earnings of both partly owned and fully owned corporations, should also be determined.

d. That major expenditures for capital additions be made only with prior Congressional approval and appropriation.

e. In order to establish a consistent practice among corporations, that all corporations, in determining the cost of construction undertaken by them, include a charge for interest on capital expended during the period of construction.

f. That where boards or part-time boards are established they be wholly advisory and be appointed by the President. Public-spirited citizens presently serve on such boards even though fees are paid only for attending meetings.

g. That where these corporations are located in the departments or major Government agencies, the heads of such agencies, or representatives designated by them, serve as ex officio chairmen of their advisory boards.

Deposit of United States Securities in the Treasury

The Government Corporation Control Act requires that all Government corporations shall carry most of their cash balances in the Treasury. A number of them invest funds in United States Government securities. Where capital funds are subscribed, or advanced by the Government or its agencies, and then invested in Government securities, the interest on these securities amounts to a subsidy by the Government. It is an indirect subsidy for the Government to provide them with capital and then to pay them interest on their otherwise idle funds. Examples of this exist in the following cases:

PRODUCTION CREDIT CORPORATIONS	HOME LOAN BANKS
FEDERAL HOUSING ADMINISTRATION	BANKS FOR COOPERATIVES
INTERMEDIATE CREDIT BANKS	PANAMA RAILROAD COMPANY

These agencies alone hold a total of over $450 million of United States securities, of which over $350 million was purchased with Government capital. The adoption of the recommendation below for the agencies listed above would thus reduce the interest-bearing debt by $350 million.

Corporations engaging in insurance operations, which require reserves to cover losses, may justifiably invest such reserves in Government securities. In these cases, the confidence of the insured may be increased by a financial statement which includes investments in Government securities. To the extent that such funds represent net premium income, or (together with interest) are held directly or indirectly in trust for beneficiaries outside the Government, income derived by investment in Government securities appears appropriate. However, this principle should not be extended to the investment of funds derived from the Treasury.

Recommendation No. 2

We recommend that all Government business enterprises be required to surrender to the Treasury all United States securities held, up to

382

the amount of the capital furnished them by the Government, and that they receive in return noninterest-bearing credit in the Treasury. They should not be allowed to invest their idle funds in any other securities except as authorized by the Congress. This recommendation does not include trust accounts.

Defects in the Organization of Unincorporated Business Enterprises

Some of the defects in Government corporations also apply to the unincorporated business enterprises, particularly those listed in sections *a*, *b*, and *c* through *f*, on pp. 380–381. Defects in the unincorporated enterprises also include the following:

a. Some of the unincorporated enterprises are operated under obsolete forms of departmental procedures. They do not enjoy the advantages of modern business practices—with the flexibility of management, budgeting, accounting, and audit—which characterize the incorporated enterprises.

b. The accounting systems of some of these agencies need revision. They have been criticized by the General Accounting Office and by our task forces.

c. A lack of uniformity and many conflicts in legal requirements characterize legislation governing these agencies.

d. Some of these enterprises do not make sufficient distinction in their accounting procedures between capital and operating items.

Some Agencies Should Be Incorporated

Certain of the unincorporated business enterprises are comparatively simple, straight-line businesses. Instances are Veterans' Life Insurance (see report on Veterans' Affairs), Washington National Airport, and Alaska Railroad.

Recommendation No. 3

We recommend that straight-line business activities be incorporated so as to secure greater flexibility in management and simpler accounting, budgeting, and auditing methods.

Some Agencies Need the Business Form without Incorporation

Some Government business enterprises, which also have other activities not wholly of the business type, should, in their business activities, have the form of operations established under the Government Corporation Control Act, but without actual incorporation. The Post Office, the Reclamation Service, and the business activities of the Maritime Commission are examples. They are discussed elsewhere.

Recommendation No. 4

We recommend to the Congress that such agencies be given the same flexibility of business practice, a business form of budget, accounting, and audit systems, which are now usually reserved for Government corporations; and that such agencies be required to set up their accounts so as to distinguish between capital expenditures and those to be charged to operations.

Subsidies through Government Payment of Administrative Expenses

Some of these business enterprises are self-supporting with regard to their administrative expenses. Some are not and appropriations from the Con gress are required for administration. Business enterprises having administrative expenses paid entirely or partly in this way include:

FEDERAL HOUSING ADMINISTRATION
CERTAIN COMPONENTS OF THE PUBLIC HOUSING ADMINISTRATION
FEDERAL CROP INSURANCE CORPORATION
FARMERS HOME ADMINISTRATION
RURAL ELECTRIFICATION ADMINISTRATION

Recommendation No. 5

We recommend that Congress require these agencies either to conduct their business so as to recover their administrative expenses, or, alternatively, to set out such subsidies as a part of their annual request to the Congress for appropriations.

Certain agencies provide direct or indirect subsidies to their clientele even aside from their failure to earn administrative expenses. They may incur losses through loans or investments, or through operating expenses. Examples are:

PUBLIC HOUSING ADMINISTRATION   POST OFFICE
COMMODITY CREDIT CORPORATION   BUREAU OF RECLAMATION
UNITED STATES MARITIME COMMISSION (ship management and loans)

Recommendation No. 6

We recommend that both incorporated and unincorporated business enterprises report specifically to Congress each year the extent to which earned income fails to cover: (a) interest on capital furnished by the Government, (b) losses on loans or investments, and (c) operating expenses. Otherwise, through the exhaustion of capital, there is a hidden subsidy, and the real financial results of governmental operations are obscured. These subsidies may not be disclosed until liquidation. Losses and subsidies should be made clear each fiscal year and passed upon by the Congress.

Diversion of Government Revenues

There are several business enterprises of the Government which directly receive and expend Government revenues arising outside their normal activities. Instances are the Bureau of Reclamation, which receives part of the revenues derived from public land sales and oil royalties, and the Commodity Credit Corporation, which receives customs duties on certain agricultural imports.

Recommendation No. 7

We recommend that, as a general principle, receipts arising outside of normal activities be paid into the Treasury, and that the sums necessary for the conduct of these agencies be appropriated by the Congress. This may require provision for some revolving funds.

Chapter Two

LENDING, GUARANTEEING, AND INSURANCE ENTERPRISES

There are 40 agencies in the Federal Government engaged in lending, guaranteeing, and insuring (other than social security and pension agencies). Nine of these agencies, with loans outstanding, have either ceased lending or are in liquidation.

As of June 30, 1948, the Federal Government had an investment of over $12.5 billion in these agencies and had further commitments to supply them with over $9 billion. Loans guaranteed by Federal agencies amount to about $8.5 billion; and the value of deposits insured by Federal agencies amounts to something over $80 billion. Life insurance underwritten by Government agencies totals approximately $40 billion.

Some of these agencies have obtained more than $2 billion of capital from private investors.

At least 35,000 employees in 300 offices and branches of these agencies are paid by the Federal Government.

Some of these activities are legacies of depression and war; some are permanent fixtures in our economic system for expanding and securing the channels of credit; and some were created to effect social rather than economic objectives.

The accompanying list includes agencies active in this field, or with loans, credit guarantees or insurance outstanding. The figures given, however, merely illustrate the importance of various undertakings of this type; because the amounts shift daily, they have been given in round numbers. The amounts listed are of June 30, 1948, as shown by reports and statements.[1]

[1] The diverse accounting and budgeting systems make it difficult to present figures on which to base comparisons. Furthermore, there is a certain amount of interagency financing, including stock subscriptions, lending, and advances, and several agencies

Housing

1. FEDERAL HOME LOAN BANKS (11 corporations)—Federal investment in capital stock, $119,800,000; loans outstanding to members, $475,000,000.
2. FEDERAL SAVINGS AND LOAN INSURANCE CORPORATION—Federal investment in capital stock, $100,000,000; insurance outstanding, $7,766,000,000.
3. FEDERAL HOUSING ADMINISTRATION—Federal investment, $107,-000,000; loan guarantees outstanding, $4,970,000,000.
4. PUBLIC HOUSING ADMINISTRATION—Federal investment, approximately $500,000,000 [2]; loans outstanding, $281,000,000.[2]
5. FEDERAL NATIONAL MORTGAGE ASSOCIATION—Federal investment, $59,000,000; loans outstanding, $64,000,000; further authorizations, over $200,000,000.
6. NATIONAL CAPITAL HOUSING AUTHORITY—Total assets, $15,528,-000; net Federal capital, $602,436.

Agricultural

7. FEDERAL LAND BANKS (12 corporations)—Federal investment, none; loans outstanding, $830,000,000.
8. FEDERAL INTERMEDIATE CREDIT BANKS (12 corporations)—Federal investment in capital stock, $60,500,000; loans and assets, $565,-000,000.
9. PRODUCTION CREDIT CORPORATIONS (12 corporations)—Federal investment, $82,000,000 [3]; loans and assets, $98,000,000.
10. BANKS FOR COOPERATIVES (13 corporations)—Federal investment in capital stock and advances, $178,000,000; loans and assets, $285,-000,000.
11. FEDERAL CROP INSURANCE CORPORATION—Federal investment in capital stock, $100,000,000.
12. FARMERS HOME ADMINISTRATION—Federal advances, about $550,-000,000; loans outstanding (less reserves), $278,000,000.

---

have substantial investments in United States securities. Many agencies are engaged in activities other than lending or guaranteeing. Only these latter functions are considered in this portion of this report. Therefore, in presenting the financial data, we have made approximate allowances for these factors. The amount of their lending in excess of amounts indicated as Federal advances is derived from private investors and surplus. These same qualifications apply equally to later detailed discussions of the activities listed here.

[2] This amount is for U. S. Housing Act programs only. Other programs—mainly emergency in nature—involved about $1,800,000,000 of appropriations.

[3] Must repay Treasury $20,000,000 prior to June 30, 1949.

13. RURAL ELECTRIFICATION ADMINISTRATION—Advances outstanding, $786,700,000 [4]; further authorizations, $380,000,000.
14. COMMODITY CREDIT CORPORATION—Federal investment in capital stock, $100,000,000; total Federal advances, $436,000,000; total authorized advances, $4,750,000,000.

Veterans

15. VETERANS' ADMINISTRATION. Guarantees outstanding on loans to veterans for home, farm, or business purposes—Investment, $9,200,-000; contingent liability, $3,176,000,000.
16. U. S. GOVERNMENT LIFE INSURANCE—Amount underwritten, $2,-242,000,000.
17. NATIONAL SERVICE LIFE INSURANCE—Amount underwritten, $37,-676,000,000.

Business or Commercial

18. FEDERAL RESERVE BANKS—Loans (guaranteed by the Treasury), $11,500,000.
19. FEDERAL DEPOSIT INSURANCE CORPORATION—Federal investment, none; authorized to borrow from Treasury, $3,000,000,000; approximate deposits guaranteed, $74,466,000,000.
20. RECONSTRUCTION FINANCE CORPORATION [5]—Federal investment in capital stock, $100,000,000; Federal advances (1950 estimate), $1,062,400,000; total authorizations, about $200,000,000.
21. UNITED STATES MARITIME COMMISSION—Loans outstanding, $516,-000,000.

Foreign Field [6]

22. EXPORT-IMPORT BANK OF WASHINGTON—Federal investment in capital stock, $1,000,000,000; advances from the Treasury, $971,-000,000; authorized total borrowing from the Treasury, $2,500,-000,000.
23. TREASURY DEPARTMENT BRITISH LOAN—$3,750,000,000.
24. ECONOMIC COOPERATION ADMINISTRATION LOANS—Federal loans authorized, $1,000,000,000; loans made, about $837,300,000.

[4] March 31, 1948.
[5] $9,313,737,000 of the Corporation's notes held by the Treasury were canceled pursuant to P. L. 860, 80th Congress. There were no notes payable to the Treasury on June 30, 1948, but the borrowings are estimated at $1,062,400,000 as of June 30, 1950.
[6] The United States has completed its subscription of $2,750,000,000 to the International Monetary Fund. It has answered the first call of the International Bank of Reconstruction and Development with $635,000,000, and has an additional commitment to invest $2,540,000,000 in the Bank's capital stock.

25. BUREAU OF INDIAN AFFAIRS—Authorization, $12,000,000; loans outstanding, $6,600,000.
26. NATIONAL CAPITAL PARK AND PLANNING COMMISSION—Loans outstanding, $251,000; further authorizations, $5,600,000.[7]
27. INLAND WATERWAYS CORPORATIONS—Wholly owned by U. S., $24,-300,000; loans outstanding, $207,000.
28. PUERTO RICO RECONSTRUCTION ADMINISTRATION—Loans outstanding, $2,600,000.
29. PUBLIC HEALTH SERVICE—FEDERAL WORKS AGENCY, Water Pollution Abatement Loans (5-year loan authority), $22,500,000 per annum.

Better Organization of Lending, Guarantee, and Insurance Agencies

In the previous chapter on "General Observation and Recommendations," we have pointed out a number of defects and recommendations which are applicable to lending corporations and insurance enterprises.

In our report on the Treasury Department, we have recommended that the Department should regularly inspect and report on all concerns in process of liquidation. The Treasury is the beneficiary of any recoveries and has an independent interest in full and rapid realization of assets.

We make the following specific recommendations.

Direct Lending to Private Persons

While some agencies in this group have additional security for their loans because private credit institutions participate in their guarantees, other agencies lend directly to private enterprise or to individuals without the participation of intermediate private agencies.

Direct lending by the Government to persons or enterprises opens up dangerous possibilities of waste and favoritism to individuals or enterprises. It invites political and private pressure, or even corruption. Emergencies may arise in depression, war, national defense, or disaster which must be met in this way. But direct lending should be absolutely avoided except for emergencies. Five agencies make direct loans at the present time.

[7] 1947 Estimate.

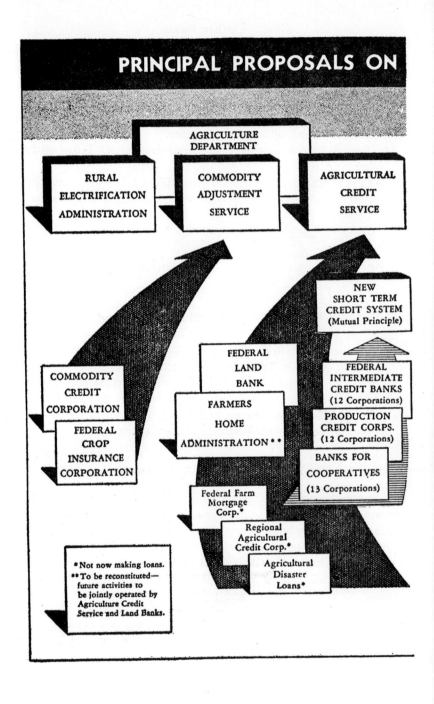

PRINCIPAL PROPOSALS ON

AGRICULTURE DEPARTMENT

RURAL ELECTRIFICATION ADMINISTRATION

COMMODITY ADJUSTMENT SERVICE

AGRICULTURAL CREDIT SERVICE

NEW SHORT TERM CREDIT SYSTEM (Mutual Principle)

COMMODITY CREDIT CORPORATION

FEDERAL CROP INSURANCE CORPORATION

FEDERAL LAND BANK

FARMERS HOME ADMINISTRATION **

FEDERAL INTERMEDIATE CREDIT BANKS (12 Corporations)

PRODUCTION CREDIT CORPS. (12 Corporations)

BANKS FOR COOPERATIVES (13 Corporations)

Federal Farm Mortgage Corp.*

Regional Agricultural Credit Corp.*

Agricultural Disaster Loans*

*Not now making loans.
**To be reconstituted—future activities to be jointly operated by Agriculture Credit Service and Land Banks.

FEDERAL BUSINESS ENTERPRISES

HOUSING AND HOME FINANCE AGENCY

NATIONAL SYSTEM OF MORTGAGE DISCOUNT BANKS

HOME LOAN BANK BOARD

NATIONAL HOUSING COUNCIL

FEDERAL HOUSING ADMINISTRATION

CORPORATION
to be formed to take over certain functions for flexible management and liquidation

PUBLIC HOUSING ADMINISTRATION

Federal Home Loan Bank System

Federal Savings and Loan Insurance Corp.

Home Owners Loan Corporation (In Liquidation)

FEDERAL NATIONAL MORTGAGE ASSOCIATION

OFFICE OF HOUSING EXPEDITER

HOME LOAN GUARANTEE FUNCTIONS OF THE VETERANS ADMINISTRATION

UNITS TO BE BROUGHT IN

Two are minor—the Agriculture Department Drought Loans, of which roughly $50 million are outstanding, and Indian Loans with $6.6 million outstanding and about $12 million authorized. These operations are in the nature of personal emergency relief, rather than business transactions.

The three major governmental agencies making direct loans are:

FARMERS HOME ADMINISTRATION   FEDERAL RESERVE BANKS [8]
RECONSTRUCTION FINANCE CORPORATION

Recommendation No. 8

We recommend (*a*) that the Congress review the power to make direct loans (excluding the two minor activities mentioned above), taking into account the problems of economy, efficiency, and integrity; (*b*) that in nonemergency periods, the Congress place restrictions on direct loans in order to insure that the normal channels of credit are utilized to the maximum extent possible or, alternatively, provide for the guarantee of loans made by private or other established agencies.

However, no guarantees of loans should be made on terms more liberal than those made on direct loans. The Government should not engage in direct lending where loans can be obtained from private sources on reasonable terms.

Business Enterprises in Housing

Inasmuch as the Congress is now dealing with basic questions of organization in the field of housing, this Commission is not in a position to present complete recommendations.

Recommendation No. 9

We do, however, recommend that all housing activities be placed in one agency under a single administrator who should be given the type of authority which we have recommended for the heads of all agencies.

Substantial progress has been made toward unifying the housing activities of the Government by the establishment of the Housing and Home

[8] Relatively inactive in lending at the present time.

Finance Agency under a single administrator. Housing activities now in this agency are:

PUBLIC HOUSING ADMINISTRATION   NATIONAL HOUSING COUNCIL
FEDERAL HOME LOAN BANK SYSTEM   HOME LOAN BANK BOARD
FEDERAL SAVINGS AND LOAN INSURANCE CORPORATION
HOME OWNERS' LOAN CORPORATION (in liquidation)
FEDERAL HOUSING ADMINISTRATION

We propose that the following functions also be included:

HOME LOAN GUARANTEE FUNCTION OF THE VETERANS' ADMINISTRATION
FEDERAL NATIONAL MORTGAGE ASSOCIATION
OFFICE OF THE HOUSING EXPEDITER

The Federal Housing Administration
Public Housing Administration

The Federal Housing Administration and the Public Housing Administration are engaged in closely related activities, that is, to stimulate the building and improvement of dwellings.

Federal Housing Administration provides insurance of home mortgages and home improvement loans on one- to four-family dwellings, on multiple-family projects, and on housing manufactured by industrial methods. The loans so insured are made by private lending institutions.

The amount of money involved in this agency is not great in proportion to its commitments. As of June 30, 1948, it had received the following financing from the Federal Government:

PAID-IN SURPLUS	$15,000,000
APPROPRIATIONS (net)	64,811,504
DEBENTURES (guaranteed by United States)	27,149,286

Its assets mainly consisted of the following items:

CASH	$45,800,150
UNITED STATES BONDS AND NOTES	136,134,893
OUTSTANDING LOANS (net)	22,680,946
ACQUIRED SECURITIES (net)	10,754,890

The Administration's principal obligation, however, is a contingent one, arising through its guarantee of home mortgages with estimated unpaid balances of about $5 billion.

Public Housing Administration engages in the following activities.

a. Federal Aid to Local Authorities in the development of low-rent housing and slum clearance. (U. S. Housing Act Program.) The financing for this program as of June 30, 1948, had come primarily from the following sources:

LOANS FROM THE TREASURY	$362,000,000
CAPITAL STOCK	1,000,000
ASSETS TRANSFERRED FROM OTHER AGENCIES	114,833,900
APPROPRIATIONS	90,966,288

The principal assets under the program were

LOANS RECEIVABLE	$281,624,723
LAND, STRUCTURES, AND EQUIPMENT	202,116,137

Under this program, there remained unused borrowing authority of $363,144,000.

This is partly a subsidizing agency. Its accounts should accord with recommendations Nos. 5 and 6 (pp. 384–385).

b. Public War Housing Program. This is one of a series of projects, either temporary or in liquidation, administered by the Public Housing Administration. Its financing, as of June 30, 1948, consisted of:

ASSETS TRANSFERRED FROM OTHER AGENCIES	$113,937,744
APPROPRIATIONS	1,266,175,751

The assets were almost entirely in land, structures, and equipment, carried on the program books at $1,308,664,787. These assets are in the process of liquidation.

c. Homes Conversion Program. This program was financed almost entirely from appropriations that, as of June 30, 1948, amounted to $68,-966,740. Its assets, carried on the books at $24,775,589, were mainly in land, structures, and equipment.

d. Veterans' Re-Use Housing Program. This program was financed almost entirely by appropriations of $449,981,082. Its assets were carried on the books, as of June 30, 1948, at $49,450,448.

e. Subsistence Homestead and Greenbelt Towns Program. These programs had been financed up to June 30, 1948, by:

TRANSFERS OF ASSETS FROM OTHER AGENCIES	$62,468,467
APPROPRIATIONS	10,335,008

The assets, consisting principally of land, structures, and equipment, were carried on the books at $39,959,430.

f. Defense Homes Corporation. This agency is in the process of liquidation under supervision of the Public Housing Administration. Estimated investment, as of July 31, 1948:

NOTES PAYABLE TO RFC	$40,870,000
EQUITY OF THE TREASURY	12,239,000

Recommendation No. 10

We recommend that the Congress give consideration to establishing one corporation under the Government Corporation Control Act of 1945, as amended, to take over the activities *b.* through *f.* above so as to afford the flexibility of management, and the simplification of budgeting, accounting, and auditing authorized under that act, and thus to expedite liquidation.

Veterans' Administration Loan Guarantees

The Veterans' Administration loan guarantee program is part of the "G. I. Bill of Rights." Under this, the Veterans' Administration guarantees loans not to exceed 50 percent up to $4,000 for varied purposes, or $8,000 for housing only. The Federal Government also pays the interest at 4 percent for the first year on the guaranteed portion of the loan. The loans may be used to acquire property, including homes and farms, or to establish businesses.

As of June 30, 1948, the Government had an exposure on guaranteed or approved loans amounting to approximately $3,175,970,000. The Government's gross investment, aside from contingent liabilities under the guarantee and excluding recaptured amounts, was roughly estimated at $9 million as of the same date, provided from current appropriations.

In our report on the Veterans' Administration we have recommended that these activities be transferred from the Veterans' Administration to the Housing and Home Finance Agency, which is engaged in almost exactly the same business. Great economies can be effected. A veteran will then be able to obtain one guarantee where now he frequently requires two. He will have to pay for only one appraisal. He will get his loan faster.

The Veterans' Administration should continue to certify veterans eligible for loans under the law.

Federal National Mortgage Association

The Federal National Mortgage Association is not included in the Housing and Home Finance Agency. It is a corporation created in 1938, with capital subscribed by the Reconstruction Finance Corporation. It has operated in the secondary market as a buyer of certain classes of mortgages insured under Federal Housing Administration programs.

As of July 31, 1948, its financing had all been supplied by the Reconstruction Finance Corporation as follows:

NOTES PAYABLE	$48,709,243
CAPITAL STOCK	10,000,000

On that date, the Association had unused borrowing authority of $243,-844,000. It held $63,795,687 worth of Federal Housing Administration-insured mortgages and was committed to acquire over $200 million more.

The Home Loan Bank Board operates directly in this field, but the Federal National Mortgage Association remains as a part of the Reconstruction Finance Corporation.

Recommendation No. 11

We recommend that the Federal Natonal Mortgage Association be placed under the Administrator of the Housing and Home Finance Agency.

Office of the Housing Expediter

The Office of the Housing Expediter is an independent agency reporting directly to the President. The Expediter enforces Federal rent control and veterans' preference requirements in the sale and rent of new housing units. Liquidation of certain provisions of the Veteran's Emergency Housing Act is also his responsibility. The President cannot give adequate time to the supervision of this agency, yet its operations have major effect upon the Nation's supply of housing—the primary responsibility of the Housing and Home Finance Agency.

Recommendation No. 12

We recommend that the Office of the Housing Expediter be placed under the Administrator of the Housing and Home Finance Agency since the work of the two agencies is closely related.

National Capital Housing Authority

This is another agency concerned with the problem of housing, but it is limited to improving housing in the Washington area. It reports to the President, who has little time for its direction. We previously listed this agency under the Office of General Services, where the Commissioners of the District of Columbia would report.

Recommendation No. 13

We recommend that the National Capital Housing Authority be placed directly under the Commissioners of the District of Columbia.

Farm Credit Enterprises

The principal farm credit activities of the Government have been brought into a major-purpose group placed under the Farm Credit Administration in the Department of Agriculture. These agencies are:

FEDERAL FARM MORTGAGE CORPORATION [9]   BANKS FOR COOPERATIVES
FEDERAL INTERMEDIATE CREDIT BANKS   FEDERAL LAND BANKS
PRODUCTION CREDIT CORPORATIONS AND ASSOCIATIONS
REGIONAL AGRICULTURAL CREDIT CORPORATION [9]

The following other lending or guarantee agencies are also connected with the Department of Agriculture:

FEDERAL CROP INSURANCE CORPORATION
COMMODITY CREDIT CORPORATION
FARMERS HOME ADMINISTRATION
AGRICULTURAL DISASTER LOANS
RURAL ELECTRIFICATION ADMINISTRATION

The Commission makes recommendations below on the following agencies:

Federal Intermediate Credit Banks are 12 wholly owned Government corporations in which the Government has invested $60.5 million. They engage in loans to facilitate the marketing of agricultural products. They report a surplus of $34,712,218 (June 30, 1948) which was partly earned by investment in United States securities. They also obtain capital by issues to private investors or Government agencies. On June 30, 1948, they had so obtained $528 million.

[9] These agencies are not making new loans and hence are declining in activity.

Banks for Cooperatives comprise a central corporation and 12 regional Government corporations. The Government has provided $178.5 million in capital and the borrowers have provided $12,642,300 of capital (June 30, 1948). They report a surplus of $43,483,695, part of which has been earned by investment in Government securities. They engage in loans to farm cooperatives mostly to aid in marketing agricultural products. Loans outstanding on June 30, 1948, were $229,275,936.

Production Credit Corporations (12 corporations) are wholly owned by the Government, with a capital of $81,635,000 (June 30, 1948) and a surplus of $16,761,000, partly earned from investment in United States securities. They engage in loans to, or investment in, local production credit associations for production purposes. The amount of such investments outstanding on June 30, 1948, was $30,875,000.

These three agencies are mainly engaged in extending short-term credit. They comprise a total of 37 Government corporations and, while their work is generally coordinated, it would strengthen them, reduce the amount of Government capital involved, and make their administration ultimately more economical if they were consolidated.

These agencies should follow the principle of mutualization of credit. This principle is old in American economy (mutual savings banks, building and loan associations, life insurance). Mutualization has been promoted admirably in several instances by wise action of the Federal Government. The Federal Reserve banks involve, in one sense, the mutualization of commercial credits. "Member" private institutions acquired the capital contingently underwritten by the Government and govern themselves subject to the Federal Reserve Board.

This same principle of mutualization and lending through "member" institutions, and the method of control by Federal boards, runs through the Home Loan banks, the Federal Land banks and, in a minor way, through the Banks for Cooperatives. They require the borrowers to purchase a small amount of stock from the Government, based upon a small percentage of the loans, and they differ from the reserve banks in that they sometimes obtain their capital (beyond the initial Government subscription which their members are gradually purchasing) by the issue of bonds to the public or the Treasury.

Recommendation No. 14

We recommend that the Federal Intermediate Credit Banks, the Banks for Cooperatives, and the Production Credit Corporations should be consolidated into a single system, with due regard for preserving the integrity of, and the availability of credit for, the

agricultural activities involved. **The merged system should adopt the principle of mutualization.** That is, borrowers should be required to purchase an amount of stock from the Government concurrently wth the granting of any loan, such purchase to be a small percentage of each loan until the Government stock is retired.

Once they are mutualized the Government's interest becomes that of regulation and inspection only.

It is recognized that these institutions may, at times, need to obtain temporary funds, beyond the amount of their capital stock, through loans from the Government. For this, they should pay current interest rates, and they should be prohibited from paying dividends to stockholders until all loans or capital advances from the Government are repaid.

Federal Crop Insurance Corporation

The Federal Crop Insurance Corporation was created in 1938 with an authorized capital of $100 million. The full amount has been subscribed by the Federal Government. The act was amended and activities somewhat restricted by legislation in 1947. It now operates on an experimental and developmental basis in 350 counties, about 12 percent of the agricultural counties in the entire country.

The major crops for which insurance protection is offered are wheat, cotton, flax, corn, and tobacco. Certain lesser crops are included under a general authorization.

Heavy losses were incurred at first but, since 1945, the Corporation has shown a surplus on insurance covering wheat, flax, and tobacco, with some losses on cotton and corn. During 1948 there was an over-all surplus on all crops.

The total capital of $100 million, subscribed by the United States Government, has been reduced by losses to approximately $30 million as of June 30, 1948. Administrative expenses are not reflected in this impairment of capital because they are covered by direct appropriations. The estimate for administrative expenses in the fiscal year 1949 is $3,725,000.

Recommendation No. 15

The Congress has required that, after a certain period, the crop insurance premiums should include an amount for administrative expenses so as to place the Corporation on a self-sustaining basis. We endorse this stipulation.

Commodity Credit Corporation

The Commodity Credit Corporation is only incidentally a lending agency. Its purpose is price support, either by loans or by buying and selling agricultural commodities for export and import or domestically.

The Corporation has an authorized capital stock of $100 million, all of which is held by the Government. It is authorized to borrow $4.75 billion from the Treasury. As of June 30, 1948, its outstanding obligations totaled about $436 million.

The act of March 8, 1938, provided for an annual appraisal of its assets and liabilities. The act further provided that, should its net worth be less than $100 million, the Secretary of the Treasury would restore the amount of capital impairment by a contribution to the Corporation. If the appraisal establishes the net worth as more than $100 million, the surplus is to be paid into the Treasury.

The Congress now requires that this agency include interest on Federal advances as a part of its expenditures.

Up to 1944, the annual losses of the Corporation were paid by Congressional appropriations to the Treasury, and totaled about $400 million, including some wartime subsidies. In the 2 years and 3 months ended June 30, 1946, the impairment of its capital was about $1.56 billion, mainly due to further wartime subsidies.

To liquidate this loss, the Treasury surrendered to the Corporation a like amount of notes of the Corporation. This practice is still authorized. In the last two fiscal years, the Corporation has shown some profits. It will probably again incur losses. The practice of liquidating losses by the surrender of its obligations by the Treasury is undesirable as it obscures actual expenditures. It is most desirable to return to the practice which was discontinued in 1944.

Recommendation No. 16

This Commission recommends that when the Commodity Credit Corporation makes these readjustments of capital on account of losses, the readjustments should be financed by Congressional appropriation and not by cancellation of notes.

Farmers Home Administration

Our task force on Agriculture has strongly urged that the activity of the Farmers Home Administration be reduced. Our task force on Government lending strongly recommends that this agency be liquidated at once.

The agency now employs over 10,000 persons, many of whom duplicate the work of the other loan services, and of the guidance and advice services of the Department of Agriculture.

The administrative expenses of this agency, $23 million annually, are currently appropriated by the Congress. In addition, large sums are appropriated by the Congress for loans. Interest on the loans is not available for purposes of the agency, but is paid into the Treasury as miscellaneous receipts.

The agency and its predecessors have expended about $2 billion, of which some $1.45 billion has been recovered out of repayments and interest. The present assets and loans represent about $550 million. Almost half the loans are delinquent with perhaps $277 million in danger of being lost, along with interest on the Government advances.

The agency does not appear to be responsive to the Secretary of Agriculture. Our task force points out that land purchases, at present values, are most hazardous and that the Department of Agriculture is advising against them.

However, it appears to this Commission that there is a valid service to be performed in this field for good tenant and other farmers. It should be put on a sounder basis. We believe a much better and more economical method can be found for effectuating the purposes of this agency.

Recommendation No. 17

In order to achieve these ends, we recommend that Congress consider giving authority to the Secretary of Agriculture to develop some such plan as the following:

a. That a modest Government corporation (which we refer to hereafter as the "Corporation") be set up under the Agricultural Credit Administrator.

b. That the tenant farmer or applicant for a loan obtain a first mortgage loan from a Land Bank on its usual terms (usually 50 percent of the appraised value of the property).

c. That the Land Bank furnish its appraisal to the Corporation.

d. That the Corporation guarantee a second mortgage loan to be made by the Land Bank, making total loans up to 90 percent of the appraised value.

e. That this second mortgage loan bear the same interest and terms as the initial Land Bank loan.

f. That no such second mortgage loan exceed $4,000.

g. That the Land Bank service these loans on behalf of the Corporation.

h. That the Department of Agriculture furnish guidance and advice to the borrower through its established county organizations.

i. That the Corporation assist the farmer to obtain production loans from the proposed agency to be formed by consolidation of short-term lending farm agencies.

j. That the Farmers Home Administration be liquidated. In the transfer of its functions, consideration should be given to the utilization of its employees.

k. That the Land Banks liquidate the outstanding loans of the Farmers Home Administration for a fee, to be deducted from principal or interest recoveries on these loans.

l. That the Agricultural Credit Administration be authorized to approve recommendations for compounding or settling outstanding loans.

Reconstruction Finance Corporation

The Reconstruction Finance Corporation performed a useful and necessary function in the days of the depression and the war. Its life was extended by the Congress on May 25, 1948. The manifest major purpose of that extension was to maintain it as a stand-by agency in case of emergencies. But it still has 31 branch offices and over 5,000 employees.

This agency is engaged in making direct loans to persons and enterprises, frequently without the participation of private agencies in its risks.

Our task force strongly recommends the liquidation of this corporation and the substitution of guarantees by the Government, operating through the Federal Reserve Banks, of loans to be made by commercial banks.

The Commission believes it preferable that the Corporation be reorganized to guarantee loans by commercial banks.

There may arise cases of needed loans which are not available from private institutions. However, this unavailability, except in the case of emergency or where the national defense is involved, arises from the fact that more than normal risk usually is involved. It may be in the public interest to provide such credit.

However, the credit of the Government should not be used to obtain lower rates of interest and easier terms than those which private institutions can properly provide.

Recommendation No. 18

We recommend that the Congress review the Reconstruction Finance Corporation in accord with our Recommendation No. 8 (p. 392).

In our report on the Treasury Department, we have recommended that the Reconstruction Finance Corporation be placed under the supervision of the Secretary of the Treasury.

A National System of Mortgage Discount Banks

Recommendation No. 19

We suggest that the Congress consider the creation of a system of National Mortgage Discount Banks to provide real-estate mortgage discount facilities for all private lending agencies over the entire real-property field. This might include the present Federal Home Loan Banks.

We make this recommendation—for reasons amplified below but within our terms of reference—because, in the long view, it would simplify and make more efficient the aid of the Government for organization of credit.

The need is shown by the host of Government agencies now in action. The Federal institutions for farm mortgages, the home loan institutions, some part of the operations of the Federal housing agencies, and the Reconstruction Finance Corporation are evidence of the need for Government effort to assure credit in the real-estate mortgage field. The Government efforts do not yet cover the whole field. Particularly, city real estate is not covered. The subject is of primary importance to the whole banking structure of the country.

A general institution of this kind would cover the whole field and gradually absorb some of the business and lessen the need for constant Government expansion into new areas.

The Home Loan Bank plan, adopted in 1932, was a segment of such a wider plan which was proposed at the time. The principles of the plan were adopted, but its field was practically narrowed to home loans. The success of the Home Loan Banks over the past 16 years gives warranty to the whole conception.

The ability of such an institution to obtain capital from the private investor would be unquestioned. Beyond its original capital stock furnished by the Government—to be purchased gradually by its borrowing institutions—it should be able to issue its bonds or debentures to investors at low rates of interest because they would be secured upon (*a*) the obligations of the institutions discounting their mortgages, (*b*) the collateral of the mortgages themselves, and (*c*) the capital stock of the discount banks. The Home Loan Banks and the Federal Land Banks have proved the soundness of such securities.

In review, there are several reasons for this proposal:

First. Such an institution would become a reservoir of capital for the Government real-estate mortgage agencies when they were unable to sell their own issues to the public, and thus avoid the necessity of drawing upon the Federal Government.

Second. It would give great strength to our whole banking and credit structure. Our banks engage in the dual function of both short-term and long-term credit. In times of stress when bank deposits are drawn down, the commercial banks are compelled to call in, or to refuse to extend, their short-term loans to business because these represent large quickly realizable assets. Thus they paralyze the commercial community, create unemployment, and accentuate the crisis. The savings institutions also are embarrassed. As their depositors draw down their savings, these institutions are forced to suspend further mortgage loans and to demand payment on expired loans. Thus the security of owners of farms and homes is jeopardized.

If there were a place where all these institutions could rediscount their long-term mortgage loans, these pressures could be greatly mitigated.

Third. The need for Government agencies would be gradually reduced. Private lending institutions would be more active if they felt that, when under pressure, they could render their assets liquid. By covering the entire real-estate mortgage field, the system would lessen the need for emergency agencies such as have been created by the Government in the past.

Fourth. This subject is so important to the continued prosperity of this country that a thorough investigation, either by the Congress or by a commission, might well precede legislation.

A National Monetary and Credit Council

We recommended, in our report on the Treasury Department, that a National Monetary and Credit Council should be appointed by the President to coordinate and direct domestic lending and guarantees by the Government. There is already a successful council concerned with foreign lending. This domestic credit council should be located in the Treasury Department under the chairmanship of the Secretary of the Treasury, with representatives of such agencies as the President may determine. This council should consider the activities of agencies in the credit field so as to secure coordination of purpose, and to avoid overlapping activities and inconsistent credit policies.

Chapter Three

ELECTRIC POWER AND
IRRIGATION ENTERPRISES

Government Operations in Electric
Power and Irrigation

The Government is engaged in extensive business enterprises in the electric power and irrigation fields.

The systematic development of irrigation and reclamation began with the Reclamation Act of 1902. Up to 1930 these works were primarily comprised of easier or less complex types of projects and furnished water to some 2,790,000 acres of land. Up to that time, some 17 small hydro-electric plants had been built by the Government as adjuncts to irrigation dams with a total installed electrical generating capacity of about 226,000 kilowatts. All of these projects were enterprises operated by irrigation districts or under lease, producing electricity as a byproduct.

With the Hoover Dam in 1930, there began an enlargement of the water development concept. This new concept entailed the storage of water by large dams which would serve the multiple purposes of irrigation, domestic water, flood control, and navigation.

In setting up the financial organization of these multiple-purpose projects, the Federal Government has established certain policies. Because flood control and navigation do not produce revenues, the portion of the capital cost attributable to them has been classed as irrecoverable. Because other features—including irrigation, power, and domestic water —do produce returns, a portion of the outlays is allocated in various amounts as recoverable by the Government.

Hydroelectric

Up to 1933 and including the Hoover Dam, the policy of the Government was to place the operation and transmission of power from these plants in the hands of private power companies, municipalities, or irrigation districts, under terms of payment and rate controls to protect the consumer. Under that arrangement, the hydroelectric power from the Hoover Dam was, in effect, sold "at the bus bar" under a contract, originally intended to return the cost of the project, with annual interest, to the Government in 50 years.

With the creation of the Tennessee Valley Authority, the Government extended its activities into the transmission and sale of power to municipalities and direct consumers, although occasionally the private power companies were used by that Authority for distribution. This change was emphasized by the subsequent purchase of private power companies and the proposals for construction of supplementary steam generating plants.

The following are the active agencies or systems engaged either in the construction and distribution of electric power or in lending money for that purpose:

ARMY CORPS OF ENGINEERS
BUREAU OF RECLAMATION
SOUTHWESTERN POWER ADMINISTRATION
RURAL ELECTRIFICATION ADMINISTRATION
COLORADO RIVER PROJECT
TENNESSEE VALLEY AUTHORITY
COLUMBIA RIVER SYSTEM

The operations of these agencies have attained great magnitude. By June 30, 1947, there had been constructed or purchased 46 hydroelectric and 10 steam power plants of an installed generated capacity of 4,909,582 kilowatts; 37 additional plants with a capacity of 8,481,400 kilowatts were under construction. The transmission lines now exceed 14,000 miles. Construction authorized by the Congress contemplates 79 more plants with a capacity of about 6,842,655 kilowatts. Thus, by about 1960 when these 172 plants would be in full operation, they would have a capacity of about 20,233,637 kilowatts.

The total installed electrical generating capacity in the Nation in June 1947, owned by private enterprise, municipalities, and the Federal Government, was about 52 million kilowatts.

The total expenditure of the Federal Government on these multiple-purpose projects is roughly estimated at $3.7 billion as of June 30, 1948. Probably $4 billion will be required for completion of those in construction and authorized. Beyond the above-mentioned plants, already authorized, several hundred other possible plants are listed as feasible. The further plants thus listed, if constructed, would involve an expenditure of over $35 billion and would have an installed generating capacity about equal to the whole of the actual capacity of the country in June 1947.

The works constructed or planned by the Corps of Engineers lie in 37 States, in every part of the country—New England, the Middle West, the South, and the Mountain and Western States. Bureau of Reclamation projects lie in 17 States, in the Western, Mountain, and Southwestern areas. The two services have projects in 14 of the same States. Other Government agencies, such as the Tennessee Valley Authority or Bonneville Power Administration, have projects which with produce or distribute hydroelectric power in many of the same States in which either the Bureau of Reclamation or the Corps of Engineers, or both, operates.

Irrigation

As we have said above, at the time the great multiple-purpose projects were inaugurated, the easier projects of irrigation had been largely completed and were furnishing water to about 2,790,000 acres. In the 18 years since that time, about 1.5 million acres of additional soil have been brought under irrigation with perhaps 550,000 acres more benefiting indirectly from the water supplied.

The Congress, in setting up the irrigation system, provided that the farmers should repay the costs of the system without interest added to the cost during construction, or subsequent interest on the cost. Experience has shown, however, that even with this indirect subsidy of interest, these projects, on the average, do not pay out, as the capital cost is too great (with a few exceptions) for the farmers to bear. It simply must be accepted that the national advantage of more farm homes and greater national productivity will offset Government expenditures.

Government Agencies and Organizations

Army Corps of Engineers

In improvement of flood control and navigation, the Corps of Engineers has constructed and is engaged in constructing a number of multiple-purpose dams of which electrical power is one important byproduct. These installations thus become Government business enterprises of importance. The business of marketing the power from Engineer Corps installations is managed in certain instances by the Department of the Interior, as in the cases of the Bonneville Power Administration and the Southwestern Power Administration. Generally this is the case in the Western and Southwestern States.

Outside this area the Engineers, however, have about 20 power plants either authorized or under construction. They will have a total installed capacity of over 1.4 million kilowatts and will cost a total of over $500 million. A portion of the costs will be assigned to power.

The actual appropriations for the civil functions of the Army Corps of Engineers were $580,635,950 for the fiscal year 1949. For 1950 the Corps has requested $754,423,700, including $20 million for the St. Lawrence Seaway and Power project.

Tennessee Valley Authority

As of June 30, 1947, the total of Federal funds for the Tennessee Valley Authority, plus the assigned value of properties transferred and a bond issue sold to the Treasury by the Authority, aggregated about $823 million. About $351 million of this total has been spent upon, or allocated to, navigation, flood control, and resource development. It therefore would not be considered reimbursable, except for certain minor revenues from sale of fertilizer and other miscellaneous income.

The enterprise had formerly been required simply to pay into the Treasury such proceeds as were not required for the purposes of its Act. By June 30, 1947, the Authority had paid about $30 million to the Treasury. The Government Corporations Appropriation Act of 1948 required that a total of $348 million, plus interest, be repaid from power revenues over a 40-year period after July 1, 1947.

Reclamation Fund

This operation of the Department of the Interior was created in June 1902. The original Reclamation Fund was to be supported from the sale of public lands in 16 Western States and territories (and after 1906, Texas), and was to be used for irrigation and reclamation of arid lands in those States. In 1920 Congress added the Government royalties and other income from certain minerals, including oil, on the public domain.

In the same year, Congress provided that 50 percent of the Government receipts from water-power licenses be added.

Our task forces estimate that, from the inception of the Fund until June 30, 1949, the Reclamation Fund will have received from appropriations a total of over $1,231 million; from sales of public lands, and from hydroelectric power, irrigation, and other revenues, a total of over $546 million—an aggregate of over $1,777 million—with further great sums required to complete works already under construction.

Other Major Projects

Certain major projects for which direct appropriations are made by the Congress and which also have monies from the reclamation, or rivers and harbors, funds are as follows:

CENTRAL VALLEY PROJECT

This California project was authorized in 1935. Construction began in 1937. The ultimate cost is estimated at $411 million, with approximately $53 million allocated to navigation and flood control as nonreimbursable, $130 million repayable by water users, and $228 million with interest repayable from power revenues.

COLUMBIA RIVER POWER SYSTEM

These projects comprise: The Bonneville Dam in Oregon, built and operated by the Corps of Engineers; the Grand Coulee Dam in Washington, built and operated by the Bureau of Reclamation; and the Bonneville Power Administration of the Department of the Interior which operates the transmission system from both dams.

The Bonneville Dam serves for navigation, flood control, and power; the Grand Coulee Dam, in addition, provides water for irrigation. The total expenditures to June 30, 1947, were $442,765,756.

The allocation of costs to different purposes is still confused.

On the basis of a 1946 agreement, Bonneville Dam's cost of $86,829,-000 would be so allocated that $58,138,000, on which interest during construction is charged at a rate of 2½ percent, would be repaid with interest from the sale of power over a 50-year period.

In the case of Grand Coulee, the total cost of $224,594,000 would be allocated as follows: $23 million to navigation and flood control, $73,-476,000 to irrigation, and $127,599,000 to power. The amortization period was placed at 80 years. Some part of irrigation costs is allocated to power.

The Federal Power Commission has established the accounting system for Bonneville but has been given no authority over Grand Coulee.

COLORADO RIVER PROJECT

The total funds made available to June 30, 1947, for the Hoover Dam and the All American Canal (its irrigation adjunct) were $186,580,000. An additional $51,300,000 is estimated to be required to complete this Colorado River project on the Nevada-Arizona border. The ultimate hydroelectric power capacity will be about 1,323,000 kilowatts. Construction costs of $25 million are apportioned to flood control. These are to be repaid out of power revenues after June 1, 1987.

Construction of Davis Dam, about 75 miles below the Hoover Dam, was authorized in 1941 but was delayed on account of the war, and the power plant was not in operation by June 30, 1947. Ultimate total construction cost is estimated at $127,691,777, of which amount $38,296,-615 had been expended by June 30, 1947. The eventual investment to be repaid from power revenues is estimated at $115,363,300.

SOUTHWESTERN POWER ADMINISTRATION

This agency acts for the Secretary of the Interior in managing the transmission and sale of power at dams constructed for the multiple purposes of electric power, flood control, and navigation in the Grand, Red, and North Fork Rivers in Oklahoma, Texas, and Arkansas. Construction and operation is directed by the Army Corps of Engineers. Three dams have been completed, and 22 more have been authorized; 10 of these are under construction. The Federal investment to June 30, 1947, was $82,927,000. The estimated ultimate cost of authorized projects is $730,907,000.

RURAL ELECTRIFICATION ADMINISTRATION

This agency was created by Executive Order 7037 of May 11, 1935, and was continued by the Rural Electrification Act of May 20, 1936. The Rural Electrification Administration is authorized to make self-liquidating loans up to 100 percent for the financing of rural electrical facilities. In making the loans, preference is given to public bodies, cooperatives, and nonprofit associations. The Rural Electrification Administration is also authorized to finance the wiring of farmsteads and the purchase and installation of electrical appliances and plumbing.

Recommendations

Individual members of this Commission have different points of view as to organizational and administrative recommendations on the Government's electric power and irrigation enterprises. There was no majority report of the Commissioners. The largest group of five Commissioners made the following observations.

Further Views on Major Multiple-Purpose Dams

Statement by Chairman Hoover, Commissioners Flemming, Mead, Kennedy, and Brown

We do not dissent from this report, but in the previous recommendation on the electrical business enterprises of the Government, it is indicated that the members of the Commission should submit their individual views as to the organization and administration of these projects. The following discussion relates solely to major multiple-purpose dams and not to the Rural Electrification Administration.

The law creating this Commission included the following injunction as to its duties and recommendations, "eliminating duplication and overlapping of services, activities, and functions . . . abolishing services, activities, and functions not necessary to the efficient conduct of Government . . . defining and limiting executive functions, services, and activities."

At once we wish to state that each of us believes in the construction of these multiple-purpose dams as a necessity in the conservation and control of the Nation's water resources. These reservoirs have one or all of four primary purposes: Domestic water, irrigation, flood control, and aid to navigation. Many of these multiple-purpose dams also produce hydroelectric power.

Defects in the Organization of These Enterprises

We have mentioned in the first chapter of this report, "General Observations and Recommendations," numerous defects in the Government business enterprises. Many of these are also prevalent in the electrical business enterprises discussed here.

From the studies of our task forces and other information, the following additional defects in organization appear.

a. These are business enterprises in their electrical and irrigation aspects, but, with the exception of the Tennessee Valley Authority, they do not have the advantages of flexibility of management, budgeting, and accounting that efficient modern business requires and that has been provided by the Government Corporation Control Act of 1945.

b. There is no effective agency in the Government for the screening and review of proposed projects to determine their economic and social worth. There is no effective review of the timing of the construction of these projects in relation to economic need or to the financial ability of the Nation to build them.

c. There is duplication and overlap of effort; and policy conflicts exist as between the Army Engineers and the Reclamation Bureau in construction of, and jurisdiction over, projects.

d. There is an inherent conflict between the most efficient operation of storage dams for the purpose of flood control and of dams used for the generation of hydroelectric power. Flood control implies empty storage space prior to the high-water season, the storage of water during the flood season, and the emptying of the dams during dry spells. The generation of hydroelectric power implies as nearly an even flow of water as is possible the year around. The irrigation cycle, which requires storage of water in the winter months and its release in the summer, also conflicts with the continuous flow of water required for electrical operation. There is again conflict in the original design of works as to whether flood control, navigation, irrigation, or electric power is the objective.

e. The proper assignment of capital costs as between irrecoverable costs attributable to flood control and navigation, on the one hand, and recoverable capital to be reimbursed from reclamation and sale of domestic water and power, on the other, is highly speculative.

f. There is no uniformity of principles guiding Congressional authorization of these projects. Some are authorized under the Reclamation Act, some under the Flood Control Act, and some projects have been created by individual legislation.

g. There are no uniform periods for amortization or uniform rates for interest payable to the Government on its investment.

h. Some of the Government electrical-projects costs do not include allowance for interest during construction, a period which usually covers years.

i. The cost of some projects has been greatly underestimated at the time of original authorization.

j. The original hopes of return of Government capital with interest from the electrical earnings in many cases are not being realized.

k. The Federal Power Commission has authority to fix rates and accounting principles for some Government projects, but not for others.

l. The accounting is subject to severe strictures by our task forces. It does not display, project by project, the full financial results of these enterprises.

m. Whether justifiable or unjustifiable, there is in all these multiple-purpose projects, in effect, a subsidy to local areas by the taxpayers of the Nation as a whole, which, in all instances, should be brought out into the open, so that the public has a clearer picture of the situation. The subsidy arises in various forms:

i. In some cases there is an underassignment of capital costs to the revenue-producing agencies;

ii. A lower rate of interest is given than that which private enterprise must pay in competing with the Government, and these lower rates are not available to other communities.

iii. These electrical agencies enjoy freedom from the excise tax and other taxes on private power, and from the income tax paid by private corporations.

iv. Even without considering taxes, some of the rates for sales of power are insufficient to amortize the cost and to pay a reasonable rate of interest to the Government on the investment assigned to the power element alone.

Priority of Use of Multiple-purpose Reservoirs

Recommendation No. 1

We recommend that the Congress define the relative priority in use, where several uses are involved. We suggest the first priority should be domestic water; the second, irrigation; the third, flood control; the fourth navigation. And finally, the generation of electrical power should be regarded as a byproduct, and be subordinate to all the other uses.

Determination of Need

We recommend elsewhere that there should be created in the Government at once a Board of Impartial Analysis comprised of men eminent in their professions.[10] Their duties should be:

[10] In our report on the Department of the Interior.

a. To review the need for and the timing of every construction project of the Government prior to its submission to the President through the Bureau of the Budget.

b. To review and determine the proportion of capital irrecoverable but appropriate to the benefits of flood control and navigation as well as the balance of the capital to be set up as recoverable.

Recommendations as to Accounting

As shown by our task force reports, the accounting of these agencies requires vigorous reorganization.

Accounting is based upon decisions as to what portion of the costs of these multiple-purpose projects is charged to each of the items of flood control and navigation on one hand, which are irrecoverable, and on the other hand, that portion which is charged to and is recoverable from domestic water, irrigation, and power. When undue amounts are written off to the irrecoverable items, the amounts which may be repaid to the Government from the recoverable items are diminished. Our task force points out that in some instances this has taken place. The corrective must be an independent Board of Impartial Analysis mentioned above.

Recommendation No. 2

We recommend:

a. That the standards of amortization and interest upon the Government investment in the electrical enterprises be determined by the Congress.

b. That the annual accounts show, project by project, the original estimated cost; the capital outlay to date; an estimate of further capital required; and the amounts assigned to irrecoverable items and to each of the recoverable items.

c. That the accounts clearly distinguish between expenditures for capital additions and expenditures for current operations. They should show operating costs and operating receipts; the amount of earnings applied to depreciation; the amount applicable to amortization and interest; and the resulting surplus or deficit in each of these items according to the standard set by the Congress. They should also show the amount of taxes which would have been paid if the project were a private enterprise.

All this is vital information if the American people are to know what amount of subsidy they are paying or what amount of returns they are receiving.

Recommendation No. 3

We recommend that the Federal Power Commission should prescribe for all governmental electrical projects, as it now does in some cases, the detailed accounting practices to be followed by those agencies so as to produce an accurate picture of results, project by project.

Flexibility in Management, Budgeting, and Accounting

Recommendation No. 4

We recommend that the Congress should establish the budgeting, accounting, and auditing of these business enterprises upon the same basis as Government corporations under the Government Corporation Control Act of 1945, thus giving both more flexibility in management and uniformity and clarity in budgeting, accounting, and auditing methods.

We do not believe it advisable to incorporate projects of the Reclamation Bureau or the Corps of Engineers. Such incorporation might, in these cases, weaken Congressional and executive control.

Rates for Electrical Power

The disposal of byproduct electric power from these multiple-purpose projects raises many difficult questions. We are not here discussing the wisdom or the nonwisdom of these ventures. But our mandate from the Congress calls upon us to report on ways to achieve the "lowest expenditures consistent with efficient performance of essential services, activities, and functions . . ."

The rates charged for power are of first importance to Government revenues and are, of course, vital to the ability of these electrical enterprises to make adequate returns of capital and interest to the Government.

The Federal Power Commission now fixes rates for some of these projects.

Recommendation No. 5

We recommend that Congress determine a national policy as to power rates in Federal projects, and that the Federal Power Commission determine rates in accordance with such policy.

Duplication and Limiting of Functions

The Government is now, in many of these projects, constructing transmission lines and is engaged in power distribution.

In certain cases, these transmission and distribution lines duplicate existing power facilities or facilities that could be provided by the private and municipal power enterprises. The result is an unnecessary expenditure of public money.

It is possible that a larger net return could be obtained for the Government power by its sale at the generating plant (the bus-bar) as in the case at the Hoover Dam. The consumers of electricity so sold are protected by public regulatory authorities.

Recommendation No. 6

We recommend that the Congress consider, in each case, whether the transmission and distribution of power can be secured under advantageous long-term contracts by selling the power at the generating plant (the bus-bar) before deciding to authorize the construction of Government transmission and distribution lines.

(Five other separate extensions of views were filed by individual Commissioners. These were published with the Commission's original reports.)

Chapter Four

MISCELLANEOUS BUSINESS ENTERPRISES

The miscellaneous business enterprises not discussed in any detail in the preceding parts of this report comprise: [11]

Incorporated

PANAMA RAILROAD COMPANY
FEDERAL PRISON INDUSTRIES, INC.
INSTITUTE OF INTER-AMERICAN AFFAIRS
TENNESSEE VALLEY ASSOCIATED COOPERATIVES, INC.
GOVERNMENT SERVICES, INC. (Government interest in profits)
INLAND WATERWAYS CORPORATION
VIRGIN ISLANDS COMPANY

Unincorporated

ALASKA RAILROAD
VETERANS' CANTEEN SERVICE
PUERTO RICO RECONSTRUCTION ADMINISTRATION
U. S. MARITIME COMMISSION (ship management, loans, etc.)
WASHINGTON NATIONAL AIRPORT
POST OFFICE

Others

There are, in addition, a number of corporate agencies (chiefly war agencies) which have either ceased operations or are in liquidation.

The total investment of the Government in these enterprises, exclusive of that in the Maritime Commission and the Post Office, is about $250

[11] The Atomic Energy Commission is excluded from the purview of this report.

million. The Maritime Commission has made enormous investments in shipping but, for the most part, these were of a war emergency character.

Many of our comments, included in "General Observations," apply to these incorporated agencies. We have made a special report on the Post Office.

Our further specific recommendations are given in the following sections.

Inland Waterways Corporation

This corporation was first an agency of World War I and thereafter its purpose was to pioneer barge traffic on the newly deepened waterways.

For 23 years, the company has operated at an almost continual loss and, as of June 30, 1947, showed an accumulated deficit of $8,192,104 from operations and insufficient depreciation reserves. The fleet is obsolete and it is estimated that about $18 million would be required for rehabilitation. Private enterprise now serves this transportation purpose, as indicated by the fact that the company carried about 3 million tons out of a total of over 40 million tons on the rivers it serves.

The Under Secretary of Commerce, in a statement to the Appropriations Committee of the House, has given an uncertain outlook for the corporation. In 1947, the Committee on Small Business of the House of Representatives recommended that the Government liquidate the business. The General Accounting Office also has recommended that the Government withdraw from this business.

Recommendation No. 20

We recommend that the corporation be put into immediate liquidation and that the annual expenditure of the Government be ended.

United States Maritime Commission

We have recommended that the whole activity of managing and selling ships, making loans, and other business activities of this Commission should be placed in the Department of Commerce.

In our report on that Department we state in full our reasons for this recommendation.

Puerto Rico Reconstruction Administration

This relief and rehabilitation business enterprise had expended about $77 million and had assets of about $18 million in 1947.

A plan for the termination and liquidation of this enterprise has been pending in the Department of the Interior since 1947. Under it, the activities of the Administration would be distributed among functional agencies operating in this field.

Recommendation No. 21

The Commission recommends that this proposal be adopted.

The Alaska Railroad

This wholly Government-owned railroad is supervised by the Division of Territories and Island Possessions of the Department of the Interior. The Division operates the Alaska Railroad, river steamers on the Yukon, transportation and lodging for Mt. McKinley National Park, and some auxiliary ocean-going and coastwise vessels.

The railroad operates as a business enterprise; its normal receipts are supplemented by direct appropriations. Together, these monies form a special fund for maintenance and operation. Direct appropriations have approximated $60 million for capital expenditure, and $17 million as subsidy for maintenance and operation from 1914 to 1948. Operating revenues of each year have been reappropriated by the Congress to the railroad. In 1948, there were operating revenues of $10,750,000 which were so reappropriated.

Recommendation No. 22

We recommend the incorporation of this enterprise under the Government Corporation Control Act of 1945.

Washington National Airport

This airport is maintained as a direct governmental operation by the Civil Aeronautics Administration of the Department of Commerce. Maintenance and operation, including access roadways and police and fire departments, is provided by direct annual Congressional appropriation.

Until 1948, the operation had always shown a small profit above the appropriation. Profits are repaid to the general fund of the Treasury, so that the operation cannot be considered as of the revolving-fund type. Construction of facilities has been provided by direct appropriation and about $16 million has been so provided up to 1948. There have been, since 1945, varying provisions for amortization of the investment and depreciation of the hangars.

Recommendation No. 23

We urge the incorporation of this enterprise to bring it under the Government Corporation Control Act of 1945.

Other Enterprises

We present no recommendation as to the following, but for the record we mention them here.

THE VIRGIN ISLANDS COMPANY

The Virgin Islands Company was granted a charter in April 1934, by the Colonial Council as an instrument of the Department of the Interior. Its operations have been largely the production of sugar and the manufacture of rum from molasses. Its corporate life will expire on June 30, 1949, but legislation providing for Federal reincorporation is under consideration.

The net operating losses aggregated $328,000 to June 30, 1948. The remaining $797,000 is primarily invested in land, structures, equipment, and an electrification project. It was authorized to borrow $500,000 from the Treasury in fiscal year 1949.

This corporation made a profit for 1943 and 1945 as a result of the whisky shortage, but has lost money ever since. The General Accounting Office has criticized its accounting in several reports. Congress extended its present local charter to June 30, 1949, because a Federal charter was not agreed upon by the Eightieth Congress.

THE FEDERAL PRISON INDUSTRIES, INC.

The Federal Prison Industries, Inc., was established January 1, 1935, with assets from the former "Prison Industries Fund" of $4,113,380. It has a board of five unpaid members appointed by the President. The net earnings to July 30, 1947, were $20,074,871 and $13 million of dividends had been paid or authorized to be paid to the Federal Government to June 30, 1948.

It operates 43 shops in Federal prisons and makes 28 different types of products, including mail sacks for the Post Office. The Government institutions absorb most of the products, and there is little competition with private enterprise. The number of prison inmates employed in 1948 was 3,157. The accounts are audited by the General Accounting Office under the Corporation Control Act of 1945.

GOVERNMENT SERVICES, INC.

This nonprofit private distributing agency was established under private auspices and operates restaurants and recreational services for Government facilities. Original capital was supplied privately, and the organization has held its present franchise from the Government since 1926. Profits are distributed, one-half to the Government in lieu of rent, and one-half to a depreciation fund. The Government has received about $1,550,000 since 1926; no profits have been made since 1945. There is no Government investment.

It is not audited in accord with the Government Corporation Control Act of 1945.

INSTITUTE OF INTER-AMERICAN AFFAIRS

This nonprofit Government corporation is the successor to certain activities of the Office of the Coordinator of Inter-American Affairs. The Institute is responsible for furthering friendship and understanding among the peoples of the American republics through collaboration with their governments in planning, initiating, assisting, and financing technical programs and projects in the fields of public health, sanitation, agriculture, and education.

Its succession is limited to August 5, 1950. On June 30, 1948, its capital was estimated at $71 million, largely provided by appropriation. Through the corporation's operations, this had been expended except for about $1 million. The operation is essentially a grant-in-aid program.

TENNESSEE VALLEY ASSOCIATED COOPERATIVES, INC.

This agency was organized in 1934 to administer a Federal Emergency Relief Administration grant of $236,000 and to organize and assist the formation of cooperatives in the Tennessee Valley. As of June 30, 1947, approximately $320,000 in loans was outstanding. It has been inactive since June 1946, and is in the process of dissolution under supervision of the Treasury.

VETERANS' CANTEEN SERVICE

This is a service of the Veterans' Administration, established in 1946 to provide articles of convenience and necessity for hospitalized and domiciled veterans. By terms of statute the service is not required to realize a profit, but a nominal operating profit has been reported. It operates as a revolving-fund agency, and funds are deposited in a checking account with the Treasurer of the United States. The original appropriation for the fund was $4,965,000 and $965,000 is being returned to the Treasury. The remaining $4 million is adequate for the purpose of this service.

It is audited by the General Accounting Office under the Government Corporation Control Act of 1945.

Liquidations

The following business enterprise agencies have either ceased active lending operations, or are in the process of liquidating loans, with the following amounts outstanding as of June 30, 1948:

Agency	Loans Outstanding
REGIONAL AGRICULTURAL CREDIT CORPORATIONS	$1,033,000
HOME OWNERS LOAN CORP.	420,970,000
TENNESSEE VALLEY AUTHORITY	85,000
TENNESSEE VALLEY ASSOCIATED COOPERATIVE LOANS (lending only)	[12] 320,000
AGRICULTURAL MARKETING ACT REVOLVING FUND	1,120,000
FEDERAL WORKS AGENCY	[13] 129,300,000
TREASURY DEPARTMENT (certain loans)	34,000,000
ARMY AND NAVY GUARANTEES OF LOANS TO CONTRACTORS	5,000,000
FEDERAL SECURITY AGENCY (loans to students)	1,800,000
FEDERAL FARM MORTGAGE CORP. (loans and assets)	124,000,000

There are also a number of war corporations which have ceased operations or are in liquidation.

In addition we have recommended that the following agencies cease functioning and be liquidated:

FARMERS HOME ADMINISTRATION (other existing agencies substituted)
INLAND WATERWAYS CORPORATION
SEVERAL FUNCTIONS OF THE PUBLIC HOUSING ADMINISTRATION

The Commission has recommended, in its report on the Treasury Department, the systematic handling of the liquidation of business enterprises which are terminated by Congress or otherwise.

Those recommendations embrace an authority to the President to assign such liquidation to any existing agency, and a requirement that the

[12] June 30, 1947.
[13] Approximate figures, due to varied reporting dates.

Treasury make a semiannual inspection of the progress of liquidation and report to the President and the Congress.

This action would assure more expeditious liquidation of agencies whose usefulness is ended, and would save administrative expenses.

Savings—Business Enterprises

The savings to the taxpayers to be made in these business agencies are very large. They can originate from consolidations; increase in rates of interest or charges for services so as to include administrative expense; proper amortization and interest return to the Government; the incorporation of some to secure more flexibility in management, accounting, and budgeting; and more speedy liquidations. Such savings amount to large sums.

If the recommendations in this report be carried out, there would be a decrease of over 30 in the number of these agencies.

XVIII

Independent Regulatory Commissions

Chapter One

ROLE OF INDEPENDENT REGULATORY COMMISSIONS

The independent regulatory commission is a comparatively new feature of the Federal Government. It consists of a board or commission, not within an executive department, and engaged in the regulation of some form of private activity. In this report, the Commission on Organization has confined itself to a discussion of the organizational problems of these agencies, and does not deal with their quasi-judicial or quasi-legislative functions.

Beginning in 1887, with the Interstate Commerce Commission, the number of independent regulatory commissions has increased until there are now nine [1] of them, covering a vast segment of national activity. They employ about 12,000 persons. The annual cost of these agencies in 1948 was roughly $57,000,000.[2] Even more important is the fact that they regulate private activity in such significant fields as labor;

---

[1] The nine commissions are:

INTERSTATE COMMERCE COMMISSION
FEDERAL POWER COMMISSION
FEDERAL TRADE COMMISSION
U. S. MARITIME COMMISSION
SECURITIES AND EXCHANGE COMMISSION
FEDERAL COMMUNICATIONS COMMISSION
CIVIL AERONAUTICS BOARD
FEDERAL RESERVE BOARD
NATIONAL LABOR RELATIONS BOARD

Chairman Herbert Hoover believes that the following independent commissions should be included in this same category:

UNITED STATES TARIFF COMMISSION
THE TAX COURT OF THE UNITED STATES

[2] This excludes the costs of the Federal Reserve System which are not a charge on the taxpayers. It also excludes the operating costs of the Maritime Commission.

transportation whether by rail, truck, pipeline, ship, or airplane; credit; banking; securities both on or off the stock exchanges; trade practices; communications, including radio, television, telegraph, and telephone; the development, sale, and distribution of electric power together with the financing of these and other enterprises.

Thousands of pages of regulations guide private activity within these areas. Controversial issues of the greatest significance to the Nation's economic development are disposed of each year by these commissions. It is clear that their efficient operation is of vital significance to the entire nation.

These commissions were created not only to provide for the orderly dispatch of complicated controversies by bodies deemed expert in their respective fields, but also to eliminate abuses that had crept in and, at the same time, to promote an adequate and healthy development of the activities subject to their control.

To achieve prompt adjudication of controversies the commissions were freed of the necessity of following the niceties of court procedures, and their decisions were final, with only limited review by the courts. Unlike courts, their duties are not merely passive. They do not wait until differences are brought to them, but they are enjoined actively to insure that their regulations are observed and that the plans they conceive are executed.

Chapter Two

WHAT IS WRONG WITH INDEPENDENT REGULATORY COMMISSIONS

This Commission believes that the independent regulatory commissions have a proper place in the machinery of our Government, a place very like that originally conceived, but that the role of these commissions as originally established has not been adequately fulfilled.

a. To achieve consistency in attaining these objectives, members of some of the boards and commissions were given tenure of office not related to the period of ascendancy of a political party. The membership of the commissions is generally required to be bipartisan. In most cases, not more than a majority of a particular commission can be of the same political party, although there is no such requirement for the National Labor Relations Board and the Federal Reserve Board.

b. Appointments to membership on these commissions are sometimes below desirable standards because of the inadequate salaries offered, or the failure of the Executive to appreciate the importance of the positions.

c. Purely executive duties—those that can be performed far better by a single administrative official—have been imposed upon these commissions with the result that these duties have sometimes been performed badly. The necessity for performing them has interfered with the performance of the strictly regulatory functions of the commissions.

d. The quantity of work in the regulatory field at the top level has been so great that the commissions have often neglected their promotional and planning functions.

e. Sufficient delegation to the staff has not occurred, due to legislative restrictions as well as to poor internal organization.

431

f. Administrative direction has not developed within the commissions. Their chairmen are too frequently merely presiding officers at commission meetings. No one has been responsible for planning and guiding the general program of commission activity.

g. Tenure of commission members is not uniform. During their terms of office, some can be removed by the President only for specified causes; others, however, can be removed at any time for any cause.

h. Unnecessary red tape has crept into their procedures causing useless delay and expense.

i. Coordination between these commissions and the general program of the executive departments is often loose and casual and sometimes non-existent.

Chapter Three

RECOMMENDATIONS

Some of the recommendations of this Commission are applicable to all of the independent regulatory commissions; others are applicable only to one or more and are so set forth.

The Commission's task force on Regulatory Agencies makes numerous recommendations which are not included in this report but which the Commission hopes will be given thorough study and consideration by both the Congress and the commissions concerned.

Commission Administration

Administration by a plural executive is universally regarded as inefficient. This has proved to be true in connection with these commissions. Indeed, those cases where administration has been distinctly superior are cases where the administrative as distinguished from the regulatory duties have been vested in the chairman. There are many of these administrative duties. Their efficient handling will frequently make the difference between a commission's keeping abreast of its work or falling woefully behind.

Recommendation No. 1

We recommend that all administrative responsibility be vested in the chairman of the commission.

It would be his responsibility to deploy the work force most effectively in order to carry out the program developed by the commission as a whole. It would similarly be his responsibility to see that business is dispatched in an orderly manner.

The volume of this administrative work will, in every instance, require the appointment of an executive director. He should be responsible to the commission through the chairman.

This recommendation does not derogate from the statutory responsibilities placed upon the other members of the commission. They remain exactly as they are, and because of the better functioning of the organization the commission members will be enabled to discharge these responsibilities much more effectively.

One consequence of this recommendation will be to center responsibility for the functioning of the commission. The chairman will be the commission's principal spokesman before the Congress as well as before the executive branch.

Terms of Commission Members

The tenure of commission members is not uniform. Some can be removed from office only for cause, while others are removable at the President's pleasure. The Commission sees no reason for uniformity in regard to the terms of commission members. Differences with regard to their dismissal seem to arise from a difference of view as to the law prior to the *Humphrey Case*.

Recommendation No. 2

This Commission therefore recommends that the law be changed to provide that the members of the following commissions, as is the case with other commissions, be removable only for cause:

a. **The Securities and Exchange Commission.**

b. **The Federal Power Commission.**

c. **The Federal Communications Commission.**

Upon the expiration of the term of a commissioner he ceases to function as such even though a successor has not been appointed and qualified, except in a few of the commissions. Unnecessary gaps in the full membership of the commission have frequently occurred, resulting in the unnecessary disruption of the commission's work. This is easy to cure.

Recommendation No. 3

This Commission recommends that the statutes be amended to provide that a commissioner, upon the expiration of his term, continue to hold office until his successor has been appointed and qualified; subject, of course, to the general statutes on "holdover" appointments.

Commission and Board Salaries

The salaries of commissioners are too low. The salaries of the Federal Trade Commissioners have not been changed since 1916. Low salaries cannot attract men of the desired caliber.

Recommendation No. 4

The Commission therefore recommends that the salaries of all of the commissioners and board members should be substantially raised.

Almost the same situation prevails among the commissions' staffs. These staff positions are not political. They require training and experience. Rotation in office is neither common nor desirable. Comments in this connection are found in our report on Personnel Management.

Recommendation No. 5

The Commission recommends increases in the salaries of staff members so as to attract persons of high professional competence to these positions.

Delegation of Authority

Each regulatory commission handles a multitude of minor matters as well as major issues. Minor matters should be delegated to staff members, but statutory authority often prevents it.

Recommendation No. 6

The Commission therefore recommends that the statutes be amended so as to permit the commissions to delegate routine, preliminary, and less important work to members of the staffs under their supervision.

Administrative Procedures

The Commission has not explored the problems of administrative problems. This general question was recently studied by the Attorney General's Committee on Administrative Procedure and some of its recommendations have been embodied in the Administrative Procedures Act.

The Commission makes no comment as to the fairness of existing administrative procedures, but the Commission is concerned with the growth of cumbersome and costly administrative procedures. All of this detail is not required for "due process," or essential for fair and full solution of the various problems. The situation, however, is not a static one. Nor is it one for which cures can be effected except by continuous and painstaking effort.

Recommendation No. 7

This Commission recommends that the Administrative Management Division of the Office of the Budget should, with the aid of carefully selected legal consultants, suggest ways and means to improve and thereby reduce the cost of disposing of business before administrative agencies.

Such studies would be concerned not only with the independent regulatory commissions but also with the administrative disposition of controversies before all Government agencies. The causes which lead to prolonged hearings, intra-agency appeals, and voluminous records, could be analyzed by the legal experts, and simpler, more efficient, and less costly methods prescribed. Administrative justice today unfortunately is not characterized by economy, simplicity, and dispatch. It remains, however, a necessity in our complex economic system.

Executive Functions

Purely executive functions too frequently have been entrusted to these independent regulatory commissions. The consequences have not been too happy, for a plural executive is not the best device for the performance of operational duties. Moreover, these duties commonly call for close integration with the broad programs of the executive branch. The quality of independence, desirable in the disposition of controversies, creates obstacles to the handling of an executive program. The recommendations of the Commission with regard to the removal of these executive functions must be specified in detail.

THE FEDERAL POWER COMMISSION

Recommendation No. 8

The Commission recommends that the power-planning functions of the Federal Power Commission be transferred to the Department of the Interior.

436

THE MARITIME COMMISSION

Recommendation No. 9

The Commission recommends that the functions of ship construction and the operation, charter, and sale of ships should be transferred to the Department of Commerce.[3]

The functions of the Maritime Commission relating to rates, conditions of service, and the grant of subsidies should remain with that Commission.

THE INTERSTATE COMMERCE COMMISSION

Recommendation No. 10

The Commission recommends that equipment inspection, and the functions of the Interstate Commerce Commission relating to safety and car service should be transferred to the Department of Commerce.

THE CIVIL AERONAUTICS BOARD

Recommendation No. 11

The Commission recommends that the promulgation of rules relating to the safety of aircraft operation, both commercial and noncommercial, including contract operations, be transferred to the Department of Commerce with a right of appeal to the Civil Aeronautics Board from the enactment of, or the refusal to enact, any particular regulation. The investigation of the probable cause of major aircraft accidents should remain with the Civil Aeronautics Board.

Other reports of the Commission call for the transfer to the Department of Commerce of certain executive functions relating to transportation. The Department of Commerce already possesses considerable statutory concern with transportation, particularly in the Civil Aeronautics Administration. In its recommendations on the Department of Commerce this Commission proposes a consolidation in that Department of the executive functions dealing with transportation.

---

[3] In our report on the Department of Labor we recommend that the Maritime Commission activities dealing with determination of the minimum wages for seamen on privately operated vessels be transferred to the Department of Labor.

Coordination of Policies

Our task force on transportation has suggested that the remaining regulatory functions dealing with transportation be consolidated into one regulatory commission. This would include the quasi-judicial and quasi-legislative functions of the Interstate Commerce Commission, the Civil Aeronautics Board, and the Maritime Commission.

This Commission does not endorse that suggestion.

The three commissions involved are already overburdened with work, the statutory approach to these three fields of transportation has been different, and entirely different techniques are needed for the solution of the problems in the various fields. Except for the common denominator that they are regulatory in nature, these functions are vastly different, and have reached different stages of maturity in their growth.

The Commission is aware that some lack of coordination of national transportation policy will arise as a result of the separate continuance of the Maritime Commission, the Interstate Commerce Commission, and the Civil Aeronautics Board. This possibility is, however, greatly minimized by centering executive transportation functions within the Department of Commerce.

Coordination will be necessary, for land, sea, and air transportation have an intimate relationship to national defense, the postal system, and foreign commerce. Thus coordination will be required not only with the Department of Commerce, but also with the National Military Establishment, the State Department, and the Post Office Department.

The coordination of policies pursued by these independent regulatory commissions with those of the executive branch as a whole has been generally loose and casual. Though the problem has not been too serious in the past, coordination can now be easily effected because the above recommendations suggest that the chairman of each commission effect liaison between their commissions and the rest of the Government. Such coordination as may be necessary—and the removal of the executive functions from these commissions will greatly minimize the area in which coordination is needed—can be effected through the proposed machinery in the President's Office and through the reorganization of the Department of Commerce.

Planning and Promotion

The chief criticism that can be made of the regulatory commissions is that they become too engrossed in case-by-case activities and thus fail to plan their roles and to promote the enterprises entrusted to their care. Typical of this is the attitude by which the Civil Aeronautics Board and the Interstate Commerce Commission have approached the problem of building a route structure for the Nation.

The lack of planning has also resulted in too great demands upon the regulatory capacity of these commissions. The Commission is aware that adequate planning cannot be decreed.

In its report on the Department of Commerce, this Commission recommends that the Secretary of Commerce be charged with developing an over-all route pattern for land, sea, and air. When proposals are made to the commissions for route changes, the Secretary of Commerce should have the authority to present his views before the commissions. He should also have the authority to initiate, by recommendation, route changes for the consideration of the commissions.

Bipartisan Membership

The independent nature of these commissions demands bipartisan representation.

Recommendation No. 12

Therefore, this Commission recommends that this general rule be extended to all commissions.

Chapter Four

CONCLUSION

The savings that could be anticipated from the above recommendations cannot be reckoned in the normal manner. Actually the budget of these independent regulatory commissions is small in comparison to the expenditures of the executive departments, amounting in the fiscal year ending in 1949 to only $57,333,000,[4] exclusive of expenditures on operating programs. Some reduction in this figure can be made.

But the real savings are to be found elsewhere. Delay and inefficiency in regulation involves large costs to the regulated industries themselves which must be passed on to the public by one method or another. Expedition will mean vast savings as well as better justice. Second, the failure to program appropriately is costly. Extensive subsidies, for example, to the air lines or to the shipping industry could probably have been greatly reduced had there been more farsighted understanding of the direction of these programs and the appropriate methods of administration. Savings of this type alone would more than outdistance the entire present cost of the regulatory program.

[4] Excluding the Federal Reserve System.

XIX

Social Security and Education

Chapter One

WELFARE ACTIVITIES

Introduction

American concern over the problems of education, health, relief of the needy, aid to the handicapped, and assistance in unemployment and old age is as old as the Republic. Responsibilities in these fields were initially considered to be those of State and local governments.

With the growth of the Nation, these problems have become wider than local and State boundaries. There is a common interest of all citizens in the eduction of every citizen. There is a common interest in the advancement of science and in the common dangers from disease. There are obligations to veterans. The problems of unemployment extend beyond State borders. There is generally a recognition of the practical problems which lie in our obligation as "our brother's keeper."

All these circumstances have contributed to bring these problems more and more to the Federal level. In dealing with these matters, except in the case of veterans, the Federal Government has usually sought to preserve the responsibilities of local government and their agencies of administration in effecting the national purpose.

It is not the province of this Commission to pass upon the policies that have evolved in these matters. We are concerned with the efficient and economical organization of the Federal agencies as we find them. The organizational problems of education, health, medical care, assistance to the handicapped and aged, and aid to the unemployed permeate every department of the Federal Government.

There is no perfect organizational arrangement for these functions. Many of them must be performed by specialized agencies like the Veterans' Administration, the Armed Forces, and the Labor Department. As the problems grow, specialization in organization will inevitably grow.

In our report on Medical Services, we have recommended a separate United Medical Administration, reporting directly to the President. That agency would embrace the major hospitalization, medical research, and public health activities of the Government and, by its creation, bring about better medical care, development of medical staff, research, and protection of public health, together with large economies in administration.

In our report on the Labor Department, we recommended the return of several agencies now in the Federal Security Agency to that Department.

There remain, however, certain most important bureaus or agencies relating to education and security which must be organized into a workable department. They are now, with one exception (the Bureau of Indian Affairs), in the Federal Security Agency.

The size of these agencies, after making the changes we have outlined, is somewhat indicated by the fact that they embrace about 20,000 employees. The administrative expenditures would be roughly $50,-000,000. The grants-in-aid to be distributed would approximate $800,-000,000.[1] For the calendar year 1948, the collections of Old-Age and Survivors' Insurance approximated $1,688,000,000, and disbursements $550,000,000. The accumulated funds on August 31, 1948, were $10,388,000,000.

While we discuss the educational problems at greater length later, it may be said here that it has long been suggested that the educational activities of the Federal Government should be given independent or Cabinet status. However, the Federal Government is not engaged in direct educational activities (except in a small way in the case of Howard University). Its function is that of stimulating educational advancement by research, issuing publications, and making grants-in-aid to the States. The administrative staff required is less than 500 persons.

We believe that the functions, including education, which we propose to assign to this department have such an important relationship to the formation of the domestic policies of the Government that the person in charge of the functions should be a member of the President's Cabinet.

---

[1] In addition, the budget request for 1950 includes $301,200,000 for Federal aid to education and $65,000,000 for the extension of public assistance programs.

We therefore recommend that a new Department to administer the
functions set forth in this report be created and headed by a
Cabinet officer.

Proposed Departmental Organization

We have urged in our first report that good departmental administration requires that the Secretary have authority to organize and control
his department, and that grants by the Congress of independent authority to subordinates or bureaus be eliminated.

Under our recommendations made elsewhere, we propose a new form
of "performance" budget for all departments.[2] We also propose that
the Department keep its own administrative accounts as prescribed by
an Accountant General in the Treasury and approved and audited by
the Comptroller General.[2] The Commission also recommends that all
personnel recruitment should be decentralized into the Department
(except possibly in lower grade positions common to all departments
and agencies), subject to standards and methods of merit selection to
be proposed by the Department, but with the approval and enforcement
of the Civil Service Commission.[3] The Commission likewise recommends that the procurement of supplies peculiar to a department should
be decentralized into the Department under standards and methods
established by the Office of General Services. Items of common use
would, of course, be handled by the Office of General Services.[4] Further, we propose that the Department should strengthen its management research unit, working in cooperation with a comparable staff
unit under the Office of the Budget.[2]

The present administrative structure of the Federal Security Agency,
with few changes as to titles and assignments, would naturally be continued and transformed into the new Department. The staff organization should comprise:

THE SECRETARY
AN UNDER SECRETARY
THREE ASSISTANT SECRETARIES, one of whom should be Administrative
    Assistant Secretary in charge of staff services

[2] Report on Budgeting and Accounting.
[3] Report on Personnel Management.
[4] Report on the Office of General Services.

445

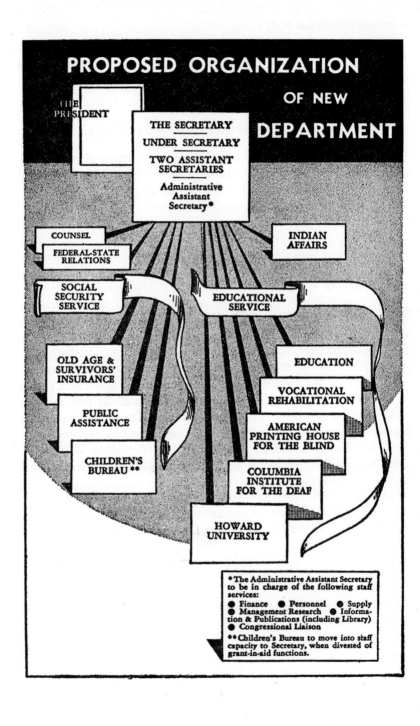

PROPOSED ORGANIZATION OF NEW DEPARTMENT

THE PRESIDENT

THE SECRETARY
UNDER SECRETARY
TWO ASSISTANT SECRETARIES
Administrative Assistant Secretary *

COUNSEL
FEDERAL-STATE RELATIONS

INDIAN AFFAIRS

SOCIAL SECURITY SERVICE

EDUCATIONAL SERVICE

OLD AGE & SURVIVORS' INSURANCE

EDUCATION

VOCATIONAL REHABILITATION

PUBLIC ASSISTANCE

AMERICAN PRINTING HOUSE FOR THE BLIND

CHILDREN'S BUREAU **

COLUMBIA INSTITUTE FOR THE DEAF

HOWARD UNIVERSITY

* The Administrative Assistant Secretary to be in charge of the following staff services:
● Finance ● Personnel ● Supply ● Management Research ● Information & Publications (including Library) ● Congressional Liaison

** Children's Bureau to move into staff capacity to Secretary, when divested of grant-in-aid functions.

Recommendation No. 2

We recommend that these officials be appointed by the President and confirmed by the Senate, but that all officials in the Department below the rank of Assistant Secretary be appointed by the Secretary.

The Administrative Assistant Secretary should preferably be appointed from the career service.

The following will indicate the opinion of the Commission concerning the arrangement of the Department. Part of this structure is already established in the Federal Security Agency. We are not, however, recommending a hard and fast rule. The Secretary should determine the organization and be free to amend it.

OFFICE OF COUNSEL
OFFICE OF FEDERAL-STATE RELATIONS
STAFF SERVICES, under the Administrative Assistant Secretary, with an officer in charge of each:

> Budgeting and Accounting
> Personnel
> Supply
> Management Research
> Information and Publications (including Library)
> Liaison with Congress

SOCIAL SECURITY SERVICES

BUREAU OF OLD-AGE AND SURVIVORS' INSURANCE
BUREAU OF PUBLIC ASSISTANCE
  (Grants-in-aid to States for Old-Age Assistance, Dependent Children and the Blind)
CHILDREN'S BUREAU

EDUCATIONAL SERVICES

BUREAU OF EDUCATION
BUREAU OF VOCATIONAL REHABILITATION
AMERICAN PRINTING HOUSE FOR THE BLIND
COLUMBIA INSTITUTION FOR THE DEAF
HOWARD UNIVERSITY, WASHINGTON, D. C.

447

The functions of the Bureau of Indian Affairs, and the reasons for its transfer from the Department of the Interior to the new department, are outlined in the report on Indian Affairs, pp. 461 et seq.

Transfers from Federal Security Agency

We elsewhere recommend the transfer from the present Federal Security Agency of the following:

BUREAU OF EMPLOYEES' COMPENSATION, to the Department of Labor.[5]

EMPLOYEES' COMPENSATION APPEALS BOARD, to the Department of Labor (These two functions relate to compensation for injuries of civilian employees of the Government).[5]

BUREAU OF EMPLOYMENT SECURITY, to the Department of Labor (These functions comprise the United States Employment Service and the Federal aspects of unemployment compensation.)[5]

PUBLIC HEALTH SERVICE, to the United Medical Administration.[6]

FOOD AND DRUG ADMINISTRATION, partly to the Department of Agriculture and partly to the United Medical Administration.[7]

General Comment

In the following section, we comment on the problems of the Department and, in doing so, we again emphasize that this Commission is not dealing with the policies of the Congress in these agencies, but purely with organizational questions.

[5] See the report on the Department of Labor.
[6] See the report on Medical Activities.
[7] See the report on the Department of Agriculture.

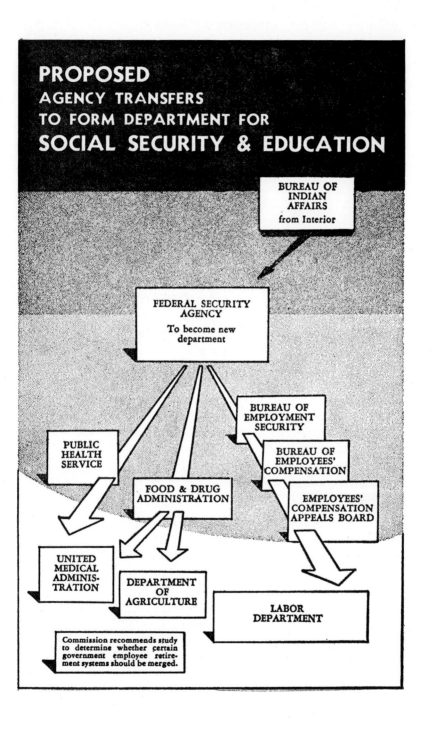

PROPOSED
AGENCY TRANSFERS
TO FORM DEPARTMENT FOR
SOCIAL SECURITY & EDUCATION

BUREAU OF INDIAN AFFAIRS
from Interior

FEDERAL SECURITY AGENCY
To become new department

BUREAU OF EMPLOYMENT SECURITY

PUBLIC HEALTH SERVICE

BUREAU OF EMPLOYEES' COMPENSATION

FOOD & DRUG ADMINISTRATION

EMPLOYEES' COMPENSATION APPEALS BOARD

UNITED MEDICAL ADMINIS-TRATION

DEPARTMENT OF AGRICULTURE

LABOR DEPARTMENT

Commission recommends study to determine whether certain government employee retirement systems should be merged.

Chapter Two

SOCIAL SECURITY

Grants-in-Aid

A considerable part of the departmental function is conducted by grants-in-aid. Total grants are as follows:

Programs		Federal grants in fiscal 1948	Average number of beneficiaries 1946–47
PUBLIC ASSISTANCE		$775,602,000	
Old Age	606,594,000		2,271,000
Dependent children	151,170,000		1,009,000
Blind	17,838,000		62,000
EDUCATION		19,171,000	*
CHILDREN		22,000,000	*
VOCATIONAL REHA-BILITATION		21,662,000	170,000**

* These two activities pertain to segments of the whole population; the numbers of beneficiaries cannot be accurately estimated.
** Aggregate—fiscal year 1947.

The methods by which these grants are distributed may be summarized as follows:

For Old Age and Blind: The Federal Government meets three quarters of the first $20 monthly, plus half of amounts between $20 and $50. States and localities pay all over $50 monthly.

For Dependent Children: The Federal Government pays three-quarters of the first $12 monthly to one child, plus half of the amount between $12 and $27. For additional children in the same household, payment per child in excess of $12 is matched up to $18. Above this level State and local governments bear the entire cost. The Federal Government reimburses the States for half of the amount expended for "proper and efficient administration."

For Vocational Rehabilitation: The Federal Government assumes 100 percent of the cost of administration and the cost of vocational counseling and placement. Other services are shared with States on a fifty-fifty basis. There is no fixed over-all participation ratio but States are expected to contribute 30 percent of total program costs except for the blind where States contribute 20 percent.

For Vocational Education: These funds are to be matched dollar for dollar by the States. Allocations to the States for different purposes are based on at least seven different formulas.

For Child Welfare: Twenty thousand dollars must be allotted to each State. The remainder is required to be allocated on the basis of approved plans in the proportion that a State's rural population bears to the rural population of the United States. There is no fixed matching ratio, but the wording of the act with reference to "cooperating" with State public welfare agencies and to paying "part" of the cost of local child welfare services clearly requires some State financial participation. In practice this is achieved by restrictions placed by the Federal administrative agency on the use of Federal funds.

Fund-matching factors differ by programs. For maternal and child health and crippled children's services, under the Children's Bureau, the law requires that one-half of Federal appropriation be matched equally by States, and that the other half be allocated at the discretion of the Administrator. This was designed to implement the development of services "especially in rural areas and areas suffering from economic distress."

The grant-in-aid system is discussed in our report on Federal-State relations.

The Children's Bureau

Recommendation No. 3

We recommend that, as soon as the integrated new Department develops a more unified approach to grants-in-aid, the Children's Bureau be divested of grant functions and the Bureau shifted to a general staff capacity to the Secretary.

The services of the Children's Bureau cut across the major areas of health, education, and welfare. The Bureau could function more effectively in a staff capacity concentrating on its functions of research, planning, and promotion. The decision as to who should take over these grants can be made at the proper time by the head of the Department.

Old-Age Assistance and Retirement

Our investigation of governmental programs in the area of Old-Age Assistance has revealed the existence of a maze of private and public pension and retirement systems. New variations are constantly being added, and there appears to be little relationship among these programs.

The flexibilities of our society encourage transfer of working skills. Therefore, the individual, in changing employment or profession, may come under a number of different pension schemes—each totally unrelated to the other—and many persons are outside the scope of any existing system. Actuarial bases, when they exist, vary tremendously.

FEDERAL PROGRAMS

The Federal Government is concerned with the following programs which bear upon support in old age:

a. The Federal Old-Age and Survivors' Insurance Program which now includes about 40 million active accounts.

b. The Old-Age portion of the Public Assistance Programs under which about $550,000,000 is disbursed annually by the Federal Government in supplement to State old-age assistance programs.

c. The veteran and military pensions and disability systems, and that for dependents of these groups, which are a direct charge on the Federal Treasury.

d. The Civil Service and Foreign Service retirement systems, also a partial charge on the Treasury.

e. The Railroad Retirement System, which is self-supporting.

OTHER PROGRAMS

In addition, a multitude of other private and governmental old-age pension and retirement systems now exist:

a. The State old-age assistance systems which are supported by State taxes and to which the Federal Treasury is a contributor (*b.* above).

b. Old-age or retirement pensions for most State and municipal employees.

c. Old-age or retirement systems set up by universities, hospitals, and various benevolent institutions.

d. A multitude of retirement or old-age pension systems set up by industries, insurance companies, and other businesses.

e. The establishment of old-age or retirement systems over whole industries by collective bargaining, such as that of the United Mine Workers.

These systems obviously overlap in the contributions from wages and salaries or from taxation, paid on a State or local basis, or passed on to the public through prices.

Operation of Federal Public Systems

Proposals are now being considered for the expansion in coverage and increase in allowances in the Federal Old-Age and Survivors' Insurance System. During the 12 years since its establishment this system has been altered. Originally a supposedly self-supporting system on an actuarial base, the system in all probability will call for appropriations from the Treasury to fulfill its obligations. Government actuaries estimate that in the absence of increases in the 2-percent pay-roll tax that has thus far been levied for the support of the system, the reserve funds will be exhausted within less than 15 years.

For the fiscal year 1950, the budget estimates of the President indicate that the administrative cost of the Old-Age and Survivors' Insurance program will amount to about $43,000,000. The administrative cost is now defrayed entirely from the receipts of the system.

For the fiscal year ended June 30, 1947, the Federal Security Agency estimated that total administrative costs amounted to 2.8 percent of contributions paid in, and to 9.6 percent of benefits paid out. About three-quarters of the administrative costs is spent for the maintenance and use of individual earnings records.

The present number of persons 65 years of age and over is about 10,600,000, or about 7.5 percent of the population. The number that will be in this age bracket 40 years hence is estimated at about 21,500,-000, or over 13 percent of the population. By 1950, it is estimated that pay-roll taxes will total a minimum of about $2.5 billion, and the disbursements to beneficiaries a minimum of over $600 million. As of August 1948 the reserve fund was estimated at $10,388,000,000.

The present costs of administration are no indication of future costs, even granting no further change is made in the system. The full administrative load is still several years ahead. At that time, large numbers of persons will become eligible for benefits. In the fiscal year 1947, the total number of beneficiaries under the system was less than 2 million persons. Even in the fiscal year 1950 it will be around 3 million. The real burden of administrative cost will become evident only when approximately the same number of persons is being added and subtracted each year.

All these problems, and others, raise the question of Congressional examination of the whole subject. Some entirely new system may be necessary if we are to provide adequate protection against the hazards of old age for the American people.

Recommendation No. 4

The Eighth Annual Report of the Board of Trustees of the Federal Old-Age and Survivors' Insurance Trust Fund has stated:

. . . There is need for a review of the old-age and survivors' insurance program covering not only the benefit formula, the coverage of the system, and the scope of protection afforded, but also contributions and financial policy.

We recommend that such a review be made.

Government Employee Systems

At the present time there are several contributory retirement systems operating within the Federal Government.

The comparative size of these systems is indicated below:

	June 30, 1948	
Retirement system	Estimated number employees covered	Balance in fund
CIVIL SERVICE	1,758,000*	$2,825,820,000
ALASKA RAILROAD	2,400	3,144,000
CANAL ZONE	4,500	13,393,000
FOREIGN SERVICE	12,400	12,134,000
TENNESSEE VALLEY AUTHORITY	10,500	19,110,000
DISTRICT OF COLUMBIA, TEACHERS	200	14,202,395
CIVILIAN TEACHERS AT NAVAL ACADEMY	200	**

* Not including employees of the legislative and judiciary branches and the District of Columbia, who number about 17,000.

** Not a trust fund. Members receive policies of commercial insurance companies.

Generally, the benefits under the Civil Service system are more comprehensive. Merger of these systems might produce economies through elimination of unnecessary accounting and duplication of legislation by the Congress. The usual experience has been that, as the Civil Service Retirement Act is amended, the other systems follow with requests for similar amendments.

While the benefits granted in all these systems differ, the Civil Service Retirement system is generally the most liberal with the exception of the Foreign Service system.

Recommendation No. 5

We recommend that a study be made to determine whether these systems, with the exception of the Foreign Service system, should be merged.

Such a merger would not be in conflict with action taken in the past two years in merging with the Civil Service system several small systems formerly operated for certain employees of the Panama Railroad Company, employees of the Comptroller of the Currency, and employees of the Smithsonian Institution.

Railroad Retirement Board

The Railroad Retirement Board was established by the Railroad Retirement Act of 1935. The other principal authority of the Board derives from the Railroad Unemployment Insurance Act of 1938, as amended. Under these two statutes, the Board administers (*a*) a retirement system for aged and disabled railroad employees and survivors, and (*b*) an unemployment insurance system including unemployment, maternity, and sickness benefits. The system takes in the railroad industry, affiliated companies and joint associations, and employees of national railway labor organizations and employee representatives. The Board is composed of three members appointed by the President by and with the advice and consent of the Senate. The President appoints the chairman independently but the other two members are nominated, one each by carrier representatives and employee representatives.

The Commission has examined the system and finds that its activities are much broader in scope than the welfare functions to be included in the new Department; that part of its functions belong with the unemployment compensation and employment service functions proposed to be placed in the Department of Labor; that essentially the system works well as located; that administratively there is no economy or efficiency to be achieved by destroying the present well-integrated system and transferring it in whole or in part to one or more agencies; and finally that the system is a uniquely administered and completely privately supported system operated under Government auspices.

The actual collection of taxes is the only part of the system financed by the Government. Of the contributions collected under the Railroad Unemployment Insurance Act 90 percent is credited for the payment of benefits and 10 percent is deposited in a special administrative fund to administer the act. The system is completely Federal. It would be possible to change it and have the railroads pay taxes to the States but nothing would be gained in efficiency by segregating the employment functions which are mingled with the retirement functions throughout the Board's organization. Unless the retirement system were extended to universal coverage, and unemployment compensation made a Federal function, the factors of efficiency, benefits, employee satisfaction, and tradition all militate against transfer of the Railroad Retirement System to either of the two departments concerned.

Recommendation No. 6

The Commission recommends the retention of the Railroad Retirement Board in its present status.

Chapter Three

EDUCATION

Federal Participation in Education Generally

Total Federal funds expended for all educational purposes, including the education of veterans, are at present at an all-time high of over $2.5 billion.

The major purposes of these expenditures may be classified as follows:

a. Federal activities concerning all levels of education—such as education of veterans, institutional on-farm training, vocational and physical rehabilitation, and education in nonmilitary subjects within the military establishment—over $2 billion.

b. Federal activities clearly related to elementary and secondary education—$166 million.

c. Federal activities clearly related to higher education—$257 million.

In addition, the Federal Government has rendered considerable assistance to education in nonbudgetary items, particularly since the recent war. For example, during approximately two years prior to May 1948, surplus property initially valued at $646,663,358 was made available to educational institutions by the War Assets Administration, Army, Navy, and Air Force, with the cooperation of the Office of Education.

With few exceptions, the Federal interest in education centers on special groups of individuals, special programs sponsored by the Federal Government, or on research and training to promote some special Federal concern such as national defense or in-service training of Federal employees. The variety of Federal activities in education is indicated by the following:

a. At elementary and secondary levels:
    I. Promotion of curricula.
    II. School lunch program.
    III. Education for dependent children of Federal employees.
    IV. Education of Indians and other native people.

b. At the level of higher education:
    I. Research grants to colleges and universities.
    II. Higher education of special groups of individuals, or individuals in special fields (Howard University, public health training, extension service of the Department of Agriculture).
    III. Special types of State higher institutions such as land-grant colleges and State Maritime academies.
    IV. International education programs.
    V. Education and training for public service.

c. Activities not specialized:
    I. Veterans.
    II. On-farm training.
    III. Vocational and physical rehabilitation.
    IV. Education in nonmilitary subjects within the military establishment.

d. Activities not connected with established educational institutions such as in-service training for government service, or programs for non-Federal employees.

e. Nonbudgetary Federal assistance through surplus property.

With respect to elementary and secondary educational activities, there has been overlapping and independent promotion of curricula in highly specialized fields, while the general curricular needs of the country have been neglected. Direct aid to local schools, with respect to curriculum development and the school lunch program, has circumvented State departments of education. There has not been sufficient coordination of the educational and nutritional aspects of the school lunch program. As regards its responsibility for the education of children of Federal employees on federally owned properties, the Federal Government does not have a consistent and comprehensive policy. There is no common policy for the education of Indians, Eskimos, and other native peoples living in our insular and mandated territories, since this responsibility is dispersed among a number of agencies of Government.

Concerning higher education, nine departments and agencies are making grants or entering into contracts for research through colleges and universities without any coordination of these programs.[8] For years the Government has made payments for agricultural research. More recently the Government has been spending huge sums in grants to higher institutions for atomic and military research. These projects are concentrated in the natural and physical sciences. The grants have an important effect on the educational system.

There are those who believe that these various educational programs should be concentrated in the Office of Education.

Recommendation No. 7

This Commission believes, however, that these educational programs must be administered by the agencies whose functions the particular programs serve to promote.

Educational Activities in the New Department

The new Department, however, should analyze the effects of expenditures and programs relating to education and assist the President in making recommendations to the Congress for the correction of deficiencies. In addition, the Department would, of course, continue to perform the historic functions of the Office of Education as follows:

a. To collect data on the condition and progress of education and to serve as a source of general information on the subject.

b. To administer certain operating functions vested in that agency by the Congress.

c. To render professional advice and service to other Government agencies.

Bureau of Indian Affairs

Due to the Bureau's diversified duties and responsibilities, there is no Department in the Government where it fits satisfactorily. Certainly with the reorientation of the Department of the Interior, which we have recommended, it has little relation to the other activities of that Department. As, however, probably the major relation of the Bureau is to education, it does have a close relationship to the educational activities of, and could be given stronger leadership in, the new Department.

[8] See our report on Federal Research.

459

Recommendation No. 8

We recommend that the Bureau of Indian Affairs be transferred from the Department of the Interior to the proposed Department which would embrace social security and educational functions.

The Commission's report on Indian Affairs follows.

XX
Indian Affairs

Chapter One

THE PROBLEM

The difficulties that face the Federal Government in guiding the affairs of the American Indians have been emphasized by recent crises. For example, the Navajo Nation, comprising some 55,000 Indians in New Mexico, Arizona, and Utah, is in severe financial straits that have caused widespread malnutrition and starvation. This has occurred at a time when the United States as a whole is enjoying prosperity and virtually full employment.

Many other Indian groups, among the estimated 400,000 in the United States face similarly severe conditions. Their standard of living is low and there is a serious problem in maintaining their health. Educating them properly has proved extremely difficult. Assistance and guidance to them has been a knotty and continuing problem of the Federal Government, whose Bureau of Indian Affairs in the Department of the Interior, has direct responsibility for their welfare.

Varying Policies

The Federal Government's policy toward the Indians has varied sharply with changing conditions.

In the early days of the Republic, attention focused on the serious military threat which the Indians presented. Through the Civil War and decades immediately following, the Indians were progressively evacuated westward; the military problem was isolated in specific areas. Eventually, it ceased to exist.

Concentration of the Indians on reservations was an integral part of Federal efforts to end their forays and wars. As the years passed, however, the reservations became the land base from which Indians extracted their living. The policy of the Federal Government has always revolved about these reservations, their use, and their disposition.

In the first quarter of the present century, the Federal Government encouraged a program of allotting tribal lands to individual Indians, but insufficient consideration was given to the capabilities of the individual Indian, or to the economic value of the lands. Since the late 1920's, the Federal Government has ceased pressing a liberal allotment policy. The Indian Reorganization Act of 1934 extended the Federal trust period indefinitely and made possible the addition of lands to tribal holdings. Loans to Indians were authorized, and the growth of Indian culture encouraged.

In very recent years, the policy of the Bureau of Indian Affairs has been directed more and more toward gradual integration of all Indians into the general population and economy, along the lines recommended by this Commission.

The Indian Population

The Indian population is no longer a pure ethnic group. Rather it represents a mélange of "full bloods" and persons of mixed ancestry. Persons classified as Indians under Federal policy and participating in tribal organizations are in many cases not Indians in the complete biological sense. This is illustrated by the following definition of "Indian" taken from the Indian Reorganization Act of 1934, the most recent definitive statement of Federal policy toward the Indians . . .

. . . The term "Indian" as used in this act shall include all persons of Indian descent who are members of any recognized Indian tribe now under Federal jurisdiction, and all persons who are descendants of such members who were on June 1, 1934, residing within the present boundaries of any Indian reservation, and shall further include all other persons of one-half or more Indian blood. For the purpose of this act, Eskimos and other aboriginal peoples of Alaska shall be considered Indians.

Government records recognize more than 100 tribes under distinct names and approximately 300 other groups who are separated either geographically or by linguistic stock. The larger groups are located as follows: Oklahoma, 110,000; Arizona, 55,000; New Mexico, 43,000; South Dakota, 30,000; North Dakota, 12,000; California, 24,000; Montana, 18,000; Minnesota, 18,000; Washington, 15,000; Wisconsin, 13,000; New York, 9,000; Oregon, 5,500; Nevada, 5,600; Michigan,

5,200; and more than 30,000 in Alaska. The Indians' cultural and economic advances vary widely because of many special circumstances—land holdings, utility of land, and others.

Federal Administration

The Bureau of Indian Affairs is charged with Federal responsibility for the Indians. It employs approximately 12,000 people; it administers approximately 5,000 statutes and 370 treaties; it operates schools and hospitals; it supervises land and management; it constructs irrigation projects; it builds roads and buildings; it assists in the growth of the political life of the Indian communities; and it handles a multitude of related activities reaching down into the most minor facets of the life of the individual Indian.

Expenditures from the Federal Treasury on Indian affairs are difficult to compute, because so many Federal agencies participate in Indian activities, and because substantial expenditures are made from trust funds, tribal funds, and other special accounts on their behalf. Appropriations to the Bureau of Indian Affairs are now in the neighborhood of $40,000,000 per annum, more than twice what they were 20 years ago. Prorating this amount on a per capita basis, these direct appropriations amount to approximately $100 per Indian. As compared with a Federal budget of $40,000,000,000, these amounts are not large, but Indian relations, from the viewpoint of the individuals involved, is a difficult and, at times, a heart-rending personal problem. Given the apparent inability of the Federal Government—over a period of more than 100 years—to free itself from responsibility for their activities, the problems loom large indeed.

The following sections of this report are devoted to the commission's analyses and recommendations regarding the conduct of Indian affairs by the Executive Branch of the Government.

Recommendation No. 1

Our task force on Indian Affairs, supported by a considerable body of thought both inside and outside the Government, advocates progressive measures to integrate the Indians into the rest of the population as the best solution of "the Indian Problem." In the opinion of the Commission this policy should be the keystone of the organization and of the activities of the Federal Government in the field of Indian Affairs.

Chapter Two

PROPOSED FEDERAL POLICY

A program for the Indian peoples must include progressive measures for their complete integration into the mass of the population as full, tax-paying citizens. The Commission has recommended that this be the firm and continuing policy of the Federal Government.

Recommendation No. 2

The Commission recommends that, pending achievement of the goal of complete integration, the administration of social programs for the Indians should be progressively transferred to State governments.

The States should receive appropriate recompense from Federal funds until Indian taxes can help carry the load. The transfer to the States should be accompanied by diminishing activities by the Bureau of Indian Affairs.

Recommendation No. 3

The Commission recommends that all agencies concerned with Indian affairs, including State and local governments, should take part in comprehensive planning of programs to carry out this policy.

Recommendation No. 4

The Commission recommends that the objectives of the proposed joint planning should include:

a. **Adequate education for the entire Indian population.**

b. **An adequate standard of living.**

c. **Progressive reduction of mortality and morbidity rates.**

d. Progressive transfer of social program responsibilities to the State and local governments, as recommended above.

e. Ultimate transfer of responsibility for medical services to local governments or to quasi-public bodies.

f. Transfer of tribal property to Indian-owned corporations.

g. Participation of Indian people in political and civic life of the States.

h. Termination of tax exemption for Indian lands.

All programs should be specific and definite dates should be set for the attainment of each major element. Costs should be estimated carefully and each area program should be subject to approval by the Commissioner of Indian Affairs, by the Department head to whom he is responsible, and by the Congress.

Recommendation No. 5

The Commission recommends that, in addition to these general efforts to improve the Indian's lot, the program of assistance toward economic stability have two parts:

a. Young employable Indians and the better cultured families should be encouraged and assisted to leave the reservations and set themselves up on the land or in business.

b. Tribal and Indian enterprises should be put on a corporate or cooperative basis as far as possible.

Recommendation No. 6

The Commission recommends the following steps be taken to establish such business enterprises:

a. Each important enterprise should have its own charter and board of directors.

b. Basic policies and objectives should be incorporated in the charter.

c. Members of the board of directors should be preponderantly drawn from the Indian community and should be held financially accountable.

d. Other members of the board should be appointed because of their business or technical competence.

e. The creation of such corporations should be a part of the comprehensive program for each area.

f. As such corporations are set up and begin to function successfully, administrative supervision by the Indian Bureau should be relaxed and eventually discontinued.

g. The accounts of these corporations should be audited annually.

The corporate device is recommended as valuable in ending the troublesome problem of "heirship" lands, which frequently cannot be utilized because so many heirs share the ownership that they cannot agree on operations.

The Commission recommends that steps be taken to strengthen the elected tribal councils on reservations and to make them more representative. Effective leadership should be strengthened; and tribal government should be regarded as a stage in the transition from Federal tutelage to the full participation of the Indians in State and local government.

Chapter Three

ADMINISTRATIVE RECOMMENDATIONS

Recommendation No. 7

Superintendents are shifted too often from one area to another. The Commission recommends:

a. That a superintendent who is inadequate or inefficient be disciplined and the policy of undue leniency in this regard be abandoned.

b. That the Washington office use more personnel with field experience.

c. That each superintendency have a range of at least two grades under the Classification Act to allow promotion based on merit at any given post.

Recommendation No. 8

The Commission further recommends:

a. That the Commissioner of the Bureau of Indian Affairs be a professional, permanent administrator; that, since the department head to whom the Indian Service is attached must assume political responsibility, he appoint the Commissioner.

b. That budget and appropriations be made upon the basis of area programs.

c. That the Commissioner of Indian Affairs be free to organize the Service. However, consolidation of field jurisdiction should not be carried too far, and the emphasis should be on geographic areas suitable for programming. Greater authority for administration should be delegated to the superintendents.

All of these suggestions are aimed at greater local autonomy. Frequent, close, and personal supervision, adequate reports, and systematic audits will be necessary.

Chapter Four

TRANSFER OF THE BUREAU OF INDIAN AFFAIRS

Recommendation No. 9

The Commission recommends that, pending discontinuance of all specialized Indian activity on the part of the Federal Government, the Bureau of Indian Affairs be transferred to the new department which we have proposed as the successor to the Federal Security Agency, thereby associating it with the new department's social services.

Federal appropriations for the Indian Bureau over the last 20 years have allocated more than 65 percent to welfare aspects of the Indian problem. The new department is best equipped to handle activities designed to assist the Indians as individuals.

Administratively, the new department will also be the Federal agency having direct contact with State welfare and education officials. More recently the Federal Security Agency has undertaken, in addition to its traditional relations with State agencies, programs of grants to the States for activities within its scope.

The professional skills and administrative relationships possessed by the new department should afford the best direction for handling the the Indian problem, recognizing: (*a*) that the executive branch lacks any agency concerned with the political organization of ethnic groups, and (*b*) that any location of the Bureau of Indian Affairs leaves problems of interdepartmental coordination.

Existing conditions which prompt transfer of the Bureau are, briefly:

Education

Improved educational conditions are recognized as a means of increasing earning power. The average 1946 income of Indian farm families was less than $1,000 and probably only about one-third that of non-Indian farm families.

The real problem of education is not in areas where public schools are available. It lies in those areas where Indian children are not being educated at all, where school facilities cannot take care of children who can and would attend. Buildings and teachers are inadequate. This denial of schooling to the Indians is inconsistent with all Federal Government commitments. New schools and new school methods are required.

Social Problems

Integration of the Indians depends, at least in part, on programs of social security which fall naturally within the scope of the Social Security Administration's various social services.

While the Commission urges transfer of the Bureau of Indian Affairs to the new department which we have proposed, for the reasons outlined, there are certain important activities of the Bureau relating to the economic status of the Indian which must be coordinated with the existing programs of other departments.

The Indian economy is now based almost exclusively on land, whether through direct management or by lease. More than this, it is for the most part a Western land economy—farming, stock raising, and forestry—heavily dependent on irrigation. Federal assistance to the Indian for irrigation, timber management and grazing will necessarily be part of the total program. This involves both the Department of Interior and the Department of Agriculture which will have to offer greater assistance to Indian owner-operators than to other private land owners.

Coordination with Other Departments

The location of the Bureau of Indian Affairs in the Interior Department has facilitated integration of land programs with general resource development. It appears to the Commission, however, that the location of the Bureau within this department has not yielded a proportionate return on the Government's investment in the Indians as a people,

471

particularly those appropriations for health, welfare, and general vocational education.

Cooperative action between Interior, Agriculture, and the new department can be mapped out when area programs for the Nation's Indian population are approved by the Congress. Area programs should be planned by Bureau superintendents with the field representatives of the Departments of Interior and Agriculture in consultation with tribal authorities and State and local officials.

Some of the activities to be coordinated and their present locations are:[1]

DEPARTMENT OF AGRICULTURE.—(a) Technical Assistance: Extension services of the Department could be of inestimable value to Indian farmers and they should be an integral part of the Department's continuing activities in cordination with the Indian Bureau's comparable functions; (b) Soil Conservation: Prevention of erosion and improved soil conditions are vitally needed on Indian lands, requiring the guidance of experienced personnel of the Department of Agriculture; (c) Credit Problems: The Department of Agriculture's standard techniques in handling the problem of credit and related subjects can also be applied to assist Indian farmers and grazers; (e) Timber: Guidance and supervision of growth and cutting for sustained yield must be continued.

DEPARTMENT OF THE INTERIOR.—(a) Irrigation: Indians have little experience with irrigated land and need assistance and guidance; (b) Grazing: Present policies must be continued to prevent overgrazing and to improve range capacity; (c) Fish and Wildlife: These resources must be protected on Indian territory while it remains part of the public lands of the United States; (d) Mineral Rights: Exploitation of mineral resources must be guided in the interests of the Indians individually and of the Nation as a whole.

In another report the Commission has recommended an executive mechanism which can be charged with the task of integrating all major resource programs, including the entire Indian program, among participating departments.

[1] Various of the listed activities would be shifted to other departments if the Commission's reports on reorganization of the Departments of Agriculture, Commerce, and Interior are carried out.

Savings

An ultimate substantial reduction in Federal expenditures in the field of Indian Affairs is possible, if the recommendations of this report are carried through. No immediate cuts can be made, however, without delaying progress and postponing the time when expenditures can be curtailed substantially. In the end, the residual Federal expenditures for Indian affairs should be quite small.

When the trust status of Indian lands has ended, thus permitting their taxation, and surplus Indian families have established themselves off the reservations, special Federal aid to State and local governments for Indian programs should end. The Indians will have been integrated, economically and politically, as well as culturally.

The length of time before expenditures can be reduced, without building up future costs, will depend largely on the vigor with which the program outlined here is pushed. A clear and consistent policy, leadership and stable financial support will be essential.

XXI
Overseas Administration

Chapter One

THE PROBLEM

Administration of Overseas Affairs

The war and its aftermath have created new and heavy operational and promotional responsibilities abroad. The magnitude of the problem is indicated by the fact that our Government is now spending over a billion dollars a year for military government and occupation costs in 4 countries and over $4 billion a year to support the economic recovery of 19 European nations. In addition, the Government continues to pursue its historical function of governing its territories, has responsibilities overseas for the disposal of surplus property, and has recently acquired new responsibilities of trusteeship in several Japanese mandated islands.

Most of the problems relating to occupation, military government, and assistance to other nations arose so rapidly that time did not permit adequate planning in terms of our total responsibilities abroad. As a result, we have had confusion, inconsistencies, and uncertainty of policy and program, with the inefficiencies which inevitably follow as a result of improvisation and lack of over-all planning.

Our overseas programs are scattered in at least four major departments, a large independent agency, and several smaller ones. The administration of military government of the occupied areas of Germany, Austria, Japan, and Korea rests with the Department of the Army. The Panama Canal is also under the supervision of the Secretary of the Army. The Trust Territories of the Pacific, Guam, and Samoa are administered by the Department of the Navy. Several territories, including Alaska, Hawaii, Puerto Rico, the Virgin Islands, and a few small islands in the Pacific are, from an organizational standpoint, part of the Department of the Interior. In the Department of State are

477

activities concerned with the liquidation of surplus property abroad, policy direction of occupied areas, and special missions. The independent agencies with operations overseas are the Economic Cooperation Administration, the American Battle Monuments Commission, the Philippine Alien Property Administration, and the Philippine War Damage Commission.

Occupied Areas

The problem of occupied areas is peculiar in several respects. In the first place, the Government's responsibility in those areas is divided, the State Department being assigned responsibility for formulation of policy and the Department of the Army for execution and administration of policy.

As we have pointed out in our report on Foreign Affairs, serious friction has existed in this arrangement from the outset.

The basic difficulty has been the uncertainty and delay in the preparation and enunciation of policy and the consequent tendency of the administrative agency, through its daily decisions, to make its own policy.

Second, it has been clearly demonstrated that at times it is impossible so draw a clear line between operations and foreign policy.

Third, the Army having completed the primary task of demilitarization in the occupied areas, and having set up civil governments under democratic constitutions, has expressed its desire to be relieved of the task of military government. The transfer of responsibility for the civil or nonmilitary aspects of administration to the State Department has been given frequent consideration during recent years, and a transfer of the American Zone in Germany, scheduled for July 1948, was indefinitely postponed.

The current view of the State Department is that it should not assume responsibilities of an operational nature except in unusual circumstances. The Department of the Army, on the other hand, admits it is ill-equipped to deal adequately with present day responsibilities of a nonmilitary nature in the occupied areas. The major purpose of the Department is to protect the security of the United States, whereas the current program in the occupied areas is concerned with advising the governments under occupation on problems of civil liberties, representative forms of government, democratic procedures, and other matters totally unrelated to the Department of the Army's major purpose, and in some instances not even compatible with it.

Apart from maintaining constabulary forces and giving logistical support, the Department's officers are not trained for the current requirements of occupied areas. While it is true that most of the purely military personnel have been replaced by civilians in the military governments, most of those who remain developed skills in military government as a result of individual initiative and hard effort after they arrived on the scene.

We are faced with the practical dilemma of having a department charged with a responsibility unsuited to its normal operations and wishing to be relieved of it, and yet having in the present executive structure seemingly no appropriate place for the function.

European Recovery

The organizational status of the Economic Cooperation Administration presents a somewhat different problem. On recommendations of the Secretary of State and Congressional Committees, the Congress decided not to place the European Recovery Program within the State Department. But because the administration of the program involves high-level United States policy, the Secretary of State has been authorized, in consultation with the Economic Cooperation Administrator, to conclude the basic agreements with the participating countries. The Economic Cooperation Administration enabling act provides that the Administrator and the Secretary of State "shall keep each other fully and currently informed on matters, including prospective action, arising within the scope of their respective duties which are pertinent to the duties of the other."

Whenever differences arise between them, having a bearing either on foreign policies or operations, which cannot be reconciled by consultation, such matters are referred to the President for decision. Here again, divided responsibility has created difficult administrative problems and has not contributed to the singleness of purpose which is so desirable in administration.

The administration of the program has also been assigned to personnel drawn from other agencies and private industry, many of whom have been engaged on a short-term basis without the security of tenure which contributes to stability of operation.

Trust Territories and Unorganized Possessions

Another type of problem is presented by our organization for the administration of the Trust Territories of the Pacific and the Island Possessions of Guam and Samoa. Responsibility for these areas was assigned to the Department of the Navy by Executive order, and they are administered by a high commissioner who is also Commander-in-Chief of the Pacific Fleet.[1]

Trusteeship for the former Japanese mandated islands of the Carolines, Marshalls, and Marianas was given to the United States by international agreement under the United Nations Charter in 1947. Under the provisions of the Charter, the United States has the obligation:

to promote to the utmost . . . the well being of the inhabitants of these territories . . . [and is directed] to develop self-government, to take due account of the political aspirations of the people, and to assist them in the progressive development of their free political institutions, according to the particular circumstances of each territory and its peoples and their varying stages of advancement . . .

Guam and Samoa, on the other hand, have been under Naval control under Executive orders for the past half century. Congress has yet to define the civil rights and political status of their inhabitants, despite the fact that the Treaty of Paris provided that this would be done, a least with respect to Guam. Here again the transfer of jurisdiction of these islands from military to civilian control has been urged on numerous occasions and has been formally approved by the Secretaries of State, War, Navy, and Interior, and by the President himself.

Our task force on Territories and Dependencies has pointed out that the principal government functions of these areas are in the fields of education, public health, social welfare, agriculture, and economic development—not to mention the more fundamental problem of working out the most fruitful relationships between advanced and backward people. These responsibilities do not fall within the special competence of the Navy Department or its personnel. The policy of rotating officer personnel every 18 months is not conducive to progressive, consistent, and stable administration. Furthermore, continuance of this function under the Department of the Navy represents a diversion of naval manpower and resources from the Navy's primary purpose. Finally, what is perhaps even more important is that it is incompatible with basic American principles to have civilians under military control for extended periods of time.

[1] The Trust Territories were assigned to the Department of the Navy by the President "on an interim basis."

Organized Territories

Still another problem of organization is presented by the location of the Division of Territories and Island Possessions in the Department of the Interior. This Division is assigned responsibility for the Territories of Alaska, Hawaii, Puerto Rico, the Virgin Islands, and several small islands in the Pacific. In another report we are recommending that the Department of the Interior be reorganized so that its major purpose will be natural resource activities and public works. Thus the retention of the territories in that Department, if not incompatible, is at least totally unrelated to the Department's major purpose.

Even within the Department of the Interior, as presently constituted, the organization for territorial administration is not satisfactory. Nowhere, either by Executive order or statute, are the powers and duties of the Division of Territories and Island Possessions enumerated. Even though required to do so by Executive order, other departments of the executive branch have consistently failed to report to the Department of the Interior on their operations in the territories. The administration of the territories has thus suffered from uncertainty of jurisdiction and from the inevitable conflicts that have arisen as a consequence.

As with other overseas areas we have failed to develop a staff of administrators with special training for this purpose. We have never had an agency in the executive branch responsible for general policy formation with respect to the territories; and if we have a policy at all it has been one of "muddling through" and "indifference."

All of these activities, despite their diversity, have in common the element of administrative planning and operation necessary to effectuate the aims of United States policy beyond the Nation's boundaries. They have a common need for a competent corps of administrators with aptitude and special training for the problems of overseas administration. While it is expected that only a few of these programs are of a definitely permanent nature, the task of overseas administration is assuredly going to be of major concern as far into the future as we can make organizational plans.

Chapter Two

RECOMMENDATIONS

The attention of our task force was directed only to the problems of the territories and possessions and a field survey was not attempted. Among the principal recommendations made by the task force was a recommendation for the creation of an Office of Territories which should be strengthened and assigned control over Guam, Samoa, and the Trust Territories of the Pacific by transfer of responsibility from the Navy Department. The functions now vested in the Division of Territories and Island Possessions in the Department of the Interior also would be included.

The location of this function was suggested in terms of three alternatives:

a. Placing the function in the President's Office.

b. Assigning it independent agency status.

c. Placing it within the Federal Security Agency, or its successor.

The Commission is taking no position on this recommendation because it represents only a partial answer to the problem of overseas administration, and we feel that a decision on this problem should not be made until some disposition is also made of the organizational questions which relate to occupied areas, the Economic Cooperation Administration, certain operating functions in the State Department, and the smaller independent agencies of the American Battle Monuments Commission, the Philippine Alien Property Administration, and the Philippine War Damage Commission.

We are suggesting at least two other alternatives which should be given serious consideration.

First: The first alternative, which also represents only a partial solution, would be to remove the responsibility for the administration of occupied areas and the Panama Canal from the Department of the Army, and Island Possessions and Trust Territories from the Department of the Navy, and assign these functions to a Special Secretary who would report directly to the Secretary of Defense.

This would at least accomplish some integration of overseas administration. It would improve the organizational status of these important responsibilities by placing them in a higher position in the Military Establishment. It would provide an answer to the objection that occupied areas and territories should not be under direct military control. It would provide another step toward unification of the Military Establishment, and could facilitate the development of a nonmilitary corps of administrators. Finally, if the Service Secretaries participation in the Security Council is eliminated, as recommended in our National Security Report, this would also indicate the advisability of bringing these problems to the Secretary of Defense level.

Such a reorganization, however, would still leave unresolved the problems of organizational status for the self-governing territories, the Economic Cooperation Administration, foreign property liquidation, and the miscellaneous agencies having administrative responsibilities overseas.

Second: Perhaps the alternative presenting the greatest possibilities for integrating overseas administrative activities would be to create a separate administration of Overseas Affairs, to which would be transferred all administrative responsibilities abroad, excluding, of course, the diplomatic and consular services of the State Department.

The Administrator would have a rank similar to that enjoyed by the Economic Cooperation Administrator and would bear the same relationship to the Secretary of State in matters involving foreign policy as is presently provided for in the statute setting up the Economic Cooperation Administration.

The new Administration would include the following activities and agencies:

a. OCCUPIED AREAS—Germany, Austria, Japan, and Korea

b. EUROPEAN RECOVERY PROGRAM

c. SPECIAL MISSIONS—Greece and Turkey

d. TRUST TERRITORIES—Carolines, Marshalls, and Marianas

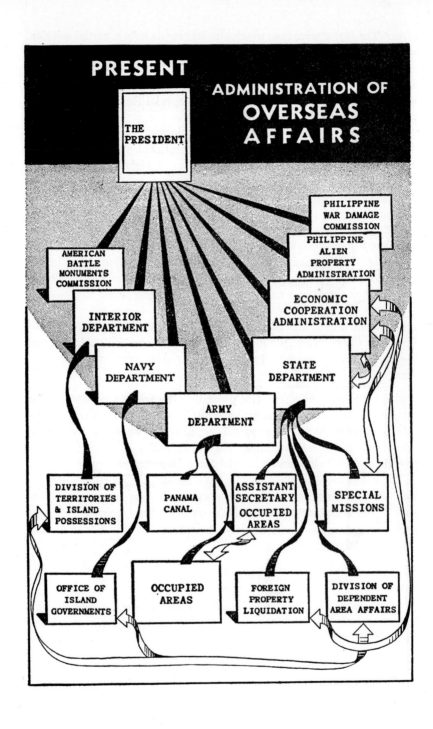

PRESENT ADMINISTRATION OF OVERSEAS AFFAIRS

THE PRESIDENT

PHILIPPINE WAR DAMAGE COMMISSION

PHILIPPINE ALIEN PROPERTY ADMINISTRATION

AMERICAN BATTLE MONUMENTS COMMISSION

ECONOMIC COOPERATION ADMINISTRATION

INTERIOR DEPARTMENT

NAVY DEPARTMENT

STATE DEPARTMENT

ARMY DEPARTMENT

DIVISION OF TERRITORIES & ISLAND POSSESSIONS

PANAMA CANAL

ASSISTANT SECRETARY OCCUPIED AREAS

SPECIAL MISSIONS

OFFICE OF ISLAND GOVERNMENTS

OCCUPIED AREAS

FOREIGN PROPERTY LIQUIDATION

DIVISION OF DEPENDENT AREA AFFAIRS

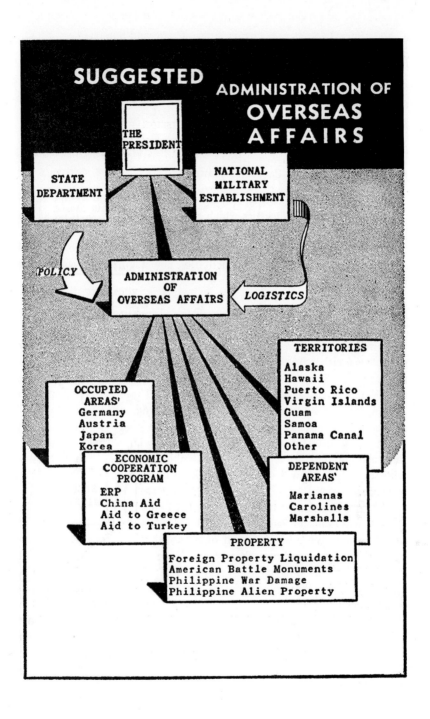

SUGGESTED ADMINISTRATION OF OVERSEAS AFFAIRS

THE PRESIDENT

STATE DEPARTMENT

NATIONAL MILITARY ESTABLISHMENT

POLICY

ADMINISTRATION OF OVERSEAS AFFAIRS

LOGISTICS

OCCUPIED AREAS'
Germany
Austria
Japan
Korea

ECONOMIC COOPERATION PROGRAM
ERP
China Aid
Aid to Greece
Aid to Turkey

TERRITORIES
Alaska
Hawaii
Puerto Rico
Virgin Islands
Guam
Samoa
Panama Canal
Other

DEPENDENT AREAS'
Marianas
Carolines
Marshalls

PROPERTY
Foreign Property Liquidation
American Battle Monuments
Philippine War Damage
Philippine Alien Property

e. NON-SELF-GOVERNING TERRITORIES—Guam and Samoa

f. SELF-GOVERNING TERRITORIES—Alaska, Hawaii, Puerto Rico, and the Virgin Islands

g. OFFICE OF FOREIGN LIQUIDATION

h. AMERICAN BATTLE MONUMENTS COMMISSION

i. PHILIPPINE WAR DAMAGE COMMISSION

j. PHILIPPINE ALIEN PROPERTY ADMINISTRATION

The creation of such a unified Administration of Overseas Affairs would resolve a number of difficulties which seem impossible of solution at the present time.

It would simplify the problem of achieving unified policy control since it would place these foreign activities, now administered separately, under one responsible head.

It would make possible the development of a corps of career men trained for foreign administration as distinguished from training for the Foreign Diplomatic Service.

As we have seen, the lack of such a corps in the past has required our dependence either upon untrained people or personnel with military experience. To the extent that we have been dependent upon such training our administrative competency has suffered. The creation of such an Administration would not only have the advantage of bringing together all foreign administrative problems into one agency, but it would facilitate the transfer of personnel from one foreign activity to another, thus making possible a variety of valuable experience in foreign administration which will serve us well both in time of war and in time of peace.

The consolidation would reduce the total number of agencies in the Government and the number reporting directly to the President. It would remove the administration of occupied areas from the Department of the Army and provide a proper place for the administration of island possessions now under Naval control; and for territories now administered by the Department of the Interior, which are unrelated to its other activities.

Although the Commission believes that the alternatives suggested are reasonable and in varying degrees provide answers to many of our troublesome problems in overseas administration, we are making no definite recommendation for reorganization since we feel that this complicated problem requires further detailed study before any definite conclusions can be reached as to the most effective organizational arrangement.

Recommendation

The Commission, therefore, recommends that the Congress direct a comprehensive study to be made of the entire problem of overseas operation and administration.

The Security Council would seem to be a logical agency for such a study since it is concerned with both defense and foreign affairs and is now considering some of the organizational problems related to occupied areas.

XXII
Federal-State Relations

Chapter One

THE PROBLEM

Federal-State relations is the cardinal question of our Federal system of government. It is not a question that can be resolved once for all time. Emphasis shifts from generation to generation as the American people fashion their Government to meet the needs of changing times and changing conditions.

Prior to 1900, the question was largely a legal problem. Since that time, it has become increasingly an economic problem.

Our Government today is very different in structure and in operation from that envisioned by the founding fathers. From a number of small semi-autonomous agricultural States, we have become a highly industrialized far-flung nation. We have become a world power with interests and responsibilities throughout the globe.

As we have grown as a nation, so have we grown as independent States; and government today—all of our governments—is a large social and economic mechanism designed to serve and operate for the welfare of the people.

As this development has taken place, two problems have been cast in bold relief:

1. How can the American type of democracy—a democracy based on individual liberty and extensive citizen participation in and control of government—be maintained and strengthened?

2. At the same time, how shall government provide the services which people increasingly demand and which are necessary for the general welfare?

These are not problems which can be solved by the States acting alone; nor can they be solved by the National Government without reference to the States. Their solution requires cooperation and team-work on the part of the States and the National Government, with understanding and support from the people at large.

The Development of Federal-State Relations

In 1913, total expenditures of the National Government were approximately $700 million, an amount which represented about one-quarter of the aggregate cost of all levels of governments in this country. Then, to a very large extent, local, State, and Federal governments established, financed, and administered their own activities.

In that same year, the National Government entered the field of income taxation on a permanent basis, thus providing the central Government with a revenue potential of great magnitude.

Almost concurrently—in 1914—we embarked upon the first large-scale, continuing cooperative project, the agricultural extension program. The pattern established for this program has been widely followed in the development of highway, vocational education and rehabilitation, public health, hospital, social security, and similar programs until today there are few major public services which are not financed and administered to some extent on a Federal-State cooperative basis.

In effect, the National Government found not only a major source of revenue, but a field of expenditure commensurate with a broadened tax base was developed. The conjoining of these two forces carried important implications for the future of Federal-State relations.

The rapidly increasing demands upon government—growing out of the development of our industrial society, out of two world wars, and a major depression—have expanded and extended public services and governmental activities far beyond those contemplated a short generation ago; and the cost of all government—Federal, State, and local—has increased from approximately $3 billion per year in 1913 to about $55 billion in 1948.

The necessity for meeting public needs and the search for revenue to meet such needs are basic to the present-day problem of Federal-State relations. We have attempted to solve this problem by the development of an extensive program of so-called grants-in-aid, and this development has had a profound effect upon our tax, fiscal, and governmental structures.

Chapter Two

GRANTS-IN-AID

"Grants-in-aid" is a term used to define a method of operation whereby funds derived from a tax levied and collected by one level of government are made available for expenditure and administration by another level, usually upon a matching basis, for some particular activity, and in accordance with definite and specific standards and requirements.

The grant-in-aid method is used extensively by both the State, with its political subdivisions, and by the Federal Government, with the States. Today, approximately 40 percent of all funds expended by local governments, and approximately 15 percent of all funds expended by State governments, are derived from grants-in-aid; and this trend toward using grants-in-aid for supporting public services is definitely on the increase.

Grants-in-aid are a part of the warp and woof of present-day government; but they cannot be considered separately from our tax and fiscal problems, nor from our Government plan and structure.

What are the assets and liabilities of this grant-in-aid method which is so large a part of the whole question of Federal-State relations?

ASSETS

a. The cooperative system based on grants-in-aid has provided needed standards of public services throughout the country in many fields— services that many States would be unable to supply. It has provided for some redistribution of resources from States that have superior means to those that lack them.

b. The plan has developed a division of responsibility: the National Government giving financial aid and establishing broad standards—the

493

State governments sharing the fiscal burden and maintaining primary responsibility for administration. In addition to decreasing inequalities of service, the grant-in-aid method has raised the level of all aided services, without transferring functions entirely to the National Government.

c. The grant-in-aid method, in fact, has added to and expanded the activities of State governments by contributing to their resources and thereby enabling them to embark upon additional or more extensive public-service programs for their own people.

d. It has stimulated States and localities to provide a number of public services deemed necessary and desirable in the national interest.

e. The cooperative method has improved the administration of many State activities. National administrative standards, as in highway and welfare programs, and national advice, as in police work, have done much to increase the professional skill and effectiveness of State administrators.

LIABILITIES

a. Grant programs are unrelated; they are uncoordinated; and they have developed in a haphazard manner without any one agency—Federal or State—concerned with the over-all impact and the over-all effects of grants-in-aid upon the general operations of government.

b. The grant-in-aid method has removed large areas of discretionary power from the hands of State officials and has transferred a measurable degree of policy-making and ultimate responsibility and control for public services to the National Government.

c. Grants-in-aid have altered State service patterns and total State programs. Available Federal funds for matching purposes stimulate or "persuade" the States in many instances to expend large sums for an aided program while, of necessity, other needed services are neglected. The public assistance program as contrasted with the general relief program is one among many examples.

d. In order to provide funds for grants-in-aid, and to adjust to war and depression, the national system of taxation has been expanded until we have extensive overlapping and conflicts on the part of Federal, State, and local governments. Of greater importance to State and local governments, the national need for revenue has caused the Congress in some instances to utilize productive tax sources that could be used just as effectively by State or local governments. In this manner, the circle widens. Under pressure to meet needs, Congress appropriates more for grants. In order to secure necessary revenues, tha national tax base is expanded which makes it more difficult for State and local governments to secure their own revenue, and hence stimulates pressure from more and more groups for more and more grants.

e. Federal grants-in-aid retard and repress the initiative of the States in financing the growing needs of State and local government, because such grants frequently result in rewarding those States which avoid their responsibility and in penalizing those which accept it.

Effect upon Executive Branch of Government

The development of cooperative government, based largely upon grants-in-aid, has had a far-reaching effect upon the executive branch.

It has enlarged the executive branch, requiring great expansion in many departments and the establishment of new administrative agencies.

It has increased national taxes.

And it has been responsible to some extent for the rapid development and extension of that fourth area of Government, known as the "regional area," serviced in large part by Federal regional offices.

Whether measured in terms of organizational set-up, personnel, or expenditures, a very large part of the executive and administrative task of the Federal Government is concerned with problems, functions, and services involving Federal-State relations.

Chapter Three

RECOMMENDATIONS

Recommendation No. 1

We recommend that the functions and activities of government be appraised to determine which can be most advantageously operated by the various levels of government, and which require joint policy making, financing, and administration.

Recommendation No. 2

We recommend that our tax systems—National, State, and local—be generally revised and that, in this revision, every possible effort be made to leave to the localities and the States adequate resources from which to raise revenue to meet the duties and responsibilities of local and State governments.

Many tax sources are exploited by both States and the Federal Government, and today there is even a triplication of taxation in the matter of incomes since many cities are now resorting to income taxes to meet their expenditures. The whole problem of duplicating and triplicating taxation is most difficult to resolve. But it is to be hoped that the Joint Committee of the Congress and the Governors' Conference will continue to explore the question of overlapping taxes.

Recommendation No. 3

We recommend that all grants-in-aid which are given to State governments directly be budgeted and administered on the Federal and State levels as are other Federal and State funds.

Recommendation No. 4

We recommend that the grant-in-aid plan and program be clarified and systematized.

A system of grants should be established, based upon broad categories —such as highways, education, public assistance, and public health— as contrasted with the present system of extensive fragmentation. There are now at least 3 separate and distinct grants in the realm of education, at least 3 in public assistance, and 10 in public health. Grants for broader categories would do much to overcome the lack of balance now readily apparent.

Recommendation No. 5

We recommend, in order to accomplish all of these things in an adequate and orderly manner, that a continuing agency on Federal-State relations be created with primary responsibility for study, information, and guidance in the field of Federal-State relations.

In cooperation with the Office of the Budget, this agency should develop a unified system of budgetary and fiscal control over the operation of all grants-in-aid.

It should make available to the Congress data and information pertaining to the problem as a whole, as well as the many and various divisions and parts thereof.

And it should be an agency which, on a continuing basis, would appraise our public needs, our resources, and ways and means for adjusting the one to the other in the interest of the American people.

* * *

The question of Federal-State relations, and the problems incident thereto, is a most important part of our governmental structure and our governmental operation. It should be studied and appraised in its overall aspects carefully and continuously if public services are to be adequately rendered, if public administration is to be efficient and economical, and if we are to maintain a strong, vital, Federal system of government.

XXIII
Federal Research

Federal Research

The Federal Government is now engaged in a wide range of research activities involving tremendous expenditures of funds. In 1947, total Federal expenditures for research, excluding atomic energy, amounted to $625,000,000.

This Commission, while recognizing that effective planning and co-ordination of research undertakings is of major importance, has not endeavored to make an independent study of organization for research in the Federal Government. This decision was based primarily on a realization that the main aspects of the problem had been recently investigated and reported on by the President's Scientific Research Board.

Nevertheless, the Commission does wish to call attention to the major issues in this field, pointing out progress which has already been achieved and further steps which should be taken.

Intradepartmental Research

The report of the Scientific Research Board makes it plain that a satisfactory coordinated research program for the National Government has not yet been realized. To be effective, an organization which will facilitate the development of research policy for the Government as a whole must have roots in each department with major research responsibilities. Every Federal agency with an extensive research program should have a staff organization, reporting to the agency head, for developing general research policy.

A number of such staff groups is now in operation. These groups include the Agricultural Research Administration, the Office of Naval Research, the Office of Research Planning of the Public Health Service, and the Research and Development Division of the Department of the Army's General Staff. While the authority, responsibility, and organizational status of these groups vary widely, they do have a number of common basic characteristics. Each is responsible to the agency head. Each maintains records of research projects conducted by all units of the agency served. Each advises the agency head on such matters of research policy as the fields in which research should be expanded or contracted, and whether research should be undertaken directly by the Federal Government or by non-Federal agencies under a grant or contract, and similar matters.

Over-all Coordination Needed

Effort along these lines within individual agencies is not enough. There is need for an organization to facilitate the development of research policy for the Federal Government as a whole. This was recognized in the report of the President's Scientific Research Board. That Board recommended, as a first step, the establishment of an interdepartmental Committee on Scientific Research and Development. Such a committee was created by Executive order in December 1947. It was directed to further the most effective administration of scientific research and development activities in the Federal Government, and was authorized to submit recommendations on research policy and administration directly to the President.

The full potentialities of this committee have not been realized since its members have not as yet attacked major problems of research policy for the Federal Government as a whole. This may be due in part to lack of staff and funds.

Creation of a National Science Foundation

An interdepartmental committee working alone and without staff is seriously limited in achieving adequate coordination and in developing over-all plans to completion. This points to the need for a National Science Foundation. The major functions of such a foundation should be (a) to examine the total scientific research effort of the Nation, (b) to assess the proper role of the Federal Government in this effort, (c) to evaluate the division of research effort among the scientific disciplines and among fields of applied research, and (d) to evaluate the key factors that impede the development of an effective national research effort. Based upon its investigations, it should advise the President as to the measures necessary to establish a sound scientific research program for the Nation.

In addition, the Foundation should be given appropriations for the support of basic research and for research fellowships in fields not adequately covered by the research grants and fellowships of other Federal Government agencies. The Foundation might administer the grant and fellowship programs for which it has received funds, or delegate administration to other Federal agencies. In addition, it should advise the President as to the proper balance among research grant and fellowship programs supported by appropriations given to other Federal agencies, and as to major policies that should govern the administration of these programs.

The National Science Foundation should consider most carefully the manner in which national policies with respect to scientific research are related to broader questions of educational policy. At present grants for research purposes are being made on a hit-and-miss basis, making the award of research grants, in effect, a new form of patronage. The awarding of research grants must be put upon a more systematic basis, with due recognition given to their impact on the educational programs of our higher institutions of learning.

Recommendation

The Commission recommends that:

a. **Authority be granted to the President to coordinate research, and to strengthen interdepartmental committee organization for this purpose.**

b. **A National Science Foundation be established.**

Acknowledgments

The Commission wishes to express its appreciation to the following task forces, whose findings have been helpful in the preparation of the Commission's recommendations in these reports.

I. GENERAL MANAGEMENT OF THE EXECUTIVE BRANCH

THE OFFICE OF THE PRESIDENT AND ITS RELATION TO THE DEPARTMENTS AND AGENCIES

DON K. PRICE, associate director, Public Administration Clearing House; assisted by Stephen K. Bailey, Wesleyan University.

H. STRUVE HENSEL, Carter, Ledyard, and Milburn, New York, and former Assistant Secretary of the Navy.

JOHN D. MILLETT, professor of public administration, Columbia University.

FEDERAL FIELD OFFICES

Contracted to

KLEIN AND SAKS, Washington, D. C.

Project Director

DR. JULIUS KLEIN, Assistant Secretary of Commerce, 1929–33.

II. BUDGETING AND ACCOUNTING

Project Director

JOHN W. HANES, member S. E. C., 1938; Assistant Secretary of the Treasury, 1938; Under Secretary of the Treasury, 1938–39; now chairman, Finance and Operating Committees, United States Lines Company.

KENYON BOOCOCK, assistant to director, New York City.

Advisers

DANIEL W. BELL, former Under Secretary of the Treasury, 1940–46; and president, American Security and Trust Company, Washington, D. C.

ROSWELL F. MAGILL, former Under Secretary of the Treasury, 1937–38; and partner, Cravath, Swaine and Moore, New York City.

A. L. M. WIGGINS, chairman of the board, Atlantic Coast Line Railroad and Louisville-Nashville Railroad, and former Under Secretary of the Treasury.

EDWARD F. BARTELT, Fiscal Secretary of the Treasury.

WALTER F. FRESE, chief, Accounting Systems Division, General Accounting Office.

FREDERICK LAWTON, assistant director, Bureau of the Budget.

ACCOUNTING PHASE

T. COLEMAN ANDREWS, director; Certified Public Accountant, Richmond, Virginia.

T. JACK GARY, JR., executive assistant and director of research; Certified Public Accountant.

IRVING TENNER, consultant; Certified Public Accountant, Chicago, Illinois.

Advisory Committee

(Members of the Committee on Federal Government Accounting, American Institute of Accountants)

EDWARD A. KRACKE, Haskins and Sells, Certified Public Accountants, New York City.

MAURICE E. PELOUBET, Pogson and Peloubet, Certified Public Accountants, New York City.

J. S. SEIDMAN, Seidman and Seidman, Certified Public Accountants, New York City.

WESTON RANKIN, Price, Waterhouse & Company, Certified Public Accountants, New York City.

HARRY HOWELL, Certified Public Accountant, Washington, D. C.

DONALD F. STEWART, Certified Public Accountant, Savannah, Georgia.

BUDGETARY PHASE

Undertaken by

INSTITUTE OF PUBLIC ADMINISTRATION, New York City.

Project Director

A. E. BUCK, Institute of Public Administration.

Assisted By

HENRY BURKE, formerly budget director of Alabama, of Tennessee, and of North Carolina.

ROWLAND EGGER, director, Bureau of Public Administration, University of Virginia.

JOHN D. MILLETT, professor of public administration, Columbia University.

S. PETER LANGHOFF, JR., vice president, Young and Rubicam, Inc., New York City.

III. STATISTICAL SERVICES

Undertaken by

NATIONAL BUREAU OF ECONOMIC RESEARCH

Research Director

FREDERICK C. MILLS, professor, Economics and Statistics, Columbia University, 1931–48; chairman, Department of Economics, 1943–48; a director, National Bureau of Economic Research; former president, American Economic Association; and former president, American Statistical Association.

Associate Director

DR. CLARENCE D. LONG, professor of economics, Johns Hopkins University, and member, National Bureau of Economic Research.

Advisory Committee

MARTIN R. GAINSBRUGH, National Industrial Conference Board, New York.

JOHN D. MILLETT, professor, Columbia University.

GEORGE SOULE, former editor New Republic Magazine, New York; a director of National Bureau of Economic Research.

P. K. WHELPTON, Scripps Foundation for the Study of Population Problems, Miami University, Oxford, Ohio.

SAMUEL S. WILKS, professor, Department of Mathematics, Princeton University.

IV.   OFFICE OF GENERAL SERVICES

RECORDS MANAGEMENT

Undertaken by

NATIONAL RECORDS MANAGEMENT COUNCIL

Research Director

E. J. LEAHY, executive director of the Council; formerly of the National Archives, and director of Records Administration, United States Navy.

Consultants

HERBERT E. ANGEL, director of Office Methods Branch, Department of the Navy.

WAYNE C. GROVER, archivist of the United States.

ROBERT H. BAHMER, assistant archivist of the United States; formerly Director of Records Management, Department of the Army.

F. M. ROOT, Westinghouse Electric Co., Pittsburgh, Pa.

EDWARD WILBER, director of the Division of Organization and Budget, Department of State.

V.   FEDERAL SUPPLY ACTIVITIES

Project Leader

RUSSELL FORBES, formerly professor and director of the Division of Research in Public Administration, New York University; Commissioner of Purchase, New York City; and consultant to the director, Bureau of Federal Supply, United States Treasury Department.

Staff Assistants

ROBERT R. NASH, formerly director, Purchase Analysis Division, Purchasing Department, Ford Motor Co., Detroit, Mich.

JOSEPH L. ERNST, formerly purchasing agent, Rochester Board of Education, Rochester, N. Y.

HERBERT L. BROWN, formerly director, Purchase Analysis of the Lincoln-Mercury Division, Ford Motor Co., Detroit, Mich.

JOHN V. O'CONNELL, formerly supervising engineer for the Bureau of Stores, Purchase Department, City of New York.

J. H. GEARY, formerly assistant manager of stores, Erie Railroad Co., Hornell, N. Y.

LEON J. JACOBI, inspection and standards engineer, the Detroit Edison Co., Detroit, Mich.

DANA M. BARBOUR, on loan from the Division of Statistical Standards, Office of the Budget.

FRANK A. CISAR and VALADIMIR S. KILESNIKOFF, Division of Statistical Standards, Office of the Budget.

KEITH G. BARR, on loan from the Property Management Section, Division of Administrative Management, Office of the Budget.

BELL AND USSERY, traffic consultants, Investment Building, Washington, D. C.

SIDNEY D. GOLDBERG, attorney, formerly associated with the Department of the Interior and the Office of the Budget.

Advisory Committee

W. Z. BETTS, director, Division of Purchase and Contract, State of North Carolina.

HARRY ERLICHER, vice president in charge of purchases, General Electric Co.

THOMAS D. JOLLY, vice president in charge of purchases and engineering, Aluminum Co. of America.

R. C. HABERKERN, vice president in charge of purchases, R. J. Reynolds Tobacco Co.

CARL ILGENFRITZ, vice president in charge of purchases, United States Steel Corp. of Delaware.

GEORGE A. RENARD, executive secretary-treasurer, National Association of Purchasing Agents.

JOHN P. SANGER, vice president in charge of purchases, United States Gypsum Co.

CHARLES E. SMITH, vice president in charge of purchases, New York, New Haven & Hartford Railroad.

VI.   PERSONNEL MANAGEMENT

Chairman

JOHN A. STEVENSON, president, Penn Mutual Life Insurance Co.

Committee

LAWRENCE A. APPLEY, president, American Management Association; former vice president, Montgomery Ward & Co.

VANNEVAR BUSH, former chairman, Research and Development Board.

HARRY F. BYRD, Senator from Virginia.

ALVIN E. DODD, honorary president, American Management Association.

COL. FRANKLIN D'OLIER, former chairman of the board, The Prudential Life Insurance Co. of America.

DR. ALVIN C. EURICH, acting president, Stanford University.

EARL G. HARRISON, former dean, University of Pennsylvania Law School; vice president of university.

DR. ROBERT L. JOHNSON, president, Temple University.

DAVID LILIENTHAL, chairman, Atomic Energy Commission.

JAMES P. MITCHELL, vice president, Bloomingdale Bros.

ROBERT RAMSPECK, executive vice president, Air Transport Association of America.

A. W. ROBERTSON, chairman of the board, Westinghouse Electric Co.

DR. GEORGE D. STODDARD, president, University of Illinois.

RAWLEIGH WARNER, chairman of the board, The Pure Oil Co.

ALFRED H. WILLIAMS, president, Federal Reserve Bank of Philadelphia.

DR. LEONARD D. WHITE, professor, Department of Political Science, University of Chicago; former Civil Service Commissioner.

Undertaken by

CRESAP, MCCORMICK, & PAGET, New York City.

Project Director

RICHARD PAGET

VII.   FOREIGN AFFAIRS

Committee

HARVEY H. BUNDY, Assistant Secretary of State, 1931–33; special assistant to the Secretary of War, 1941–45; and partner, Choate, Hall & Stewart, Boston, Mass.

JAMES GRAFTON ROGERS, Assistant Secretary of State, 1931–33; professor of law and Master of Timothy Dwight College, Yale University, 1935–42; deputy director, Office of Strategic Services, 1942–44; and president, Foreign Bondholders Protective Council, 1943 to date.

Adviser

HENRY L. STIMSON, Secretary of State, 1929–33, and Secretary of War. 1911–13 and 1940–45.

Executive Secretary and Staff Director

JOHN F. MECK, JR., treasurer, Dartmouth College, Hanover, N. H.

Staff

EVERARD K. MEADE, JR., Alexandria, Va., assistant staff director.

GEORGE A. LATIMER, Richmond Exploration Company, San Francisco, Calif., director, Interdepartmental Study.

DONALD W. BROWN, University of Chicago Law School, Chicago, Ill.

DANIEL S. CHEEVER, Harvard University, Cambridge, Mass.

PETER H. B. FRELINGHUYSEN, JR., Morristown, N. J.

H. FIELD HAVILAND, JR., Harvard University, Cambridge, Mass.

LOUIS W. KOENIG, Bard College, Annandale-on-Hudson, N. Y.

CLARENCE E. THURBER, Brookings Institution, Washington, D. C.

WILLIAM E. VOGELSANG, Washington, D. C.

Consultants

HAROLD GUETZKOW, University of Michigan, Ann Arbor, Mich.

DONALD H. MCLEAN, JR., Socony-Vacuum Oil Company, New York, N. Y.

JOHN W. MASLAND, Dartmouth College, Hanover, N. H.

WALLACE J. PARKS, Washington, D. C.

HAROLD STEIN, staff director, Committee on Public Administration Cases, Washington, D. C.

VAN LEAR WOODWARD, Van Lear Woodward & Co., New York, N. Y.

VIII.   NATIONAL SECURITY ORGANIZATION

Chairman

FERDINAND EBERSTADT, president, F. Eberstadt & Co., New York City; chairman, Army and Navy Munitions Board, 1942; and former vice chairman, War Production Board 1942–43.

Committee

RAYMOND B. ALLEN, president of the University of Washington.

THOMAS ARCHER, vice president, General Motors Corp.

HANSON W. BALDWIN, of the New York Times.

CHESTER I. BARNARD, president, Rockefeller Foundation.

DR. CHARLES W. COLE, president of Amherst College.

JOHN COWLES, president, Minneapolis Star and Tribune.

JAMES KNOWLSON, president of Stewart-Warner Corp.

JOHN J. MCCLOY, president, International Bank for Reconstruction and Development.

DR. FREDERICK A. MIDDLEBUSH, president of the University of Missouri.

ROBERT P. PATTERSON, of Patterson, Belknap & Webb.

LEWIS L. STRAUSS, Commission member, Atomic Energy Commission.

J. CARLTON WARD, JR., chairman of the board, Fairchild Engine & Airplane Corp.

GEN. ROBERT E. WOOD, chairman of the board, Sears, Roebuck & Co.

Military Advisory Committee

ADMIRAL R. S. EDWARDS	MAJ. GEN. GILBERT R. COOK
ADMIRAL BEN MOREELL	MAJ. GEN. EDWARD P. CURTIS
LT. GEN. JAMES H. DOOLITTLE	MAJ. GEN. ROBERT W. HASBROUCK
LT. GEN. IRA C. EAKER	COL. TRUMAN SMITH
VICE ADM. JOHN H. TOWERS	

Consultants

GENERAL OF THE ARMY DWIGHT D. EISENHOWER

FLEET ADM. ERNEST J. KING

FLEET ADM. CHESTER W. NIMITZ

GEN. CARL SPAATZ

LT. GEN. STANLEY D. EMBICK

MAJ. GEN. FREDERICK L. ANDERSON

JOHN M. HANCOCK, of Lehman Bros., New York City.

MRS. OVETA CULP HOBBY, executive vice president, the Houston Post.

CHARLES E. WILSON, president, General Electric Co.

Staff Members

WILLIAM ARNSTEIN	MATTHEW RADOM
JOHN A. BROSS	MISS JESSIE PEARL RICE
DR. ROBERT H. CONNERY	DR. HOWARD RUSK
ELMER T. CUMMINS	DR. E. DWIGHT SALMON
DR. CHARLES FAIRMAN	COL. LEWIS SANDERS
ELLIS J. GROFF	FRANZ SCHNEIDER
JAMES E. HOLLINGSWORTH	RICHARD W. SEABURY
ROY THOMAS HURLEY	MASON SEARS
ALMET JENKS	WILLIAM H. STRONG
DR. RICHARD L. MEILING	ARTHUR SUTHERLAND
CARROLL F. MILES	DR. EDWARD F. WILLETT

IX.   TREASURY DEPARTMENT

FISCAL, BUDGETING AND ACCOUNTING

(See report on Budgeting and Accounting.)

TREASURY PHASE

A. E. Buck, Institute of Public Administration.

Montgomery B. Angell; Davis, Polk, Wardwell, Sunderland & Kiendl of New York City.

Daniel W. Bell, president, American Security & Trust Co., and formerly Director of the Bureau of the Budget and Under Secretary of the Treasury.

William T. Sherwood, former Deputy Commissioner of Internal Revenue.

X.   THE POST OFFICE

Undertaken by

Robert Heller & Associates, Inc., management engineers, Cleveland, Ohio.

Project Director

F. L. Elmendorf, vice president.

XI.   DEPARTMENT OF AGRICULTURE

Chairman

H. P. Rusk, dean, Illinois State College of Agriculture, Urbana, Ill.

Committee

H. W. Martin, dean, School of Agriculture, Rutgers University, New Brunswick, N. J.

Dr. D. Howard Doane, Doane Agricultural Service, St. Louis, Mo.

F. W. Peck, executive director, Farm Foundation, Chicago, Ill.

John Gaus, professor, Harvard University, Cambridge, Mass.

W. A. Schoenfeld, dean, Oregon State College, Corvallis, Oreg.

Chester Davis, president, Federal Reserve Bank, St. Louis, Mo.

William Rhea Blake, executive vice president, National Cotton Council, Memphis, Tenn.

Research Director

G. HARRIS COLLINGWOOD

Consultants

FREDERIC P. LEE, member of Alvord and Alvord, attorneys, Washington, D. C.

GENERAL H. P. SEIDEMANN, former treasurer, Brookings Institution, Washington, D. C.

XII. DEPARTMENT OF INTERIOR

NATURAL RESOURCES

Chairman

LESLIE MILLER, former Governor of Wyoming.

Committee

HORACE ALBRIGHT, former director, National Park Service.

DR. ISAIAH BOWMAN, president emeritus, Johns Hopkins University.

RALPH CARR, former Governor of Colorado.

PROFESSOR SAMUEL T. DANA, dean, School of Forestry and Conservation, University of Michigan.

JOHN DEMPSEY, former Governor of New Mexico.

DONALD H. McLAUGHLIN, president, Homestake Mining Corporation.

DR. GILBERT WHITE, president, Haverford College.

PUBLIC WORKS

Chairman and Director

ROBERT MOSES, chairman of the New York State Council of Parks and of the Triborough Bridge and Tunnel Authority.

Advisory Committee

R. H. BALDOCK, president, American Association of State Highway Engineers, State of Oregon.

S. D. BECHTEL, president, Bechtel Corporation, San Francisco, Calif.

GILMORE D. CLARKE, Clarke, Rapuano and Holleran, consulting engineers.

RICHARD E. DOUGHERTY, vice president, New York Central Railroad.

GANO DUNN, president, J. G. White Engineering Corp.

AYMAR EMBURY II, architect, City of New York; and consultant to Port of New York Authority.

THOMAS F. FARRELL, chairman, New York City Housing Authority.

THOMAS K. FINLETTER, Coudert Brothers; and recently chairman, President's Air Policy Commission.

G. DONALD KENNEDY, vice president, Automotive Safety Foundation.

BEN MOREELL, president, Jones and Laughlin Steel Corp.

ROBERT P. PATTERSON, former Secretary of War.

CHARLES H. PURCELL, director, Department of Public Works, State of California.

JOHN A. REILLY, president, General Contractors Association; vice president, the Arundel Corp.

THORNDIKE SAVILLE, dean, College of Engineering, New York University.

CHARLES H. SELLS, superintendent, New York State Department of Public Works.

LUTHER C. STEWARD, president, National Federation of Federal Employees.

Consultants

W. EARLE ANDREWS, Andrews & Clark, consulting engineers, New York, N. Y.

WILLIAM N. CAREY, executive secretary, American Society of Civil Engineers.

WILLIAM S. CHAPIN, consulting engineer, Triborough Bridge and Tunnel Authority.

FREDERIC A. COLLINS, special counsel.

G. FRANK DOUGHERTY, counsel, Long Island State Park Commission.

HOLDEN A. EVANS, JR., executive assistant to superintendent, New York State Department of Public Works.

WILLIAM F. HEAVEY, consultant engineer, New York City Department of Marine and Aviation.

ARTHUR S. HODGKISS, executive officer, New York City Department of Parks.

ARTHUR E. HOWLAND, chief engineer, Long Island State Park Commission, Jones Beach Parkway Authority, Bethpage Park Authority.

WILLIAM S. LEBWOHL, deputy corporation counsel, City of New York, N. Y.

M. J. MADIGAN, Madigan-Hyland, Engineers.

EMIL PRAEGER, chief engineer, Madigan-Hyland, Engineers.

JOHN C. RIEDEL, chief engineer, Board of Estimates, City of New York, N. Y.

SIDNEY M. SHAPIRO, deputy engineer, Long Island State Park Commission.

ARTHUR V. SHERIDAN, commissioner of Borough Works, the Bronx, N. Y.

GEORGE E. SPARGO, general manager, Triborough Bridge and Tunnel Authority; Deputy Construction Coordinator, New York, N. Y.

HARRY TAYLOR, assistant general manager, Triborough Bridge and Tunnel Authority; director, Office of Construction Coordinator, New York, N. Y.

AGRICULTURE ACTIVITIES

(See report on Department of Agriculture.)

XIII. DEPARTMENT OF COMMERCE

REGULATORY COMMISSIONS

Committee

ROBERT R. BOWIE, professor of law, Harvard Law School since 1945; formerly partner, Bowie and Burke, Baltimore; War Department Procurement Legal staff, 1942–45; special assistant to the Military Governor of Germany, 1945–46.

OWEN D. YOUNG, former chairman of the board, General Electric Company; and former chairman, Second Committee of Experts appointed by Reparations Commission, 1929.

Project Director

ROBERT R. BOWIE

Executive Officer

HAROLD LEVENTHAL, of Ginsburg & Leventhal, Washington, D. C.

Survey Officers

GEORGE L. BACH, professor and head of departments of economics and industrial administration, Carnegie Institute of Technology, Pittsburgh, Pennsylvania.

JAMES M. BURNS, assistant professor of political science, Williams College, Williamstown, Massachusetts.

CARL F. FARBACH, former associate, Cravath, Swaine and Moore.

WALTER GALENSON, assistant professor of economics, Harvard University.

WILLIAM W. GOLUB, associate, Shearman & Sterling & Wright.

C. HERMAN PRITCHETT, associate professor of political science, University of Chicago.

EDWARD C. SWEENEY, editor of the Journal of Air Law and Commerce; professor of law, Northwestern University.

IRENE TILL, economist; formerly economic adviser in the Foreign Economic Administration and member of the Interdepartmental Cartel Committee.

ERNEST W. WILLIAMS, lecturer in transportation, Columbia University.

TRANSPORTATION

Undertaken by

BROOKINGS INSTITUTION

Project Director

DR. CHARLES DEARING, Brookings Institution.

Assistant Project Director

DR. WILFRED OWEN, Brookings Institution.

XIV.   DEPARTMENT OF LABOR

CONSULTANT TO THE COMMISSION

GEORGE W. TAYLOR, professor of labor relations, University of Pennsylvania; former chairman, National War Labor Board.

PUBLIC WELFARE

Undertaken by

BROOKINGS INSTITUTION

Research Directors

LEWIS MERIAM, vice president, Brookings Institution—director of Relief and Social Security Phase.

AVERY LEISERSON, assistant professor, University of Chicago—director of Employment Phase.

REGULATORY COMMISSIONS

Committee

ROBERT R. BOWIE, professor of law, Harvard Law School; former partner, Bowie and Burke, Baltimore; and former special assistant to the Military Governor of Germany.

OWEN D. YOUNG, former chairman of the board, General Electric Company; and former chairman, Second Committee of Experts appointed by Reparations Commission, 1929.

Task Force

ROBERT R. BOWIE—project director.

HAROLD LEVENTHAL, executive officer—partner, Ginsburg & Leventhal, Washington.

WALTER GALENSON, National Labor Relations Board phase—assistant professor of economics, Harvard University.

DEPARTMENTAL MANAGEMENT

H. STRUVE HENSEL, Carter, Ledyard and Milburn, New York; former Assistant Secretary of the Navy.

JOHN D. MILLETT, professor of public administration, Columbia University.

STATISTICAL SERVICES

Undertaken by

NATIONAL BUREAU OF ECONOMIC RESEARCH

Directors

FREDERICK C. MILLS, project director—chairman, Department of Economics, Columbia University; former president, American Economics Association and American Statistical Association.

CLARENCE D. LONG, associate director—professor of economics, Johns Hopkins University.

Advisory Committee

MARTIN R. GAINSBRUGH
JOHN D. MILLETT
GEORGE SOULE
P. K. WHELPTON
SAMUEL S. WILKS

FIELD OFFICES

Undertaken by

Klein and Saks

Project Director

Julius Klein, former Assistant Secretary of Commerce.

XV. MEDICAL ACTIVITIES

MEDICAL SERVICES

Chairman

Tracy S. Voorhees, Assistant Secretary of the Army.

Secretary

Rear Admiral Joel T. Boone (MC), USN, executive secretary, Committee on Medical and Hospital Services in the Armed Forces.

Members

Frank R. Bradley, M. D., director, Barnes Hospital, St. Louis, Mo.

Robin C. Buerki, M. D., vice president in charge of medical affairs, University of Pennsylvania, Philadelphia, Pa.

Edward D. Churchill, M. D., professor of surgery, Harvard Medical School, Harvard University, Boston, Mass.

Michael E. DeBakey, M. D., professor of surgery, Baylor University, Houston, Tex.

Goldwaite H. Dorr, of Dorr, Hammond, Hand & Dawson, New York, N. Y.; former special assistant to Secretary of War Henry L. Stimson.

Paul R. Hawley, M. D., chief executive officer, Associated Medical Care Plans, Chicago, Ill.; former chief surgeon, European Theater of Operations.

Henry P. Isham, president, board of trustees, Passavant Hospital, Chicago, Ill.

Hugh R. Leavell, M. D., professor of public health practice, School of Public Health, Harvard University, Boston, Mass.

William C. Menninger, M. D., the Menninger Foundation, Topeka, Kans.

Hugh J. Morgan, M. D., professor of medicine, Vanderbilt University, Nashville, Tenn.

O. H. Perry Pepper, M. D., professor of medicine, University of Pennsylvania, Philadelphia, Pa.

ALFRED NEWTON RICHARDS, Ph.D., president, National Academy of Sciences; vice president emeritus in charge of medical affairs, University of Pennsylvania, Philadelphia, Pa.

CHARLES F. ROWLEY, former trustee of Massachusetts Investors Trust, Boston, Mass.

ALLEN O. WHIPPLE, M. D., clinical director, Memorial Hospital, New York, N. Y.

RAY LYMAN WILBUR, M. D., Stanford University, Palo Alto, Calif.

Executive Director of Staff

HOWARD M. KLINE, Washington, D. C.

Consultants

On Medical Research

A. R. DOCHEZ, M. D., College of Physicians and Surgeons, Columbia University, New York, N. Y.

On Tuberculosis

ESMOND R. LONG, M. D., director, Henry Phipps Institute, University of Pennsylvania, Philadelphia, Pa.

ROBERT PLUNKETT, M. D., New York State Department of Health, Albany, N. Y.

On Hospitalization

BASIL MCLEAN, M. D., director, Strong Memorial Hospital, Rochester, N. Y.

MAXWELL E. LAPHAM, M. D., dean, School of Medicine, Tulane University, New Orleans, La.

On Medical Supply

HERMAN HANGEN, J. C. Penney & Co., New York, N. Y.

C. W. HARRIS, Horder's, Inc., Chicago, Ill.

General Consultants to the Committee

GENERAL EDWARD S. GREENBAUM, Greenbaum, Wolff and Ernst.

ELI GINZBERG, M. D., Columbia University, New York, N. Y.

GILBERT BEEBE, M. D., National Research Council, Washington, D. C.

WELFARE ACTIVITIES

DR. GEORGE W. BACHMAN, public health aspects—research staff, the

DR. LEWIS MERIAM, vice president, the Brookings Institution.

XVI. VETERANS' AFFAIRS

Chairman

COL. FRANKLIN D'OLIER, First National Commander, American Legion; Director, U. S. Strategic Bombing Survey of Germany and Japan (1944–46); and former chairman of the board, the Prudential Life Insurance Co. of America.

Advisory Committee

JOHN STEVENSON, president, Penn Mutual Life Insurance Co., Philadelphia, Pa.

EDMUND FITZGERALD, president, Northwestern Mutual Life Insurance Co., Milwaukee, Wis.

PAUL CLARK, president, John Hancock Mutual Life Insurance Co., Boston, Mass.

Survey Director

VALENTINE HOWELL, vice president and actuary, The Prudential Life Insurance Co. of America.

ASSISTED ON INSURANCE PHASE BY

ALBERT F. JACQUES, vice president, The Prudential Life Insurance Co. of America.

WILLIAM R. CUNNINGHAM, Paul C. Sanborn Associates, New York City.

ROLAND MANGINI, manager, Planning Department, John Hancock Mutual Life Insurance Co., Boston, Mass.

MASON SEARS, Boston, Massachusetts.

VICTOR HENNINGSEN, comptroller, Northwestern Mutual Life Insurance Co., Milwaukee, Wis.

ASSISTED ON ACTIVITIES OTHER THAN INSURANCE AND HOSPITALIZATION BY

Director

THOMAS M. SEARLES, president, Equity Co., Philadelphia.

Research undertaken by

TRUNDLE ENGINEERING CO., Cleveland, Ohio.

XVII. FEDERAL BUSINESS ENTERPRISES

FEDERAL BUSINESS ENTERPRISES AND REVOLVING FUNDS

MAJ. GEN. ARTHUR H. CARTER, project director—former fiscal director, Army Service Forces.
COL. ANDREW STEWART, research director—former deputy fiscal director, Army Service Forces.
  (Haskins & Sells, certified public accountants)

WATER RESOURCES PROJECTS

COL. A. B. ROBERTS, consulting engineer, Cleveland, Ohio.

LENDING AGENCIES

PAUL GRADY, former Assistant to the Secretary of the Navy.
THEODORE HERZ, assistant to Mr. Grady.
  (Price, Waterhouse & Co., certified public accountants)

Advisory Committee

PAUL BESTOR, president, The Trust Co. of New Jersey.
DONALD D. DAVIS, president, Minnesota & Ontario Paper Co.
WALTER J. CUMMINGS, chairman of the board, Continental Illinois National Bank & Trust Co., Chicago, Ill.
WALTER D. FULLER, president, the Curtis Publishing Co.
GEORGE L. HARRISON, president, New York Life Insurance Co.
ARNOLD B. KELLER, senior consultant, International Harvester Co.
WALTER B. LICHTENSTEIN, financial and economic consultant, Chicago.

PUBLIC WORKS

(See report on Department of Interior, *Chairman* and
Advisory Committee.)

NATURAL RESOURCES

(See report on Department of Interior.)

AGRICULTURE

(See report on Department of Agriculture.)

XVIII. INDEPENDENT REGULATORY COMMISSIONS

REGULATORY COMMISSIONS

(See report on Department of Commerce.)

XIX. SOCIAL SECURITY AND EDUCATION

DR. LEWIS MERIAM, vice president, Brookings Institution.
DR. HOLLIS P. ALLEN, education aspects—Claremont Graduate School, California.
DR. AVERY LEISERSON, employment aspects—University of Chicago.

XX. INDIAN AFFAIRS

Chairman

GEORGE GRAHAM, professor, Department of Political Science, Princeton University.

Committee

JOHN R. NICHOLS, president, New Mexico College of Agriculture and Mechanic Arts.
CHARLES J. RHOADS, former Commissioner of Indian Affairs.
REV. DR. GILBERT DARLINGTON, treasurer of the American Bible Society.

XXI. OVERSEAS ADMINISTRATION

RUPERT EMERSON, professor of government, Harvard University, and former director, Division of Territories and Island Possessions, Department of the Interior.
BENJAMIN RIVLIN, research assistant.

XXII. FEDERAL-STATE RELATIONS

Chairman

THOMAS JEFFERSON COOLIDGE, chairman of the board, United Fruit Company; Under Secretary of the Treasury, 1934–36.

Committee

JOHN BURTON, director of the budget, State of New York.
WILLIAM ANDERSON, professor, University of Minnesota.
SENATOR HARRY F. BYRD, Virginia.
GOVERNOR FRANK CARLSON, Kansas.
WILLIAM L. CHENERY, publisher, Collier's Weekly.

JOHN W. DAVIS, senior partner, Davis, Polk, Wardwell, Sunderland and Kiendl; Ambassador to Great Britain, 1918–21; Democratic nominee for President, 1924.

CHARLES A. EDISON, Governor of New Jersey, 1941–44; Assistant Secretary of the Navy, 1939–40; president, Thomas A. Edison, Inc.

WILLIAM L. MYERS, dean, Cornell University.

SINCLAIR WEEKS, former Senator from Massachusetts.

CHARLES STOCKTON, secretary of the committee on Federal-State Relations.

STANFORD SCHEWEL, consultant.

ROSWELL F. MAGILL, consultant; former Under Secretary of the Treasury; partner Cravath, Swaine and Moore.

Project Undertaken by

COUNCIL OF STATE GOVERNMENTS

Project Director

FRANK BANE, executive director, Council of State Governments.